Quest for
Quranic Knowledge

DR FATHIMUNNISA BEGUM

BLUEROSE PUBLISHERS
India | U.K.

Copyright © Dr Fathimunnisa Begum M Sc M Phil Ph D 2025

All rights reserved by author. No part of this publication may be reproduced, stored in a retrieval system or transmitted in any form or by any means, electronic, mechanical, photocopying, recording or otherwise, without the prior permission of the author. Although every precaution has been taken to verify the accuracy of the information contained herein, the publisher assumes no responsibility for any errors or omissions. No liability is assumed for damages that may result from the use of information contained within.

BlueRose Publishers takes no responsibility for any damages, losses, or liabilities that may arise from the use or misuse of the information, products, or services provided in this publication.

For permissions requests or inquiries regarding this publication, please contact:

BLUEROSE PUBLISHERS
www.BlueRoseONE.com
info@bluerosepublishers.com
+91 8882 898 898
+4407342408967

ISBN: 978-93-5741-740-2

Cover design: Yash Singhal
Typesetting: Namrata Saini

First Edition: January 2025

Dedication

This book is dedicated to my beloved parents though no more; to all my loving family members and to all my group members, with whom I had already shared this subject.

Language Editor: Syed Tajuddeen Madani, Senior Advocate {55 years experience in Practicing] Triuchirappalli District Courts, Tiruchirappalli, Tamil Nadu, India

Acknowledgement

Abu Huraira, in Jami`at-Tirmidhi [2682] had declared, "Who takes a path upon which he seeks knowledge, then Allah سبحانه وتعالى makes a path to Paradise easy for him. And indeed the angels lower their wings in approval to the one seeking knowledge. Indeed, forgiveness is ought for the knowledgeable one by whomever is in the heavens and whomever is in the earth, even the fish in the waters."

Glory to my Creator, for granting me the required wisdom and perception; to embark in my effort to share what ever knowledge I acquired. His thoughts were embedded within me always; brought me nearer to Him; and to realize His Greatness and to serve Him. I shall remain ever grateful for His gracious guidance; for the time granted to understand His dictates; coupled with the required health to implement my efforts along with an aptitude to share it, with others. The required help, to work without any hitch or hindrance, is His Grace. With His blessings, my family, understood my efforts by extending its fullest co-operation in providing the needed encouragement, along with the technical support. In all humility, I feel indebted to everyone, who helped me in accomplishing this humble effort.

I immensely thank my husband, Syed Tajuddeen Madani, M.A., B.L., for his sincere effort to publish this book in its present form. I also thank my niece Anees Fathima, B.Com., for helping me in checking out errors.

Last but not the least, I thank the Blue Rose Publishers who have consented to convert my dream into reality.

Contents

1. See the picture and mention the Ayath. 1
2. Who are they? 21
3. Search the Surah, mention the Ayath 36
4. During which situation, these verses have been revealed? 53
5. Rapid round 69
6. To whom it refers..80
7. Who statesments are these? 102
8. Prophets...122
9. Persons other than Prophets mentioned in Quran..148
10. Angels..172
11. Communities...194
12. Quranic verses...209
13. Enemies 240
14. Resurrection and the Day of Resurrection 269
15. About Surah 295
16. Miscellaneous..316

بِسْمِ ٱللَّهِ ٱلرَّحْمَٰنِ ٱلرَّحِيمِ

1. See the Picture and Mention the Ayath.

1. See the picture and mention the verse from the Quran.

Answer: Surah Fatir, verse 27

[أَلَمْ تَرَ أَنَّ ٱللَّهَ أَنزَلَ مِنَ ٱلسَّمَاءِ مَاءً فَأَخْرَجْنَا بِهِ ثَمَرَٰتٍ مُّخْتَلِفًا أَلْوَٰنُهَا ۚ وَمِنَ ٱلْجِبَالِ جُدَدٌ بِيضٌ وَحُمْرٌ مُّخْتَلِفٌ أَلْوَٰنُهَا وَغَرَابِيبُ سُودٌ]

"See you not that Allah sends down water (rain) from the sky, and We produce there with fruits of varying colors, and among the mountains are streaks white and red, of varying colors and (others).........." (35:27)

The heaven and the earth and all that are found between the two belong to Allah ﷻ. He created them, fashioned them, designed them just for a purpose which we are not aware of. There are different varieties of plants, animals, objects, celestial bodies and human beings. No two objects/beings are same. Even though there is homogeneity and uniformity among them, the differences are quiet obvious.

For example, on the earth there are innumerable varieties of fruit bearing trees. All the trees intake the same water, pour from the sky or sent down as rain. Same earth produces different trees, which in turn produce fruits with different colors and tastes. Even the fruits from the same tree are at times different in color, size and taste.

Similarly, there are mountains, that are used as pegs (78:7) on the earth. Normally the mountains appear brown or grey from distance. On closer look, one can see "streaks of white and red, of varying colors." It is due to the differences in the mineral composition of the sediments of its rocks.

The mountains are built up over millions of years by movement of tectonic plates, by the deposition layers of sediments, sand-stone and minerals. Colours are developed due to the oxidation of minerals with the presence of water and by erosion due to freezing and thawing, wind etc. The varieties of colours are green, yellow, orange, pink, red, brown, white and black. Iron oxides impart dark red colours. Oxidized limonite or goethite will produce brown or yellow stains. Black staining of sandstones is due to magnetite. Iron sulfide forms metallic yellow colour. Green colour is due to chlorite/iron silicates. There are several mountains in the world, called rainbow mountains, which show distinctly, brilliant coloured stripes or masses on sunny days.

This kind of wonderful rainbow mountains and sandstones are seen at the following places in the world:

★ Vinicunca Rainbow Mountains, Peru, South America with colored stripes ranging from turquoise to lavender to maroon and gold.

★ Vermilion Cliffs National Monument, called 'Painted Desert', Arizona, U.S.

★ Zhangye Danxia Land Form Geological Park, China. This 'Earth's Paint Palette' is seen with red, yellow, green and blue striped mountains.

★ Landmannalaugar Mountain, Iceland. It contains hot springs.

★ Coloured Canyon in Nuweiba, Sinai, Egypt.

★ Colourful mountains of Tabriz, Iran.

★ Serranía de Horonocal fourteen colored mountain range of limestone, Argentina.

The existence of countless, limitless, wonderful, unimaginable designs and creations like these; are due to the great wisdom of Allah - a Wise Planner, a Unique Creator, a Matchless Fashioner, a Maker of varieties of masterpieces without any previous models, but with immense, uncomparable Power and Authority.

As William Cowper quoted, "Variety is the spices of life!" Variety and change is the key to an interesting life. Allah says further in this ayath: "And of men and moving living creatures, beasts and cattle, in like manner of various colours. It is only those who have knowledge among His slaves that fear Allah. Verily, Allah is All Mighty, Oft Forgiving." (35:28). So fear Allah Subhanahuthala!

One who fears Allahuthala, without seeing Him, turns to Him and keeps away from what makes Him angry, is said to be more knowledgeable!

2. Relate the ayath of the Quran with this picture.

Answer: In surah Yunus, verse 92. (10:92).

[فَالْيَوْمَ نُنَجِّيكَ بِبَدَنِكَ لِتَكُونَ لِمَنْ خَلْفَكَ آيَةً وَإِنَّ كَثِيرًا مِّنَ النَّاسِ عَنْ آيَاتِنَا لَغَافِلُونَ]

"So this day We shall deliver your (dead) body (out from the sea) that you may be a sign to those who come after you! And verily, many among mankind are heedless of Our Ayath." (10:92).

Allah Subhanahuthala, left innumerable proofs for the people of future generations to learn how arrogance, disbelief, evil and rejections of Allah's message bring severe punishment in this worldly life and the Hereafter. Among them is the Nuh (AS)'s ship; the city of Lut (AS) that was turned upside down and the dead body of Firaun

Allah (SWT) commanded Musa (AS) and his brother Harun (AS), "Go, both of you, to Firaun, verily, he has transgressed. And speak to him mildly, perhaps he may accept admonition or fear Allah." (20:43 and 44). Hence, they went to Firuan and said: "Verily, we are Messengers of your Lord, so let the Children of Israel go with us, and punish them not; indeed, we have come with a sign from your Lord! And peace will be upon him who follows the guidance!" (20:46)

Claiming himself to be God, Firaun rejected their teachings. Even after getting signs after signs and the series of life threatening signs from Allahuthala, Firaun was defient and proud. He denied and declined the exitance of the Creator. (20:56). As an arrogant tyrant, he caused lots of trouble to the believers. He transgressed all bounds with regards to disbelief and disobedience. He devised a plan (20:60) with his skilled magicians. That plan turned against him, because his magicians, realizing the power of Almighty Allah, became His believers.

To rescue the followers of these messengers and the Children of Israel, Allah ﷻ inspired Musa (AS) and said "Travel by night with My slaves and strike a dry path for them in the sea, fearing neither to be over-taken nor being afraid of drowning in the sea." (20:77). Then Firaun pursued them with his hosts, in oppression and enmity, (10:90), but the sea-water completely overwhelmed them and covered them up." (20:78). While drowning, he said: "I believe that none has the right to be worshipped but Allah, in Whom the Children of Israel believe, and I am one of the Muslims." (10:90). But it was too late! The repentance of an evil person on the approach of his death is of no use. Allah [عَزَّ وَ جَلَّ] asked him: "Now (you believe?) while you refused to believe before and you were one of the evil-doers/corrupts." (10:91).

Allah ﷻ preserved his dead body as a sign for the future generations (10:92). Allah [سبحانه وتعالى] punished him before death and after death along with his followers. The Quran holds that: "Evil punishment encompassed Firaun's people" (40:45) in this world. "And they are exposed to the Fire, morning and afternoon, and on the Day when the Hour will be established" (it will be said to the angels): "Cause Firaun's people to enter the severest punishment!" (40:46). The severest punishment was waiting for him and his people in Jahannum.

Ibn Abbas and others from among the Salaf have said: "Some of the Children of Israel doubted the death of Firaun so Allahuthala commanded the sea to throw his body - whole, without a soul - with his known armor plate, to a high place on the land so that the people of those time could confirm his death and destruction. According to their customs they mummified that body and buried in their burial ground. This happened, more than 3000 years ago.

During the excavation work in the "Valleys of the King", towards the end of nineteenth Century, Firaun's mummy was recovered from a wooden coffin, with a name engraved Ramsses II. Another set of mummies were obtained from another place. All the mummies collected from these two places in Egypt were kept in the Medical School of Cairo University. It was noticed in 1979 that the mummy of Ramsses II was losing its shape, due to fungal attack. So they sent that mummy to France, with due care and respect. A group of French Scientists preserved those mummies with nuclear radiation and sent them back to Cairo.

The government of Egypt called highly qualified experts for a research of these mummies. One of them was Dr. Moarses Bucaille, who along with his team concluded that the mummy of Ramsses II; died because of drowning in the sea. It was quiet distinct from other mummies with the deposition of salt in many places. In order to prove his statement, he traced its history. He has been reading the holy Scriptures - Taurath, Bible and Quran. He was impressed by the clear story of Musa (AS) and the Pharaoh in the Holy Quran with a definite prediction about the preservation of the body of Firaun after his drowning. In 1979, he published a book on "Quran, Bible and Science"; where he openly highlighted the fact to the whole world that the mummy of Ramsses II was that of Pharaoh of Musa (AS)'s period. Dr. Moarses, who was a Christian, became a Muslim after such a research.

Even now, the preserved body of Firaun is kept in the Royal Mummies Great Museum in Cairo, Egypt. It is one of the mighty miracles of the Holy Quran. It is a sign for those who strongly believe in Allah.

الحمدلله

3. By seeing this picture, can you recollect two ayaath from Quran, which has the same meaning?

Answer: Surah Kahf, 18:109 and Surah Luqman, 31:27

Surah Al-Kahf, 18:109:

[قُل لَّوْ كَانَ ٱلْبَحْرُ مِدَادًا لِّكَلِمَـٰتِ رَبِّى لَنَفِدَ ٱلْبَحْرُ قَبْلَ أَن تَنفَدَ كَلِمَـٰتُ رَبِّى وَلَوْ جِئْنَا بِمِثْلِهِۦ مَدَدًا]

"Say (O Muhammad ﷺ to man kind), if the sea were ink for writing the words of my Lord, surely, the sea would be exhausted before the Words of my Lord would be finished, even if we brought (another sea) like it for its aid."

Surah Luqman, 31:27:

[وَلَوْ أَنَّمَا فِى ٱلْأَرْضِ مِن شَجَرَةٍ أَقْلَٰمٌ وَٱلْبَحْرُ يَمُدُّهُ مِنۢ بَعْدِهِۦ سَبْعَةُ أَبْحُرٍ مَّا نَفِدَتْ كَلِمَٰتُ ٱللَّهِ ۗ إِنَّ ٱللَّهَ عَزِيزٌ حَكِيمٌ]

"And if all the trees on the earth were pens and the sea (were ink wherewith to write), with seven seas behind it to add to its (supply), yet the Words of Allah would not be exhausted. Verily, Allah is All-Mighty, All-Wise."

Which means that the pens would break and the trees will be exhausted and the ink would run dry, if we continue to keep writing the Glory of Allah Subhanahuthala. There is no limit with regard to the signs, words, meticulous work, the excellence and the wonders arising out of His Power and Wisdom. Allah's Majesty, His Might, His pride, His Power, His Knowledge, His beautiful Names, His sublime Attributes and His Perfect Words; about which no human being nor even angels or other creations, know their essence or their nature or number.

As the Prophet ﷺ narrated:

[لَا أُحْصِي ثَنَاءً عَلَيْكَ أَنْتَ كَمَا أَثْنَيْتَ عَلَى نَفْسِكَ] "I cannot praise You enough; You are as You have praised Yourselves." His praise does not run out by writing. Numbers are not enough to express the amount of the beings He created. Remember and Glorify daily the supremacy of our Creator in order to get much closer to Him.

[سُبْحَانَ اللهِ وَبِحَمْدِهِ عَدَدَ خَلْقِهِ، وَرِضَا نَفْسِهِ، وَزِنَةَ عَرْشِهِ، وَمِدَادَ كَلِمَاتِهِ] "How perfect his Creation; His pleasure by the weight of His throne and ink of His words."

الحمدلله

4. Can you find out the ayath related to this picture.

Answer: Surah Ghafir, ayath 67. (40:67) Stages of man

[هُوَ ٱلَّذِى خَلَقَكُم مِّن تُرَابٍ ثُمَّ مِن نُّطْفَةٍ ثُمَّ مِنْ عَلَقَةٍ ثُمَّ يُخْرِجُكُمْ طِفْلًا ثُمَّ لِتَبْلُغُوٓا۟ أَشُدَّكُمْ ثُمَّ لِتَكُونُوا۟ شُيُوخًا ۚ وَمِنكُم مَّن يُتَوَفَّىٰ مِن قَبْلُ ۖ وَلِتَبْلُغُوٓا۟ أَجَلًا مُّسَمًّى وَلَعَلَّكُمْ تَعْقِلُونَ]

"He, it is Who has created you (Adam) from dust, then from a Nutfah [mixed semen drops of male and female discharge] then from a clot (a piece of coagulated blood), then brings you forth as children, then (makes you grow) to reach the age of full strength, and afterwards to be old (men and women), though some among you die before, and that you reach an appointed term, in order that you may understand." (40:67)

There is another ayath similar to it. "Verily We created man from a product of wet earth; then placed him as a drop (of seed) in a safe lodging; then We fashioned the drop into a clot, then We fashioned the clot into a little lump, then We fashioned the little lump into bones, then clothed the bones with flesh, and then produced it another creation. So blessed be Allah, the Best of Creators!" After that, surely, you will die. Then (again), surely, you will be resurrected on the Day of Resurrection." (23:12-16)

Allah (SWT) describes the stages of man from dust to death, by the following ayaath:

[18:37] "Do you deny Him Who created you out of dust, then out of a sperm-drop, then fashioned you into a man?"

[32:7-8] "Who made all things good which He created, and He began the creation of man from clay. And made his progeny from a quintessence of the nature of a fluid despised."

[80:19] "From a sperm-drop He had created him, and then moulds him in due proportions"

[6:5 – 7] "Now let man but think from what he is created. He is created from a drop emitted. Proceeding from between the backbone and the ribs."

[77:20 -22] "Have We not created you from a fluid (held) despicable?" Placing it in a secure place, until an appointed time?

[16:4 and 36:77] "He (Allah) has created man from a sperm-drop; and behold this same (man) becomes an open disputer!"

[76:2] "Verily We created Man from a drop of mingled sperm, in order to try him. So We gave him Hearing and Sight."

[53:45-46] "That He did create in pairs - male and female, from a seed when lodged (in its place)"

[30:54] "It is Allah Who created you in a state of (helpless) weakness, then gave (you) strength after weakness, then, after strength, gave (your weakness and a hoary head: He creates as He wills and it is He Who has all knowledge and power."

[36:68] "If We grant long life to any, 'We' cause him to be reversed in nature: Will they not then understand?"

[16:70] "It is Allah who creates you and takes your souls at death; and of you there are some who are sent back to a feeble age, so that they know nothing after having known (much): for Allah is All-Knowing, All-Powerful."

[3:185] "Every self will taste death."

[31:34] "No soul perceives in what land it will die. Indeed, Allah is Knowing and Acquainted."

[16:61] "When their specified time arrives, they cannot delay it for a single hour nor can they bring it forward."

Hadhees about the determination of destiny and stages of man:

Narrated Abdullah (RA): Allah's Messenger (ﷺ), the true and truly inspired said: "(As regards your creation), every one of you is collected in the womb of his mother for the first forty days, and then he becomes a clot for another forty days, and then a piece of flesh for another forty days. Then Allahuthala sends an angel to write four words: The angel writes his deeds, time of his death, means of his livelihood, and whether he will be wretched or blessed (in the Hereafter). Then the soul is breathed into his body. So a man may do deeds characteristic of the people of the (Hell) Fire, so much so that there is only the distance of a cubit between him and it, and then what has been written (by the angel) surpasses; and so he starts doing deeds characteristic of the people of Paradise and enters Paradise. Similarly, a person may do deeds characteristic of the people of Paradise, so much so that there is only the distance of a cubit between him and it, and then what has been written (by the angel) surpasses, and he starts doing deeds of the people of the (Hell) Fire and enters the (Hell) Fire." (Sahih Al Bukhari, Vol.4, Hadith No.549).

Allah ﷻ says in Quran that a man after his fortieth year, will pray: "My Lord, enable me to be grateful for Your favor which You have bestowed upon me and upon my parents and to work righteousness of which You will approve and make righteous for me my offspring. Indeed, I have repented to You, and indeed, I am of the

Muslims." (46:15). This is a prayer which a man offers for his parents, for himself and for his offspring.

الحمدلله

5. Mention the ayath related to this picture showing the jugular vein

Answer: Surah Qaf, verse 16. (50:16).

[وَلَقَدْ خَلَقْنَا الْإِنسَانَ وَنَعْلَمُ مَا تُوَسْوِسُ بِهِ نَفْسُهُ وَنَحْنُ أَقْرَبُ إِلَيْهِ مِنْ حَبْلِ الْوَرِيدِ]

Once a group of companions of the Prophet ﷺ asked him, 'Is our Lord nearby so that we should talk to Him secretly, or is He far away, so that we should call out to him?', and the following was revealed: "And Indeed, 'We' have created man, and We know what his own self whispers to him. And We are nearer to him than his jugular vein (by Our Knowledge)." (50:16). Not only the whisper but Allah knows even what we are thinking in our mind. When people can read the mind, why not Allahuthala?

Similar Quranic quotes are:

"And when My servants ask you (O Muhammad ﷺ concerning Me, then answer them), I am Indeed, near (to them by My knowledge). I respond to the invocations of the supplicant when he calls on Me (without any mediator or intercessor). So let them obey Me and believe in Me, so that they may be led a right" (2:186).

"Call upon Me, I will respond to you. Surely those who are too proud to worship Me will enter Hell, fully humbled." (40:60).

"My mercy encompasses all things" (7:156)

"Allah comes in between a person and his heart" (8:24).

"Is not Allah Best Aware of what is in the breast of the Alamin." (29:10).

"No doubt! They did fold up their breasts, that they may hide from Him. Surely, even when they cover themselves with their garments, He knows what they conceal and what they reveal. Verily, He is the All-Knower of the (innermost secrets) of the breasts?" (11:5).

Imam Ahmad reported that Abu Musa Al-Ashari (RA) stated that "We were in the company of Allah's Messenger ﷺ during a battle. Whenever we climbed a high place, went up a hill or went down a valley, we used to say, `Allahu Akbar,' raising our voices. The Prophet ﷺ came by us and said: "O people! Be merciful to yourselves (i.e., don't raise your voices), for you are not calling a deaf or an absent one, but One Who is All-Hearer, All-Seer. The One Whom you call is closer to one of you than the neck of his animal." Furthermore, Imam Ahmad recorded that Anas (RA) said that the Prophet ﷺ said: "Allah the Exalted said, `I am as My servant thinks of Me, and I am with him whenever he invokes Me'."

الحمدلله

6. With the clues given in the picture, find the name of the Prophet.

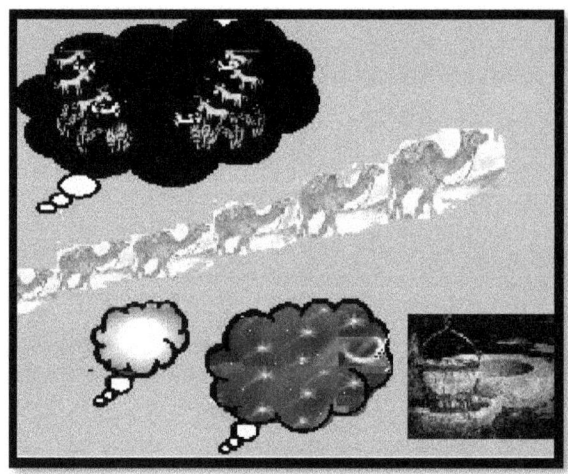

Answer: Nabi Yusuf (AS).

Allah [عَزَّ وَ جَلَّ] declares that the story of Yusuf (AS): "was the best story revealed in Quran" (12:3); with "Ayaath for those who ask". (12:7). "And there is a lesson in their story, for men of understanding." (12:111). This surah was revealed to Prophet ﷺ during the difficult situation, when Quraysh were planning to exterminate or exile him. Moreover, Jews were repeatedly asking him a question, thinking that he being an Arab cannot answer – "Why did Israelites go to Egypt?". This surah gave strength to Mohammad ﷺ and his companions. They came to know about how the Prophets of past underwent difficulties and problems and how they faced them by trusting Allah, patiently.

Lessons learnt from surah Yusuf:

★ **Allahuthala prepares the good doers to face difficulties:** Out of jealousy when his brothers, threw Yusuf (AS) in the well, Allahuthala inspired, prepared and consoled Yusuf (AS) that one day he will inform them about their deeds (12:15). Allah is the one who gives strength to men to bear the difficulties.

★ **Allah [SWT} protect those who seek refuge:** Allah ﷻ will prevent human beings from committing wrongs, when we seek refuge with Him, (12:23) during trials/difficulties.

★ **Wrong doers and betrayers never succeed:** "Wrong and evil-doers will never be successful." (12:23). Allah [عَزَّ وَ جَلَّ] guides not the plot of the betrayers. (12:52)

★ **Pray during the times of difficulties, Allah [سبحانه وتعالى] will prevent one from committing sins:** When the wife of Aziz said, "If he refuses to obey my order, he shall certainly be cast into prison, and will be one of those who are disgraced." (12:32). Yusuf (AS) prayed: "O my Lord! Prison is more to my liking than that to which they invite me. Unless You turn away their plot from me, I will feel inclined towards them and be one of the ignorant." (12:33).

★ **Allah ﷻ hears your invocations:** "Allah the All-Hearer, the All-Knower answered his invocations and turned away Yusuf (AS) from their plot." (12:34)

★ **Allah ﷻ is predominant over our affairs:** Allah ﷻ has full power and control over His creation's affairs, but most of us know not. (12:21). It was Allahuthala's plan to shift Yusuf (AS) early from his Bedouin's life, to life in Egypt, where he had more opportunities to learn many things. Thus Allah ﷻ equipped with him wisdom and knowledge (12:22). All decision comes only with Allah. (12:67). Allahuthala planned for Yusuf (AS) to take his younger brother by the law of the king. (12:76)

★ **Patience is beautiful and put trust in Allah ﷻ for everything:** Yusuf's (AS) father Yaqub (AS) patiently bearing the separation of his beloved son with Allahuthala's help. (12:18). When Yaqub (AS) sent his youngest son to get another camel load of grain he said: "In Him, I put my trust and let all those that trust, put their trust in Him." (12:67). When Yaqub (AS) came to know that his youngest son is retained in

Egypt itself he said: "Patience is most fitting (for me). May be Allah will bring them (back) all to me." (12:83)

★ **Complain the grief and sorrow to Allah [SWT] alone:** Yaqub (AS) lost his sight because of the suppressing grief for Yusuf (AS) (12:84). His sons were conveying to him that "By Allah! You will never cease remembering Yusuf (AS) until you become weak with old age, or until you be of the dead." (12:85). He replied to them: "I only complain of my grief and sorrow to Allah, and I know from Allah that which you know not." (12:86)

★ **Do not despair on the Mercy of Allah ﷻ:** Yaqub (AS) told his sons: "O my sons! Go you and enquire about Yusuf (AS) and his brother, and never give up hope of Allah's Mercy. Certainly no one despairs of Allah's Mercy, except the people who disbelieve." (12:87).

★ **Shaitan is an open enemy to us:** 'Shaitan is an open enemy to man', (12:5). 'He sows enmity between the members of the family' (12:100). And Shaitan made his prison-mate to forget to mention about Yusuf (AS) to his master. Thus he prolonged his stay in prison for few more years. (12:42)

★ **Be thankful to Allah [SWT] for making us as believers:** Belief in Allah is from the Grace of Allah to us, but most men thank not. (12:38). Abandon the religion of disbelievers of Allah. (12:37). And follow the religion of Ibrahim (AS), Ishaque (AS) and Yaqub (AS) and do not attribute any partners to Allah. (12:38).

★ **Whenever you can, let others know about the Oneness of Allah [عَزَّ وَ جَلَّ]:** Even in prison Yusuf (AS) was teaching his prison mates about Oneness of Allah. (12:39)

★ **Allahuthala rewards Muhsinun, both in this world and in Hereafter:** The skill of interpretation of dreams of Yusuf (AS) became known to many at the right time. (12:47 - 49). Time has come to prove Yusuf (AS) truthfulness (12:51) and loyalty to his master. He has not betrayed his master even in secret. (12:52)

Allah ﷻ make not to be lost the reward of Al-Muhsinun (12:22 and 56). And the king of Egypt said: "this day, you are with us high in rank and fully trusted." (12:54). "The reward of the Here-after is better for those who believe and used to fear Allah and keep their duty to Him." (12:57)

When his brothers asked Yusuf (AS): "Are you Yusuf?" He said: "Yes. I am Yusuf. Allah has indeed been gracious to us. Verily, he who fears Allah with obedience to

Him and is patient, then surely, Allah makes not the reward of the good-doers to be lost." (12:90).

"Understand, the home of the Hereafter is the best for those who fear Allah and obey Him." (12:109)

★ **Allah [SWT] bestows His mercy on whom He please:** The human self is inclined to evil, except upon those, whom Allah bestows His mercy (12:53). Yusuf (AS) took charge over the storehouses of the land; and guarded them with full knowledge (12:55).

Allah gave full authority to Yusuf (AS) in the land, to take possession therein, as when or where he likes. (12:56). We raise to degrees whom We please. (12:76).

★ **Be kind to even those who caused difficulties to you:** Yusuf (AS) recognized his brothers, behaved as best host when they came to him and gave full measures of grains (12:59), gave their goods back, so that they can bring their younger brother. (12:61)

★ **Ask forgiveness from Allah when you do and realize a sin:** After knowing that he was his brother Yusuf (AS), his brothers told: "By Allah! Indeed, Allah has preferred you above us, and we certainly have been sinners." (12:91). Yusuf (AS) said: "No reproach on you this day, may Allah forgive you, and He is the Most Merciful of those who show mercy! (12:92)

They even asked forgiveness for their sins with their father and asked him to pray for them. (12:97) He replied: "I will ask my Lord for forgiveness for you, verily He! Only He is the Oft-Forgiving, the Most Merciful." (12:98).

Father's prayer is always accepted by Allah and his (Yaqub's) offspring are known as "The Children of Israel" to whom Allah has bestowed many favors.

★ **Allah guides all of us, through Yusuf (AS) how to pray:** "My Lord! You have indeed bestowed on me of the sovereignty, and taught me the interpretation of dreams; The only Creator of the heavens and the earth! You are my Wali in this world and in the Here-after, cause me to die as a Muslim and join me with the righteous." (12:101).

★ **Yusuf (AS) raised his family's status and became an example to others:** And he raised his parents to the throne and his dream came true when they and his brothers prostrated before him, as it was a practice in those days (12:100). He told others about

His Lord who is the Most Courteous and Kind (12:100) to him by bringing out from prison and removing the enmity of his brothers by forgiving them with the name of His Lord, who is Merciful. (12:101). All his brothers then became good Muslims.

★ **Quran as a reminder and a guide:** The Quran is no less than a reminder and an advice unto the 'Alamin (12:104). Quran confirms Allah's other Scriptures which contain detailed explanation of everything; a guide and a 'Mercy' for the people who believe. (12:111).

الحمدلله

7. Can you relate an ayath from Quran with this picture?

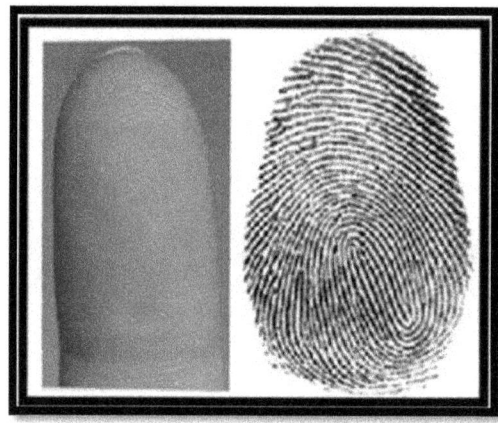

Answer: The ayath related to fingertip is: [بَلَىٰ قَادِرِينَ عَلَىٰ أَن نُّسَوِّيَ بَنَانَهُ]

"Yes! We are Able to put together in perfect order the tips of his fingers." (Al Qiyama, 75:4).

Revelation of these verses:

Once a man named Adiy bin Rabiah went to the Prophet Muhammad ﷺ and asked, "O Muhammad (ﷺ)! Let us challenge the Day of Resurrection, when will it happen and how?" The Prophet ﷺ told him about that day, then, Adiy said, "If I saw that day, we do not believe and do not believe in you." He further enquired, "How did Allah unite the bones?" Then Allahuthala replied with these verses of the Holy Quran: "Does man (a disbeliever) think that 'We' shall not assemble his bones? Yes! We are Able to put together in perfect order the tips of his fingers." (75:3 and 4). Our Creator who created us for the first time has the power to recreate the same finger-tips that we had in this world.

The disbelievers of different times, were enquiring the same with their Messengers:

"When we are bones and fragments should we really be resurrected (to be) a new creation?"(17:49 and 98; 23:35 and 82; and 37:16; 56:47 and 66:46).

"Who will give life to these bones when they have rotted away and became dust?" (36:78)

"Shall we indeed be returned to (our) former state of life? Even after we are crumbled bones?" (79:10 and 11)

"There is no (other life) but our (present) life of this world, and never shall we be resurrected (on the Day of Resurrection)." (6:29)

"Far, very far is that which you are promised. There is nothing but our life of this world! We die and we live! And we are not going to be resurrected!" (23:36 and 37).

"This is a strange thing! (50:2). This is only the tales of the ancients!" (23:82)

"There is nothing but our first death, and we shall not be resurrected. If so "Then bring back us our forefathers, if you speak the truth!" (44:35 and 36).

"Thus the disbelievers still have doubt in the Resurrection." (6:2)

Allah answered to all these questions by confirming:

"Does man (a disbeliever) think that We shall not assemble his bones? Yes! We are Able to put together in perfect order the tips of his fingers. (Al Qiyama, 75:3 and 4).

"He will give life to them Who created them for the first time! And He is the All-Knower of every creation!" (36:79).

Allah warns men: "but (you men) love the present life of this world, and leave (neglect) the Hereafter." (75:20 and 21).

Importance of Fingertips:

At the time of revelation of Quran, fingertips were known to contain ordinary curves of fingertips without any specific importance. Allah is specifically referring to the fingertips because it carries the identity of an individual, that is the "finger print" or a natural signature. The Creator only knows about the importance of what He had created. If Allah has mentioned in Quran means, it is of utmost significance with some uniqueness.

Its importance has only been fully understood in the nineteenth century. In 1856, Genn Ginsen, found out that the pattern of finger prints is unique to individuals. Sir Francis Golt, the cousin of famous Charles Darwin did a research on the uniqueness of fingerprint. "No two people have ever been found to have the same finger prints, including identical twins." Each finger of the same person shows a unique print. The probability of two persons having exactly same fingerprints will be one in 64 billion persons.

Scientific facts about finger prints:

Fingerprints are minute curvatures or friction ridges, following whorls and valley pattern. Each ridge contains pores from the sweat glands present below the skin. They are formed at the fourth month of a fetus. The movement of fetus in the watery medium of womb, create pressure and the friction also causes the formation of ridges on the tiny fingers. The ridges thus formed are due to the fusion of epidermis with dermis. They remain permanent and distinct till death. The type of the pattern of a person is inherited, but the unique arrangements of the ridges is not genetically linked.

The pattern of curves in the palm and fingers on touching, leave a mark on any dry object with rough or smooth surface. From these marks we can identify the person who has touched it. In 1880 finger printing became the scientific method of identification in forensic science. Edward Henry first categorized the fingerprints into three basic types - whorl, loop, (most common) and arch (rare). FBI (Federal Bureau of Investigation) further subdivided this to nine types. The Automated Fingerprint Identification System (AFIS) is used widely to obtain, store and analyze the fingerprints by various departments. Finger tip patterns of employees of offices, hospitals and industries, are recorded in biometric attendance machine to check the time of entry and exit.

Fingerprints are one of the signs of Allah:

Allah has designed these ridges in the palm, foot and fingers and toes, relatively in small area of few square centimeters of our body. Uniqueness and diversification of its pattern is a sign of His Power and Greatness. It is one of the wonderful and miraculous sign in our body. The fingerprint is the most honest and powerful evidence for an individual in this world; and the most genuine testimony in the Hereafter also. There will not be any confusion of individuals after Resurrection.

The creation of this highly diversified pattern is an extraordinary creativity by the Almighty. Recreating the same image, after the complete destruction of its tissue is super ordinary. Seemingly insignificant tip of fingers may carry some information of our body [الله اعلم!] which future discoveries may/will reveal something more significant.

As Allah asserts, "We will show them Our Signs in the universe and in their own selves, until it becomes manifest to them that this (the Quran) is the truth. Is it not sufficient in regard to your Lord that He is a Witness over all things?" (41:53). Yes! He is Allah, the Creator, the Inventor of all things (59:24), the Bestower of all forms! He is Allah All-Mighty, the Compeller, the Supreme! Glory be to Him! (59: 23).

الحمدلله

8. Mention the appropriate Ayath related to this picture.

Answer: Al-Araf, 7:40.

[لَا تُفَتَّحُ لَهُمْ أَبْوَابُ السَّمَاءِ وَلَا يَدْخُلُونَ الْجَنَّةَ حَتَّىٰ يَلِجَ الْجَمَلُ فِي سَمِّ الْخِيَاطِ] "The doors of heaven shall not be opened for them, nor shall they enter the garden until the camel pass through the eye of the needle"

Allah عز وجل says in Surathul Araf: Those who reject or deny Our revelations and turn away from them arrogantly, when they die and when their souls are taken to the heaven, the doors of heaven will not open for their soul. They cannot enter into Paradise. Allah compares their situation with a camel. It is impossible for a camel (جَمَلٌ) to pass through the eye of a needle (سَمَّ الْخِيَاطِ). Likewise, the arrogant deniers who disbelieve, Allah, the Messenger and their Message, it is not possible for them to pass through the gates of Paradise. It is a hyperbole, a figure of speech that exaggerates and lays emphasis.

There is claim that the word (جَمَل) in this ayath is translated as "camel" should actually be a "cable or rope'"' Mujahid and Ikrimah said that Ibn Abbas used to recite this Ayah this way, "Until the thick rope goes through the eye of the needle,"

Ibn Jarir reported that Al-Bara said that the Messenger of Allah ﷺ mentioned, "the capturing the soul of the `Fujjar'(الفُجَّار) (the wicked sinner or disbeliever), and that his/her soul will be ascended to heaven and the angels, there will ask, "Who's wicked soul is this?" They will reply, `The soul of so-and-so,' calling him by the worst names he was called in this life. When they reach the (lower) heaven, they will ask that its door be opened for the soul, but it will not be opened for them." This is a part of a long Hadith which was also recorded by Abu Dawud, An-Nasa'i and Ibn Majah.

The same camel and needle example also is referred in the Bible (New Testament) at three places. (Matthew 19:24; Mark 10:25; Luke 18:25).

Once a rich young man approached Jesus and asked, "What it took to have eternal life?" (Matthew, 19:16). Jesus then told him if he wanted to be perfect, sell all his owned property, give it to the poor, and follow him! After hearing these words, the rich man went away sadly. He did not wish to part with his property. (Matthew 19:23). The Bible then refers to this camel example. Then Jesus said, "Truly I say to you, it is extremely difficult for a rich man to enter into the kingdom of heaven. And again I say to you, it is easier for a camel to pass through the eye of a needle than for a rich man to enter into the kingdom of God" (Matthew,19:24). With man, this is impossible, but not with God; all things are possible with God" (Matthew 19:26).

Blessed are the poor in spirit, for theirs is the Kingdom of Heaven. (Matthew 5:3)

Here the meaning is if God wishes, He can make impossible thing to become possible. Upon His Grace, Mercy and Forgiveness He allows even the sinners to enter into Paradise, when they repent at right time. [الله اعلم !] Once the Prophet ﷺ warned his companions, saying, "You should know that you will not get entry into Paradise merely by virtue of your deeds". They asked "Is it we or you also?" He replied, "Yes, I too shall enter Paradise, merely by Allah's Grace and Mercy."

So repent for your sins and pray to Almighty Allah for Jannah in the Hereafter as guided in the Quran:

★ "And make me one of the inheritors of the Paradise of Delight." [Ash-Shuara, 26:85]

★ "My Lord! build for me a house with Thee in the garden" [At-Tahrim, 66:11[[

★ "O Allah! I ask for Jannah"

Ya Allah! Make our whole family enter into Jannathul Firdhouse! Ameen Ya Rubb!

الحمدلله

9. Can you relate this picture of two seas, to any one of two verses of Quran?

Answer: [مَرَجَ ٱلْبَحْرَيْنِ يَلْتَقِيَانِ o بَيْنَهُمَا بَرْزَخٌ لَّا يَبْغِيَانِ] "He has let loose the two seas meeting together. Between them is the barrier which none of them can transgress" (Ar Rahaman, 55:19, 20).

[وَهُوَ ٱلَّذِى مَرَجَ ٱلْبَحْرَيْنِ هَذَا عَذْبٌ فُرَاتٌ وَهَذَا مِلْحٌ أُجَاجٌ وَجَعَلَ بَيْنَهُمَا بَرْزَخًا وَحِجْرًا مَّحْجُورًا] " And it is He who has set free the two seas one is palatable and sweet and the other is salty and bitter; and He has set a barrier and a complete partition between them" (Al Furqan, 25:53)

In the Gulf of Alaska, the heavy sediment laden water from Glaciers and rivers pour into the open ocean. One is light colored, less dense, mineral rich and sediment laden and other is dark blue with high salinity content. The temperatures of two waters are also different. Due to these differences they never mix, even in depth but their intersecting borders are not static.

Similarly,

- ❖ In the northern Jutland Denmark, the Baltic Sea and North Sea meet marking a line of white foam.
- ❖ The Atlantic Ocean and Indian Ocean show such partition in Cape Agulhas.
- ❖ The Atlantic Ocean meets with the Mediterranean Sea at Gibralter with such barrier.

- ❖ Such barrier and partition zone is deduced when any river flows into the sea but cannot be seen by human eye. The Oceano-graphers call this zone as pycnocline zone.

For men of understanding these are indeed the signs of Allah. "Those who remember Allah standing, sitting and lying down on their sides and think deeply about the creation of the heavens and the earth (say): "Our Lord! You have not created this without purpose, glory be to You. Give as salvation from the punishment of Fire." (Al-Imran, 3:191).

Allah says, "Travel in the land and see how (Allah) originated the creation and then Allah will bring forth the creation of the Hereafter. Verily Allah is able to do all things." (Al-Ankabut, 29:20). "So glorify with praises the name of your Lord, the Greatest!" (Al-Waqiah, 56:96). [الله اعلم !]

الحمدلله

بِسْمِ ٱللَّهِ ٱلرَّحْمَٰنِ ٱلرَّحِيمِ

2. Who are They?

1. "By time! Verily! Man is in loss" Who are those who are an exception to this?

Answer: They are:

1. those who believe in Allah [سبحانه وتعالى] and do righteous good deeds,

2. those who recommend one another to the truth and

3. those who recommend one another to patience.

With these three verses, the essence of the Quran is revealed about utilization of time given to us, in one surah. Ibn Kathir says, "It is a warning to believers not to waste time or they could be humiliated or even ruined." Abu Madinah reported: 'Whenever two men among the companions of the Prophet ﷺ would meet, they would not part until one of them recited to the other, "By time, surely man is in loss" (103:1 and 2) and the other would bid him farewell with peace.'

1. Allah asserts in Quran, "Those who believe" are:

Those who say, "Our Lord! Verily, we have heard the call of one (Muhammad ﷺ) calling to Faith: 'Believe in your Lord' and we have believed." (3:193). Allahuthala has provided the definition of believers in the Quran: "The believers are only those who, when Allah is mentioned, feel a fear in their hearts and when His Verses are recited unto them, they increase their Faith; and they put their trust in their Lord" (8:2). He commands to the believers: "O My slaves who believe! Be afraid of your Lord and keep your duty to Him. Good is for those who do good in this world" (39:10).

Allah ﷻ mentions the qualities of believers as:

"Al-Birr is (the quality of) the one who believes in Allah, the Last Day, the Angels, the Book, the Prophets and gives his wealth, in spite of love for it, to the kinsfolk, to the orphans, and to the poor, and to the wayfarer, and to those who ask, and to set slaves free, performs As-Salath and gives the Zakat, and who fulfill their covenant when they make it, and who are As-Sabirin in extreme poverty and ailment (disease) and at the time of fighting. Such are the people of the truth and they are Al Muttaqun." (2:177)

Allah [SWT] has promised that "We will indeed make victorious Our Messengers and those who believe in this world's life and on the Last Day" (40: 51). "Moreover, Shaithan has no power over those who believe and put their trust only in their Lord" (16: 99).

2. And those who believe and fulfill righteous good deeds are:

"The best of creatures." (98:7). 'They remember Allah much' (26:227). 'They humble themselves (in repentance and obedience) before their Lord' (11:23). Allah, the Ghafoor, will give them "forgiveness and Rizqun Karim." (34:4) 'He will guide them through their Faith' (10:9). 'He, the Noor, may take them, from darkness to light' (65:11) and a "great reward" (5:9).

'He will bestow love for them (in the hearts of the believers)' (19:96). 'He will remit from them their evil deeds' (29:7). 'He will change their sins into good deeds' (25:70). 'He grants them succession to (the present rulers) in the earth' (24:55). 'He may reward them out of His Bounty' (30:45) 'with an endless reward' (41:8) and promised 'to dwell in Paradise forever.' (2:82)

3. Recommend each other to the truth:

Let us list the truths mentioned in the Quran.

Allah is Wahid [One]:"In truth He (Allah) is the only one Ilah (God)" (6:19). "He has created the Heavens and the Earth with truth, and He shaped you (man) and made good your (his) shapes, and to Him is the final Return." (64:3).

His words are true: "And whose words can be truer than those of Allah? (Of course, none)" (4:122). "He further says, "O mankind! Verily, there has come to you the Messenger (Muhammad ﷺ) with the truth from your Lord, so believe in him, it is better for you." (4:170). "Verily, it (this Quran) is an absolute truth with certainty" (69: 51). It is the Word that separates (the truth from false-hood) (86:13)."

His Promise is true: "Allah's Promise is the truth, and there is no doubt about the coming of the Hour." (45:32). On the day of resurrection: "The earth will shine with the light of its Lord (Allah, when He will come to judge among men) and the Book will be placed (open) and the Prophets and the witnesses will be brought forward, and it will be judged between them with truth, and they will not be wronged." (39:69).

"The Muttaqun (pious), will be in a seat of truth (i.e. Paradise)," (54:54 and 55). "Paradise is a promise of truth, which they have been promised." (46:16). "On the Day when those who disbelieve will be exposed to the Fire (it will be said to them): "Is this not the truth?" They will say: "Yes, By our Lord!" (46:34). Understand that Allahuthala has provided a long list relating to truth, to the humanity and the Jinn; through Quran. Adhere to them in your day today life. Recommend such truth to others also. It is a command to you from Allah, your Creator, your Sustainer, your All in All.

4. Recommend each other to patience:

Allah [SWT] say to the believers: "O you who believe! Seek help in patience and Salath. Truly! Allah is with As-Sabirin (patient one)" (2:153). "There will be forgiveness and a great reward (Paradise)" (11:11), for the patient ones. "The Reward of Allah (in the Hereafter) is better for those who believe and do righteous good deeds and this none shall attain except those who are patient (in following the truth)." (28:80) "Only those who are patient shall receive their rewards in full, without reckoning." (Az-Zumar, 39:10). Allah [عَزَّ وَجَلَّ] repeated the same in Surah Balad: "Those who made effort to pass on the path that is steep, then he became one of those who believed, and recommended one another to perseverance and patience, and (also) recommended one another to pity and compassion." (90:11 and 17).

The Prophet ﷺ said, "Loose no time to perform good deeds before you are caught up by one of seven calamities awaiting you": (At-Tirmidhi).

1. A starvation, which may impair your wisdom;

2. A prosperity, which may mislead you;

3. An ailment, which may damage your health;

4. An old age, which may harm your senses;

5. A sudden death;

6. Coming of Dajjal or

7. Doomsday, which is indeed the hardest one and most bitter.

May Allah Subhanahuthala bless and enable us to utilize the time, so that we are in a position to fulfill His command!

الحمدلله

2. Allah (عَزَّوَجَلَّ) has commanded in Quran "sit not with them." Who are those people referred by Him?

Answer: Those who deny and mock the verses of Allahuthala; and those who are engaged in false conversation, about the verses of Quran.

In the - 140th ayath of surah Nisa of Quran Allah (عَزَّوَجَلَّ) states: "And it has already been revealed to you in the Book (this Quran) that when you hear the Verses of Allah being denied and mocked at, then sit not with them, until they engage in a talk other than that (but if you stayed with them) certainly in that case you would be like them. Surely, Allah will collect the hypocrites and disbelievers all together in Hell."

"Already revealed to you" here refers to the ayath 68 of Surah Al-Anam: "And when you (Muhammad ﷺ) see those who engage in a false conversation about Our Verses (of the Quran) by mocking at them, stay away from them till they turn to another topic. And if Shaitan causes you to forget, then after the remembrance sit not you in the company of those people who are the Zalimun (polytheists and wrong-doers, etc.).

Allah سبحانه وتعالى forbids a believer from joining the company of such people, who deny and mock His ayaath. Because it amounts to participating along with them in mocking and denying. By joining them, the believer will be availing the burden of sin, similar to those people who were mocking.

Allah (SWT) also commands the believers not to stay with those people who are engaged in false conversation and mocking of the verses of Quran, till they shift to another topic. Because such people are heedless and reckless. Instead of falling into that sin along with them, it is better to leave such people as a sign of disapproval of their behaviour.

When a believer stays away, there may be a chance of the mockers realising their mockery. Or they may avoid such discussion and never repeat it again. Even if a believer forgets about this by the work of Shaithan; and as and when he remembers he will leave the company of those Zalimun. A hadhees informs, "My Ummah was forgiven unintentional errors, forgetfulness and what they are coerced to do." May Allah [عَزَّ وَ جَلَّ] protect us!

الحمدلله

3. "So did We restore him to his mother, that she might be delighted, and that she might not grieve, and that she might know that the Promise of Allah is true." Who is that mother?

Answer: Mother of the Prophet Musa (AS).

Firaun, the Pharaoh the tyrant king of Egypt, came to know either through a dream or from his kingdom's learned scholars of previous scriptures that a son from Israelites, on growing up, will overthrow him. So he commanded to kill all the boy babies born therafter to prevent this prediction. Seeing this cruel command, the experts from Pharaoh's court requested him: "If it is continued Pharaoh will lose manpower of enslaved Israelites. They suggested instead to kill boy babies in the alternate years."

Therefore, Harun (AS) the elder brother of Musa (AS) was born in such an alternate year where the killing of boy babies had been spared. Musa (AS) was born in a year, in which boys were slaughtered. Firaun appointed midwives to inform the birth of boy babies and soldiers to slain such babies.

Allah ﷻ described, the birth of Musa (AS) in surah Qasas: "Verily, Firaun, the tyrant king weakened the Children of Israel by killing their sons and letting their females live." (28:4). "Allah favoured these weak, oppressed group to be rulers making them the inheritors of their land" (28:5). "And to establish them in the land, and We let Firaun and Haman and their hosts receive from them that which they feared." (28:6).

When Musa (AS) was born, Allah inspired the mother of Musa (AS), by saying: "Suckle the baby but when you fear for him, then cast him into the river and fear not, nor grieve. Verily! We shall bring him back to you, and make him one of Our Prophets." (28:7). She obeyed immediately the divine revelation, she arranged to make a basket for Musa (AS), nursed him, put him into the basket and placed that in Nile river.

"Then the household of Firaun picked him up, that he might become for them an enemy and the cause of grief. Verily! Firaun and Haman and their hosts were sinners." (28:8). "And the wife of Firaun said: "A comfort of the eye for me and for you. Kill him not, perhaps he may be of benefit to us, or we may adopt him as a son." "And they perceive not the result of that." (28:9).

"And the heart of the mother of Musa (AS) became empty from every thought, except the thought of the baby. She was very near to disclose his case, but Allah strengthened her heart with Faith, so that she might remain as one of the believers." (28:10).

She said to Musa's (AS) sister: "Follow him." So his sister watched him from a far place, secretly, while they perceived not (28:11). Allah had already forbidden the other foster suckling mothers for him, until his sister came up and said: "Shall I direct you to a household who will rear him for you, and sincerely they will look after him in a good manner?" (28:12)

Ibn Kathir, in his Tafsir recorded that the soldiers took her to the household she referred, after a complete enquiry, brought the baby there. The baby accepted suckling of the woman of that household! No body suspected her, as the baby's real mother. Musa (AS)'s mother was so happy about the situation, which turned to her favour; with ease. Firaun's wife was also happy and she rewarded generously with gifts to the mother. Musa's (AS) mother kept her child in her house because she had the responsibility of looking after her husband and two children. The wife of Firaun agreed to that also.

Therefore, Allah [SWT] fulfilled His promise to the mother of Musa (AS). Allahuthala relieved the worry and distress of the entire family since it obeyed His command. In a hadhees, the Prophet ﷺ has said: "He who works to earn his livelihood and keeps in view Allah's good will also has a likeness with the Musa's (AS) mother, who suckled her own son as well as received her wages for the service, too."

The baby was named "Moses" in Pharaoh's house. It is a Coptic word, which means, "I drew him out of the water", for 'mo' means water and 'oshe' means rescued. As suckling was over, he was taken to the palace and grew up as a prince.

Allahuthala stated that: "So did We restore him to his mother, that she might be delighted, and that she might not grieve, and that she might know that the Promise of Allah is true. But most of them know not." (28:13). This decree of Allah helped Musa (AS) to attain his full strength, with religious knowledge of Israelites and reared up with the honour of an Egyptian prince.

The two other mothers, as mentioned in Quran are:

1. Bibi Marium's mother, when she begot a girl baby, prayed to protect her and her offspring from Shaitan. There is no report of a single incidant of Shaitan's whisper to either Marium or Isa ibn Marium (AS).

2. While Bibi Marium went alone for her child's birth, to a place where there was no one, Allah [عَزَّ وَ جَلَّ] provided her with food and drink. She was advised to fast and not to say anything to her society, if they enquire about her baby. The baby spoke to them by "saying of truth about which they dispute." (19:34).

O, believing mothers! Allahuthala will bless you and your children if you intend and take effort to bring them as good Muslims. Allah will provide you with good reward in return, beyond your expectations.

Lesson from the mother of Musa (AS):

★ Before any trail, Allah Subhanahuthala will prepare the faithful believers, to go through the situation.

★ After the hardship, Allahuthala will reward them beyond their imagination.

★ Take necessary precautions and arrangements (actions according to the situations and prayer) to convert the difficult time, to seek Allah's Mercy.

★ Realize that Allah سبحانه وتعالى will not cause any difficulty, beyond the tolerance level.

★ "It may be that you dislike a thing and Allah ﷻ brings through it a great deal of good." (4:19).

★ Thus, Allah [SWT] will always reward the good doers (48:14).

★ Understand, that the difficulties and trails are only temporary. They will pass away.

الحمدلله

4. Who are Hawariyyun?

Answer: They are the disciples/helpers of Isa ibn Marium (AS).

The root word "hawr" means to whiten, to bleach, to purify, to clean, to change, to transform, to amend and to alter etc. Hawariyyun means, "He who whitens cloth" or "He who has been appointed chosen and purified from all kinds of defects" or "a companion and a helper".

Hawariyyuns are mentioned in three surahs of Quran. In Ala-Imran, when Isa ibn Marium (AS) came to know the disbelief of his people, he exclaimed: "Who will be my helpers in Allah's cause?" Al-Hawariyyun said: 'We are the helpers of Allah; we believe in Allah, and bear witness that we submit to Allah. "Our Lord! We believe in what You have sent down and we follow the Messenger; so write us down among those who bear witness." Because of their belief, Allah made them superior than the other believers and disbelievers.' (3:52 and 53). The same is repeated again as in another ayath, "And when I (Allah) inspired Al-Hawariyyun to believe in Me and My Messenger, they said: 'We believe. And bear witness that we are Muslims.' in surah Al-Maidah. (5:111) Similarly, Allah mentioned the victory of these "Allah's helpers" in surah As- Saff (61:14).

Once the Al-Hawariyyun asked Isa ibn Marium (AS)': "O Isa, son of Marium (AS)! Can your Lord send down to us table spread (with food) from the heaven? " Isa ibn Marium (AS) said: "Fear Allah, if you are indeed believers" (5:112). They said: "We wish to eat thereof and to satisfy our hearts (to be stronger in faith) and to know that you have indeed told us the truth and that we ourselves be its witnesses." (5:113).

The best sustainer Allah [ٱلرَّزَّاقُ] sends down the table spread as a festival and sign, on condition that if any one still disbelieves a great punishment will be given. (5:114 and 115). After Isa ibn Marium (AS) these helpers went to different places and spread his message. The followers of Isa ibn Marium (AS) were called as Christians (in Quran they are referred as Nasara) and the Hawariyyun as "Apostles".

الحمدلله

5. "If you both turn to Allah; then indeed your hearts are already inclined (to this)." (At-Tahrim, 66: 4). Who are those two?

Answer: The Prophet's ﷺ wives, Hafsa (RA) and Ayesha (RA).

"And when the Prophet ﷺ secretly communicated a piece of information to one of his wives - but when she informed (others) of it, and Allah made him to know it, he made known part of it and avoided a part; so when he informed her of it, she said: 'Who informed you of this?' He said: 'The Knowing, the one Aware, informed me.' (66:3). Allahuthala said to them, "It will be better if you wives both turn to Allah in repentance, for your hearts are already inclined. But if you continue to collaborate against him, then know that Allah Himself is his Guardian; Jibreel (AS), the righteous believers, and the angels are all his supporters as well." (66: 4).

In this ayath Allahuthala has not mentioned as to:

- ❖ what is that secret?

- the names of the wives and
- whom it has been shared?

From Umar bin Kattab's (RA) narrations, we come to know that one of the wives mentioned was his own daughter Hafsa (RA), who shared the information to Ayesha (RA).

Abdullah bin Abbas narrated: 'I had been eager to ask Umar (RA) about the two ladies from among the wives of the Prophet ﷺ regarding whom Allah said: "If you two turn in repentance to Allah your hearts are indeed so inclined (66.4)", till I performed Hajj along with Umar (RA). He went aside (to answer the call of nature) and I also went aside along with him carrying a tumbler of water. When he had answered the call of nature and returned. I poured water on his hands from the tumbler and he performed ablution. I enquired, "O, Chief of the believers! Who were the two ladies from among the wives of the Prophet ﷺ in ayath 66:4 of Quran?"

Umar (RA) stated that "I am astonished at your question, O Ibn Abbas. They were Hafsa (RA) and Ayesha (RA). Then Umar (RA) went on relating the narration and said. "I and an Ansari neighbour of mine from Bani Umaiya bin Zaid who used to live in Awali Al-Madina, used to visit the Prophet ﷺ in turns. He used to go one day, and I another day. When I went I would bring him the news of what had happened that day regarding the instructions and orders and when he went, he used to do the same for me.

We, the Quraish, used to have authority over women, but when we came to live with the Ansar, we noticed that the Ansari women had the upper hand over their men, so our women started acquiring the habits of the Ansari women. Once I shouted at my wife and she paid me back in my coin and I disliked that she should answer me back. She said, 'Why do you take it ill that I retort upon you? By Allah, the wives of the Prophet ﷺ retort upon him and some of them may not speak with him for the whole day till night.' What she said scared me and I said to her, 'Whoever amongst them does so, will be a great loser.' Then I dressed myself and went to Hafsa (RA) and asked her, 'Does any of you keep Allah's Messenger ﷺ angry all the day long till night?' She replied in the affirmative. I said, 'She is a ruined losing person (and will never have success)! Doesn't she fear that Allah may get angry for the anger of Allah's Messenger ﷺ and thus she will be ruined? Don't ask Allah's Messenger ﷺ too many things, and don't retort upon him in any case, and don't desert him. Demand from me whatever you like, and don't be tempted to imitate your neighbour (i.e. Ayesha [RA]) in her behavior towards the Prophet ﷺ for she is more beautiful than you, and more beloved to Allah's Messenger ﷺ.

In those days it was rumored that Ghassan, (a tribe living in Sham) was getting prepared their horses to invade us. My companion went to the Prophet ﷺ on the day of his turn, went and returned to us at night and knocked at my door violently, asking whether I was sleeping. I was scared (by the hard knocking) and came out to him. He said that a great thing had happened. I asked him: "What is it? Have Ghassan come?" He replied that it was worse and more serious than that, and added that Allah's Apostle had divorced all his wives. I said, Hafsa (RA) is a ruined loser! I expected that would happen someday.' So I dressed myself and offered the Fajr prayer with the Prophet ﷺ. Then the Prophet ﷺ entered an upper room and stayed there alone.

I went to Hafsa (RA) and found her weeping. I asked her, 'Why are you weeping? Didn't I warn you? Have Allah's Messenger ﷺ divorced you all?' She replied, 'I don't know. He is there in the upper room.' I then went out and came to the pulpit and found a group of people around it and some of them were weeping. Then I sat with them for some time, but could not endure the situation. So I went to the upper room where the Prophet ﷺ was and requested to a black slave of his: "Will you get the permission of for Umar (RA) (to enter)? The slave went in, talked to the Prophet ﷺ about it and came out saying, 'I mentioned you to him but he did not reply.' So, I went and sat with the people who were sitting by the pulpit, but I could not bear the situation, so I went to the slave again and said: "Will you get he permission for Umar (RA)? He went in and brought the same reply as before.

When I was leaving, behold, the slave called me saying, "Allah's Messenger ﷺ has granted you permission." So, I entered upon the Prophet ﷺ and saw him lying on a mat without mattress on it, and the mat had left its mark on the body of the Prophet, ﷺ and he was leaning on a leather pillow stuffed with palm fibres. I greeted him and while still standing, I said: "Have you divorced your wives?" He raised his eyes to me and replied in the negative. And then while still standing, I said chatting: "Will you heed what I say, 'O Allah's Messenger ﷺ We, the people of Quraish used to have the upper hand over our women, and when we came to the people whose women had the upper hand over them..." Umar (RA) told the whole story (about his wife). "On that the Prophet ﷺ smiled." Umar (RA) further said, "I then said, 'I went to Hafsa (RA) and said to her: "Do not be tempted to imitate Ayesha (RA) for she is more beautiful than you and more beloved to the Prophet ﷺ." The Prophet ﷺ smiled again. When I saw him smiling, I sat down and cast a glance at the room, and by Allah, I couldn't see anything of importance but three hides. I said him, "Invoke Allah to make your followers prosperous for the Persians and the Byzantines have been made prosperous and given worldly luxuries, though they do not worship Allah?'

The Prophet ﷺ was leaning then and said, 'O Ibn Al-Khattab! Do you have any doubt (that the Here-after is better than this world)? These people have been given rewards of their good deeds in this world itself.' I asked the Prophet ﷺ 'Please ask Allah's forgiveness for me.' The Prophet ﷺ did not go to his wives because of the secret which Hafsa (RA) had disclosed to Ayesha (RA), and he said that he would not go to his wives for one month as he was angry with them when Allah admonished him (for his oath that he would not approach Maria). When 29 days had passed, the Prophet ﷺ went to Ayesha (RA) first of all. She said to him, 'You took an oath that you would not come to us for one month, and today only twenty-nine days have passed, as I have been counting them day by day.' The Prophet ﷺ said, "The month is also of 29 days." "That month consisted of 29 days."

Ayesha (RA) said, "When the Divine revelation of Choice was revealed, the Prophet ﷺ started with me, saying to me, 'I am telling you something but you need not hurry to give the reply till you can consult your parents." Ayesha (RA) knew that her parents would not advise her to part with the Prophet ﷺ. The Prophet ﷺ said that Allah had said: 'O Prophet! Say to your wives; 'If you desire The life of this world and its glitter, ... then come! I will make a provision for you and set you free in a handsome manner. But if you seek Allah and His Apostle, and The Home of the Here-after, then Verily, Allahuthala has prepared for the good-doers amongst you a great reward.' (33:28) Ayesha (RA) said, 'Am I to consult my parents about this? I indeed prefer Allah, His Apostle, and the Home of the Hereafter.' After that the Prophet ﷺ gave the choice to his other wives and they also gave the same reply as Ayesha did." (Sahih al-Bukhari, 2468)

So Umar (RA) advised them saying, "Either stop bothering Allah's Messenger ﷺ or Allah [SWT] might provide him better wives than you." Imam Ahamed, Muslim, At-Tirmidhi and An-Nasa'i also collected this Hadith using various chains of narrations.

After all, the wives of the Prophet ﷺ are the normal human beings. They, out of affection to their husband tried to attract his attention towards them. So Allah warns them in Quran, for such intensions. Allah, the most Gentle, reminds to the Prophet ﷺ's wives that their husband was not an ordinary person. The wives of Prophets ﷺ

will always have a high status in the society and they must not act against their husband, the Prophet ﷺ.

Therefore, Allah, the most Forbearing, required them, to turn to Him and ask forgiveness for their deeds. Even if the wives caused harm to the Prophet ﷺ, Allah assured of guarding him through Jibreel (AS), his faithful companions and lots of angels. (66:4)

The Prophet's wives irritated him to such an extent that he wished to be away from them. And if he divorces them, Allahuthala will provide better women - who would be as defined in the ayath: [مِنكُنَّ مُسْلِمَاتٍ مُؤْمِنَاتٍ قَانِتَاتٍ تَائِبَاتٍ عَابِدَاتٍ سَائِحَاتٍ ثَيِّبَاتٍ وَأَبْكَارًا]. "It may be if he divorced you (all) that his Lord will give him instead of you, wives better than you, Muslims (who submit to Allah), believers, obedient to Allah, turning to Allah in repentance, worshipping Allah sincerely, fasting or emigrants (for Allah's sake), previously married and virgins" (66:5). By this ayath Allah عَزَّ وَجَلَّ expected the Prophet's wives to be submissive, faithful, obedient, penitent, adorers and fasters.

Why Allahuthala has brought the private/family matter of the Prophet into the public? To guide the believers, both men and women. Allah openly warns the believers, "O you who believe! Save yourselves and your families from a fire whose fuel is men and stones." Therfore, repent and turn to Him for the sins committed - small or big!

الحمدلله

6. Who are the people of Al-Araf?

Answer: The people whose good and bad deeds are equal on the Day of Judgement. They are gathered on Al-Araf - an elevated spacious barrier between Heaven and Hell.

According to Ibn Jarir, "Every elevated piece of land is known by Arabs as Urf". And Araf is plural form of "Urf." As-Suddi is of opinion that "Al-Araf is so named because its residents recognize (يَعْرِفُونَ) people." Al-Araf is a heightened barrier wall between the Hell and the Heaven. It prevents the people of the Hell from reaching the Heaven.

There is another ayath in Quran, referring about this wall: "So a wall will be put up between them (believers and hypocrites), with a gate therein. Inside it will be mercy, and outside it will be torment." (57:13).

On this wall will be those, who are referred as the people of "Al Araf". Their good deeds and bad deeds will weigh equal. Their evil deeds will prevent them from entering Paradise and their good deeds will enable them to avoid the Hell. They will be awaiting the judgement of Allah on the wall.

The men of Al-Araf, as they are in an elevated place, will be in a position to recognize; even talk to the "Dwellers of Paradise" and will be able to greet them with Salam. They can talk to the "Dwellers of Hell-fire" and will wonder how their great number and wealth did not bring any benefit in their Here-after, due to their arrogance in the worldly life. If the men of Al-Araf pray; and on its acceptance they will be granted Jannah. With the Mercy of Allah, they will enter the Heaven.

Allah provides a clear picture about the events that will happen after the Day of Judgement and about the consequence of their deeds in this world.

Quran records:

"And between them will be a barrier screen and on Al-Araf (a wall with elevated places) will be men (whose good and evil deeds would be equal in scale), who would recognise all (of the Paradise and Hell people), by their marks. They will call out to the dwellers of Paradise, "Salamun Alaikum" and at that time they (men on Al-Araf) will not yet have entered it (Paradise), but they will hope to enter (it) with certainty." (7:46).

"And when their eyes will be turned towards the dwellers of the Fire, they will say: "Our Lord! Place us not with the people who are Zalimun." (7:47)

"And the men on Al-Araf will call unto the men whom they would recognize by their marks, saying: "Of what benefit to you were your great numbers (and hordes of wealth), and your arrogance against Faith?"(7:48).

"Are they those, of whom you swore that Allah would never show them mercy. (Behold! It has been said to them): "Enter Paradise, no fear shall be on you, nor shall you grieve." (7:49).

The last ayath refers to the characteristic of the people of "Al Araf". Those are the people who had committed sin; unable to enter Heaven. The people in the world had sweared that Allah will not show them any Mercy, but if Allahuthala wills they will enter Heaven.

There are number of opinions about these ashabul Araf:

1. These people are the sinners among Muslims,

- ❖ who committed major sins (like murder, or getting riba [interest], people not doing their prescribed duties) but not repenting to Allah for their sins.
- ❖ who went to Jihadh disobeying their parents.
- ❖ who committed lot of minor sins but not having enough good deeds.
- ❖ who had not paid their debts, before death.
- ❖ who performed good deeds for Allah's sake but claimed about such deeds proudly to others.

2. Or those people who are innocent, not sinful but they are not being righteous. Those who have followed their ancesters. The people who lived before or after coming of any of the Prophets. [الله اعلم !]

Therefore, O believers!

★ Fear Allahuthala, while you are in this world! Increase your good deeds as they erase your bad deeds and your balance should be heavy with good deeds, while you leave this world!

★ Thank Allah [سبحانه وتعالى] for He has promised Paradise for the righteous ones. Seek Allah's guidance to be among the righteous!

★ Forget not that Allah ﷻ will put the wrong doers and disbelievers in Hell-fire!

★ Seek Allah's forgiveness and also refuge from Hell-fire.

★ Realize that Allah [سبحانه وتعالى] will be always Merciful. Turn to Him in repentance. He is ready to accept your repentance, even if your sins are many.

★ Unlike the prayers of "Dwellers of Hell-fire"; the prayers of men of Al-Araf will be always accepted, as Allah [SWT] is always extremely Merciful!

الحمدلله

7. Who are the slaves of the Most Beneficent Allah?

Answer: The slaves of the Most Beneficent (Allah) are:

★ "Those who walk on the earth in humility and sedateness" (Al-Furqan, 25:63)

★ "When the foolish address them (with bad words) they reply back with mild words of gentleness." (Al-Furqan, 25:63)

★ "And those who spend the night before their Lord, prostrate and standing" (25:64).

★ And those who say: "Our Lord! Avert from us the torment of Hell. Verily! Its torment is ever an inseparable, permanent punishment." (25:65).

★ "And those, who, when they spend, are neither extravagant nor niggardly, but hold a Medium (way) between those (extremes)." (25:67).

★ "And those who invoke not any other ilah (god) along with Allah [عَزَّ وَجَلَّ],

★ nor kill such life as Allah ﷻ has forbidden, except for just cause,

★ nor commit illegal sexual intercourse (25:68)

★ Except those who repent and believe (in Islamic Monotheism), and do righteous deeds, for those, Allah will change their sins into good deeds, and Allah is Oft-Forgiving, Most Merciful. (25:70)

★ And those who do not witness falsehood, and if they pass by some evil play or evil talk, they pass by it with dignity. (25:72)

★ And those who, when they are reminded of the Ayath of their Lord, fall not be blind there at (25:73).

Such slaves pray like this:

"Our Lord! Bestow on us from our wives and our offspring who will be the comfort of our eyes, and make us leaders for the Muttaqun" (25:74). "Those will be rewarded: with the highest place (in Paradise) because of their patience. Therein they shall be met with greetings and the word of peace and respect." (25:75). "Abiding therein; excellent it is as an abode, and as a place to dwell." (25:76).

This is a checklist to enter paradise. Find out as to whether you will be eligible to enter Heaven with this checklist.

الحمدلله

بِسْمِ ٱللَّهِ ٱلرَّحْمَٰنِ ٱلرَّحِيمِ

3. Search the Surah, Mention the Ayath

1. Search the surah 17 and mention the ayaath that explain about how to spend the wealth.

Answer: 26, 27, 28, 29 Ayaath.

"And give to the kindred his due and to the Miskin (poor) and to the wayfarer. But spend not wastefully your wealth in the manner of a spendthrift." (17:26). "Verily, spendthrifts are the brothers of Shaitan and the Shaitan is ever ungrateful to his Lord" (17:27).

"And if you (O Muhammad ﷺ) turn away from them (kindred, poor, wayfarer, etc. whom We have ordered you to give their rights, but if you have no money at the time they ask you for it) and you are awaiting a mercy from your Lord for which you hope, then, speak unto them a soft kind word (i.e. Allah will give me and I shall give you)." (17:28). "Let not your hands be tied like a miser to your neck, you become blameworthy and if stretch it forth to its utmost reach like a spend-thrift, you will face severe poverty." (Al-Isra, 17:29)

Therefore:

🎈 Do not be like a miser who does not spend anything.

🎈 Do not be a spend-thrift. Lest, you may face poverty.

🎈 Be moderate with regard to the manner of spending!

Allah سبحانه وتعالى asserts: "But surely, the slaves of the most beneficent Allah, when they spend, are neither extravagant nor niggardly, but hold a medium way between those extremes" (Al-Furqan, 25:67).

When you spend,

▶ Spend for a good cause. Specially for Allah's cause.

▶ Do not count the money while spending for a good cause.

▶ Let no extravagance or pride be mixed up, when you spend.

- Be grateful to Allah for giving you a chance to spend.
- Do not look down upon those who accepts your charity, as they are providing you a favor by its acceptance.
- Neither you expose their dependance on you, nor you expect anything in return.
- Pay your Zakath to needy. This is your savings for your Hereafter.

Most of the companions and the Prophet ﷺ shared their provisions whatever available without saving it for future. Their needs were simple and little. Rich people at the time of Umar (RA) used to walk long distances, in search of persons who required charity. Every rich person has more accountability than a poor person.

Allah, ٱلْهَادِي guides us by informing: "They ask you (O Muhammad ﷺ) what they should spend. Say: Whatever you spend of good must be for parents and kindred and orphans and Al-Masakin (the poor) and the way- farers, (2:215) and to free the captives; and for those in debt; (9:60) and for the unlucky who has lost his property and wealth (70:25). "Charity is for the needy who are too engaged in the cause of Allah to move about in the land for work. Those unfamiliar with their situation will think they are not in need of charity because they do not beg. You can recognize them by their appearance. They do not beg people persistently" (2:273)

Always remember these ayaath from Quran:

"Surely your Lord gives abundant or limited provisions to whoever He wills." (Al-Isra, 17:30). If your provision is insufficient, patiently wait till your Lord enlarges the provisions. If your provision is in abundance, do not think that it is yours! It is Allah's! "Obey Allah and be polite! Those who spend their wealth (in Allah's Cause) by night and day, in secret and in public, they shall have their reward with their Lord. On them shall be no fear, nor shall they grieve." (2:274).

الحمدلله

2. Search the Surah 49, mention the ayath which refers to suspicion, spying and back biting.

Answer: Al- Hujraat, 49:12

"O, you who believe! Avoid much suspicions, indeed some suspicions are sins. And spy not, neither backbite one another. Would one of you like to eat the flesh of his dead brother? You would hate it (so hate backbiting). And fear Allah

Subhanahuthala! Verily, Allah is the One Who accepts repentance, Most Merciful!" (49:12)."

Suspicion:

Allahuthala commands the believers to avoid suspicion, spying and back biting. He calls upon us "O you who believe! Avoid". All these three aspects are acts of thinking, acting and talking ill, about other persons. By such activity, we may harm the person concerned. If we are suspicious about a person, we may develop a wrong feeling about all his deeds and start hating him. We may be persuaded to avoid and neglect him. Some times our suspicion may amount to a sin.

Prying and spying:

It is human nature to pry the secrets, defects, family matters and the deeds of others. People try to get information by listening secretly to the private conversation, by watching the neighbour's house and by attempting to read their communications. Such actions arise out of their curiosity or may be with evil intention, are highly immoral; that may lead them into trouble. Sometimes people immediately communicate, what they hear, to others and thus spread bad name ageist him in the society. It is a wastage of their accountable time. They will not be benefitted by such activities. It prevents them from remembering Allah. They become the friends of Shaitan, who guides them to become astray. Knowledge of certain aspects, make us feel as to why we came to know about it.

To get a clarification of our suspicion, we spy. Spying is an equal evil. Being ignorant of the existence of certain things is a reward. When we spy, we only come to know about a part of the problem. We wrongly decide, at times due to incomplete information. So spying is henious. We may opt to call the concerned person and seek clarity about our doubts. Such an act is far better than spying.

The hidden evil of spying can be learnt from the incidence of Umar (RA):

As a Calipha, once Umar (RA) was in his night rounds. He heard a person singing in his house. Upon curiosity he climbed over the wall of the house and observed a man with wine and woman. He shouted at the man. The man told, "O, Commander of faithful! I committed only one sin and you have done three forbidden things: spying, entering my house – climbing over the wall and not through door, and entering my house without my permission." Hearing this, Ammerul Mumeeneen confessed his mistakes. He made him to promise that he would never repeat this evil deed again. (Abi Bakr Muhammad bin Jafar al- Kharaiti, Makarim al-Akhlaq). By indulging in one wrong act, without our knowledge, we commit many minor sins.

Back biting:

Imam Malik has recorded in Muwatta, on the authority of Muttalib bin Abdullah: "A person asked the Prophet ﷺ: "What is ghibat? (back biting)." The Prophet ﷺ replied: "It is talking of your brother in a way irksome to him." He asked: "Even if it is true, O Messenger of Allah ﷺ? He replied: "If what you said was false, it would then be a slander." Back biting is forbidden in Islam.

Back biting is explained as:

- A kind of gossip, common in human society.
- It is condemned as the worst of the mortal sins.
- It is a kind of insult to the concerned person.
- Some people to cover their mistakes, they talk ill of others.
- It hurts the person affected.
- It spreads a bad name for that person.
- It destroys the 'life of the soul'
- It is used to divert the blame for establishing their place in the dominance of hierarchy.
- It is considered as a form of guilt, arising from inferiority complex.
- It attracts Divine anger.
- It amounts to eating the flesh of one's own dead brother.

The very words are condemnable and the act is much worse than that. Allahuthala has further quoted in Quran as: "Woe to every slanderer and backbiter" (Al-Humaza, 104:1).

How to nullify the effect of back biting?

➢ A backbiter must first realize that he has caused backbiting.

➢ Seek repentance from Allahuthala, for such act is forbidden.

- Never ever indulge in this forbidden act.
- He should compensate the damage caused to the backbitten person.
- If backbitten person is already dead, one who caused the back biting should seek Allah's forgiveness.
- If one is backbitten and alive; if the backbiting is false one who caused the back biting, is bound to refute before the public or seek pardon from the backbitten person.
- And if such fact was true, he should never speak ill of backbitten person in future.

Therefore, the believers must remember this ayath (49:12). Even if you forget and indulge in such an act on being induced by others, never continue it. As soon as you are reminded, depart from that place or part the company of those who are talking. Islam is the way of life! Live as a follower of Islam!

Be aware! Fear Allah Subhanahuthala!

الحمدلله

3. Read the Surah 49 and mention the ayath, which commands neither to scoff nor insult anyone by use of nick names.

Answer: Surah Al-Hujraat, 49:11

"O, you who believe! Let not a group scoff at another group, it may be that the latter are better than the former; nor let (some) women scoff at other women, it may be that the latter are better than the former, nor defame one another, nor insult one another by nicknames. How bad is it, to insult one's brother after having Faith? And whosoever does not repent, then such are indeed Zalimun" (49:11).

This is another proof of "Islam is the way of life" and that "Islam brought social reformation."

Scoffing:

Some people like to make fun of others, mimic them, make pointed reference to them, laugh at their words, work, appearance, dress, defect or shortfalls found in them. Such act amounts to humiliating the affected person. It is not good to hurt anyone by facial expressions, which may expose their faults in public.

A person will scoff other person for the following reasons:

◊ due to his weak faith,

◊ because, their fear of Allahuthala is poor,

◊ spending much time in gossip,

◊ seeking praise from others,

◊ forgetting that they will be inviting punishment from Allah [عَزَّ وَ جَلَّ], by indulging in such acts, as He hates such activity.

Scoffing is forbidden in Islam:

People treat the act of scoffing lightly, though it is forbidden in Islam. Persons who scoff at others, are wrong doers. Such an act may hurt the person affected. Because of scoffing, enmity is produced. Words of scoffing, on being spread in the society may convert a person into a criminal. That is the reason for Allah to forbid such acts, among believing men and women.

Sometimes it pushes the person to Hell-fire. For example, Allahuthala loves a person for his good thoughts, good deeds, or for such acts preferred by Allah. If we make a mockery of such person whom Allah [عَزَّ وَ جَلَّ] loves, by use of undesirable words; we invoke the wrath of Allah ﷻ. Such mockery becomes a greater sin. We know that the Mushrikun were making fun of Rasullullah ﷺ and other companions. We are aware that Allah ﷻ loved them immensely. We are also aware as to what happened to those who made fun of the Prophet ﷺ.

Allah [SWT] asserts in Surah Thowba, "Those who defame such of the believers, they mock at them, Allah will throw back their mockery on them, and they shall have a painful torment" (9:79).

Allah ﷻ also refers to such a behavior in the Surah Al-Mumenoon, "Verily! There was a party of My slaves, who used to say: "Our Lord! We believe, so forgive us, and have mercy on us, for You are the Best of all who show mercy". But you took these people for a laughing stock, so much so that they made you forget My Remembrance while you used to laugh at them. Verily! I have rewarded them this Day for their patience, they are indeed the ones that are successful." (23:109 -111)."

Hadhees about prying:

"O people, who have professed belief verbally, but faith has not yet entered your hearts: Do not pry into the affairs of the Muslims, for he who will pry into the affairs of the Muslims, Allah will pry into his affairs, and he whom Allah follows inquisitively, is disgraced by Him in his own house." (Abu Dhawud).

Muawiyah says that he himself heard the Prophet ﷺ claims: "If you start prying into the secret affairs of the people, you will pervert them, or at least drive them very near perversion." (Abu Dhawud). In another hadhees, he has stated: "When you happen to form an evil opinion about somebody, do not pry about it." (Al-Jassas, Ahkam al-Quran).

According to still another hadhees, the Prophet ﷺ had asserted that: "The one who saw a secret affair of somebody and then concealed it is as though he saved a girl who had been buried alive." (Al-Jassas).

Calling by a nick name:

Again calling one by a nick name also causes humiliation, condemnation or disgrace to the person so called. Nicknames suppress their identity. The personality of theirs is misjudged by referring them with nick-names. Some really hate being called with their nicknames.

When the Messenger of Allah ﷺ migrated to Al-Madhina, every man residing there had two or three nicknames. On the Prophet ﷺ calling a man by one of his nick names, people would exclaim, "O Allah's Messenger ﷺ! He hates that nickname." Only after such incidents, the above ayath was revealed. On embracing Islam, calling one's brother of faith with abusive nickname; such act is regarded as evil and if that person concerned fails to repent, he is considered as a wrong doer.

But the nicknames which serve as a mark of recognition arising out of love and affection; those who are called by such names themselves on approving it, like Abu Hurairah (Father of the kitten); Abu Turab (Father of the dust); Ameerul Mominoon to Umar bin Khathab; Zun Noorain to Uthman bin Affaan etc.; such reference is permissible.

الحمدلله

4. Peruse the Surah 24; mention the ayaath regarding "obtaining permission to enter the houses, of other than yours."

Answer: An-Noor, 24:27-29.

"O, you who believe! Enter not houses other than your own, until you have asked permission and greeted (Salam) those in them, that is better for you, in order that you may remember (24:27)." "And if you find no one therein, still, enter not until permission has been given. And if you are asked to go back, go back, for it is purer for you, and Allah is All-Knower of what you do (24:28)." "There is no sin on you that you enter (without taking permission) houses uninhabited, when you have any interest in them. And Allah has knowledge of what you reveal and what you conceal" (24:29).

The manner of seeking permission:

- Greeting as "Assalaamu alaikum" in moderate voice.
- Before entering the house of others, knocking the door gently or ringing the bell is required or if the door is left open; seek permission politely as "May I enter?"
- One should seek permission three times, to enter. If permission is not granted, one can leave.
- If someone enters without seeking permission, it is preferable to require him to depart.
- It is better to inform your name; if the people inside the house enquire about the visitor, instead of replying, "It's me."
- Knocking the door continuously or ringing the bell repeatedly, should be avoided.
- It is Sunnah to avoid standing by facing the door. Standing at either of its sides, will prevent knowing or viewing something that takes place inside the house.

While rescuing someone or preventing an evil like murder or adultery; no need to seek permission.

Even within our own house; for entering into other's private portion, permission should be sought during three occasions:

"O, you who believe! Let your legal slaves and slave-girls, and those among you who have not come to the age of puberty ask your permission on three occasions; before Fajr prayer and while you put off your clothes for the noonday, and after the 'Isha' prayer. These three times are of times of privacy for you, other than these times there is no sin on you or on them to move about, attending you each other. Thus Allah makes the ayath clear to you. And Allah is All-Knowing, All-Wise (24:58)."

"And when the children among you come to puberty, then let them also ask for permission, as those senior to them Thus Allah makes clear His ayath for you. and Allah is All-Knowing, All-Wise (24:59)."

Thus the Holy Quran teaches us to respect the privacy of others. Such simple act will help to avoid many evils.

الحمدلله

5. Mention the ayaath about "Quran is made easy for remembrance" by searching the surah 54.

Answer: 54:17, 22, 32 and 40.

Explanation of this ayath [وَلَقَدْ يَسَّرْنَا ٱلْقُرْءَانَ لِلذِّكْرِ فَهَلْ مِن مُّدَّكِرٍ]

"And We have certainly made the Quran easy for remembrance, so is there any who will remember?" These are the repeated verses in this surah. By saying many times, Allahuthala insist on its importance. Ibn Khathir observes in his tafsir, "that the Qur'an has been made easy [يَسَّرْنَا] to the extent of memorizing it and paying heed to its advice and warnings, [لِلذِّكْرِ]" A learned scholar or an unlearned person, young or old, all may be benefitted with this. Allahuthala is asking [فَهَلْ مِن مُّدَّكِرٍ] "Is there any that will remember?" As-Sadi interpret this verse as: "We [i.e. Allah] have made this Quran easy and simplistic: its words for memorization and recitation, and its meanings for understanding and knowledge... and this is the beneficial knowledge, if a person seeks it, he will be helped to achieve it."

Quran is a verbal revelation, easy to memorize by many:

Allah Subhanahuthala, took responsibility of revealing the content of Holy Quran to Ummi Nabi ﷺ by Himself. He made his Prophet ﷺ to recite what was revealed. Hundreds of companions at once memorized it. The Prophet ﷺ arranged a team of intellectuals to write it. Most of the Sahabas were reciting Quran from their memory without referring to any written script. The memorization continues from that time onwards till now in every age, every person and in every part of the world. The Quran was preserved in the hearts of the Hafiz. No other Allahuthala's scripture is memorized 'by heart' other than the Holy Quran. It is easy for both, the intellectuals and laymen. All can benefit from its admonition.

Allah sent His Prophets to the communities which were astray:

It is indeed Allah's Grace that He has sent His Prophets to the communities which were on the wrong path; warned them if they transgress; punished them severely, saving those who followed the Prophet's guidance. In this surah Allah ﷻ has mentioned four communities.

1. Community of Nuh (AS): The verses 9 to 15 states as to how the people of Nuh (AS) denied him; therefore, he sought the help of his Lord to save him. Allah poured water from heaven; gushed forth water from earth; He saved the messenger and his followers in a ship safely but drowned the disbelievers.

2. Community of Hud (AS): The verses from 18 to 20 explains how Aad people belied their Prophet, Hud (AS). Allah destroyed the disbelievers like a hollow trunks of palm trees with the blow of furious wind for seven nights and eight days in succession.

3. Community of Salih (AS): The verses from 23 to 31 says, Thamud people also belied the warnings of Salih (AS). Allah sent a she-camel as a test and required them to share their water, whereas they killed her. "A single Saihah (awful cry), and the disbelievers became like the dry stubble of a fold-builder."

4. Community of Lut (AS): The verses from 33 to 38 explain that the people of Lut (AS) belied the warnings. Therefore, Allah ﷻ destroyed them with a violent storm of stones marked with name by sparing the family of Lut (AS).

Allah questioned:

"How (great) was then My punishment and My warning?" [فَكَيْفَ كَانَ عَذَابِيْ وَنُذُرِ] (54: 16, 21, 30). He pointed out: "So taste My punishment and My warning."[ذُوقُوا عَذَابِى وَنُذُرِ] (54:39). Subsequent to each of these four ayaath, Allah has repeated the following ayath four times "And We have certainly made the Quran easy for remembrance, so is there any who will remember?"

Similar guidance was provided to the present and future communities through Quran:

In another verse, Allah asserts, "(This is) a Book which We have sent down to you, full of blessings, that they may ponder over its ayath, and that men of understanding may remember." (38:29). Similarly, He continues, "So We have made this (the Quran) easy in your own tongue, only that you may give glad tidings to those who have Taqwa and warn with it the most quarrelsome people." (19:97)

Hadhees about reciting and memorizing the Quran:

Abu al-Qasim reported: Abu Umamah (RA) had narrated, "Recite the Quran and do not be deceived by depending on the written copies. Verily, Allah will never punish a heart that has memorized the Quran." [Musannaf Ibn Abi Shaybah, 34044]. Abu Hurairah (RA) says: "In the house where the Quran is read the house hold members increase; virtues and blessings multiply; angels descend upon the house and Shythan quits the home." (Fazail-e-Quran).

Abu Huraira (RA) narrated that Rasulullah ﷺ conveyed: "There is no jealousy but of two men: A man whom Allah has taught the Quran and he recites it during the hours of the night and during the hours of the day, and his neighbour listens to him and says: "I wish I had been given what has been given to so-and-so, in order that I might do what he does" (Sahih Bukhari Vol. 6, Book 61, Hadhees 544). Abdullah ibn Masud narrated that Rasulullah ﷺ said: "He who reads one letter of the Quran it (becomes) for him a good deed and a single good deed is rewarded (by Allah) by ten times the like thereof. I am not saying that 'الم' is one word, but that 'ا' is a separate letter, 'ل' is a separate letter, and 'م' is a separate letter." (Tirmidhi)

If anybody claims that he cannot understand Quran or that he cannot remember Quran, then he has to check himself as to whether he is:

- ❖ Ignorant.
- ❖ Arrogant.
- ❖ His heart and his eyes are screened by Allah.
- ❖ Cursed by Allah.

Allahuthala thus holds, [هَلْ مِن مُّدَّكِرٍ] "so is there any who will remember?" Therefore, be among the one, who remembers the Quran.

Hence, dear brothers and sisters of Islam, read the Quran daily in Arabic, understand its meaning in your mother tongue or in your regional language. Get the rewards easily from Allah سبحانه وتعالى for every Arabic letter you recite! The position in the Hereafter of a person depends the last verse he recited from Quran. Remember and ponder over it's ayaath and follow it in your day today life! Don't be among the ignorant! Do not waste your life time! Let us pray to Allahuthala that we recite, understand and memorize the Quran and also remind the others to follow the same.

الحمدلله

6. "Wealth and children are trial", by searching the surah 64, mention this ayath.

Answer: [64:15]– "Your wealth and your children are only a trial, whereas Allah! With Him is a great reward!"

Allahuthala tests the mankind through various means, judges them as to how far they follow the straight path. The love for wealth, leads mankind to deviate from the right path. Wealth makes a person self-sufficient but at times make him forget Allah. Excessive wealth, makes a man proud. Excessive love for wealth, affects sincerity and faith of a person; thus leading him towards hypocrisy, treachery and dishonesty.

Similarly, when a man fullfils his responsibilities to his children and family, such effort drives him away from the straight path. Love towards them overwhelms a man and thereby becomes a hindrance to the relationship with Allah and his loyalty to Islam. One should not ruin his eternal life for the sake of the betterment of his children's worldly life.

If anybody illtreats his wife and children, his domestic life becomes miserable, lacking peace and wretched. By avoiding the temptations and allurement of wealth and children; he succeeds in maintaning the love for Allah, attracting rewards from Him.

Allah mentions in another place, "O, you who believe! Verily, there are enemies to you from among your spouses and your off-spring, so beware of them. But if you forgive and overlook their offences and pardon them, then surely Allah is Most Forgiving, Most Compassionate. (64:14). Your wealth and your children are only a trial, whereas Allah! With Him is a great reward." (64:15).

If you peruse the next ayath of 8:28 and 64:15, it provides a remedy for this trail/test:

"O, you who believe! If you obey and fear Allah, He will grant you Furqan a criterion [to judge between right and wrong, or making a way for you to get out from every difficulty] and will expiate for you your sins, and forgive you, and Allah is the Owner of the Great Bounty (8:29)."

"So keep your duty to Allah and fear Him as much as you can; listen and obey; and spend in charity, that is better for yourselves. And whosoever is saved from his own covetousness, then they are the successful ones." (64:16)

Allahuthala then records in another ayath: "Beautified for men is the love of things they covet; women, children, much of gold and silver (wealth), branded beautiful horses, cattle and well-tilled land. This is the pleasure of the present world's life; but Allah has the excellent return with Him." (3:14)

Therefore, Allah {SWT} warns the believers as: "O you who believe! Let not your properties or your children divert you from the remembrance of Allah and whosoever does that then they are the losers." (63:9).

Thereupon, Allah guides the believers by referring to their rewards: "Shall I inform you of things far better than those? For the pious there are Gardens with their Lord, underneath which rivers flow. Therein (is their) eternal (home) and purified mates or wives. And Allah will be pleased with them. And Allah is All-Seer of (His) slaves". (3:15).

Imam Ahmad recorded that Buraydah (RA) narrated that: "The Messenger of Allah ﷺ was delivering a Khutbah to us when Al-Hasan and Al-Husain came, wearing red shirts, walking and falling down. So the Messenger of Allah ﷺ descended from the Minbar and carried them, and placed them in front of him. Then he said: 'Allah spoke the Truth: Indeed, your wealth and your children are a trial. I looked at these two children walking and falling down, and I could not bear patiently anymore until I interrupted my talk and picked them up." This was recorded by the Sunan compilers, and also At-Tirmidhi {3774}. Hasan Gharib claimed, "Allah and His Messenger ﷺ said the truth."

He grants wealth and children to a man, to test whether he becomes grateful and obedient to Him or busy and dedicated to them by ignoring Him. Allahuthala said in another Ayah, "And We shall make a trial of you with evil and with good" (21:35).

Therefore, Allah's reward being the Paradise, is better for you than the wealth and children in this world.

الحمدلله

7. Read the Surah Naml and mention how many times the following verse is available: [ءَاِلٰهٌ مَّعَ اللهِ] "Is there any ilah (god) with Allah?"

Answer: Five times. (27:60 to 64)

[27:60] "Is not He (better than your gods) Who created the heavens and the earth, and sends down for you water (rain) from the sky, whereby We cause to grow wonderful gardens full of beauty and delight? It is not in your ability to cause the growth of their trees. **Is there any ilah (god) with Allah?** Nay, but they are a people who ascribe equals (to Him)!"

[27:61] "Is not He (better than your gods) Who has made the earth as a fixed abode, and has placed rivers in its midst, and has placed firm mountains therein, and has set a barrier between the two seas (of salt and sweet water). **Is there any ilah (god) with Allah?** Nay, but most of them know not."

[27:62]. "Is not He (better than your gods) Who responds to the distressed one, when he calls Him, and Who removes the evil, and makes you inheritors of the earth, generations after generations. **Is there any ilah (god) with Allah?** Little is that you remember!"

[27:63] "Is not He (better than your gods) Who guides you in the darkness of the land and the sea, and Who sends the winds as heralds of glad tidings, going before His Mercy (rain)? **Is there any ilah (god) with Allah?** High Exalted be Allah above all that they associate as partners (to Him)!"

[27:64] "Is not He (better than your so-called gods) Who originates creation, and shall thereafter repeat it, and Who provides for you from heaven and earth? **Is there any ilah (god) with Allah?**"

We all know that Allah Subhanahuthala is incomparable. Allahuthala asserts with the disbelievers; "I am the One who -

- ❖ Created you and your surroundings,
- ❖ Controlling everything efficiently,
- ❖ Providing with all needs,
- ❖ Helping you during your difficulties; and will
- ❖ Resurrect you in the same form, as I created you earlier"

Is there any ilah (god) who can be compared with Allah in doing all these things? **Is He not superior** than your gods?

Allah [عَزَّ وَجَلَّ] is challenging them:

Allahuthala requires the Prophet ﷺ to claim, "Bring forth your proofs, if you are truthful." Not only the Quraish, even the disbelievers of all time could not bring evidence to prove their stand. On being required to mention any of their gods who will perform such type of work; they could not refer the names of any of their deities.

Observe these verses of Allah in the Quran:

[43:9] "If you ask them, who has created the heavens and the earth?" they will surely say: "The **All-Mighty**, the All-Knowing One has created them."

[43:87] "And if you ask them, who has created them?" they will surely say, '**Allah**'.

[29:63] "If you ask them, who sent down rain water from the sky and thereby raised the dead earth back to life?" they will surely say, '**Allah**'.

[10:31] "Ask them, who provides for you from the heavens and the earth? who has power over these faculties of hearing and sight? who brings forth the living from the dead and the dead from the living? who controls and directs the system of the universe?" they will surely say, '**Allah**'."

Then He demands; "What is the need of associating partners with Allah?"

While Prophet ﷺ reciting the verses from 27:60 to 64, he immediately asserts that: "Nay, but **Allah** is better, He alone is the Everlasting, Exalted and High."

الحمدلله

8. Recite the 40th surah Ghafir and refer the ayath about "Calling Allah".

Answer: Ghafir, 40:60

And your Lord demands: "Call on Me; I will answer your (Prayer): but those who are too arrogant to serve Me will surely find them-selves in Hell, in humiliation!" (Ghafir, 40:60).

Allah responds to the invocations of man, so plead with Him:

[7:55] "Invoke your Lord with humility and in secret. He likes not the aggressors."

[7:56] "Invoke Him with fear and hope; Surely, Allah's Mercy is (ever) near unto the good-doers."

[2:186] "And when My servants ask you concerning Me, then surely I am very near; I answer the prayer of the suppliant when he calls on Me, so they should answer My call and believe in Me that they may walk in the right way."

[42:26] "And He answers (the invocation of) those who believe and do righteous good deeds, and gives them increase of His Bounty."

[11:61] "Ask forgiveness of Him, and turn to Him (in repentance): for my Lord is Near, the Answerer (of prayers)."

[22:11] "And among mankind is he who worships Allah as it were, upon the very edge (i.e. in doubt); if good befalls him, he is content therewith; but if a trial befalls him, he turns back on his face. He loses both this world and the Here- after. That is the evident loss."

[65:2 and 3] "And for those who fear Allah, He (ever) prepares a way out. And He provides for him from (sources) he never could imagine. And whosoever puts his trust in Allah, then He will suffice him."

[17:11] "And man invokes (Allah) for evil as he invokes (Allah) for good and man is ever hasty."

[94:8] "And to your Lord (Alone) turn (all your intentions and hopes and) your invocations."

[27:62] Allah asks the disbelievers about their own experiences: "Who is it that responds to the distressed when he calls out to Him, and who removes the ill and has made you inherit the earth? Could there be any divine power besides Allah?"

Before seeking any obligation, you must be informed that:

- Allah Subhanahuthala loves to respond to our prayers.
- All good is as per His command.
- Allahuthala knows exactly what is best for us.
- Allah [SWT] will not be unjust to one, who turns towards Him.

To get your obligations fulfilled:

★ perform all duties with sincerity,

★ perform righteous deeds,

★ repose more faith in Him and remain patient,

★ be humble and sincere in prayers,

★ seek humility, with fear and hope,

★ let not our demands be specific; as we are not aware as to what is good for us,

★ seeking help from Allah; at the right time that is before and after fasting; subsequent to all farz prayers, after 'asr' prayers on Friday; during the third part of the night; at dawn; between Azan and Iqamath and also during any emergency.

Ahadhees about supplications:

That is why `Umar (RA) used to say: "I do not worry that my supplications will be answered. I worry about my supplications themselves." "The kindness of Allah does not annul His wisdom; it is for this reason that not all supplications are answered." [Ali ibn Abi Talib (RA)].

الحمدلله

بِسْمِ ٱللَّهِ ٱلرَّحْمَٰنِ ٱلرَّحِيمِ

4. During which situation, these verses have been revealed?

1. During which situation, the last two verses of Al-Baqara have been revealed?

Answer: When our Prophet ﷺ visited Allah, in the seventh heaven.

The meaning of these verses (2:285 and 286) are:

"The Messenger (Muhummad ﷺ) believes in what has been sent down to him from His Lord, and (so do) the believers. Each one believes in Allah, His angels, His Books, and His Messengers. (They say) "We make no distinction between any one of His Messengers" and they say, "We hear, and we obey. (We seek) Your forgiveness, Our Lord, and to You is the return (of all)" (2:285).

"Allah burdens not a person beyond his scope. He gets reward for that (good) which he has earned, and he is punished for that (evil) which he has earned. "Our Lord! Punish us not if we forget or fall into error, our Lord! Lay not on us a burden greater than we have strength to bear. Pardon us and grant us forgiveness. Have mercy on us. You are the Protector and give us victory over the disbelieving people" (2:286).

The above verses were revealed to the Prophet ﷺ during his visit to seventh heaven:

When our Prophet ﷺ went on the night journey along with Jibreel (AS) he heard the sound of a door opening which has never opened before. (Ibn Abbas). An angel descended down and said to Prophet ﷺ: "I bring you, the good tidings of two lights which have been given to you and no other Prophet before you have ever received them." (Narrated by Ibn Abi Laila). The Messenger of Allah ﷺ said: "I was given Fatihat al Kitab (Surah Fatiha) and the final verses of Surathul Baqara, from a treasure beneath the Throne (Arsh) of Allah!" Ibn Mardawaih said: "He required us to recite them." Allah proclaims, "Thus We have made of you a just and the best nation that you may be witnesses over mankind and the Apostle (Muhammad ﷺ) will be a witness over yourselves." (2:143).

The Ummath of the Prophet ﷺ is the best among the communities of other Prophets:

★ Because they have been informed about Allah and believed in Him.

★ They always believe in all the Prophets, without any distinction.

★ They believe not only Quran but also all the Scriptures of the other Prophets.

★ They believe in all the angels.

★ They always seek pardon, only from Allah.

★ They believe in returning back to Him.

★ They know that Allah does not test beyond one's capacity. Hence, they face all the difficulties with patience.

★ They perform lot of good deeds, as they know that it will lead them to heaven.

★ They avoid the evil deeds, as such deeds lead them to hell.

★ On indulging in any sin, they turn towards Allah and repent.

★ They always praise and pray to Allah.

Benefits of reading the last two verses of Al-Baqara:

The Prophet ﷺ further asserted: "Whoever recites the last two verses of surathul Baqara at night, it will be sufficient for him" (Bukhari). "Allah wrote something before He created the heaven and earth, He [سبحانه وتعالى] sent down from it, two verses with which He ended surathul Baqara and if they are not recited in any house for three nights Shaithan approaches it" (An-Nu'man Ibn Basheer).

It is reported by Abu Huraira (RA) that the Prophet ﷺ said: Allah [سبحانه وتعالى] assured that "Yes. I have already done so." Shukur Alhumdhulillah! We are born as Muslims!

Those who have not yet memorized, memorise and recite it daily and then you will be the most successful person. [الله اعلم !].

الحمدلله

2. Say: (O Muhammad ﷺ) "Come, let us call our sons and your sons, our women and your women, ourselves and yourselves - then we pray and invoke the Curse of

Allah upon those who lie."(3:61). Under which circumstance Allahuthala revealed this ayath?

Answer: 60 Christian delegates from Najran, came to know about Islam to Madhina. They had long discussion about Isa (AS) with our Prophet ﷺ. Even after reciting the verses of Quran about Isa (AS), they were stubborn in their belief about Isa (AS), as being their God; as God's son and their concept of Trinity. Then Allah revealed this ayath, requiring the Prophet ﷺ to call them for "Mubahalah."

Quran says:

"Then whoever disputes with you concerning him [Isa ibn Marium (AS)], after the knowledge that has come to you, say (O Muhammad ﷺ): "Come, let us call our ....then we pray and invoke the Curse of Allahuthala upon those who lie." (3:61). This verse is called as "The verse of Mubahalah". Mubahalah means "invocation of God's curse".

After the conquest of Makkah, Prophet Muhammad ﷺ wrote letters through delegates to various neighbouring and distant Countries. He sent a letter to Najran, located in south-west Saudi Arabia near Yemen border. Initially the people of that town were idol worshippers. Then a Christian priest went there and converted most of them to Christianity.

The following is from the famous Seerah by Muhammad bin Ishaq bin Yasar:

"The delegation of Christians from Najran came to the Messenger of Allah ﷺ. The delegation consisted of sixty horse-men, including fourteen of their chiefs who make decisions. Three of these men were chiefs of this delegation: Al-Aqib, their leader and to whom they referred for advice and decision; As-Sayyid, their scholar and leader in journeys and social gatherings and Abu Harithah bin Alqamah, their patriarch, priest and religious leader. Abu Harithah was an Arab, who embraced Christianity. The Romans and their kings honored him and built churches at his instance. They also supported him financially and provided him servants, because they knew how firm his faith in their religion was.

The priest Abu Harithah knew about the advent of; and the description of the Messenger of Allah ﷺ from the prior Divine Books. In view of his high position, to enjoy its previleges, he concealed the truth and remained as Christian."

Ibn Ishaq narrated that Muhammad bin Jafar bin Az-Zubayr said that, "The (Najran) delegation wearing rich robes and garments came to the Messenger of Allah ﷺ after he completed the 'Asr' prayer in Al-Madinah, entered the Masjid. They were accompanied with a caravan of camels, led by Bani Al-Harith bin Ka`b. The Companions of the Messenger of Allah ﷺ who saw it, felt astonished as they had never witnessed a delegation like that.

The leaders spoke to the Messenger of Allah ﷺ. For more than three days, they had long arguments and discussions. They were stubborn in their 'Trinity' concept and were not convinced with the truth revealed in Quran, about Isa ibn Marium (AS)."

Ibn Ishaq continued, "Judging between him and the People of the Book, Allah commanded the Prophet ﷺ to call them to the Mubahalah, if they still refused the truth." Thus the Prophet ﷺ called them to the Mubahalah to react a decisive solution with regard to the dispute.

The delegation said, `O Abu Qasim! Let us think about this matter and get back to you with our decision as to what we want to do.' They left the Prophet ﷺ and conferred with Al-Aqib, with whom they saught advice.

They consulted him,"O Abdul-Masih! What is your advice?" He said, `By Allah, O Christian fellows! You know that Muhammad ﷺ is a Messenger and that he brought you the final word regarding your Isa (AS). You also know that no Prophet conducted Mubahalah with any people, and the old persons among them remained safe and the young people grew up. Indeed, it will be the end of you if you do it. If you have already decided that you will remain in your religion and your creed regarding Isa (AS), then enter into a treaty with that man and go back to your land.'

Al-Bukhari recorded that Hudhayfah said, "Al-Aqib and As-Sayyid, two leaders from Najran, came to the Messenger of Allah ﷺ at the appointed time." On seeing the Prophet ﷺ coming, carrying Husayn in his arm, holding Hasan by his hand, followed by Fatima (RA) and Ali (RA) behind. Seeing this, they were really worried and frightened and said to Prophet ﷺ: "O Abu Qasim! We decided that we cannot do Mubahalah with you and that you remain on your religion, while we remain on our religion. However, send with us a man from your companions whom you are pleased with to judge between us regarding our monetary disputes, for you are acceptable to us in this regard."

As per wish the Prophet Muhammad ﷺ appointed Abu 'Ubaydah ibn Al-Jarrah as a representative. According to Muhammad Husayn Tabataba'i in Tafsir al-Mizan, the

Prophet ﷺ said that the Najrans escaped being turned into monkeys and pigs or otherwise all of Najran would have perished within a year of the mubahala.

Shia Muslims celebrate this event as "Eid Mubahala" on 24th Dhu al Hijja.

الحمدلله

3. "....... the companions of Musa (AS) said: "We are sure to be overtaken." Musa (AS) said: "Nay, verily! With me is my Lord, He will guide me." (26:61 and 62) During what situation Musa (AS) stated this?

Answer: When Musa (AS) gathered the Children of Israel and escaped from Egypt, by Allah's command; Firaun's large army followed them behind. They came to the shore of Red sea. In front of them was the sea, behind them was Firaun's army. And they thought there was no way to escape. At such a situation, one of Musa's (AS) companion stated the above verse.

Almighty Allah decided to put an end to the Paraoh's torture, to the Children of Israel. Allahuthala had offered several chances to Firaun and his people to believe and accept Him. But Firaun remained arrogant, even after witnessing several clear signs. Thereupon, Allah inspired Musa (AS) by directing: "Take away My slaves by night, (from Egypt) verily, you will be pursued." (Ash-Shuara, 26:52). During the darkness of night, Musa (AS) led them towards the Red Sea.

When Firaun became aware of their departure, he sent callers to all the cities (26:53). Claiming, "Verily! These indeed are but a small band (26:54). And verily, they have done what has enraged us (26:55). But we are host all assembled, amply fore-warned." (26:56).

Allah ﷻ claimed: "So, 'We' expelled them from gardens and springs, (26:57) treasures, and every kind of honourable place (26:58). Thus [We turned them (Pharaoh's people) out] and We caused the Children of Israel to inherit them." (26:59). "So they pursued them at sunrise" (26:60).

And when the two hosts saw each other, the companion (Joshua Ibn Nun) of Musa (AS) exclaimed: "We are sure to be over-taken." (26:61) "In front of us is this barrier, the sea and behind us the enemy; surely death cannot be avoided!" Musa (AS) with strong faith in Allah said: "Nay, verily! With me is my Lord, He will guide me." (26:62).

Then Allah [SWT] inspired Musa (AS) by directing: "Strike the sea with your stick." And it parted, and each separate part of that sea water became like the huge, firm mass of a mountain" (26:63). And We took the Children of Israel across the sea. Then We brought near the Firaun's party in oppression and enmity, till when drowning over-took him. Firaun said: "I believe that La ilaha illa Huwa, in Whom the Children of Israel believe and I am one of the Muslims that is those who submit to Allah's Will" (Yunus, 10:90). Allah [سبحانه وتعالى] asked Him, "Now (you believe) while you refused to believe before and you were one of the evil doers" (10:91).

Allahuthala further recorded in Quran, "So this day We shall deliver your (dead) body (out from the sea) that you may be a sign to those who come after you! And verily, many among mankind are heedless of Our ayath" (10:92).

"And We saved Musa (AS) and all those with him (26:65). Then We drowned the others (26:66) especially the elite of Pharaoh's tyrannical kingdom." "Verily! In this is indeed a sign, yet most of them are not believers" (26:67).

That is the destiny of disbelievers! The waves threw his body upon the western sea shore. The Egyptians saw their god whom they followed and worshipped. Thereupon, preserved his body as per the custom of those days. It was designed to serve as a sign for all time!

الحمدلله

4. At which situation the verse, "Verily, 'We' have given you (O Muhammad ﷺ) a manifest victory" (48:1), was revealed?

Answer: When Prophet ﷺ and his companoions were returning after entering the treaty at Hudaibiyah.

On coming to Madhina, during the sixth year of Hijrah, the Prophet ﷺ had a dream. In that dream he saw that he and his followers were circumambulating the holy Kaba and coming out of it with their head shaven. The Prophet ﷺ used to be provided with the information from Allah, either through a Wahi or a dream. The Prophet ﷺ thought that it was Allah's command. Thereupon, he informed his companions about this dream and told that whoever wishes, can accompany Him. Those who migrated from Makkah, were immensely happy as they could visit their homeland.

Prophet ﷺ left Madhina in the state of Iharam, along with 1400 Muslims and 70 camels for sacrifice, towards Makkah for performing Umrah. They carried only self defence weapons with them. On hearing this, the Quraish sent 200 soldiers under the leader ship of Khalid bin Walid, for preventing them from entering Makkah.

To avoid this army, Prophet ﷺ changed the route and came to a lesser-known place called Hudaibiyah, which is on the western edge of the city and halted there. The Quraish sent Urwah bin Masud to negotiate with the Prophet ﷺ. After meeting the Prophet ﷺ, he said to the Quraish about the love and respect, his followers exhibited towards him. He further declared, "I have visited the royal courts of Persians, Roman and Ethiopian kingdoms, but I have never seen the kind of respect and high esteem as the followers of Mohammad ﷺ have for him. They have come only for worship. Let them enter the holy city." But the the leaders of Makkah never heeded his advice.

The holy Prophet ﷺ sent Uthman bin Affan (RA) who had good contacts in Makkah to inform the Makkans that they have come to perform Umrah and not to fight. They detained him unnecessarily, with their long discussions. Rumors spread about Uthman (RA) having been killed by the Quraish. This was a great challenge to the Prophet ﷺ and Muslims. They came here to perform Umrah. There were no weapons carried by them. They were far away from their home city. Hence, he called all the companions and took an oath of allegiance under a tree by placing their hands upon his hand, to assure him that they will fight till their death. This is called as "Baithul Rhithwan", the act which pleased Allah.

This news quickly reached Makkans. They released Uthman (RA). They sent Sohayl bin Amr Al-Thaqafi to negotiate the terms of peace with the Prophet Muhammad ﷺ. Sohayl was a very strict person. Ali (RA) was writing the treaty. He wrote "Bismillah hirrrahamn niraheem" on the top of the treaty. Sohayl asked to remove that because they know not who is Rahaman. Ali (RA) hesitated. The Prophet ﷺ collected the material on which the treaty was to be written; rubbed the heading with his own hand. He also told them not to write Rasulullah after the Prophet's ﷺ name and instructed them to write Mohammad ibn Abdullah. The Muslims were all restless and were angry with such a behaviour.

These were the conditions of peace between Muhammad (ﷺ), son of Abdullah, and Sohayl ibn Amr, the envoy of Makkah:

1. There will be an armistice between the two parties and ther will be no fighting for the next 10 years.

2. Any person or tribe who wishes to join Muhammad (ﷺ), and desires of entering into any agreement with him, is free to do so. Likewise, any person or tribe who wishes to join the Quraish and to enter into any agreement with them, is free to do so.

3. If any Makkan goes to Madinah, then Muslims would return him to Makkah, but if any Muslim from Madinah goes to Makkah, he would not be returned.

4. If any young man, whose father is alive, goes to Muhammad (ﷺ), without the permission of his father or guardian, should be returned to his father or guardian. But if anyone goes to the Quraish of Makkah, he will not be returned.

5. That year the Muslims will go back without entering Makkah. But next year onwards Muhammad (ﷺ), and his followers can enter Makkah and perform the Umrah by spending three days.

Apparently, it was an agreement that went against the wishes of the Muslims. The Prophet ﷺ showed extreme patience by accepting all these terms as dictated by Sohayl. But the sahabas were least satisfied. They were so dejected that they were prevented to perform Umrah after travelling a long distance from their dwellings with Iharam.

This treaty is known as the "Treaty of Hudaibiyah." When Sohayl was signing the treaty, Sohayl's own son known as Abu Jandal (RA), a Muslim, appeared in chains crying for help. Sohayl cried, "Here is the test of this treaty, you cannot take this man. You have to return him to me." The holy Prophet ﷺ, agreed and consoled Abu Jandal (RA), "We have just concluded a treaty with Quraish in the name of Allah and we honor it. Be patient and resign yourself to the will of Allah. He will provide you relief." Abu Jandal (RA) was handed over to his father. But he escaped soon from Makkah and came to Madhina. All the companions watched this, with their blood boiling. The Prophet ﷺ, signed the treaty.

All the sahabas were so shocked and disappointed that they never moved from their place. As per Quranic instruction in Surah Baqara, Muslims were commanded, "But if you are prevented (from completing/proceeding Hajj and Umrah), sacrifice a Hady (animal, i.e. a sheep, a cow, or a camel, etc.) such as you can afford, and do not shave your heads until the Hady reaches the place of sacrifice," (2:196), the Prophet ﷺ told the companions to sacrifice the camels, get their head shaved or hair cut and come out of ihram. He conveyed this message thrice, but they did not obey him.

The Prophet ﷺ entered his tent and told his wife, Umm Salma (RA), about the reluctance of sahabas. She politely advised him, "The people are in shock to lose their Umrah and the entry to the Holy City. You first do as planned. They will follow you." The Prophet ﷺ came out, slaughtered his camel and got his head shaved. Sahabas followed him and they all set out towards Madhina with a heavy heart.

As all were returning from Hudaibiyah, the Prophet ﷺ received the revelation from Allah:

[48:1] "Verily, 'We' have given you (O Muhammad ﷺ) a manifest victory." [إِنَّا فَتَحْنَا لَكَ فَتْحًا مُبِينًا]

[48:18] "Indeed, Allah was pleased with the believers when they gave their Bai'a (pledge) to you (O Muhammad ﷺ) under the tree, He knew what was in their hearts, and He sent down As-Sakinah (calmness and tranquility) upon them, and He rewarded them with a near victory."

[لَّقَدْ رَضِيَ اللَّهُ عَنِ الْمُؤْمِنِينَ إِذْ يُبَايِعُونَكَ تَحْتَ الشَّجَرَةِ فَعَلِمَ مَا فِي قُلُوبِهِمْ فَأَنزَلَ السَّكِينَةَ عَلَيْهِمْ وَأَثَابَهُمْ فَتْحًا قَرِيبًا]

The benefits of Treaty of Hudhaibiyah:

- Prophet Mohammed ﷺ was recognized as a leader of the Madhina.
- Muslims were allowed to move freely talk and preach openly, about Islam.
- Muslims were equally allowed to make alliances with other tribes.
- Islam reached to the other parts of Arabian Peninsula, faster.
- It was the masterpiece of leadership, patience, wisdom and farsightedness.

After the Treaty of Hudhaibiyah, the Muslims realized the eventual triumph of Islam. Many [in thousands] entered the fold of Islam. The Hudaibiyah Treaty, proved to be a prelude to the conquest of Makkah with less bloodshed after 22 months. This was a great gift availed through the Hudaibiyah Treaty.

الحمدلله

5. "Indeed Allah has heard the statement of her that disputes with you [Prophet ﷺ] concerning her husband, and complains to Allah." (Al-Mujadila, 58:1) What is the complaint to Allah and the Prophet ﷺ, about her husband?

Answer: Her husband pronounced the Zihar on her.

In the narration that Ibn Abi Hatim collected, Ayesha (RA) said, "Blessed is He, whose hearing has encompassed all things. I heard what Khawlah bint Thalabah said while some of it I could not hear. She was complaining to Allah's Messenger ﷺ about her husband. She said, `O Allah's Messenger ﷺ! He spent my wealth, exhausted my youth and my womb bore abundantly for him. When I became old, unable to bear children, he pronounced the Zihar on me! O Allah! I complain to you.' Soon after, Jibril (AS) brought down this ayath, "those among you who make their wives unlawful to them by Zihar, they cannot be their mothers. None can be their mothers except those who gave them birth. And verily, they utter an ill word and a lie. And verily, Allah is Oft-Pardoning, Oft-Forgiving." Al-Bukhari collected this Hadhees without a chain of narration in the Book of Tawhid, in his Sahih. An-Nasa'i, Ibn Majah, Ibn Abi Hatim and Ibn Jarir also recorded this Hadith.

The people involved in this:

Khawlah bint Thalabah from the Khazraj tribe, was the woman who disputed with the Allah's Messenger ﷺ. Her husband was Aus bin Samit Ansari, brother of Ubadah bin Samit, the chief of the Aus tribe.

The problem that has been complained is 'Zihar':

There was a custum in Arabs, during the quarrel between husband and wife, the husband used to declare zihar to his wife. The husband proclaiming to his wife, "You are for me as the back of my mother." This proclaiming is worse than divorce because the Arabs thought that reunion was impossible after declaring zihar. Allah wished to remove this practice from Arabs as they shamelessly compare the wife to their mother. The mother had given birth to the man. She is sacred and prohibited. How a woman (wife) who has not delivered him, become his mother? By declaring zihar; the wife becomes forbidden for him like his mother. A man may treat a woman as his wife as long as he likes but when he dislikes, starts claiming her as his mother.

Allah required to abolish this custom and sent clear rulings about Zihar. In this case Khawlah bint Thalabah was complaining about her husband and reported that "My husband has pronounced the Zihar on me!" She pleaded with the Prophet ﷺ to suggest a solution to save her and her children from ruin. The Prophet ﷺ consoled her and required her to "Be patient"; not knowing what to say. She called upon lastly "O Allah! I complain to you."

Allahuthala immediately heard her statement and revealed the following ayaath:

[58:1] "Indeed Allah has heard the statement of her (Khawlah bint Thalabah) that disputes with you (O Muhammad ﷺ) concerning her husband (Aus bin As-Samit), and complains to Allah. And Allah hears the argument between you both. Verily, Allah is All-Hearer, All-Seer."

[58:2] "Those among you who make their wives unlawful (Az-Zihar) to them by saying to them "You are like my mother's back." They cannot be their mothers. None can be their mothers except those who gave them birth. And verily, they utter an ill word and a lie. And verily, Allah is Oft-Pardoning, Oft-Forgiving."

Allah Subhanahuthala also revealed the expiation of zihar:

[58:3] "And those who make unlawful to them (their wives) (by Az-Zihar) and wish to free themselves from what they uttered, (the penalty) in that case (is) the freeing of a slave before they touch each other. That is an admonition to you (so that you may not return to such an ill thing). And Allah is All-Aware of what you do."

[58:4] "And he who finds not (the money for freeing a slave) must fast two successive months before they both touch each other. And for him who is unable to do so, he should feed sixty of Miskin (poor). That is in order that you may have perfect Faith in Allah and His Messenger. These are the limits set by Allah. And for disbelievers, there is a painful torment."

After the revelation the above verses the Prophet ﷺ called her husband and explained about the expiation. He said that he was not so rich to free a slave. So the Prophet ﷺ asked him to observe fast. He and even his wife told that he cannot fast continuously for two months. So he selcted the third option. The Prophet ﷺ helped him by giving dates and his wife also helped him in feeding the poor.

After this incidence Khawlah bint Thalabah was honoured very much by the companions. She earned an esteemed position. This because her grievance had been heard by Allah Almighty and the the divine command was revealed immediately.

The following ahadhees proved her status:

"Ibn Abdul Barr has related in Al-Istiab, this tradition from Qatadah: When Umar (RA), while he was the Caliph; came across this lady on his way, he greeted her. After answering his greeting, she said: "O Umar (RA), there was a time when I saw you at the Ukaz festival. Then you were called Umair. You tended goats with the shepherd's staff in your hand. Then, not very long after this, you began to be called Umar (RA). Then a time came when the people began addressing you as "Commander of the faithful".

So, fear Allah with regard to your subjects, and remember that the one who fears Allah's punishment, for him the stranger also is like a close kinsman and the one who fears death, may well lose that very thing which he wants to save." At this Jarud Abdi, who was accompanying Umar (RA), said: "O woman, you have talked insolently to the Commander of the faithful." Thereupon Umar (RA) said: "Let her say whatever she has to say. Do you know who she is? She was heard at the seventh heaven. Hence, she deserves to be heard longer and with greater attention by Umar (RA)."

"Ibn Abi Hatim and Baihaqi have related that once Umar (RA) was on his way out with some companions came across a woman who stopped him. He immediately stopped proceeding further; listened to what she had to say patiently with his head bent down and did not move till she finished. One of the companions said: "O Commander of the faithful, you held back the Quraish chiefs for such a long time for the sake of this old woman!" Umar (RA) said: "Do you know who she is? She is Khawlah bint Thalabah, the woman whose complaint was heard at the seventh heaven. By God, even if she had kept me standing till the night, I would have kept standing. I would only have excused myself at the prayer times."

الحمدلله

6. "You show friendship to them (Quraish) in secret, while I am All-Aware of what you conceal and what you reveal. And whosoever of you does that, then indeed he has gone astray, from the Straight Path." [60:1]. Do you know the back ground history of the revelation of this verse?

Answer: It has been revealed when a Sahaba due to the anxeity of the safety of his children and wealth at Makkah, sent a secret letter to Quraish, informing about the Prophet ﷺ's secret plan to attack Makkah.

Hatib bin Abu Baltaah (RA) was a Sahabha, the early emigrant, who participated in the battle of Badr. He had children and wealth in Makkah, but he was not from the tribe of Quraysh. Rather, he was an ally of Uthman (RA). When the Messenger of Allah ﷺ decided to conquer Makkah, after its people violated the peace treaty between them. He ordered the Muslims to mobilize their forces to attack Makkah, and then said, "O Allah! Keep our news concealed from them."

Hatib (RA) wrote a letter and sent it to the people of Makkah, through a woman from the tribe of Quraish, informing them of the Messenger's ﷺ intent to attack them. He wanted them to be indebted to him so that they would grant safety to his family in Makkah. Allah, the Exalted conveyed this matter to His Messenger ﷺ, because He accepted the Prophet's ﷺ invocation, to Him to conceal the news of the attack. The Prophet ﷺ sent someone after the woman and retrieved the letter. This occurance was collected from the Two Sahihs.

Let's follow the hadhees, as narrated by Ali (RA) himself:

"Allah's Messenger ﷺ sent me, Zubayr and Al-Miqdad saying, "Proceed until you reach Rawdat Khakh, where a lady will be carrying a letter. Collect that letter from her." Hence, we proceeded on our way, with our horses galloping, until we reached the Rawdah. There we found the lady and said to her, `Take out the letter.' She replied, `I am not carrying any letter.' We said, `Take out the letter, or else we will take off your clothes.' So she took it out of her braid, and we brought the letter to Allah's Messenger ﷺ. The letter was addressed from Hatib bin Abu Baltaah to some pagans of Makkah, informing them about what Allah's Messenger ﷺ intended to do." (Imam Ahmad recorded this hadhees as Hasan bin Muhammad bin Ali said that Abdullah bin Abu Rafi or Ubaydullah bin Abu Rafi informed that he heard what Ali (RA) said).

The conversation between Hatib (RA) and the Prophet ﷺ, as narrated by Ali (RA):

"Allah's Messenger ﷺ said, "O Hatib! What is this?" Hatib (RA) replied, `O Allah's Messenger ﷺ! Do not make a hasty decision about me. I was a person not belonging to Quraish, but I was an ally to them. All the emigrants who were with you have kinsmen in Makkah, who can protect their families. So I wanted to do them a favor, so they might protect my relatives, as I have no blood relation with them. I did not do this out of disbelief or to renegade from my religion, nor did I do it to choose disbelief after Islam.' Allah's Messenger ﷺ said to his companions, "Regarding him, he has told you the truth."

Umar (RA) said, `O Allah's Messenger ﷺ! Allow me to chop off the head of this hypocrite!' The Prophet ﷺ said, "He attended Badr. What can I tell you, perhaps Allah looked at those who attended Badr and said, "O the people of Badr, do what you like, for I have forgiven you." The Group with the exception of Ibn Majah, collected this

Hadith using various chains of narration that included Sufyan bin Uyaynah. Al-Bukhari added the above narration in the chapter, on the Prophet's ﷺ battles.

Then Allah revealed the following verses in Surah Al-Mumtahina:

"O, you who believe! Take not My enemies and your enemies (i.e. disbelievers and polytheists, etc.) as friends, showing affection towards them, while they have disbelieved in what has come to you of the truth and have driven out the Messenger ﷺ and yourselves (from your homeland) because you believe in Allah your Lord! If you have come forth to strive in My Cause and to seek My Good Pleasure, (then take not these disbelievers and polytheists, etc., as your friends). You show friendship to them in secret, while I am All-Aware of what you conceal and what you reveal. And whosoever of you (Muslims) does that, then indeed he has gone (far) astray, (away) from the Straight Path." (Al Mumtahina, 60:1)

الحمدلله

7. "Fitna is worse than killing." At what occasion this verse was revealed?

The Arabic word 'Fitnah' means 'persecution', 'corruption', 'sedition'. The word 'Fitnah' is used in verse 2:191 and 193, which means 'persecution'

The following two verses says "fitna" is worse than killing:

"And kill them wherever you overtake them and expel them from wherever they have expelled you, and fitnah is worse than killing." (2:191). "Fighting therein is great [sin], but averting [people] from the way of Allah and disbelief in Him and [preventing access to] Al-Masjid Al-Haram and the expulsion of its people therefrom are greater [evil] in the sight of Allah. And fitnah is greater than killing." (2:217).

To persecute the Muslims, Quraish adopted the following methods:

★ They prevented people from following the path of Allah.

★ They refused to accept the Oneness of Allah.

★ They prevented people from performing Thawaf around Kabah.

★ Tortured and expelled Muslims from Makkah.

★ By adapting various methods, they diverted people from accepting Islam.

Associating partners to Allah (Shirk) and deviating from His path; is a much greater evil and disastrous than killing. The torture and torment; these disbelievers caused to the Muslims and deviated them away from their Deen, is far worse a crime than killing, during the sacred month.

There is a historical event connected to the revelation of the above ayath:

"After the battle of Badr Allah's Messenger ﷺ sent a small group under the leadership of Abdullah bin Jahsh. He gave him a written instruction to read after the second day of their march. He should not force anybody in his team to accompany him. He has been ordered to go to a place called Nakhlah, watch the movements of the caravan of Quraish and inform about them. Abdullah bin Jahsh did so. Sad bin Abu Waqqas and Utbah bin Ghazwan left the team in search of their camel which they were riding in turns.

When they came to Nakhlah they happened to meet the caravan. The companions discussed amongst themselves. That was the last day of Holy month of Rajab. They cannot kill those in the caravan in that holy month. If they are allowed to pass, they will enter into the Sacred area. Initially they hesitated, but later decided to kill those in the caravan. They killed one amongst them but another one managed to escape, while the two amongst them were captured as prisioners along with their belongings and brought to Madhina.

Allah's Messenger ﷺ was harsh with them because they killed a person during the holy month. He never required them to attack or kill. Committing such an act was not assigned to them. Prophet ﷺ refused to accept the booty. The team felt depressed. Criticism was raised from Quraish that Muhammad (ﷺ) and his Companions violated the rule of killing during the holy month. Muslims of Madhina also criticized them. The Jews were also pleased on knowing about the act of killing, which was prohibited during that month. The act of Quraish in preventing people's access to al-Masjid al-Haram; the torturing and expulsion of people from their homes; were also the violations of the rule. When the people were discussing continuously about this incidant, Allahuthala revealed to His Prophet ﷺ the ayath 2:217 i.e. "Al-Fitnah is worse than killing."

Then Allah's Messenger ﷺ forgive the members of the team. He accepted possessions from the caravan and the two prisoned. He arranged the payment of the blood money to the family of the Quraish killed. Ibn Ishaq said: "When Abdullah bin Jahsh and his companions were relieved from their depressing thoughts, after the ayath was revealed about this subject, they received the reward of Jihadh."

This incident proved the greatness of the Prophet ﷺ:

- When an army committed a harmful act, which was not assigned to them, he was strict with them.
- He refused to accept the booty, they brought before the revelation of the above mentioned ayath.
- After revelation ot the ayath, he arranged to compensate the loss caused due to the mistake of his army.
- He paid the blood money to the family of the killed.
- He forgave the team members, who brought about a slur to the reputation of the Prophet ﷺ.

الحمدلله

بِسْمِ ٱللَّهِ ٱلرَّحْمَٰنِ ٱلرَّحِيمِ

5. Rapid Round Questions

Set: 1. As referred in the Holy Quran:

1. **Which animal has the 'Harshest voice'?**
   Answer: Donkey - (31:19)

2. **Which house of animal is 'Frailest house'?**
   Answer: The spider's house - (29:41)

3. **Whose hold is the "Firmest hold"?**
   Answer: Allah's hold - (2:256 and 31:22)

4. **According to Allah which sin is the "Greatest sin"?**
   Answer: Associating partners with Allah - (4:48 and several places)

5. **Who is mentioned as "Devoutly obedient woman" in Quran?**
   Answer: Bi bi Marium - (66:12)

6. **According to Allah who are the "Worst of creatures"?**
   Answer: The disbelievers amongst the 'people of the Scripture'; and the polytheists - (98:6)

7. **Who are "Best of creatures"?**
   Answer: Those who believe Allah and do good deeds - (98:7)

8. **Which is the "Promised day" for mankind?**
   Answer: The Promised Day is the Day of Judgement - (85:2)

9. **Which days are referred as "Witnessing and Witnessed day" in Quran?**
   Answer: The witnessing day refers to "Friday" and witnessed day refers to "The day of Arafath"

10. Which is the "Best of abodes" for those who have achieved supreme success?
    Answer: The Paradise - (3:14)

الحمدلله

Set 2: Surahs of the Quran:

1. Which is the last surah revealed?
    Answer: Surah An-Nasr.

2. Which two surahs are recited in Fajr prayer?
    Answer: Surah Kafirun and Surah Iqlas.

3. Which surah is the hump of Quran?
    Answer: Surah Baqara

4. Which two surahs are often recited in two rakaths of Friday Obligatory prayer?
    Answer: Surah Ala and Surah Ghashiya.

5. Which Surah of the Quran protects from the punishment of grave?
    Answer: Surah Mulk.

6. Which are the two surahs on recitation protects from Black magic, envy and evils.
    Answer: Surah Nass and Surah Falaq.

7. Which of the two surahs on the Day of Resurrection will come as two clouds/ shades/ flocks of birds pleading for those who recite them.
    Answer: Surah Baqara and surah Ala-Imraan

8. The revelation of which surah has been delayed because the Prophet ﷺ never said "In sha Allah"
    Answer: Surah Kahaf.

9. Which surah was revealed by Jibreel (AS) along with 70,000 angels?
    Answer: Surah Al Anam

10. Which surah has to be recited for being protected from enemies?
    Answer: Surah Kauthar.

الحمدلله

Set 3. From the hints provided below find out who are these persons:

1. His punishment in this life will be that he will say: "Touch me not"
   Answer: Samiri - (20:97)

2. King's golden bowl was traced from his bag therefore he was retained with his brother.
   Answer: Bunyamin and Yusuf (AS) - (12:76)

3. "Strike the wife with bundle of thin grass and break not your oath."
   Answer: Ayyub (AS) - (38:44)

4. "Bring me molten copper to pour over it."
   Answer: Zul-Qarnain - (18:96)

5. "She saw it, she thought it was a pool and she (tucked up her clothes) uncovering her legs."
   Answer: Queen of Saba - (27:44)

6. "Will You place on earth someone who will spread corruption there and shed blood while we glorify Your praises and proclaim Your Holiness?"
   Answer: Angels to Allah (سبحانه وتعالىٰ) - (2:30)

7. They said, "We wish to eat from it and let our hearts be reassured and know that you have been truthful to us and be among its witnesses."
   Answer: The disciples of Isa (AS) - (5:113).

8. "And speak to him mildly, perhaps he may accept admonition or fear Allah."
   Answer: Allah (سبحانه وتعالىٰ) said to Musa (AS) and Harun (AS) while going to Firaun - (20:44)

9. "Have you seen him who prevents, a slave when he prays?"
   Answer: Abu Jahal prevents the Prophet ﷺ to pray – (96:9 and 10)

10. "Would that my people knew! That Allah has forgiven me and made me of the honoured ones!"
    Answer: A man from the farthest end of the city came, rushing. He advised, "O my people! Follow the messengers. Follow those who ask no reward of you, and

are rightly guided." This is from the story of the three Prophets mentioned in the Surah Yaseen but he was killed by his Society- (36:26 and 27). After enteing the Paradise, he narrated these words.

Set 4. Furnish the other name for the following:

1. Surah Fathiha
Answer: It is called by the following names.
  1. Umm Al-Kitab - "Mother of the Book"
  2. Umm Al-Quran - "Mother of the Quran"
  3. Sab'a al Mathani - "Seven repeated verses" (15:87)
  4. Al-Hamd -"Praise"
  5. As-Shifa - "The Cure",
  6. Ar-Ruqyah - "Remedy" or "Spiritual cure",
  7. Al-Asas, "The Foundation" for the entire Quran.

2. Surah At-Tauba
Answer: Al Baraath

3. Surah Al Isra
Answer: Bani Israel

4. Surah Ghafir
Answer: Momin

5. Surah Fussilath
Answer: Hameem Sajdha

6. Surah Muhammad (ﷺ)
Answer: Qithal

7. Surah Al Mulk
Answer: Thabarak

8. Surah Al Qalam
Answer: Noon - (ن)

9. **Surah Al Insan**
   Answer: At Dhar, Hal Ata

10. **Surah Al Iqlas**
    Answer: At-Tawhid

11. **"Al-Mu'awwidhateyn"**
    Answer: Surah Falaq and Surah Naas together are called (المعوذتين) - meaning. "the two (surahs) for seeking refuge and protection"

الحمدلله

Set 5: From the clues provided identify the Prophets:

1. **His death was made known by the little worms of earth**
   Answer: Sulaiman (AS).

2. **Without knowing his worth, was sold for a very little price.**
   Answer: Yusuf (AS).

3. **She camel was sent to**
   Answer: Salih (AS).

4. **Stayed for three days in a small cave, along with his friend.**
   Answer: Muhammad ﷺ and his friend Abu Bakr (RA)

5. **Always sang the praise of Allah with his sweet voice.**
   Answer: Dawood (AS).

6. **Born with the pronouncement of the word "Qun"**
   Answer: Isa (AS).

7. **Propogated the Divine message through his brother.**
   Answer: Musa (AS) through Haroon (AS).

8. **Caused him to die and resurrected after 100 years.**
   Answer: Uzaer (AS).

9. **Named by Allah before his birth.**
   Answer: Yahya (AS).

10. **Ram was placed for sacrifice due to his and his father's obedience.**
    Answer: Ismail (AS).

الحمدلله

Set 6: From the clues furnished, identify the woman/women:

1. **Here are my daughters: they are purer for you (if you marry).**
Answer: The daughters of the society of Lut (AS).

2. **Became refreshed by shaking date palm tree, by eating its fruits and drinking water from the stream that formed near her feet.**
Answer: Bi bi Marium.

3. **Prayed to Allah to build a house in the Paradise.**
Answer: Firaun's wife Asia

4. **Followed the brother, on the bank of the river Nile, as to know where he is going?**
Answer: Sister of Musa (AS).

5. **Instead of cutting fruits they cut their fingers**
Answer: Guests of Aziz's wife on seeing Yusuf (AS).

6. **Around her neck will be a rope of palm-fibre**
Answer: Wife of Abu Lahab

7. **"Her heart was empty she would have almost disclosed, it had We not strengthened her heart so that she might be of the believers."**
Answer: Mother of Musa (AS)

8. **O my (dear) father! engage him on wages: truly the best of men for thee to employ is the (man) who is strong and trust worthy.**
Answer: Wife of Musa (AS).

9. She said: "Kings, when they enter a country, despoil it, and make the noblest of its people its meanest thus do they behave"
Answer: Queen of Saba

10. "O my Lord! I do dedicate into Thee what is in my womb for Thy special service."
Answer: Imran's wife

11. "They were both under two of Our righteous servants, but they acted treacherously towards them"
Answer: Wife of Nuh (AS) and Wife of Lut (AS).

الحمدلله

Set 7. Name the surahs:

1. Surahs named with single arabic letter:

   Answer: 1. Noon (ن)
             2. Qaf (ق)
             3. Sad (ص)

2. Surahs titled with the names of animal beings:

   Answer: 1. Al-Baqara
             2. Al-Anaam
             3. An-Nahl
             4. An-Naml
             5. Al-Ankabooth
             6. Al-Feel.

3. Surah that contain longest aya:
   Answer: Al-Baqara, Verse 282.

4. Surahs titled with the names of Prophets:

   Answer: 1. Yunus (AS)
             2. Hud (AS)
             3. Yusuf (AS)
             4. Ibrahim (AS)

    5. Mohammad (SAW)
    6. Nooh (AS).

5. **Surahs titled with names of Holy people:**
   Answer: 1. Ala-Imran
            2. Marium
            3. Luqman.

6. **Surah titled with the arabic name of a metal**
   Answer: Al-Hadith.

7. **Second surah that was revealed.**
   Answer: Al-Muddasir 1 to 7.

8. **Surah that was revealed twice.**
   Answer: Al-Fathiha.

9. **Surah titled with the name of Allah.**
   Answer: Ar-Rahaman.

10. **Shortest surah**
    Answer: Al-Kauther.

الحمدلله

Set 8. With reference to Hell:

1. **How many angels are guarding the Hell?**
   Answer: 19 angels.

2. **How many gates are there in Hell?**
   Answer: 7 gates.

3. **What is the fuel of hell fire?**
   Answer: Men and stones.

4. **Where is the bridge of Siraath?**
   Answer: Over the Hell.

5. What is the food of dwellers of fire?
   Answer: Zaqqum, Dari and Pus.

6. What is their drink?
   Answer: Boiling water.

7. In the hell which one appears like the head of Shayatin?
   Answer: Zaqqum tree.

8. Who are ashabul Naar?
   Answer: The dwellers of hell.

9. Who are ashabul jaheem?
   Answer: The dwellers of the blazing fire.

10. Those who hoard gold and silver without spending in the way of Allah, what type of punishment they will get in the hell?
    Answer: In the Hell fire the gold and silver will be heated up and placed on their foreheads, flanks, and backs, and will be told "so taste what you used to hoard."

الحمدلله

Set 9. What is that mentioned, only once in the Quran?

1. Which is the only day of a week, named as surah in the Quran?
Answer: Al- Juma (Friday).

2. Which is the only women's name mentioned in the Quran?
Answer: Bi bi Marium

3. Which is the only sahaba's name referred in Quran?
Answer: Zaid bin Harith (RA)

4. Which is the only community which repented on watching the punishment from Allah and escaped from it?
Answer: Community of Yunus (AS) (10:98)

5. Which is the only name of the enemy of Allah and His Messenger ﷺ mentioned in Quran?
Answer: Abu Lahab, the uncle of the Prophet ﷺ (111:1)

6. The only community which transgressed, for which punished by being converted into animals?
Answer: Community which transgressed by fishing on Sabbath. (2:65).

7. Name the house, where all the angels created, perform only once tawaf (Circumambulation)?
Answer: Baithul Mamur (52:4)

8. Mention the only animal that acts as Messenger for Allah.
Answer: Beast from earth (دَابَّةً مِّنَ الْأَرْضِ) that will speak to mankind (27:82).

9. Which is the only Sajdha ayath, when recited by the Prophet ﷺ, all Kafir of the Makka performed Sajdha?
Answer: The last ayath of Surah Najm: [فَاسْجُدُوا لِلَّهِ وَاعْبُدُوا] (53:62).

10. What is the only ayath revealed inside the Kabah?
Answer: "Verily! Allah commands that you should render back the trusts to those, to whom they are due; and that when you judge between men, you judge with justice. Verily, how excellent is the teaching which He (Allah) gives you! Truly, Allah is Ever All-Hearer, All-Seer." (4:58)

الحمدلله

Set 10. Mention the surah in which the following famous ayaath are located:

1. "Surely to Allah we belong and to Him we will all return to Him."
[إِنَّا لِلَّهِ وَإِنَّا إِلَيْهِ رَاجِعُونَ]
Answer: Surah Baqara (2:156)

2. "His command is only when He intends a thing that He says to it, "Be," and it is."
[إِنَّمَا أَمْرُهُ إِذَا أَرَادَ شَيْئًا أَن يَقُولَ لَهُ كُن فَيَكُونُ]
Answer: Surah Yasin (36:82)

3. "So, surely with hardship comes ease. Surely with that hardship comes more ease." [إِنَّ مَعَ ٱلْعُسْرِ يُسْرًا فَإِنَّ مَعَ ٱلْعُسْرِ يُسْرًا]
   Answer: Surah Al-Inshirah (94:5 and 6).

4. "Remember Me; I will remember you. And thank Me, and never be ungrateful." [فَٱذْكُرُونِىٓ أَذْكُرْكُمْ وَٱشْكُرُوا۟ لِى وَلَا تَكْفُرُونِ]
   Answer: Surah Al-Baqara (2:156).

5. "This is what Allah has willed! There is no power except with Allah!" [مَا شَآءَ ٱللَّهُ لَا قُوَّةَ إِلَّا بِٱللَّهِ]
   Answer: Surah Al-Kahaf (18:39)

6. "Read, O Prophet, in the Name of your Lord Who created. Created humans from a clinging clot." [ٱقْرَأْ بِٱسْمِ رَبِّكَ ٱلَّذِى خَلَقَ خَلَقَ ٱلْإِنسَٰنَ مِنْ عَلَقٍ]
   Answer: Surah Alaq (96:1 and 2).

7. "My Lord! Increase me in knowledge." [رَّبِّ زِدْنِى عِلْمًا]
   Answer: Surah Taha, (20:114)

8. Your Lord has proclaimed, "Call upon Me; I will respond to you." [وَقَالَ رَبُّكُمُ ٱدْعُونِىٓ أَسْتَجِبْ لَكُمْ]
   Answer: Surah Ghafir, (40:60)

9. "He is with you wherever you are. And Allah, of what you do, is Seeing." [وَهُوَ مَعَكُمْ أَيْنَ مَا كُنتُمْ ۚ وَٱللَّهُ بِمَا تَعْمَلُونَ بَصِيرٌ]
   Answer: Surah Hadid (57:4).

10. "O you who have believed, let not your wealth and your children divert you from remembrance of Allah. And whoever does that – then those are the losers."
    [يَٰٓأَيُّهَا ٱلَّذِينَ ءَامَنُوا۟ لَا تُلْهِكُمْ أَمْوَٰلُكُمْ وَلَآ أَوْلَٰدُكُمْ عَن ذِكْرِ ٱللَّهِ ۚ وَمَن يَفْعَلْ ذَٰلِكَ فَأُو۟لَٰٓئِكَ هُمُ ٱلْخَٰسِرُونَ]
    Answer: Surah Al Munafiqun (63:9)

الحمدلله

بِسْمِ ٱللَّهِ ٱلرَّحْمَٰنِ ٱلرَّحِيمِ

6. To Whom it refers

1. According to Quran, whom all Allah ﷻ dislikes? (إِنَّ اللَّهَ لَا يُحِبُّ)

Allahuthala dislikes the following persons.

- disbelievers
- traitors
- treacherous and ungrateful
- transgressors
- sinning disbelievers
- wrong doers
- arrogant persons
- those who corrupt
- those who boast
- sinning deceivers
- those who speak evil words, in public
- those who commit excess.

1. إِنَّهُ لَا يُحِبُّ الْكَافِرِينَ - He does not like the disbelievers. (30:45).

2. إِنَّ اللَّهَ لَا يُحِبُّ الْخَائِنِينَ - Indeed, Allah does not like traitors. (8:58).

3. إِنَّ اللَّهَ لَا يُحِبُّ كُلَّ خَوَّانٍ كَفُورٍ - Allah does not like every treacherous and ungrateful. (22:38)

4. إِنَّ اللَّهَ لَا يُحِبُّ الْمُعْتَدِينَ - Allah likes not the transgressors. (2:190)

5. وَاللَّهُ لَا يُحِبُّ الْفَسَادَ - And Allah likes not corruption. (2:205).

6. وَاللَّهُ لَا يُحِبُّ كُلَّ كَفَّارٍ أَثِيمٍ - And Allah does not like every sinning disbeliever. (2:276).

7. وَاللَّهُ لَا يُحِبُّ الظَّالِمِينَ - Allah does not like the wrong-doers. (3:140) (42:40)

8. إِنَّهُ لَا يُحِبُّ الْمُسْتَكْبِرِينَ - He does not like the arrogant. (16:23).

9. إِنَّ اللَّهَ لَا يُحِبُّ الْفَرِحِينَ - Indeed, Allah does not like the prideful. (28:76).

10. إِنَّ اللَّهَ لَا يُحِبُّ الْمُفْسِدِينَ - Allah does not like corrupters. (28:77).

11. إِنَّ اللَّهَ لَا يُحِبُّ مَن كَانَ خَوَّانًا أَثِيمًا - Indeed, Allah loves not one who is a habitually sinful deceiver. (4:107)

12. إِنَّ اللَّهَ لَا يُحِبُّ كُلَّ مُخْتَالٍ فَخُورٍ – Allah does not like everyone self-deluded and boastful. (31:18 and 57:23)

13. لَّا يُحِبُّ اللَّهُ الْجَهْرَ بِالسُّوءِ مِنَ الْقَوْلِ إِلَّا مَن ظُلِمَ – Allah does not like the public mention of evil except by one who has been wronged. (4:148).

14. إِنَّهُ لَا يُحِبُّ الْمُسْرِفِينَ - Indeed, He does not like those who commit excess. (6:141) (7:31)

الحمدلله

2. Whom all Allah ﷻ loves?

Allah سبحانه وتعالى **loves:**

★ The good-doers (الْمُحْسِنِينَ)
★ Those who turn unto Him, in repentance (التَّوَّابِينَ)
★ Those who purify themselves. (مُتَطَهِّرِينَ)
★ The pious (الْمُتَّقِينَ)
★ The patient ones (الصَّابِرِينَ)
★ Those who repose their trust in Him (الْمُتَوَكِّلِينَ)
★ Those who are clean and pure (الْمُطَّهِّرِينَ)
★ Those who are equitable/who deal with equity (الْمُقْسِطِينَ).

Al Quran says:

1. اللَّهَ يُحِبُّ الْمُحْسِنِينَ – Allah loves the doers of good. (2:195) (3:134 and 148)

2. إِنَّ اللَّهَ يُحِبُّ التَّوَّابِينَ وَيُحِبُّ الْمُتَطَهِّرِينَ Allah loves those who turn unto Him in repentance; and loves those who purify themselves. (2:222).

3. فَإِنَّ اللَّهَ يُحِبُّ الْمُتَّقِينَ - Allahuthala loves those who fear Him. (3:76) (9:4 and 7).

4. وَاللَّهُ يُحِبُّ الصَّابِرِينَ - And Allah loves As-Sabireen (the patient ones, etc.). (3:146).

5. إِنَّ اللَّهَ يُحِبُّ الْمُتَوَكِّلِينَ - Verily, Allah loves those who put their trust (in Him). (3:159).

6. وَاللَّهُ يُحِبُّ الْمُطَّهِّرِينَ - And Allah loves those who are clean and pure. (9:108).

7. إِنَّ اللَّهَ يُحِبُّ الْمُقْسِطِينَ - Indeed, Allah loves those who act justly. (49:9) and (60:8).

Prayer:

O Allah Subhanahuthala! Make us pious, make us perform good deeds; make us turn towards you in repentance; purify us; make us just; finally, we should be made to repose trust in You and thereby admit us in Paradise, along with all our near and dear ones. Ameen!

الحمدلله

3. To whom Allahuthala refers to "as better in speech", in Quran?

Answer: And who is better in speech than he who [says: "My Lord is Allah," and then stands straight and invites (men) to Allah's, and does righteous deeds, and says: "I am one of the Muslims." (Fussilath, 41:33).

Allahuthala refers to those, who are better in speech -

★ openly accepts that their Lord is Allah who is Wahid [ألْوَاحِدٌ].

★ by standing straight, that is, boldly without any fear, they call men towards Allah.

★ they will be always good, performing the righteous deeds. Their character is revealed in their goodness.

★ they totally submit themself to their Lord.

★ they are always very humble and never consider them as great.

This ayath was revealed as an encouragement, glad tidings and guidance to our Prophet Mohammad ﷺ and his followers, who propagated Islam amidst the strong opposition of arrogant and stubborn Quraish. Prophet Mohammad ﷺ was called a liar, mad man and sorcerer. After Hamza bin Abdul Mutalib (RA), the Prophet's uncle embraced Islam, the Quraish became greatly distressed and grieved. They decided to do something, to stop the growth of Islam.

Utbah bin Rabia, an honoured Quraish leader met the Prophet ﷺ, enquiring whether the Prophet ﷺ required money or kingship or the best woman in the city. He offered to make arrangement to fulfill such a requirement. He further observed that if the Prophet ﷺ was under the inspiration of a Jinn or a devil, he offered to arrange the best physicians for cure.

After waiting for him to finish; and after enquiring whether he had completed; the Prophet ﷺ started reciting Surah Fussilath (the other name is Hameem Sajdha) with

بِسْمِ اللهِ الرَّحْمٰنِ الرَّحِيْمِ He recited till he reached the ayath 38, a verse of Prostration. He prostrated and rose up and said that was his answer.

On hearing that recitation, Utbah's face changed because he heard the truth and he went to his people and said "Leave Muhammad (ﷺ), if other tribes of Arab overcome him then you would be saved of not causing any harm to him and if Muhammad (ﷺ) overcomes them his victory will be yours and his honour will be yours." With the encouragement and glad tidings from Allah, understand how strongly and calmly the Prophet ﷺ faced his enemy.

In fact, this ayath is a guidance to all those who make a call towards Islam.

- ❖ They must have a strong faith in Allah [سبحانه وتعالىٰ].
- ❖ They must practice what they teach.
- ❖ Their character must prove that they are true Muslims.
- ❖ Their words and deeds must be uncomparable.
- ❖ They must be knowledgeable.
- ❖ They should stand firmly against opposition, as with the commencement of preaching; even the friends and relatives become their enemies.
- ❖ They should perform righteous deeds and further they must be humble enough to face anything.
- ❖ They must be amongst those who submit to Allah [عَزَّ وَ جَلَّ]. Speech of such people, is better and beautiful.

الحمدلله

4. "If you dislike them, it may be that you dislike a thing and Allah brings through it a great deal of good." [4:19]. In this ayath to whom Allahuthala refers as "them"?

Answer: Them refers to wives of Muslims.

"O, you who believe! You are forbidden to inherit women against their will, and you should not treat them with harshness, that you may take away part of the Mahr you have given them, unless they commit open illegal sexual intercourse. And live with them honourably. If you dislike them, it may be that you dislike a thing and Allah brings through it a great deal of good." {An Nisa, 4:19}.

Allah ﷻ advises men:

[30:21] "And among His Signs is this, that He created for you wives from among yourselves, that you may find repose in them, and He has put between you (both) affection and mercy. Verily, in that are indeed signs for a people who reflect."

[4:20 and 21] If you desire to replace a wife with another and you have given the former even a stack of gold as a dowry, do not take any of it back. Would you still take it unjustly and very sinfully? And how could you take it back after having enjoyed each other intimately and she has taken from you a firm commitment?

[4:34] "Men are the protectors and maintainers of women, because Allah has made one of them to excel the other, and because they spend (to support them) from their means..."

[4:34] "As to those women on whose part you see ill-conduct, admonish them (first), (next), refuse to share their beds, (and last) beat them (lightly, if it is useful), but if they return to obedience, seek not against them means (of annoyance)."

The opinion of the Messenger of Allah ﷺ about wives of beleivers:

"A believer must not hate (his wife) believing woman; if he dislikes one of her characteristics he will be pleased with another". (Muslim)

"Best men are those who get good name from wife"

"All objects in earth are to enjoy. Among those, is a wife with good conduct"

It was narrated by Jaabir (RA) from the Farewell Sermon of the Prophet ﷺ:

"Fear Allah concerning women! Verily you have taken them on the security of Allah, and intercourse with them has been made lawful unto you by words of Allah. You too have rights over them, and that they should not allow anyone to sit on your bed [i.e., not let them into the house] whom you do not like. But if they do that, you can chastise them but not severely. Their rights upon you are that you should provide them with food and clothing in a fitting manner. Treat women well, for they are [like] helpers ('awan) with you and do not possess anything for themselves. You have taken them only as a trust from God, and you have made the enjoyment of their persons lawful by the word of God" (Muslim, 1218).

Allahuthalas's instructions towards women:

[4:19] "the righteous women are devoutly obedient (to Allah and to their husbands), and guard in the husband's absence what Allah orders them to guard." (e.g. their chastity and their husband's property, etc.).

[2:228] "And women have rights similar to the rights of men in a just manner and the men have a degree (of advantage) over them to what is reasonable."

[4:128] "And if a woman fears cruelty or desertion on her husband's part, there is no sin on them both if they make terms of peace between themselves; and making peace is better. And human inner- selves are swayed by greed. But if you do good and keep away from evil, verily, Allah is Ever Well-Acquainted with what you do."

[24:31] "and not to show off their adornment except only that which is apparent (like palms of hands or one eye or both eyes for necessity to see the way, or outer dress like veil, gloves, head-cover, apron, etc.), and to draw their veils all over Juyubihinna (i.e. their bodies, faces, necks and bosoms, etc.) and not to reveal their adornment except to their husbands, their fathers, their husband's fathers, their sons, their husband's sons, their brothers or their brother's sons, or their sister's sons, or their (Muslim) women (i.e. their sisters in Islam), or the (female) slaves whom their right hands possess, or old male servants who lack vigour, or small children who have no sense of the shame of sex. And let them not stamp their feet so as to reveal what they hide of their adornment. And all of you beg Allah to forgive you all, O believers, that you may be successful."

[33:59] "Tell your wives and your daughters and the women of the believers to draw their cloaks (veils) all over their bodies (i.e. screen themselves completely except the eyes or one eye to see the way). That will be better, that they should be known (as free respectable women) so as not to be annoyed."

[66:10] "Allah sets forth an example for those who disbelieve, the wife of Nuh (AS) and the wife of Lut (AS) .... both betrayed their (husbands), and it was said: "Enter the Fire along with those who enter!"

[66: 11] "And Allah has set forth an example for those who believe, the wife of Firaun."

[66:12] "And Marium, the daughter of 'Imran who guarded her chastity; and We breathed into through Our Ruh and she testified to the truth of the Words of her Lord and His Scriptures, and she was of the Qanitin (i.e. obedient to Allah)."

Ahadheese about women:

★ "Abu Hurayrah (RA) narrated that the Prophet ﷺ declared that: "When a man calls his wife to his bed and she refuses, and he went to sleep angry with her, the angels will curse her until morning." (Al-Bukhari, 3065; Muslim, 1436).

★ "It is not permitted for a woman to fast when her husband is present without his permission, or to admit any one into his house without his permission and whatever she spends (in charity) of his wealth without his consent." (Al-Bukhari, 4899, Muslim, 1026).

★ "Treat women nicely, for a woman is created from a rib, and the most curved portion of the rib is its upper portion, so, if you should try to straighten it, it will break, but if you leave it as it is, it will remain crooked. So treat women nicely."

★ "If prostation was allowed then I would ask wives to prostrate themselves infront of their husbands." This hadhees indicates the importance of husband.

Allah [سبحانه وتعالى] further asserts:

If both the husband and wife follow all the above instructions, Allah ﷻ will be satisfied with them and hold that: "Enter Paradise, you and your wives, in happiness." (43:70)

الحمدلله

5. "And verily, you are on an exalted standard of character." (68:4) As to whom Allahuthala points out, in this ayath?

Answer: To Mohammad ﷺ

The Prophet Mohammad ﷺ was bestowed by Allah [SWT], an exemplary character and righteous thoughts. But his enemies referred him as a mad man. To console His Prophet ﷺ, Allahuthala revealed the following ayath:

"You (O Muhammad ﷺ) are not, by the Grace of your Lord, a madman. And verily, for you (O Muhammad ﷺ) will be an endless reward. And verily, you are on an exalted standard of character. Which of you is afflicted with madness? Verily, your Lord knows better, who (among men) has gone astray from His Path, and He knows better those who are guided." (Al Qalam, 68: 2 to 7).

Imam Al-Bukhari recorded that Al-Bara had claimed that: "The Prophet ﷺ had the best behaviour of all of the people." Imam Ahmad also recorded from Abu Hurayrah

(RA) that the Prophet ﷺ conveyed, "I have only been sent to perfect the righteous behaviour."

Prophet ﷺ was very simple, kind, gentle, modest, soft spoken, considerate, brave and with every other good character. Every single characteristic of his was at the highest pinnacle. He was close to the people, listening, teaching, advising and correcting. He was granted with complete intellect; always rendering sound judgment and a brevity in speech. The Prophet ﷺ:

★ accepted invitations without hesitation and used to comply with it,
★ fulfilled the needs of those, who approached him,
★ will not decline or disappoint them,
★ comforted and consoled all those in misery,
★ never imposed his opinion, on others,
★ always sought other's opinion,
★ consulted and instructed those concerned, accordingly,
★ forgave those who insulted him,
★ was never harsh to anyone,
★ would tolerate the incompetency of others with complete fortitude,
★ exposed kindness towards his companions; provided the best and complete companionship.

"It has been mentioned that Sad bin Hisham (RA) enquired Ayesha (RA) about the character of the Messenger of Allah ﷺ. She responded: `Have you not read the Quran?' Sad (RA) said: `Of course.' Then she clarified: `Verily, the character of the Messenger of Allah ﷺ was the Quran." Abdur- Razzaq conveyed the same message; so also Muslim refers to such a statement. Prophet ﷺ always followed the command of Quran and avoided the acts prohibited therein. Allah [عَزَّ وَجَلَّ] also blessed him with noble characteristics. Allah, the Exalted also appreciated his characteristics.

The following Quranic verses are proof for that:

[7:199] "Show forgiveness, enjoin what is good, and turn away from the foolish."

[3:159] "And by the Mercy of Allah, you dealt with them gently. And had you been severe and harsh hearted, they would have broken away from about you; so pass over (their faults), and ask (Allah's) Forgiveness for them; and consult them in the affairs. Then when you have taken a decision, put your trust in Allah."

[9:128] "It grieves him (Muhammad ﷺ) that you should receive any injury or difficulty. He is anxious over you (to be rightly guided, to repent to Allah, and beg Him to pardon and forgive your sins, in order that you may enter Paradise and be saved from the punishment of the Hell-Fire), for the believers (he is) full of pity, kind, and merciful."

[33:21] "Indeed in the Messenger of Allah (Muhammad ﷺ) you have a good example to follow"

[31:22] "Submits his face to Allah .... has grasped the most trustworthy hand-hold."

[4:135] "Stand out firmly for justice"

[2:177] "fulfil their covenant when they make it, and who are As-Sabirin in extreme poverty and disease and at the time of battles."

[25:64] "spent the night before their Lord, prostrate and standing."

[2:283] "let the one who is entrusted discharge his trust (faithfully)"

[28:54] "repel evil with good"

[42:38] "who (conduct) their affairs by mutual consultation"

[2:83] "speak good to people".

Anas (RA) confirmed in the Two Sahihs that: "I served the Prophet ﷺ for ten years, and he never said a word of displeasure to me (Uff), nor did he ever say to me concerning something I had done: `Why did you do that?' And he never said to me concerning something I had not done: `Why didn't you do this?' He had the best character."

Imam Ahmad recorded that Ayesha (RA) had claimed, "The Messenger of Allah ﷺ never struck a servant of his with his hand, nor did he ever hit a woman. He never hit anything with his hand, except for when he was fighting Jihad in the cause of Allah."

Al-`Awfi reported from Ibn Abbas that it also means "Verily, you are on a great religion, and it is Islam." Many of the scholars have agreed with this opinion.

Allahuthala showers His blessings upon the Prophet ﷺ, the angels also pray for him and He commands the Muslims to send salawath on him. "Indeed, Allah showers His blessings upon the Prophet, and His angels pray for him. O believers! Invoke Allah's blessings upon him, and salute him with worthy greetings of peace." (33:56).

الحمدلله

6. "Construct a building over them". Them refers to whom?

Answer: Dwellers of cave (Ashabul Kahaf).

Allahuthala commences the story of dwellers of cave in Sura Kahaf as: "Do you think that the dwellers of Al-Kahf (cave and Ar-Raqim - the place/mountain/valley at which the cave is located) were a wonder among Our signs" (18:9). No! Allah's signs are countless in heavens and earth and in between them both. Allah continues, "We relate to you O Prophet ﷺ their story in truth. They were youths who truly believed in their Lord." (18:13).

According to the scholars who furnished Tafsir, that those youths were from the families of king and his leaders. Arrogant and tyrannical King Decacias, was their ruler. The people of the city used to celebrate a festival every year, all gathering outside the city. They worshipped their idols and offered sacrifices to them. Those beleiving young men, totally disliked their idol worship. Guided and inspired by Allah, they left their elders, gathered one by one in a place without consulting each other. They were total strangers and gathered by the Will of Allah.

Ibn Kathir said, "Allah guided them and inspired them to fear Him, so they recognized His Oneness, and bore witness that there is no god besides Him." Then they said to one another, "These people of ours have taken gods besides Allah. Why do they not produce a clear proof of them? Who then does more wrong than those who fabricate lies against Allah?" (18:15). Allah recorded, "And We strengthened their hearts when they stood up and declared, "Our Lord is the Lord of the heavens and the earth. We will never call upon any god besides Allah, or we would truly be uttering an outrageous lie." (18:14).

Ibn Kathir in his Tafsir explains: "It was said that when they called their king to believe in Allah, he refused, warned and threatened them. He commanded them to be stripped of their clothing bearing the adornments of their people, then he gave them some time to think about the situation, hoping that they would return to their former religion. This was a way that Allah showed kindness for them, because during that time they managed to escape from him and flee from persecution for the sake of their religion. This is what is prescribed in the Shariah during times of trial and persecution - a person who fears for his religion should flee from his persecutors,"

Those young men fled, taking refuge in a cave and prayed, "Our Lord, grant us from Yourself mercy and prepare for us from our affair right guidance." Their Lord extended His mercy on them and accommodated them in a spacious cave along with their dog (18:16). Allah mentioned this in Quran as: "And you would have seen the sun, as it rose, inclining away from their cave to the right, and as it set, declining away from them to the left, while they lay in its open space. That is one of the signs of Allah. Whoever Allah guides is truly guided. But whoever He leaves to stray, you will never find for them a guiding mentor." (18:17).

Allah describes their deep sleep as, "So We sealed up their hearing in the Cave for a number of years." (18:11). "And you would have thought they were awake, though they were asleep. We turned them over, to the right and left, while their dog stretched his forelegs at the entrance. Had you looked at them, you would have certainly fled away from them, filled with horror" (18:18). Thus Allah protected them from any disturbance.

Regarding the number of years about their sleep, it was stated that: "they remained in their cave for three hundred years, adding nine." (18:25). Allah proclaimed, "O Prophet, Allah knows best how long they stayed. With Him alone is the knowledge of the unseen of the heavens and the earth. How perfectly He hears and sees! They have no guardian besides Him, and He shares His command with none." (18:26).

"And so We awakened them so that they might question one another. One of them exclaimed, 'How long have you remained asleep?' Some replied, "Perhaps a day, or part of a day." They said to one another" "Your Lord knows best how long you have remained. So send one of you with these silver coins of yours to the city, and let him find which food is the purest, and then bring you provisions from it. Let him be exceptionally cautious, and do not let him give you away." (18:19). "For, indeed, if they find out about you, they will stone you to death, or force you back into their faith, and then you will never succeed." (18:20).

"That is how We caused them to be discovered so that their people might know that Allah's promise of resurrection is true and that there is no doubt about the Hour. When the people disputed with each other about the case of the youth after their death some proposed, "Build a structure around them. Their Lord knows best about them." Those who prevailed in the matter said, "We will surely build a place of worship over them." (18:21).

During the life of Prophet Mohammed ﷺ, the Jews knew this story while Arabs were ignorant of it. When Quraish approached the Jewish scholars to know what their scripture had recorded about the coming of a Prophet at Makkah. The Jewish scholars required the Qurash to ask the Prophet ﷺ about "What happened to the young men who took refuge in the cave and how many of them?"

The Prophet ﷺ replied them that he would furnish answer on the next day, with out mentioning "in sha Allah." Allah revealed the full story through Jibreel (AS), after a long wait. The story was exact as it was known by Jews. Allah declared that the exact number of men in the cave was known to Him only. 'Number seven' was not mentioned in the Holy Quran. Instead Allah informed the Prophet ﷺ, through this verse, to assert: "My Lord knows best their exact number. Only a few people know as well. So do not argue about them except with sure knowledge, nor consult any of those who debate about them" (18:22).

Allah recorded that "And thus We made their case known to the people, that they might know that the Promise of Allah is true, and that there can be no doubt about the Hour." (Remember) when they (the people of the city) disputed among themselves about their case, they said: "Construct a building over them, their Lord knows best about them," (then) those who won their point said (most probably the disbelievers): "We verily shall build a place of worship over them." (18:21).

There is a cave commonly known as "the cave of seven sleepers." located in Amman of Jordan, freely open to tourists. This is one of the seven sites attributed to legends of ashabul kahaf. The other sites are said to be located in Syria (Mar Musa), Turkey (Ephesus, Izmir and Kahramanmaras), Tuisia (Chenini) and even in China (Turpan). [الله اعلم !].

الحمدلله

7. To whom Allahuthala command "to lower the gaze?"

Answer: Believing men and women.

" [O Prophet ﷺ!] Tell the believing men to lower their gaze and guard their chastity. That is purer for them. Surely Allah is All-Aware of what they do." (An Noor, 24: 30)

"And tell the believing women to lower their gaze and guard their chastity, and not to reveal their adornments except what normally appears. Let them draw their veils over their chests, and not reveal their hidden adornments except to their husbands, their fathers, their fathers-in-law, their sons, their stepsons, their brothers, their brothers' sons or sisters' sons, their fellow women, those bondwomen in their possession, male attendants with no desire, or children who are still unaware of women's nakedness. Let them not stomp their feet, drawing attention to their hidden adornments. Turn to Allah in repentance all together, O believers, so that you may be successful." (An Noor, 24:31).

الحمدلله

8. "Allah will not speak to them on the Day of Resurrection, nor purify them, and theirs will be a painful torment." To whom Allah will not speak on the Day of Resurrection?

Answer: "Surely those who conceal any part of the Book that Allah has revealed and take for it a small price, they eat nothing but fire into their bellies, and Allah will not speak to them on the day of resurrection, nor will He purify them, and they shall have a painful torment." (2:174)

"(As for) those who take a small price for the covenant of Allah and their own oaths - surely they shall have no portion in the hereafter, and Allah will not speak to them, nor will He look upon them on the day of resurrection nor will He purify them, and they shall have a painful torment." (3:77).

Reason for revealing these ayaath:

1. Verse 2:174:

At the time of the Prophet ﷺ was in Makkah, the Rabbis [الرَّبَّانِيُّونَ] and scholars [وَالْأَحْبَارُ] were living in Madhina with great pomps and luxury. The whole Madhina was under the authority of these Jews. The Arabs respected them much thinking that they were intellectually high and used to send them their precious gifts.

But the Jews concealed the entire information about the description and coming of the Prophet ﷺ available in their Book Taurath. When the Prophet ﷺ commence his preaching at Makkah, ignorant Arabs approached these Jews, who denied the Truth. They distarted certain verses in their Scripture, fearing of loosing their authority, power and wealth. So Allahuthala warned them through several ayaath.

2. Verse 3:77:

There was a quarrel over a land among a Jew and a Muslim. They both went to the Prophet ﷺ and after listening to them he said: "Whoever makes an oath knowing well that he is lying in order to usurp the property of another, Allah will be angry with him when he meets Him." At this moment this ayath (3:77) was revealed.

In several places of the Quran, Allah warns the Jews:

[2:40 to 42] "O children of Israel! Call to mind My favor which I bestowed on you and be faithful to (your) covenant with Me, I will fulfill (My) covenant with you; and of Me, Me alone, should you be afraid." "And believe in what I have revealed, verifying that which is with you, and be not the first to deny it, neither take a mean price in exchange for My communications; and Me, Me alone should you fear." "And do not mix up the truth with the falsehood, nor hide the truth while you know (it)."

[2:79] "So woe to those who write the 'scripture' with their own hands, then say, 'This is from Allah, in order to exchange it for a small price. Woe to them for what their hands have written and woe to them for what they earn."

[3:187] "And when Allah made a covenant with those who were given the Book: 'You must make it clear to the people and not conceal it.' But they threw it away behind their backs and exchanged it for a small price. And wretched is that which they purchased."

[5:44] "Indeed, 'We' sent down the Taurath, in which was guidance and light. The prophets who submitted [to Allah] judged by it for the Jews, as did the rabbis and scholars by that with which they were entrusted of the Scripture of Allah, and they were witnesses thereto. So do not fear the people but fear Me, and do not exchange My verses for a small price. And whoever does not judge by what Allah has revealed – then it is those who are the disbelievers."

[16:95] "And do not exchange the covenant of Allah for a small price. Indeed, what is with Allah is best for you, if only you could know."

[3:199] "And indeed, among the People of the Scripture are those who believe in Allah and what was revealed to you and what was revealed to them, [being] humbly submissive to Allah. They do not exchange the verses of Allah for a small price. Those will have their reward with their Lord. Indeed, Allah is swift in account."

[9:9] "They have exchanged the signs of Allah for a small price and averted [people] from His way. Indeed, it was evil that they were doing."

Thus, many of those Rabbis and Scholars earned Allah's wrath, for misguiding ignorant people in return of worldly benefits.

In the authentic book of hadhees, it is recorded that various acts of sins if committed, will result in Allah عَزَّ وَجَلَّ not looking at such sinners on the Day of Resurrection. He will not purify them and such sinners will have a painful punishment, in the Hereafter.

Hadhees 1:

Allah's Messenger ﷺ proposed that: "There are three persons whom Allah will neither talk to nor look at, nor purify from (the sins), and they will have a painful punishment. (They are):

- ❖ A man possessed superfluous water on a way [some versions say 'in a desert'] and he withheld it from the travelers.
- ❖ a man who gives a pledge of allegiance to a Muslim ruler and gives it only for worldly gains. If the ruler gives him what he wants, he remains obedient to his pledge, otherwise he does not abide by it, and
- ❖ a man bargains with another man after the "Asr prayer and the latter takes a false oath in the Name of Allah claiming that he has been offered so much for the thing and the former (believes him and) buys it." (Sahih Bukhari – Book 52, hadith 34).

In one version of the hadith, it adds the words: Allah will say on the Day of Resurrection, 'Today I withhold My Blessings from you as you withheld the superfluous part of that (water) which your hands did not create.' (Sahih Bukhari, Book 97, Hadith 72).

Hadhees 2:

The Messenger of Allah ﷺ claimed: "There are three at whom Allah will not look on the Day of Resurrection: The one who disobeys his parents, the woman who imitates men in her outward appearance and the cuckold [husband of an adulterous wife]. And there are three who will not enter Paradise: The one who disobeys his parents, the drunkard, and the one who reminds people of what he has given them." (Sunan al-Nasai, 2562).

Hadhees 3:

The Prophet ﷺ stated: "There are three at whom Allah عَزَّ وَجَلَّ will not look on the Day of Resurrection, nor will He sanctify them and theirs' will be a painful torment: the one who does not give anything except that he reminds (the recipient of his gift), the one who drags his garment (below the ankles), and the one who sells his product by means of false oaths." (Sunan an-Nasa'i Hadith Number 4464).

Hadhees 4:

The Messenger of Allah ﷺ further stated: "Three (are the persons) with whom Allahuthala would neither speak, nor would He absolve them on the Day of Resurrection. Abu Muawiya added: "He would not look at them and there is grievous torment for them: the aged adulterer, the liar king and the proud destitute." (Sahih Muslim, Book 1: Hadith 195).

الحمدلله

9. According to Quran on whom the Shayatheen descends?

Answer: Shall I inform you upon whom the devils descends? They descend upon every sinful liar. They pass on what is heard and most of them are liars. [لَكٰذِبُوْنَ] (26:221 to 23).

Allahuthala here declares to the disbelievers of Makkah that the recipient of the Quran is not a sorcerer nor liar or madman. The Quran is not the work of a poet. It is the Truth. It is a sign by itself. It is not something that the Prophet ﷺ who had made it up by himself. It is not a work of Shaithan nor it came to him in visions from the Jinn. In fact, the Shaithan descends upon those who are like him - the fortune-teller. They pass on the lie they hear.

The devils overhear from the angels in the heaven. They fabricate what they had heard and convey it to the fortune tellers; who add to it a hundred lies and pass it on to the human beings. Thus, most of the fortune-tellers are liars!

This was recorded in an authentic Hadhees of Ayesha (RA). She said, "The people enquired the Prophet ﷺ about fortune-tellers", and the reply was: 'They are nothing.' They responded: "O Messenger of Allah ﷺ they say things that come true." The Prophet ﷺ said: "That is a word of truth which the Jinn snatches, then he gabbles it like the clucking of a chicken into the ear of his friend, but he mixes it with more than one hundred lies." (Al-Bukhari and Muslim).

In another hadhees Ayesha (RA) assert that: "The angels speak in the clouds about some matter on earth, and the Shayatin overhear what they say, so they tell it to the fortune-teller, gurgling into his ear like (a liquid poured) from a glass bottle and he adds to it one hundred lies."

Abu Hurayrah (RA) narrated, in another hadhees that the Prophet ﷺ said: " When Allah Subhanahuthala decrees a matter in heaven, the angels beat their wings in submission to His decree, like a chain beating on a rock. And when the fear in their hearts subsides, they say: "What is it that your Lord has said". They say: "The truth. And He is the Most High, the Greatest."

Then when the Jinns who are listening out, one above the other, when they hear this, they pass it on from one to another, until it is passed to the fortune-teller or soothsayer. The shooting star may strike the Jinn before he passes it on or he may pass it on after he is struck and he adds to it one hundred lies, thus it is said: "Did he not tell us that on such and such a day, such and such would happen" So they believe him because of that one which was heard from the heavens. (Al-Bukhari and Muslim).

★ **What Quran records about lies:**

Allah commanded us to avoid false words (22:30). He also says, do not mix (and confuse) the truth with falsehood. Do not suppress the truth knowingly. (2:42)

★ **What Quran refer about liars?**

- "Saying a lie against Allah and His revelation is a grave sin. The liars tell a lie against Allah knowingly." (3:75)
- "The liars are the criminals" (10:17).
- "See how they forge the lie against Allah, and this is sufficient as a manifest sin." (4:50)
- "Who is more unjust than he who forges a lie against Allah (18:15) or says: "It has been revealed to me; while nothing has been revealed to him, and he who says: I can reveal the like of what Allah has revealed?" (6:93)
- "They will indeed swear that their intention is nothing but good; But God doth declare that they are certainly liars." (9:107).
- "Knowingly they lie about Allah, by altering the Scripture with their tongues." (3:78).
- "And whoever invents lie about Allah, truly they are wrong doers." (3:94)
- "Allah does not guide a liar, and a disbeliever." (39:3).
- "He who forges a lie against Allah should lead astray men without knowledge." (6:144).

- But soon "Allah eliminates the falsehood and establishes the truth by His words." (42:24)
- Allah said to His Prophet ﷺ "if they give you the lie, then say: Your Lord is the Lord of All-encompassing mercy; & His punishment cannot be averted from the guilty people." (6:147).

★ **What will happen to the liars?**
- ❖ 'Allah will seal over their hearts.' (42:24)
- ❖ 'Allah never guides them.' (6:144 and 39:3).
- ❖ 'They will not be successful.' (6:21 and 10:17)
- ❖ 'Nobody will believe them.' (23:38).
- ❖ Allah says, "When they will be presented before their Lord, and the witnesses will say, 'These are the ones who lied against their Lord.' Unquestionably, the curse of Allah is upon them. (11:18)
- ❖ 'Allah will exterminate them with a punishment' (20:61) of humiliation.' (6:93)
- ❖ 'They will be put in the Hell.' (29:68)

★ **Aahadhees about lies:**
- A person came to the Prophet ﷺ and humbly enquired: 'O Beloved Prophet! What is that action which leads to Hell?' The Prophet ﷺ replied: 'When a bondsman speaks a lie, he commits a sin and when he commits a sin he shows ingratitude and when he shows ingratitude he enters Hell.' (Al-Musnad Imam Ahmad Bin Hanbal, vol. 2, pp. 589, Raqm 6652)
- The Prophet ﷺ declares that the greatest of the mortal sins are: "Shirk, disobeying parents and lying."
- Lying is opposite to Iman. (Al-Musnad Imam Ahmad Bin Hanbal, vol. 1, pp. 22, Hadees 16)
- The Prophet ﷺ said, "Falsehood leads to Al-Fajur (i.e. wickedness, evil-doing), and Al-Fajur (wickedness) leads to the (Hell) Fire, and a man may keep on telling lies till he is written before Allah, a liar." (Sahih Al-Bukhari – Book 73 Hadith 116).
- Destruction is for the one who speaks lies to make people laugh (Sunan-ut-Tirmizi, vol. 4, pp. 142, Hadees 2322).

- Whoever lies in order to make people laugh, falls into Hell at a distance more than the distance between the sky and the earth. (Shuab-ul-Iman, vol. 4, pp. 213, Hadees 4832).

- When a person speaks a lie, the angel moves a mile away from its foul smell. (Jami Tirmizi, vol. 3, pp. 392, Hadees 1979).

- A person's face turns dark due to Lying. (Shuab-ul-Iman, vol. 4, pp.208, Hadhees 4813).

- Narrated Sufyan ibn Asid al-Hadrami: I heard the Apostle of Allah ﷺ said: 'It is great treachery that you should tell your brother something and have him believe you when you are lying.' (Sunan of Abu-Dawood – Book 41, Hadith 4953)

- Telling a lie is the greatest treachery. (Abi Dawood, vol. 4, pp. 381, Hadees 4971).

- The Prophet ﷺ said, "Who ever does not give up forged speech and evil actions, Allah will not accept his fasting." (Sahih Al-Bukhari – Book 31 Hadith 127).

- Saying a false thing is a major sin (Al-Mu'jam-ul-Awsat, vol. 18, pp. 140, Hadhees 213).

- Telling a lie is one of the signs of a hypocrite. (Sahih Muslim, pp. 50, Hadhees 106)

- On the Day of Judgment, liars will be included amongst the most hated people in the sight of Allah عَزَّوَجَلَّ (Kanz-ul-Ummal, vol. 16, pp. 39, Hadhees, 44037)

★ **Some common opinions about lies, liars and lying:**

¶ Lying is worse than consuming alcohol.

¶ Lying is an ailment or a disease.

¶ Do not accuse one as a liar, until you know he is lying.

¶ Do not make a liar, a witness.

¶ Liars are hypocrites.

¶ People lie to prove that they are superior.

¶ Lying is transgression.

¶ Lying destroys faith.

¶ Lying causes destruction.

¶ True believer will not lie.

¶ All the evils are locked in a room and its key is lying.

★ Quran provides a clue to the fact that the front part of the brain is responsible for lying:

Recently it has been proved that area of the brain behind the forehead, is responsible for planning, motivating and initiating good and sinful behavior; and is responsible for the telling lies and truth. Quran has recorded this fact with reference to Abu Jahal: "Nay! if he desists not, 'We' would will certainly smite his forehead (بِالنَّاصِيَةِ) A lying, sinful forehead." (96:15 and 16)

★ Allah commands the believers to stand by truth and justice:

"O ye who believe! stand out firmly for justice, as witnesses to Allah, even as against yourselves, or your parents, or your kin, and whether it be (against) rich or poor: for Allah can best protect both. Follow not (your) low desires, lest you deviate; and if you deviate or turn aside, then surely Allah is aware of what you do." (4:135).

Dear Muslims! Never swear a false oath; never tell a lie; never harm anyone; and never take anyone's belongings; for all such evils Shaitan will sit over you, bring your destruction, in both the worlds! Repent and seek forgiveness of Allah and refuge from Shaitan.

الحمدلله

10. "And recite to them the episode of him to whom We gave Our ayath, but he threw them away; so Shaitan followed him up, and he became of those who went astray." (7:175) To whom does it refers?

Answer: Balam bin Baura

Ibn Khathir narrated this episode, of a so called holy man Balam bin Baura, who lived in the Bayt al-Muqaddas (Jerusalem) as follows:

About him:

He is from the Children of Israel. He was sent to the King of Madyan by Musa (AS); to pass on the message of Allah. He knew Allah's Greatest Names and provided with the knowledge of Allah's ayaath. Because of his holiness, people sought his help at times of difficulty through his supplications. On receipt of lands and the gifts from the king, he rejected Allah's ayaath

His people asked him to supplicate against Musa (AS):

Those in Jerusalam, on hearing the news of the arrival of the army of Musa (AS) near Jerusalem, they were very much afraid because they may be chased out from their land. Those people came to Balam to supplicate against Musa (AS) and his followers.

Balam, very well knew that if he supplicates to Allah against the Prophet, then he will lose the life of this world and the Hereafter. So he expressed his desire to perform Isthiqara and later supplicate. But he was aware that he cannot supplicate against Musa (AS). But his people lured him with lot of wealth and begged him, until he was tempted to perform the supplication.

In spite of all the hurdles, he supplicated and received the punishment from Allah:

He went with his donkey towards Mount Husban. On reaching the base of the the mount, the donkey refused to proceed further and sat down. He tried his best to persuade it to stand up, by beating it. Even after such an effort the donkey refused to proceed upwards. Thereupon he managed to climb up and started supplicating against Musa (AS) and his army. Allah made him to supplicate against his own people, instead of Musa (AS). On hearing this, his people were shocked. They asked him, "O Balam! What are you doing? You are supplicating for them and against us!" He said, "It is against my will. This is a matter that Allah has decided." After this incident his tongue was made to hang out of his mouth till his breast, like a panting dog. He then informed them that "Now I have lost this life and the Hereafter."

Even after receiving punishment, he gave suggestion to his people:

Even after such a punishment from Allah, he advised his people to adorn and beautify their women; for being sent to entertain the army of Musa (AS). Allah honoured him but he ignored it. Shaitan treating such a situation in his favour; persuaded him to deviate from the Allah's path. So he joined those, who went astray.

He became the loser:

Allah continues further in the Quran by saying, "And had We willed, 'We' would surely have elevated him therewith, but he clung to the earth and followed his own vain desires. So his parable is the parable of a dog: if you drive him away, he pants, or if you leave him alone, he (still) pants. Such is the parable of the people who rejected Our ayath. So relate the stories, perhaps they may reflect" (7:176). "Evil is the parable of the people who rejected Our ayath, and used to wrong themselves." (7:177).

He became an example of a dog which hangs out it's tongue, while it was resting or running. Allah provided him with faith and knowledge but he misused it. He has to be treated as an example of an evil. Because of his misdeeds, he became the loser.

"Whomsoever Allah guides, he is the guided one, and whomsoever He sends astray, those! They are the losers." (7:178). May Allah Subhanahuthala bless every Muslim not to go astray after getting a clear guidance from Quran.

الحمدلله

بِسْمِ اللهِ الرَّحْمٰنِ الرَّحِيمِ

7. Whose Statements Are These?

1. "Would you exchange that which is better for that which is lower? Go you down to any town and you shall find what you want!" Who said this?

Answer: Musa (AS) asserted to Bani Israel. They want to exchange Manna and Salwa, the divine food with variety of worldly food. (2:61).

Allah [SWT] blessed Bani Israel with lots of favours:

After their enemy Firaun and his soldiers were drowned in front of their eyes (2:50), the children of Israel were favored with lots of Allah's Bounty and Grace. Allah says: "And We divided them into twelve tribes (as distinct) nations. We directed Musa (AS) by inspiration, when his people asked him for water, (saying): "Strike the stone with your stick", and there gushed forth out of it twelve springs: each group knew its own place for water. We shaded them with the clouds and sent down upon them Al-Manna and the quails (saying): "Eat of the good things with which We have provided you. They harmed Us not but they used to harm themselves." (7:160).

Manna is a kind of food, sweeter than honey and whiter than snow. It descends from heaven from dawn to sunrise, like the snow and it remains on plants and rock as dew drops. The people can collect them without much effort in the early morning. Salwa is a quail like bird, when it is caught in the hands; it turns into roasted meat. This food was descending on daily basis. People with greed, used to store it for the next day. It used to become rotten. Once the Holy Prophet ﷺ said that 'had the Bani Israel not existed, neither food would get spoiled nor would meat have rotten'. (Tafseer Ruh-ul-Bayan; part 1, Surah Al-Baqarah, verse 57).

They were provided with a high quality, pure, special and tasty food; which was easily available. It decended from heaven, without any effort. There was no need for them to earn for their food nor any need to cook. Forgetting Allah's generosity and kindness, they turned mean and became disgusted with the same type of food. They did not know the worth of such a food. Becoming ungrateful, they desired for worldly, low quality food which is made of cultivated vegetable products. They could not forego such a food, even for some time. They wished to satisfy their tongues which demanded taste. Musa (AS) himself refused to fulfill such a request. He never opted to arrange such a food, which was commonly and easily available. Instead, he required them to go to any town and get such a food as they desired.

But they enquired Musa (AS) to bring varieties of earthly food:

"They said, 'O Musa! We cannot endure one kind of food! So invoke your Lord for us to bring forth for us of what the earth grows, its herbs, its cucumbers, its Fum (wheat or garlic), its lentils and its onions.' Musa (AS) replied, 'Would you exchange that which is better for that which is lower? Go you down to any town and you shall find what you want!" (2:61).

They were the people who required a variety and a change. Such people were inconsistent in their thoughts, lacked steadfastness and lived without any purpose in their lives. They lacked commitment towards their religion. To those people Allah said, "They did not wrong Us but they wronged themselves." (2:57).

Allah continues in Quran by referring the consequences of their deeds: "They were covered with humiliation and misery, and they drew on themselves the Wrath of Allah. That was because they used to disbelieve the ayath of Allah and killed the Prophets wrongfully. That was because they disobeyed and used to transgress the bounds and commit crimes and sins." (2:61).

Lesson to be learnt:

Even in our life, blessed with many of the favors of Allah, we are not satisfied at most of the times. We aspire for big houses; with all the facilities but not at all interested in building a house in Paradise. We spend much of our time in worldly aspects but not in worshipping. We love to accumulate money but do not intend spending on Allah's cause. We compare ourselves with others; feel dissatisfied without knowing His plans for us. We forget that Allah understands us far better than we could realize. Allah Subhanahtuthala knows as to what favors that will be beneficial for us.

Always be satisfied with the blessings of Allahuthala! Allah [عَزَّ وَ جَلَّ] is aware as to what should be and what not to be provided; the right time of its being provided; and where and how it should be provided and also to whom.

الحمدلله

2. "Peace be upon me the day I was born, and the day I die, and the day I shall be raised alive" Who said these words?

Answer: Isa (AS) ibn Marium.

Like Adam (AS), Allah, the Creator [الْخَالِقُ] created Isa (AS) with the word "Qun (Be)" in the womb of virgin Marium (AS). Bi Bi Marium carried her baby Isa [AS] after his birth to her people. By seeing her with the new born, they said: "O Marium! Indeed, you have brought an amazing thing! O sister of Aaron! [not Musa (AS)'s brother] Your father was not a man who used to commit adultery, nor your mother was an unchaste woman" (19:28).

Bi Bi Marium was commanded by Allah not to speak to her people. The Lord intended the baby to reply, instead. When her people enquired her about the baby, she pointed her finger towards the baby. They said: "How can we talk to one who is an infant in the cradle?" The baby said: "Verily! I am a slave of Allah (Abd Allah), He has given me the Scripture and made me a Prophet. And He has made me blessed (Mubarakan) whosoever I be, and has enjoined on me Fast, Salath and Zakath, as long as I live." (19:30 and 31) "And dutiful to my mother and made me not arrogant, unblest. And Peace be upon me the day I was born (not on Christmas Day; as Christians believe), and the day I die (after his descend to the world, not on the day of crucification as Christians believe), and the day I shall be raised alive!" (on the Day of Resurrection). (19:32 and 33).

Thus Isa (AS) ibn Marium, spoke to his people while he was in the cradle. He performed innumerable miracles, with the permission of Allah. These are the signs for those who believe. (19:49). "Such is 'Isa (AS), son of Bi Bi Marium. It is a statement of truth; about which they dispute" (19:34). "It befits not (the Majesty of) Allah that He should beget a son. Glorified (and Exalted Be He above all that they associate with Him). When He decrees a thing, He only says to it, "Be!" and it is." (19: 35). Thus Allah has revealed clearly in the Quran the truth about the birth of Isa Ruhullah (AS).

Safyan bin Uyaynah recorded that a man feels loneliness in three situations: on the day he was born; on the day he dies after that he will not see people anymore; on the day when he was resurrected, he sees himself in great gathering. These three situations are most difficult situations for human beings. However, the son of Marium the Isa (AS) will have peace in these three situations!

In the same surah, Allahuthala has also sent down to us the strikingly an identical ayath (Marium, 19:14 and 15) with reference to Yahya (AS). He was also born by

Allah's Grace to the aged Zakariya, who was the care taker of Bi Bi Marium. He was her aunt's husband. Through his prayers, he wanted to be blessed with a child, at such an old age. Allah provided him with glad tidings about the birth of a son to be named as Yahya.

It was said to Zakariya's son: "O Yahya (AS)! Hold fast the Scripture [the Taurath] And Allah gave him wisdom while yet a child. And (made him) sympathetic to men as a mercy (or a grant) from Us, and pure from sins and he was righteous." (19:12 and 13). He was noble, pious, from among the righteous and had no inclination to do sins. He was "dutiful towards his (Yahya's) parents, and he was neither arrogant nor disobedient (to Allah or to his parents). So Peace be on him the day he was born, the day that he dies and the day that he will be raised up to life (again)!" {Note the ayath is expressed in second person, whereas the above ayath (19:33) which Isa (AS) says is in first person}

الحمدلله

3. "Come both of you willingly or unwillingly." They both said: "We come, willingly." Who said these verses?

Answer: The first verse is by Allah. And the second verse is by heaven and earth. (Fussilath, 41: 11)

All creations are under Allahuthala's Control:

Unlike man and Jinn, all the creations of Allahuthala willingly and unwillingly obey His command and praise, worship in their own way and remember Him. "Obeying of Allah Almighty's command by heaven and earth is one of His Signs" (30:25). "And to Him belongs whoever is in the heavens and earth, all are subject to His Will. (30:26).

Creation of heaven and earth in six days:

Allah سبحانه وتعالى "created the heavens and earth and what is in between them in six days ((7:54, 10:3, 11:7, 25:59, 32:4, 50:38 and 57:4) and then He Istawa (rose over) the Throne (really in a manner that suits His Majesty)." Here the day means a long length of period, an epoch [probably a 1000 years (32:5) or 50,000 years (70:4)], [الله اعلم !] quite different from "our day" between sun rise and sun set or 24 hours.

Allah has stated earlier that the heaven and earth were joined together (21: 30); then He separated the earth from the sun. He fashioned the earth in two days as a dwelling place (41:9). Then He directed Himself to the heaven while it was smoke and said to it and to the earth, "Come [into being], willingly or unwillingly." They have answered, "We have come willingly." (41:11).

As He was creating earth, He simultaneously turned to heaven and fashioned seven heavens with harmony (2:29) in two days. Thus He raised the heaven as a canopy (2:22) without any pillars (13:2) and proportioned it as a ceiling to earth. (79:28). Blessed is He Who made the constellations in the heavens and made therein sun as lamp and a shining moon. (25:61) Then, He has subjected the sun and the moon, each orbiting for an appointed term. (13:2). He created stars, made all of them subservient to His command (7:54). And He darkened its night and extracted its brightness (79:29). And He it is Who made the night and the day to follow each other (25:62). He adorned the lower heaven with lamps and firmly secured it (41:12). And the earth, He expanded it simultaneously. (79: 30). He placed on the earth firmly set mountains over it's surface, and He blessed it and determined therein it's [creatures'] sustenance, water and pasturage in four days without distinction - for those who ask. (41:10 and 79:31 to 33).

No clear-cut sequence of creations of heaven and earth are provided in Quran:

We come to know something through hadhees the sequences of earth and its objects: Abu Huraira (RA) reported that Allah's Messenger ﷺ took hold of my hands and said: "Allah, the Exalted and Glorious, created the clay on Saturday and He created the mountains on Sunday and He created the trees on Monday and He created the things entailing labour on Tuesday and created light on Wednesday and the animals to spread on Thursday and He created Adam (AS) after 'Asr' on Friday; the last creation at the last hours of Friday, i.e. between afternoon and night." (Sahih Muslim, Chapter 2, Book 39, Number 6707).

Allah asserts to humanity, that He is "The Supreme" in creation:

'Is not He Who created the heavens and the earth able to create the like of them? Thus He is the Supreme Creator and the All-Knower' (36:81) 'When He intends to create a thing, His command is to say, "Be." Then it is created.' (2:177,16:40, 36:82 and 40:68). And Allah says His command is but one, like a glance of the eye (54:50). 'And He did not create the heaven and the earth and what is between them for play' (21:16) 'but in truth,' (15:85, 16:3, 29:44, 39:5, 44:39, 45:22 and 46:3). Allah, has created heaven and earth and all that is seen between them from nothing. He brought all non existence to existence. Still He is expanding the universe. People observe new species everyday.

Heaven and earth are the greatest signs of Allah:

Allah conveys in surah Ghafir, "The creation of the heavens and the earth is indeed greater than the creation of mankind, yet most of mankind know not" (40:57). In another ayath He asks mankind, "Are you a more difficult creation or is the heaven?" (79:27).

He requires the believers to observe, "What is before them and what is behind them, of the heaven and the earth. If We will, 'We' shall sink the earth with them, or cause a piece of the heaven to fall upon them. Verily, in this is a sign for every faithful believer, who believes the One-ness of Allah, and turns to Him" (34:9).

"He created the heaven and earth and what is in between them in six days". Allah repeated this verse seven times in Quran. Along with this verse, every time Allah tries to lay emphasis on the following:

1. His is the creation and the command; blessed is Allah, the Lord of the worlds. (7:54).

2. He is regulating all the affairs, therefore serve Him. (10:3)

3. Surely man has to be raised up after death (11:7)

4. He, the Most Merciful, Well informed, established Himself above the Throne (25:59)

5. There is no other guardian or intercessor besides Him. (32:4)

6. He was not tired after the creation of heaven and earth in six days. (50:38). Whereas, the people of Scripture claim that 'On seventh Day God took rest.'

7. He is with you wherever you are and sees whatever you do. (57:4)

Narrated Abu Huraira (RA): Allah's Apostle ﷺ said, "When Allah completed the creation, He wrote in His Book which is with Him on His Throne, "My Mercy overpowers My Anger."

الحمدلله

4. He said to his companion: "Be not sad (or afraid), surely Allah is with us." Who said this? Who is his companion?

Answer: 'He' refers to Muhammad ﷺ and his companion was Abu Bakr (RA).

Allah [SWT] mentioned in the Quran: "If you help him (Muhammad ﷺ) not (it does not matter), for Allah did indeed help him when the disbelievers drove him out, the second of two, when they were in the cave, and he ﷺ said to his companion: "Be not sad, surely Allah is with us." (9:40)

The Prophet ﷺ was propagating Islam and teaching Quran to the community of Quraish, for thirteen long years. Quraish, identical to the treatment meted out to the other prophet's communities; opposed him and his followers strongly. They adopted several methods to ill-treat the Prophet ﷺ and his followers. They caused innumerable troubles to the Muslims. They insulted and tortured them by, also claiming that their Prophet ﷺ was a madman, a sorcerer and a liar etc. Similar to the exiling of Prophets by earlier communities, the Quraish intended to exile or exterminate him.

Finally, they formulated a scheme. With the evil intention of exterminating the Prophet ﷺ, the Quraish selected a volunteer from each tribe. They as a group, surrounded the house of Prophet ﷺ during the night. Allah made known their evil plan, to the Prophet ﷺ. Therupon he collected all the belongings which were entrusted with him by his people. After handing over the same to Ali (RA), required him to pass it on to those, to whom it belonged. He requested Ali (RA) to sleep in his bed, on that night. Reciting few verses of Yasin, he took some dust in his hand and threw it towards the people who were awaiting, his exit. Allah put a veil on their sight, thereafter he walked out of the house, unnoticed.

As it was planned previously, the Prophet ﷺ went to Abu Bakr (RA)'s house, who was keeping two camels ready for travel. They headed towards the opposite direction of Yathrib (old name of Madhina); towards the mountain Thawr.

While departing, he turned towards Makkah reciting a Dua; that was taught by Allah: "Say {O Muhammad ﷺ}, My Lord! Let my entry (to the city of Al-Madhina) be good, and likewise my exit (from the city of Makkah) be good. And grant me from You an authority to help me " (17:80).

The mountain Thawr had so many caves. They selected a crevice like small cave, that could accommodate two people. Abu Bakr (RA) entered the cave first to check whether it is safe and the Prophet ﷺ followed him.

Accompanying them; was Abu Bakr (RA)'s eldest son Abdullah (RA). He was a teenager, at that time. After leaving them at the cave, he returned home with the two camels. He was instructed to collect the news relating to the enemies and convey it the following night. The freed servant of Abu Bakr (RA), named Amir ibn Fuhayrah

(RA), lead his flock of sheep during the morning up and down many a times, in order to erase the camel's foot prints. So that the enemies could not trace the path treaded by the Prophet ﷺ.

Quraish, learning that the Prophet ﷺ had escaped, sent searching groups on horses towards different directions, specially the routes proceeding to Yathrib. They declared that anyone who brings either the Prophet ﷺ or Abu Bakr (RA) alive or dead, will be rewarded with 100 camels.

Every night Asma (RA), the daughter of Abu Bakr (RA) accompanied by her brother, visited them carrying milk, food and water. They passed on the information about the activities of the Quraish. Two days passed without any disturbance. On the third day, the Quraish hired an expert searching group, which somehow traced the foot prints leading to mount Thawr. Many people went to mount Thawr in search of the Prophet ﷺ, intending to claim the reward.

The Prophet ﷺ and Abu Bakr (RA) heard faint noises of men searching, down below. Fear engulfed Abu Bakr (RA). Thereupon the Prophet ﷺ was reassuring him about the Power of Allah by asserting, "Be not be sad, surely, Allah is with us."

Two men approached the entrance of the cave, eager to trace Prophet ﷺ. On looking at the cave they found that an undisturbed spider's web and a bird's nest with eggs were found at the entrance of the cave. On watching these, they concluded that none could have entered the cave within the past two days. So they gave up their pursuit! Subhanallah!

Imam Ahmad recorded from Anas (RA) that Abu Bakr (RA) later informed him. "I said to the Prophet ﷺ when we were in the cave, 'If any of them looks down at his feet, he will see us.' The Prophet ﷺ said, 'What do you think, O Abu Bakr, about two, when Allah is third with us?' "

These details are referred in several books of Seerah, including Ibn Khathir. It is not considered to be an authentic hadhees but a weak one by some scholars. There is another weak hadhees claiming that the entrance of the cave was closed with the wing of an Angel. Allah knows Best! [! الله اعلم]

Allah refers to this incident through this ayath, "If you help him not (it does not matter), for Allah did indeed help him." Thus the Prophet ﷺ was miraculously helped by the Divine forces; not visualized by human beings.

Allah completes the above ayath as: "Then Allah sent down His calmness, upon him, and strengthened him with forces (angels) which you saw not, and made the word of those who disbelieved the lowermost, while it was the Word of Allah that became the uppermost, and Allah is All-Mighty, All-Wise." (9:40).

Yes! Allah alone can help the Messengers and those who believe in Him. He never let down His believers whenever they faced the disbelievers. On the Prophet ﷺ praying with Allah; his exit from Makkah was comparably made easy and his entry into Madhina was rewarded with love and respect by all. Later, after about ten years he conquered Makkah, without any war or bloodshed.

As per assertion of Allah, the Exalted: "They plotted a plot, and We planned a plan, while they perceived not. Then see how was the end of their plot! " (16:50 and 51). Allah is the best planner!

الحمدلله

5. "And verily, we used to sit there in stations, to a hearing, but any one who listens now will find a flaming fire watching him in ambush." Who said these words?

Answer: Jinn.

Meaning of the word Jinn:

The word "jinn" is derived from the Arabic word "janna" meaning to hide or conceal. Jinn are invisible to human beings. In the Quran they are mentioned as Marid (37: 7), Ifrit (27:39), Jinn (72:1) and as Shayateen in many places.

Creation of Jinn:

Allah declares: "And the jinn We created before from scorching fire." (نَارِ السَّمُومِ) (15:27). Note the word "before", it means the jinn were created even before Adam (AS). "And He created the jinn from a smokeless flame of fire. [مَّارِجٍ مِّن نَّارٍ]" (15:55). The purpose of creation of jinn and man is for worshipping Allah. "And I did not create the jinn and mankind except to worship Me". (51:56).

Allah has warned both of them in this world through the same Messengers:

Quran records, "O company of jinn and mankind, did there not come to you messengers from among you, relating to you My verses and warning you of the meeting of this Day of yours?" They will say, 'We bear witness against ourselves'; and the worldly life had deluded them, and they will bear witness against themselves that they were disbelievers." [6:130]

"Many are the Jinns and men we have made for Hell: They have hearts wherewith they understand not, eyes wherewith they see not, and ears wherewith they hear not. They are like cattle - nay more misguided: for they are heedless (of warning)." (7:179).

Their life:

They live in this world along with us. But they have different dimensions, different time frame, different type of food and even animals, which Allah only knows. Man has no knowledge about it. They also need sustenance from Allah. They eat, they drink, they marry, they have their family, children, tribes etc. Their life span is more than us; extending about to 1000 or 1500 years. They will also die similar to human beings and will be resurrected on the Day of Judgement similarly.

They follow the religion, like human beings:

Unlike angels, Allah created them by providing free will, ordered them to worship Him; instructed and guided them through our messengers. Allah had created Hell and Heaven for them also. According to their deeds, they either enter Jannah or Jahannum.

A group of Jinns heard the recitation of Holy Quran by Prophet ﷺ, which fact was not known to the Prophet ﷺ himself.

Allah commands the Prophet ﷺ, to inform his people by revealing through these ayaath:

"Say, [O Muhammad ﷺ] It has been revealed to me that a group of the jinns listened and said, 'Indeed we have heard an amazing Quran. It guides to the right course and we have believed in it. And we will never associate with our Lord anyone." [72:1, 2]

In another part of Quran Allah states: "And (remember) when We sent towards you (Muhammad ﷺ) nafran (a group numbering three to ten) of the jinn, (quietly) listening to the Quran, when they stood in the presence thereof, they said: "Listen in silence!" and when it was finished they returned to their people, as warners." (46:29)

The jinns who listened returned to their people declared:

[72:3] "Now, we believe that our Lord — Exalted is His Majesty — has neither taken a, a wife, nor a son."

[72:4] "And that the foolish amongst us used to forge extravagant things against Allah".

[72:5] "And that we thought that men and jinns did not utter a lie against Allah".

[72:6] "And that persons from among men used to seek refuge with persons from among jinns, so they increased them in wickedness."

[72:7] "And that they (human) thought as you think, that Allah would not raise any one".

[72:12] "And that we know that we cannot escape Allah on the earth, nor can we escape Him by flight."

[72:13] "And that when we heard the guidance, we believed in it; so whoever believes in his Lord, he should neither fear loss nor being overtaken (by disgrace)."

Categories of the Jinn:

Allah declares in Quran that Jinns after listening to the recitation of Quran, they went and informed their people:

"There are among us some that are righteous, and some the contrary; we are groups each having a different way" (religious sect, etc.) (72:11) "So whoever submits, these aim at the right way" (72:14). "And as to the deviators, they are fuel of hell" (72:15).

The disbeliever Jinns are considered as the followers of "Shaitan". Such jinns are known as Shayateen.

One type of Jinn presents an appearance of snakes, dogs and other animals. Another type keeps flying around us but they are harmless. The third type live with us without causing hindrance. Some Jinns reside in filthy places, such as dirty bathrooms etc.

Their powers and weaknesses:

They are faster, sometimes super fast; stronger than man and change into any form. From the Seera of Prophet ﷺ we come to know that Iblis came taking over the form of Surakha during the battle of Badr; again as an old man while the Quraish were plotting to assassinate the Prophet ﷺ and also appeared as poor begger to steal the treasure guarded by Abu Huraira (RA). In spite of the fact that he was a habitual liar; he referred to the truth as to the power of Ayathul Kursi, to Abu Huraira (RA). The Jinnath are visible to human beings, only when they opt to reveal themselves.

Since they have less wisdom provided by Allahuthala comparable to Adam (AS), Allah [عَزَّ وَجَلَّ] directed the angels and jinns to prostrate before him.

Sulaiman (AS) and Jinns:

By the permission of Allah, jinns served the Prophet Sulaiman (AS). "They made for him what he pleased of fortresses and images, and bowls (large) as watering-troughs and cooking-pots that will not move from their place." (34:13). He had also soldiers from jinn. (27:17). And of the rebellious shaitan were those who dived for him and did work other than that. And We kept guard over them." (21:82)

Eavesdropping of jinnath:

Jinns are interested in listening to the discussions by angels in heavens about the life of human beings. Formerly they claimed that they had special sitting places in the lowest heaven. Sitting comfortably, they hear all discussions of angels; convey these discussions to fortune tellers, adding some lies and in turn those fortune tellers repeat it to the human beings, by adding many more lies.

Quran clarifies in surah Jinn: "And we have sought to reach the heaven; but we found it filled with stern guards and flaming fires. (72:8). And verily, we used to sit there in stations, to (steal) a hearing, but anyone who listens now will find a flaming fire watching him in ambush (72:9). And we know not whether evil is intended for those on the earth, or whether their Lord intends for them guidance." (72:10).

In Surah As-Saaffat Allah further states, "Verily! We have adorned the near heaven with the stars (37:6). And to guard against every rebellious devil (37: 7). They can't listen to the higher group (angels) for they are pelted from every side (37:8). Except such as snatching away something by stealing and they are pursued by a flaming fire of piercing brightness (37:10). They are, "Outcast, and their's is a constant or painful torment" (37:9).

It was reported in the hadhees of Ibn Abbas (RA) as, "While we were sitting with the Prophet ﷺ a shooting star flashed in the sky. The Prophet ﷺ enquired, "What did you all used to say about this?" We replied, "We used to say that a great person has been born or a great person has died." The Prophet ﷺ said, "This is not so, rather whenever Allah decrees a matter in the heaven..." and then Ibn Abbas (RA) started narrating the rest of the hadhees by continuing: Allah's Messenger ﷺ went out along with a group of his companions towards Ukaz Market. At that time something intervened between the devils and the news of the Heaven, and flames were sent down upon them, so the devils returned. Their fellow-devils said, "What is wrong with you? "They said, "Something has intervened between us and the news of the Heaven, and fires (flames) have been shot at us." Their fellow-devils said, 'Nothing has intervened between you and the news of the Heaven, but an important event has happened. Therefore, travel all over the world, east and west, and try to find out what has happened.' And so they set out and travelled all over the world, east and west, looking for that thing which intervened between them and the news of the Heaven. Those of the devils who had set out towards Tihama, went to Allah's Messenger ﷺ at Nakhla, (a place between Mecca and Taif) while he was on his way to Ukaz Market. (They met him) while he was offering the Fajr prayer with his companions. When they heard the Holy Quran being recited (by the Prophet ﷺ, they listened to it and said (to each other). This is the thing which has intervened between you and the news of the Heavens."

Arabs seek refuge with jinn during the period of Ignorance:

There was a custom in Arabs to seek refuge with jinn as they thought that jinn were mightier than them and are capable of causing harm/evil/good to human beings. As-Suddi said, "A man used to set out with his family (on a journey) until he came to a piece of land where he would settle. Then he would say, "I seek refuge with the master Jinn of this valley to save myself, my wealth, my children or my animals from any harm." Qatadah said, "When they sought refuge with him instead of Allah, the Jinn would overcome them with harm." Ibn Abi Hatim recorded from Ikrimah that he said, "The Jinn used to fear humans just like humans fear them, or even worse. So whenever humans would come to a valley, the Jinns would flee. So the leader of the people would say, 'We seek refuge with the leader of the inhabitants of this valley.' So the Jinn said, 'We see these people fleeing from us just like we flee from them.' Thus, the Jinn started coming near the humans by afflicting them with insanity and madness."

The evil shayatheen and jinn; when they whisper or cause harm, recite the ayaath revealed by Allahuthala in the Quran, so that no harm or whisper affects us! [!الله اعلم] Allah knows best!

الحمدلله

6. "And you take vengeance on us only because we believed in the ayath of our Lord when they reached us! "Our Lord! pour out on us patience, and cause us to die as Muslims." Who said these words?

Answer: Magicians gathered by Firaun (Al-Araf, 126).

When Musa (AS) was provided with clear signs from Allah, he displayed them in front of Firaun. He claimed that it was magic. He collected all the magicians of his kingdom, to beat out Musa (AS), on their festival day. The magicians wished to know from Firaun: "Indeed there will be a (good) reward for us if we are the victors." His reply was: "Yes, and moreover you will (in that case) be of the nearest (to me)." (7:113 and 114)

The magicians exclaimed to Musa (AS): "O Musa (AS)! Either you throw (first), or shall we have the (first) throw?" Musa (AS) said: "Throw you (first)." "When they threw, they bewitched the eyes of the people, and struck terror into them, and they displayed a great magic." (7:115 and 116). "Then behold, their ropes and their sticks, by their magic, appeared to him as though they moved fast." (20:66) It was an illusion which was not real, at all!

So Musa (AS) concealed a fear in himself. (20:67). We (Allah) said: "Fear not! Surely, you will have the upper hand. (20:68). And throw that which is in your right hand! It will swallow up that which they have made. That which they have made is only a magician's trick, and the magician will never be successful, no matter whatever amount (of skill) he may attain." (20:69)

"And when Musa (AS) threw the stick, it swallowed up straight away all the falsehoods which they showed. Thus truth was confirmed, and all that they did was made of no effect. So they were defeated there and then, and were returned disgraced. And the sorcerers fell down prostrate." (7:118 to 120).

At that tremendous moment, Allah differentiated between 'Truth' and 'Falsehood'. The magicians realized that this was from heaven and was by no means magic. They fell in prostration and proclaimed, "We believe in the Lord of Alamin. The Lord of Musa (AS) and Harun (AS) (20:70)." "Had Musa (AS) been a magician, he would not have prevailed over us." (7:121 and 122).

Watching that, Firaun said: "You have believed in Musa (AS) before I give you permission. Surely, this is a plot which you have plotted in the city to drive out its people, but you shall come to know. Surely, I will cut off your hands and your feet from opposite sides and then I will crucify you all." (7:123 and 124) and you shall surely know which of us [I (Firaun – Pharaoh) or the Lord of Musa (AS) (Allah)] can give the severe and more lasting torment." (20:71).

The magicians asserted, "Verily, we are returning to our Lord." They further continued, "We are now sure that we will go back to Allah. Certainly, Allah's punishment is more severe than your punishment and His torment for what you are calling us to, this day, and the magic you forced us to practice, is greater than your torment. Therefore, we will observe patience in the face of your punishment today, so that we are saved from Allah's torment." Then they prayed to the Lord of Musa (AS) and Harun (AS), "Our Lord! pour out on us patience and cause us to die as Muslims." (7:125 and 126,)

They also conveyed to Firaun, "So decide whatever you desire to decree, for you can only decide for the life of this world. Verily, we have believed in our Lord, that He may forgive us our faults, and the magic to which you did compel us. And Allah is better to reward and more lasting in punishment. Verily, whoever comes to his Lord as a criminal, then surely, for him is Hell, wherein he will neither die nor live. But whoever comes to Allah as a believer, and has done righteous good deeds, for such are the high ranks in the Here-after." (20:72-75). The magicians commenced the day as sorcerers and ended as honorable martyrs!

"Allah sends astray whom He wills and He guides on the straight path whom He wills." (Al-Anaam, 6:39).

الحمدلله

7. "Even if you kill me I will not even raise my hand to defend because you are my brother." Who said this?

Answer: Habil the yougest son of Adam (AS)

Habil and Qabil are the sons of Adam (AS). Qabil is the eldest son but not worthy. Habil eventhough younger had all good qualities with piety. Adam (AS) tried to test his sons by requiring them to provide a sacrifice for the sake of Allah. Only Habil's sacrifice was accepted by Allah. Learning about it, Qabil become jealous and decided to kill his brother. But Habil informed his brother that he will never even raise his arms, to resist. Qabil killed him. He does not know what to do with his brother's corpse. A raven exihibited a method to dig the soil. Then he dug the soil and buried his brother's body. Thereafter, Qabil cried very much for his deed.

Quran records this incident, as follows:

[5:27]. "And (O Muhammad ﷺ) recite to them (the Jews) the story of the two sons of Adam [Habil (Abel) and Qabil (Cain)] in truth; when each offered a sacrifice (to Allah), it was accepted from the one but not from the other. The latter said to the former: "I will surely kill you." The former said: "Verily, Allah accepts only from those who are pious."

[5:28] "If you do stretch your hand against me to kill me, I shall never stretch my hand against you to kill you, for I fear Allah; the Lord of the Alamin (mankind, jinns, and all that exists)."

[5:29] "Verily, I intend to let you draw my sin on yourself as well as yours, then you will be one of the dwellers of the Fire, and that is the recompense of the wrong-doers."

[5:30] "So the Nafs (self) of the other encouraged him and made fair-seeming to him the murder of his brother; he murdered him and became one of the losers."

[5:31] "Then Allah sent a crow who scratched the ground to show him to hide the dead body of his brother. He (the murderer) said: "Woe to me! Am I not even able to be as this crow and to hide the dead body of my brother?" Then he became one of those who regretted."

[5:32] "Because of that We ordained for the Children of Israel that if anyone killed a person not in retaliation of murder, or (and) to spread mischief in the land – it would be as if he killed all mankind, and if anyone saved a life, it would be as if he saved the life of all mankind. And indeed, there came to them Our Messengers with clear proofs, evidences, and signs, even then after that many of them continued to exceed the limits (e.g. by doing oppression unjustly and exceeding beyond the limits set by Allah by committing the major sins) in the land!"

Even in the first generation the human beings on earth, fall as the victim of Shaithan by showing jealousy, vengeance and murder.

الحمدلله

8. "O our father! Verily, your son has stolen, and we testify not except according to what we know, and we could not know the unseen!" (12:81). Say the name of the father mentioned in the above verse.

Answer: Israel or Yaqoob (AS).

Allah سبحانه وتعالى narrates the life of Yusuf (AS) commencing with:

"We relate unto you (Muhammad ﷺ) the best of narrations through Our Revelations unto you, of this Quran." (12:3). When Yusuf (AS) was put in charge of the granary, his brothers came to collect the grains. He required them to bring their younger brother Bunyamin. He returned their goods expecting them to return. The brothers of Yusuf (AS), pleaded with their father. Yaqub (AS) insisted, "I will not send him with you until you give me a solemn oath by Allah that you will certainly bring him back to me, unless you are totally overpowered." Then after they had given him their oaths, he concluded, "Allah is a Witness to what we have said." Then Yusuf's brothers brought Bunyamin to Egypt.

The Quran then narrates the events that happened, as follows:

Yusuf (AS) detained his brother, Buniyamin:

[12:69] Yusuf (AS) stated to his brother, "Verily! I am your brother, so grieve not for what they used to do."

[12:70] So when he had furnished them forth with their pro-visions, he put the golden bowl into his brother's bag, then a crier cried: "O you the caravan! Surely, you are thieves!"

[12:71] They [brothers of Yusuf (AS)] turning towards them proclaimed: "What is it that you have missed?".

[12:72] Yusuf (AS)'s men replied: "We have missed the golden bowl of the king and for him who produces it is the reward of a camel load; I will be bound by it.".

[12:73] They [brothers of Yusuf (AS)] said: "By Allah! Indeed, you know that we came not to make mischief in the land, and we are no thieves!"

[12:74] Yusuf (AS)'s men enquired: "What then shall be the penalty of him, if you are proved to be liars."

[12:75] Yusuf's (AS) brothers responded: "The penalty should be that he, in whose bag it is found, should be held for the punishment. Thus we punish the Zalimun!"

[12:76] "So Yusuf (AS) began the search in their bags before the bag of his brother. Then he brought it out of his brother's bag. Thus did We plan for Yusuf (AS). He could not take his brother by the law of the king except that Allah willed it. We raise to degrees whom We please, but over all those endowed with knowledge is the All-Knowing Allah."

[12:77] To distance themselves Yusuf (AS)'s brothers argued: "If he steals, there was a brother of his [Yusuf] who did steal before him." But these things did Yusuf (AS) keep in himself, revealing not the secrets to them. He said within himself: "You are in worst case, and Allah knows best the truth of what you assert!"

His brothers pleaded with Yusuf (AS) to take away anyone of them instead of Buniyamin:

[12:78] They appealed: "O ruler of the land! Verily, he has an old father (who will grieve for him); so take one of us in his place. Indeed, we think that you are one of the good-doers."

[12:79] Yusuf (AS) responded: "Allah forbid, that we should take anyone but him with whom we found our property. Indeed, if we did so, we should be wrong-doers."

[12:80] So, when they despaired of him, they held a conference in private. The eldest among them said: "Know you not that your father did take an oath from you in Allah's Name, and before this you did fail in your duty with Yusuf (AS)? Therefore, I will not leave this land until my father permits me, or Allah decides my case by releasing Bunyamin and He is the Best of the judges.".

They told to their father about the theft:

[12:81] They return to your father and say, "O our father! Verily, your son (Bunyamin) has stolen, and we testify not except according to what we know and we could not know the unseen!"

[12:82] "And ask the people of the town where we have been, and the caravan in which we returned, and indeed we are telling the truth."

Yaqub (AS) become highly emotional and complained his grief to Allah and asked them to go and find both of his sons:

[12:83] Yaqub (AS) cried: "Nay, but your ownselves have beguiled you into something. So patience is most fitting for me. May be Allah will bring them back all to me. Truly He! only He is All- Knowing, All-Wise."

[12:84] And he turned away from them and said: "Alas, my grief for Yusuf!" And he lost his sight because of the sorrow that he was suppressing.

[12:85] They said: "By Allah! You will never cease remembering Yusuf (AS) until you become weak with old age, or until you be of the dead.".

[12:86] He replied: "I only complain of my grief and sorrow to Allah, and I know from Allah that which you know not."

[12:87] "O my sons! Go you and enquire about Yusuf and his brother and never give up hope of Allah's Mercy. Certainly no one despairs of Allah's Mercy, except the people who disbelieve."

Yusuf (AS) revealed about him to his brothers:

[12:89] He enquired: "Do you know what you did with Yusuf and his brother, when you were ignorant?"

His brothers regretted for their sins:

[12:90] They asked in shock: "Are you indeed Yusuf (AS)?" He said: "I am Yusuf and this is my brother Bunyamin. Allah has indeed been gracious to us. Verily, he who fears Allah with obedience to Him and is patient, then surely, Allah makes not the reward of the good-doers to be lost."

[12:91] They admitted: "By Allah! Indeed, Allah has preferred you above us, and we certainly have been sinners."

He forgave all his brothers:

[12:92] He said: "No reproach on you this day, may Allah forgive you, and He is the Most Merciful of those who show mercy!"

He forgave all his brothers, who jointly threw him in the well. The Most Merciful, Allah also forgave them. All of them proceeded to settle down in Egypt. Their families and offspring were known as the "Children of Israel"

The lessons learnt from this incident, are:

★ Allah [SWT] raises the degree of whom He is pleased with.

★ Allah's plans of our life, is always best.

★ Obey the laws of nation you live in.

★ Allah [أَلْعَلِيْمُ] is All-Knower.

★ Allah [الْحَكَمُ] is the best judge.

★ Patience is most fitting during any loss.

★ Complain your grief and sorrow, to Allahuthala only.

★ Indeed Allah has been gracious to those who fear Him.

★ Never give up hope in Allah's Mercy.

★ Allah ﷻ does not allow the reward of the good-doers, to be lost.

★ Allah [التَّوَّابُ] forgives when one repents for his sins, however great the sins are.

الحمدلله

بِسْمِ ٱللَّهِ ٱلرَّحْمَٰنِ ٱلرَّحِيمِ

8. Prophets

1. What was the test Sulaiman (AS) underwent, as per the surah Sad, verse number 34?

Answer: A jasadan (جَسَدًا - dead body) was placed on his throne.

"And, indeed We did try Sulaiman (AS) and We placed on his throne Jasadan (dead body) but he did return to Allah with obedience and in repentance." (38:34). This verse has been interpreted, in a variety of ways, by different Scholars.

There are five possible theories suggested by Fakhr al-Din al-Razi based on the stories and explanations of "Ulama":

1. King Sulaiman lost his throne to a demon, as a punishment for the idol-worship of one of his wives.

2. He lost his throne because the demon acquired his ring of sovereignty, by trick.

3. His son's dead body was placed on the throne due to some mistake committed by the Prophet Sulaiman (AS), himself.

4. Due to some kind of illness, he appeared as a weak person just like a dead body.

5. Affected by fear, he resembled a frail body on the throne.

Such mention is lacking in the Quran:

¶ That there was a devil on his throne.

¶ That there was a ring of sovereignty.

¶ That he had a son

¶ That he was ill.

¶ That he was engulfed with fear

Allahuthala alone is aware as to why he tested Sulaiman (AS)! [الله اعلم !]

Persuent to the test by Allahuthala, Sulaiman (AS) repented: "My Lord! Forgive me, and bestow upon me a kingdom such as shall not belong to any other after me: Verily, 'You' are the Bestower." (38:35)

Allah سبحانه وتعالى mentions about him in Quran as:

★ "We inspired and guided Sulaiman (AS), like other Prophets" (4:163, 6:84)

★ "How excellent a slave! Verily, he was ever Oft-returning in repentance (to Us)!" (38:30).

★ "Sulaiman (AS) did not disbelieve, but the Shayatin (devils) only disbelieved." (2:107)

Allah ﷻ bestowed on him:

★ A unique kingship.

★ Hukman (right judgement of the affairs), Prophet hood and knowledge. (21:79).

★ He has been taught the language of birds and bestowed with everythings. (27:16)

★ Wind blew gently as per his orders, where-so-ever he willed (38:36)

★ Shayateen and the jinns, being builders and divers; along with others bound in fetters, were under his control (38:37 and 38);

★ for all such gifts, no account will be required. (38:39)

★ And verily, he enjoyed a near access to Us (Allahuthala), and a good final return (that is Paradise) (38:40).

Even the world history mentions him, as "Salomon, The Great"

Allah [SWT] also had tested Sulaiman (AS) by presenting the throne of the Queen of Saba in his front:

"One Jinn, who had the knowledge of the Scripture claimed: 'I will bring it (throne of the Queen of Saba) to you within the twinkling of an eye!' then when [Sulaiman (AS)] saw it placed before him, he said: 'This is by the Grace of my Lord to test me whether I am grateful or ungrateful! And whoever is grateful, truly, his gratitude is for (the good of) his own-self, and whoever is ungrateful, (he is ungrateful only for loss of his own self)'. Certainly! My Lord is Rich (Free of all wants), Bountiful." (27:40).

No negative aspect of the Sulaiman (AS) has been mentioned in the Holy Quran. But there are lots of negative stories spread, by his own people Jews and Christians, especially about his wives, his ring, his throne, his control over Shayatheen. Allah alone knows the best! [! الله اعلم]. The Quran records that Allah rewarded him in this world with all goodness in view his gratefulness and repentance. So also in the Hereafter, with nearness to Allah and Paradise. (38:40).

There is a hadhees about his prayer and also about Shaithan:

Abu Darda (RA) reported: Allah's Messenger ﷺ stood up (to pray) and we heard him say: "I seek refuge in Allah from thee." Then said: "curse thee with Allah's curse" three times, then he stretched out his hand as though he was taking hold of something. When he finished the prayer, we asked: Messenger of Allah ﷺ, we heard you say something during the prayer which we have not heard you say before, and we saw you stretch out your hand. He replied: "Allah's enemy Iblis came with a flame of fire to put it in my face, so I said three times: 'I Seek refuge in Allah from thee'. Then I said three times: "I curse thee with Allah's full curse." But he did not retreat (on any one of these) three occasions. Thereafter I meant to seize him. I swear by Allah that had it not been for the supplication of my brother Sulaiman he would have been bound and made an object of sport, for the children of Madhina." (Sahih Muslim, Book 4, Number 1106).

Abu Huraira (RA) reported that he heard the Messenger of Allah ﷺ saying: "A highly wicked one amongst the Jinn escaped yester night to interrupt my prayer, but Allah gave me power over him, so I seized him and intended to tie him to one of the pillars of the mosque in order that you, all together or all, might look at him, but I remembered the supplication of my brother Sulaiman: "My Lord, forgive me, give me such a kingdom as will not be possible for any one after me". (Sahih Muslim, Book 8, Number 1104)

Lessons from the life of Sulaiman (AS):

(1) Even the chosen Prophets were not exempted from committing errors, on being influenced by the Shaithan.

(2) If anybody, after realizing that they had committed an error on their repenting, Allah [SWT] will always forgive them.

(3) Do not allow Shaithan to control us.

(4) Keep seeking refuge with Allahuthala, against the outcast, the Shaithan.

(5) Seek whatever you want from Allah [SWT]. He will provide you, if it is best of your interest.

(6) If anybody prays further after repenting, Allah [عَزَّ وَجَلَّ] will accept it and bless him with more favours.

الحمدلله

2. "O Prophet! Why do you prohibit yourself from what Allah has made lawful to you, seeking to please your wives?" (Surah Tahrim, 66:1). What is the aspect the Prophet ﷺ wished to avoid for himself?

Answer: Drinking honey/avoiding conjugal relationship, with Mariyah, in future.

This ayath is a warning to the Prophet ﷺ! Being a religious leader, it is not good to treat a lawful matter, as unlawful one. When every action of his was followed by his companions, as Sunna, Allah سبحانه وتعالى knew that his Umma will follow it. So He warned His Prophet ﷺ not to ban honey and make expiation for his oath. (66:2).

Yaqub (AS) forbade himself the meat and milk of camels because he did not like their taste. The Children of Yaqub treated those two, as forbidden. Allah refers in Quran, "All food was lawful to Children of Israel, except that which Israel (AS) had forbidden to himself, before the Taurath was revealed." (3:93).

Allah ﷻ does not mention what the Prophet ﷺ banned for himself, to please his wives.

According to some scholars there were two different events, which brought about the revelation of this ayath.

1. Avoidance of the use of honey, by him.

2. Denying him, the relationship with the slave girl Mariyah Qibiyyah.

1. Avoidance of the use of honey:

From two of the ahadhees, we come to know that the Prophet ﷺ banned honey.

(i) From Sahih al-Bukhari 6691:

As narrated by Ayesha (RA): "The Prophet ﷺ used to stay (for a period) in the house of Zainab bint Jahsh [RA] (one of the wives of the Prophet ﷺ) and he used to drink honey in her house. Hafsa (RA) and I decided that when the Prophet ﷺ entered upon either of us, she would say, "I smell in you the bad smell of Maghafir (a bad smelling raisin). Have you eaten Maghafir?" When he entered upon one of us, she said that to him. He replied (to her), "No, but I have drunk honey in the house of Zainab bint Jahsh (RA), and I will never drink it again." Then the following verse was revealed: 'O Prophet ﷺ! Why do you ban (for you) that which Allah has made lawful for you? (up to) If you two (wives of the Prophet ﷺ turn in repentance to Allah.' (66.1-4) The two were `Ayesha (RA) and Hafsa (RA). And also the Statement of Allah: 'And (Remember) when the Prophet ﷺ disclosed a matter in confidence to one of his wives!' (66.3) i.e., his saying, "But I have drunk honey." Hisham said: It also meant his saying, "I will not drink anymore, and I have taken an oath, so do not inform anybody of that."

(ii) From Sahih al-Bukhari- 6972

As narrated by Ayesha (RA): Allah's Messenger ﷺ used to like sweets and also used to like honey, and whenever he finished the `Asr' prayer, he used to visit his wives and stay with them. Once he visited Hafsa and remained with her longer than the period he used to stay, so I enquired about it. It was said to me, "A woman from her tribe gave her a leather skin containing honey as a present, and she gave some of it to Allah's Messenger ﷺ to drink." I said, "By Allah, we will play a trick on him." So I mentioned the story to Sauda [RA} (the wife of the Prophet ﷺ) and said to her, "When he enters upon you, he will come near to you whereupon you should say to him, 'O Allah's Messenger ﷺ! Have you eaten Maghafir?' He will say, 'No.' Then you say to him, 'What is this bad smell? ' And it would be very hard on Allah's Messenger ﷺ that a bad smell should be found on his body. He will say, 'Hafsa (RA) has given me a drink of honey.' Then you should say to him, 'Its bees must have sucked from the Al-`Urfut (a foul smelling flower).' I too, will tell him the same. And you, O Saifya (RA), say the same." So when the Prophet ﷺ entered upon Sauda (RA) (the following happened). Sauda (RA) said, "By Him except Whom none has the right to be worshipped, I was about to say to him what you had told me to say while he was still at the gate because of fear from you. But when Allah's Apostle ﷺ came near to me, I said to him, 'O Allah's Messenger ﷺ! Have you eaten Maghafir?' He replied, 'No.' I said, 'What about this smell?' He said, 'Hafsa (RA) has given me a drink of honey.' I said, 'Its bees must have sucked Al-`Urfut.' " When he entered upon me, I told him the same as that, and when he entered upon Safiya (RA), she too told him the same. So when he visited Hafsa (RA) again, she said to him, "O Allah's Messenger ﷺ! Shall

I give you a drink of it (honey)?" He said, "I have no desire for it." Sauda (RA) said, Subhan Allah! We have deprived him of it (honey)." I said to her, "Be quiet!"

Thereupon, Allah revealed an ayath: "O Prophet ﷺ! Why do you ban (for yourself) that which Allah has made lawful to you?" (Surah Tahrim, 66:1). [الله اعلم !]

Allah knows best!

2. To have no conjugal relation with Mariyah:

Anas (RA) said: "The Messenger of Allah ﷺ had a female-slave with whom he had intercourse, but Ayesha (RA) and Hafsah (RA) would not leave him alone until he said that she was forbidden for him. Then Allah, the Mighty and Sublime, revealed this ayath." (Sunan an-Nasa'i, 3959). Only an-Nasa'i narrates this hadhees. No other authentic collections of the ahadees has this information. All will know that Allah blessed a son, Ibrahim, through Mariyah, and made the Prophet ﷺ enjoy the fatherhood in his late fifties. It was Allah's decree.

Allah [عَزَّ وَجَلَّ] continued the first ayath in surah Taharim as "You seek to please your wives; and Allah is Forgiving, Merciful." (66:1). Al-Quran says further to the Prophet ﷺ, "Allah indeed has ordained for you the expiation of your oaths and Allah is your Protector, and He is the Knowing, the Wise." (66:2).

As Allah ﷻ has reminded the Prophet ﷺ about the ayath which had been already revealed: "He calls you to account for the making of deliberate oaths; so its expiation is the feeding of ten poor men out of the middling (food) you feed your families with, or their clothing, or the freeing of a neck of a slave; but whosoever cannot find (means) then fasting for three days; this is the expiation of your oaths when you swear; and guard your oaths. Thus does Allah make clear to you His communications, that you may be grateful." (5:89). Thus Allah [الْعَلِيمُ الْحَكِيمًا] guided, protected and forgave the Prophet ﷺ when he forbade a lawful thing on account of his jealous wives.

Allah [عَزَّ وَجَلَّ] also warned Ummul Momineen (the Mothers of believers) and directed them to repent and declared, "if you back up each other against him, then surely Allah it is Who is his Guardian, and Jibreel (AS) the believers that do good, and the angels after that are the helpers." (66:4). Allah ﷻ made his wives realize their delicate responsibilities and position; as the "Mothers of Muslims"

Allah [SWT] then warns the believers about the Hell, "O believers! Protect yourselves and your families from a Fire whose fuel is people and stones, overseen by formidable and severe angels, who never disobey whatever Allah orders—always doing as commanded." (66:6). It is our duty to guide our family members to protect them from Hell-Fire.

May Allahuthala guide us and forgive our sins which we do without knowing and protect us from the Hell-Fire! Ameen! [! الله اعلم]

الحمدلله

3. Which Nabi's death was informed by the little worm of earth?

Answer: Sulaiman (AS)

"Then when We decreed death for Sulaiman (AS), nothing informed jinn of his death except a little worm of the earth, which kept gnawing away at his stick, so when he fell down," Surah Saba, (34:14).

Sulaiman (AS) was blessed by Allahuthala, with favours in abundance:

Allahuthala bestowed Sulaiman (AS) with keen knowledge (27:15) and fine judgement (21:74). He knew the language of ants (27:19) and language of birds and had been provided with all kind of things with His manifest grace. (27:16). He had a flowing molten brass (34:12). He had many horses (38:31), a big army of the jinn, men and birds, (27:17), a big beautiful unique palace (27: 44). Allah made subservient to Sulaiman (AS); the rebellious Shayatheen, divers, workers and guards (21: 82) to work under him by His Will. (34:12). They made for him whatever he desired of sanctuaries, statues, basins as large as reservoirs, and cooking pots fixed into the ground (34:13). To him, Allah [SWT] subjected the wind: its morning stride was a month's journey and so was its evening stride (34:12).

Al-Hasan Al-Basri said, "Sulaiman (AS) set out from Damascus in the morning, landed in Istakhar where he ate a meal, then flew on from Istakhar and spent the night in Kabul." In between Damascus and Istakhar, is an entire month's travel for a swift rider and so also between Istakhar and Kabul.

He always praised his Lord and was known for his gratitude towards the Grace of his Lord (27:15). He was honoured by Allahuthala as a most excellent servant, as he always returned in repentance to Him (38:30). Allah responded to His prayer which sought, "bestow upon me a kingdom such as shall not belong to any other after me" (38:35). Thus he was recognized as "Saloman, The Great"

During Sulaiman (AS)'s reign, Jinn were claiming themselves as to have acquired the knowledge of unseen. As Allah had asserted in the Quran that: "the jinn used to sit in some of the sitting places in the sky thereof to steal a hearing from above" (72:9). With that knowledge they used to foretell the future of the people - good and bad. So the people used to turn to jinn, they make them associates with Allah (4:100) and worshipped them (34: 41) and used to forge extravagant things against Allah (72:4).

The death of Sulaiman (AS):

Sulaiman (AS) used to sit, holding his stick as a support and used to watch the activities of the Jinn. In that position Allah decreed the death for Sulaiman (AS). None was aware of his death. The Jinn were toiling, under the impression that he was watching them. Allah, the Exalted, commanded the little creature of earth (termites) to eat his stick and thereupon his body, fell to the ground. Then only human beings and jinn became aware of his death. They approached him and realized that he was dead long ago. Nobody was aware, excepting Allah, as to how long he was sitting in that position. "The jinn realized that if they had really known the unseen, they would not have remained in such humiliating servitude." (34:14).

Such a death, is a guidance to those people who believe that the future is neither known to the jinn nor to the prophets/great persons, but to Allah alone. "Allah is the Knower of the unseen! He does not reveal His secrets to any" (72:26).

الحمدلله

4. "Verily he was a man of truth and a Prophet and We raised him to a lofty station." (19:56 and 57). Who was he?

Answer: Prophet Idris (AS) or Enoch.

Allahuthala testifies that Idris (AS) as a truthful (19:56); a patient and a good human being (21:85). He was the third Prophet, after Adam (AS) and Sheeth (AS). He was from the sixth generation of Adam (AS). Allah ﷻ for his exemplanary deeds raised him to the lofty station, which is the fourth heaven. Allah ﷻ states in Quran: "And Ismail, Idris and Zulkifl; all were of the patient ones; and We caused them to enter into Our mercy, surely they were of the good ones." (21:85 and 86).

He was the first one to use the pen; a pioneer tailor who stiched his own clothes. It was recorded that thirty portions of Allah's sacred scriptures, were revealed to him. Some claim that he was teaching the 104 revelations of Sheeth (AS). Allah knows best! He was the inventor of the science of astronomy and also arithmetic. [الله اعلم !]

During his time, the entire humanity was believing in Allah [SWT] but some embarked on corrupt activities. He was the first one to participate in jihadh. With his horsemen and army, he was fighting against the people of Qabil (Adam's son who murdered his brother Habil), who were corrupt.

Ibn Kathir narrated that "During the Night Journey of Prophet Mohammad ﷺ, he was met and greeted by Idris (AS), in the fourth heaven." In a hadees Ibn Abbas (RA) required Ka'b to furnish explanation to the following verse, "We raised him to a lofty station." Ka'b explained: Allahuthala revealed to Idris (AS): "I would raise for you every day the same amount of deeds of all Adam's children". So Idris (AS) decided to increase his deeds and devotion. A friend of his from the angels visited Idris (AS), to whom he informed about Allahuthala's revelation, "could you please speak to the angel of death, so I would increase my deeds."

So the angel carried him in his wing and went up to the fourth heaven. There, they met the angel of death, who was descending down to earth. The angel spoke to him about what Idris (AS) had stated to him. The angel of death exclaimed, "But where is Idris?" The reply was, "He is on my back". Then the angel of death exclaimed: "How astonishing! I was sent and told to seize his soul in the fourth heaven. I kept thinking how could I seize it in fourth heaven when he was on earth?" Thereupon, he took his soul out of his body. [الله اعلم !]

Allah knows best!

الحمدلله

5. "O mountains! Sing praises with him and the birds" (34:10). Him refers to which Prophet?

Answer: Nabi Dawud (AS).

Apart from this ayath, Allah refers the same content in two other places in the Holy Quran: "Indeed, 'We' subjected the mountains [to praise] with him, exalting [Allah] in the [late] afternoon and [after] sunrise." (38:18). "And the birds gathered together; all joined in singing with him." (38:19). "We made the mountains, and the birds to celebrate Our praise with Dawud (AS)". (27:79).

Dawud (AS) was gifted with a sweet voice. He was singing the praise of Allahuthala at the sun rise as well as at the sunset. Allah [SWT] had ordered mountains and the gathering of the birds to sing along with Dawud (AS). The mountains are still echoing and the birds are still singing in their own way during early morning and evening. Prophet Dawud (AS) was a divinely guided leader and the most excellent servant of Allah ※. Even though he was a king, he was never proud. He was always grateful and thankful for all the talents and gifts from Allah ※ and used his power at Allah's will.

Allah ※ refers in Quran about Dawud (AS) as:

★ "Allah gave him kingdom and wisdom, and taught him of what He pleased." (2:251)

★ "And We strengthened his kingdom and We gave him wisdom and a clear judgment." (38:20) "and knowledge" (27:15) "and excellence from Us" (34:10)

★ "We have made some prophets to excel others, and to Dawud (AS) We gave a scripture Zabur." (17:55 and 4:163).

★ "He was rewarded for his goodness" (6:84)

★ "We were bearers of witness to their (his as his son's) judgment." (27: 78)

Quran mentions 'that Dawud (AS) and his son Sulaiman's (AS) prayed as: "Praise be to Allah, 'Who' has made us to excel many of His believing servants." (27:15).

Allahuthala softened the iron for him, with which Dawud (AS) prepared iron coats to be worn during wars, weapons of war and many other useful materials. During his period there were very many wars and his talent in making iron armor, became very much useful. When he took over the position of a King, Allah ※ said to Dawud (AS), "O Dawud! surely We have made you a ruler in the land; so judge between men with justice and do not follow desire, lest it should lead you astray from the path of Allah." (38:26). His judgement was tested by Allah [SWT], through two litigants.

"There come to you the story of the litigants, when they made an entry into the private chamber by ascending over the walls? When they entered in upon Dawud (AS) and he was frightened at them, they said: Fear not; two litigants, of whom one has acted wrongfully towards the other, therefore decide between us with justice, and do not act unjustly, and guide us to the right way." (38:21 and 22). "Surely this is my brother; he has ninety-nine ewes and I have a single ewe; but he said: 'Hand it over to me, and he over powered me in speech against me." (38:23). Dawud (AS) immediately said:

"Surely he has been unjust to you in demanding your ewe to add to his own ewes; and most surely most of the partners' act wrongfully towards one another, save those who believe and do good, and very few are they." (38:24).

The two men disappeared like a cloud. He realized that they were two angels sent to him to teach him a lesson. He should not have passed a judgement without hearing the opposing party. "And Dawud (AS) realized that Allah ﷻ had tested him. He fell down prostrating himself and turned towards Him repenting." (38:24). "So Allah forgave his sins. He had a nearness to Us (to Allah) and an excellent resort. (that is Paradise)" (38:25)

When the Quraish idolaters pleaded, "Our Lord, hasten for us our share of the punishment before the Day of Account" (38:16). Allah Subhanahuthala provided the example of Dawud (AS) to the Prophet Muhammad ﷺ as: "Be patient over what they say and remember Our servant, Dawud (AS), the possessor of strength; indeed, he was one who repeatedly turned back [to Allah]." (38:17)

Every believer has to learn a lesson from Dawud (AS) as found in the following ahadhees:

Narrated Abdullah bin Amr: Allah's Messenger (ﷺ) said to me, "The most beloved fasting to Allah was the fasting of (the Prophet) Dawud (AS) who used to fast on alternate days. And the most beloved prayer to Allah was the prayer of David who used to sleep for (the first) half of the night and pray for 1/3 of it and (again) sleep for a sixth of it." [Sahih al-Bukhari 3420, Book 60, Hadith 92]. "He would not flee on facing the enemy" [Sahih al-Bukhari 3419: Book 60, Hadith 91]

Narrated by Abu Huraira (RA): The Prophet ﷺ stated, "The reciting of the Zabur (i.e. Psalms) was made easy for Dawud (AS). He used to order that his riding animals be saddled, and would finish reciting the Zabur before they were saddled. And he would never eat except from the earnings of his manual work." (Sahih al-Bukhari 3417, Book 60, Hadith 89).

الحمدلله

6. "When he ran away to the laden ship. And he drew lots and was among the losers." (37:140 and 141) Or "When he went off in anger and imagined that we shall not punish him" (21:87). Who is that Prophet?

Answer: Nabi Yunus (AS) or Dhun-Nun (Fish man)

Yunus (AS) was sent as a Prophet to a community of Nineveh town of the Mawsil (northern Iraq). His community was adhering to idolatry. The Prophet required them to worship 'One Allah'. They argued and continued to persist in disbelief; involved in all wrong doings.

Frustrated with their stubbornness, disbelief and meaningless argument, he warned by threatening them of facing Allah's punishment within three days. Without waiting for Allah's instructions he left them, with anger and impatience. He never thought that it is an act of disobedience and without realizing that Allah will punish for such an act, he ran away from his town. Allah ﷻ says in the Quran: "And (remember) Dhun-Nun (Yunus AS) when he went off in anger and imagined that we shall not punish him" (21:87).

"Then he boarded into the ship that was fully laden" (37:140). It sailed in calm waters for some time and suddenly, a storm started blowing and continued. To reduce the load of the ship they threw the baggage into the sea. Still the ship was heavy. According to the tradition practiced then, it was decided to draw a lot in order to remove at least one person from the ship. He agreed for the casting of lots. (37:141)

Yunus (AS)'s name appeared. Being the most noble man of their society, they wished to select some other person to be thrown into the sea. So they drew a lot second time. Again his name appeared. They repeated for the third time. Unfortunately, again his name was drawn. Realizing his mistake of running away impatiently, without fulfilling his mission, he accepted their selection and jumped into the sea.

Allah عزّ وجل ordered a big fish to enter into that green Mediterranean Sea and commanded it to swallow him. Allah recorded that "So the fish swallowed him while he did that for which he blamed himself" (37:142). He was covered with three layers of darkness. The darkness of night, the darkness of sea and the darkness of fish's stomach.

Realizing that he was still alive, he said: "O Lord, I have taken this as a place of worship to You; place which no other person has reached." He cried and glorified Allah Subhanahuthala; repenting for his act. He recited the thasbhi: [لَا إِلَٰهَ إِلَّا أَنتَ سُبْحَانَكَ إِنِّي كُنتُ مِنَ الظَّالِمِينَ] - "There is no God except You. Glory be to You! Verily, I have been of the wrong doers." (21:87). All the creatures of the sea, heard the voice of the Yunus (AS) and began to glorify the praise of Allahuthala in their own way. There are several views regarding the period of his stay in the belly of the fish.

Qatadah says it was three days, Jafar As-Sadiq said - 7days, Abu Malik - 40 days and Mujahid said, "It swallowed him in the morning and cast him forth in the evening." Allah knows best! [الله اعلم !]

Allahuthala responds: "So We answered his call and delivered him from the distress. And thus We do deliver the believers" (21:88). Allah [SWT] has promised in the Quran to the believers that whoever calls Him during distress with sincere effort, through this dua, Allahuthala will remove such distress and provide unexpected reward. Allah [عَزَّ وَ جَلَّ] also further states: "Had he not been of them who glorify Allah, he would have indeed remained inside the belly of the fish till the Day of Resurrection." (37:143 and144).

Allah ﷻ continues: "But We cast him forth on the naked shore while he was sick and We caused a plant of gourd to grow over him. And We sent him to a hundred thousand (people) or even more and they believed; so We gave them enjoyment for a while" (37:145 - 148).

This dua is referred as "Thasbi of Yunus" or "Ayathul Kareema" and whoever recites this, Allah the Merciful forgives their sins and remove their distress. Narrated from Ibn Abbas (RA), he said: "Remember Allah during times of ease and He will remember you during the times of difficulty."

His people, when he left, saw the black cloud approaching them. They realized that their Prophet was telling the truth. They went out with their children and animals and pleaded to Allahuthala, to save them from the punishment.

Allah ﷻ says: "Was there any town that believed (after seeing the punishment), and its faith saved it except the people of Yunus; when they believed, 'We' removed from them the punishment of disgrace in the life of the world, and permitted them to enjoy for a while." (10:98)

From this story we learn the following lessons:

★ To be patient in all affairs.

★ Mistakes committed should be realized.

★ Thereafter repent for one's mistake.

★ Glorify Allah Subhanahuthala, at times of ease.

★ That act helps, during the times of difficulty.

★ Have strong faith in Allah's Mercy.

★ Fear Allah [سبحانه وتعالى].

★ Save yourself from Allah's punishment.

★ Zikir is a very powerful form of prayer.

★ Glorifying Allahuthala with sincere effort during distress will provide unexpected reward after distress.

Ahadhees about Yunus (AS):

'This cry of repentance (of Yunus [AS]) was heard up to the Great Throne, where angels asked Allah ﷻ, "O Lord, this is the voice of one who is weak but known, in a far-away strange land."

Allah, the Exalted, enquired, "How do you know this?"

They wished to know, "O Lord, who is he?"

Allah [عَزَّ وَ جَلَّ], the Exalted, said, "My servant Yunus."

They said, "Your servant Yunus, from whom there kept coming acceptable deeds and supplications which were answered!"

They said, "O Lord, will You not have mercy on him for what he did during his time of ease, and save him from this trial and tribulation?"

He said, "Of course."

So, He commanded the great fish, and it cast him forth on the naked shore.'

Allahuthala advised the Prophet Mohammad ﷺ: " So wait patiently for the judgment of your Lord, and be not like the companion of the fish, when he cried while he was in distress." (68: 48). "Were it not that favor from his Lord had overtaken him, he would certainly have been cast down upon the naked ground while he was blamed." (68:49).

Imam Ahmad recorded that Sad bin Abi Waqqas, (RA) had narrated: "I passed by Uthman bin Affan, (RA) in the Masjid, and greeted him. He stared at me but did not return my Salam. I went to Umar bin Al-Khattab (RA) and said: `O Commander of the faithful, has something happened in Islam!' I said that twice. He said, `No, why do you ask?' I said, `I passed by Uthman (RA) a short while ago in the Masjid and greeted him, and he stared at me but he did not return my Salam.'

Umar (RA) sent for Uthman (RA) and asked him, `Why did you not return your brother's Salam?' He said, `That is not true.' Sad (RA) said, `Yes it is.' It reached the point where they both swore oaths.

Then Uthman (RA) remebered and said, `Yes, you are right, I seek the forgiveness of Allah and I repent to Him. You passed by me a short while ago but I was preoccupied with thoughts of something I had heard from the Messenger of Allah ﷺ, which I never think of but a veil comes down over my eyes and my heart.'

Sad said: `And I will tell you what it was. The Messenger of Allah ﷺ told us the first part of the supplication then a Bedouin came and kept him busy, then the Messenger of Allah ﷺ got up and I followed him. When I felt worried that he would enter his house, I stamped my feet. I turned to the Messenger of Allah ﷺ, who said, "Who is this. Abu Ishaq?" I said, "Yes, O Messenger of Allah ﷺ." He said, 'What is the matter?' I said, "Nothing, by Allah, except that you told us the first part of the supplication, then this Bedouin came and kept you busy." He said, "Yes, the supplication of Dhun-Nun when he was in the belly of the fish: " No Muslim ever prays to his Lord with these words for anything, but He will answer his prayer." It was also recorded by At-Tirmidhi, and by An-Nasa'i in Al-Yawm wal-Laylah.

Ibn Abi Hatim had recorded that Sad stated that the Messenger of Allah ﷺ asserted: "Whoever offers supplication in the words of the supplication of Yunus (AS), will be answered." Abu Sa`id said: The Prophet ﷺ was referring to the verse 21:88: "And thus we do deliver the believers".

الحمدلله

7. At which place the ship of Nuh (AS) rested finally?

Answer: Mount Judi.

Nabi Nuh (AS) was sent as a warner, to the people who were involved in idol worship. "He called them night and day" (71:5). 'He required them to worship Allah and ask forgiveness of most forgiving' (71:10), 'Pointing out Allah's blessings' (71: 12-20). "He also reminded them of the torment of the painful day." (Hud,11:26).

'He called them publicly and privately' (71:9). 'But his call has only made them flee the more' (71:6). 'They thrust their fingers into ears or covered themselves with clothes and they persisted in their pride.' (71:7) They said "You have prolonged the dispute with us, now bring upon us what you have threaten us if you are truthful" (11:32).

"He stayed among them for 950 years" (29:14). Only poor and helpless labourers were attracted by him. They threatened him: "If you cease not you will be stoned to death." (26:116). Thereupon, "He grieved and invoked, 'O my Lord! Help me because they denied me' (23:26). I have been overpowered, so help me" (54:10). And Nuh (AS) supplicated: "My Lord! leave not upon the land any dweller from among the unbelievers. For surely if You leave them they will lead astray your servants, and will not beget any but immoral, ungrateful children." (71:26 and 27).

Then Allah [سبحانه وتعالى] commanded him "to construct a ship under His eyes with Our Revelation" (11:37). "As he was making a ship with planks and nails in a place far away from sea, the people were mocking at him whenever they passed by him." (11:38). "Until when Our command came and water came forth from the valley, 'We' said: Carry in it two of all things, a pair, and your own family - except those against whom the word has already gone forth, and those who believe. And there believed not with him but a few" (11:40).

After you embarked on the ship, you then say: "All the praises and thanks be to Allah, who saved us from Zalimun". And pray, "My Lord! Allow me a blessed landing, for You are the best accommodator." (23:28 and 29). And it moved on with them amid waves like mountains; and Nuh (AS) called out to his son, and he was aloof: "O my son! Embark with us and be not with the unbelievers." He said: "I will betake myself for refuge to a mountain that shall protect me from the water." Nuh (AS) said: "There is no protector today from Allah's punishment but He Who has mercy; and a wave intervened between them, so he was of the drowned. (11:42 and 43).

"Sailing, before Our eyes, a reward for him who was denied." (54: 14). And it was said: "O earth! swallow down your water, and O cloud! clear away; and the water was made to abate and the affair was decided and the ark rested on the mount Judi" and it was said: "Away with the unjust people." (11:44). 'So We delivered him and the inmates of the ark, and made it a sign to the nations.' (29:15) 'We made them rulers' (10:73). 'We drowned those who rejected Our communications; surely they were a blind people.' (71:64). 'See then what was the end of the (people) warned.' (10:73).

Bible also refers to Noah's ark:

The sixth chapter Genesis - The New International Version -Verse 13 to 21 states:

[6:13] "So God said to Noah, "I am going to put an end to all people, for the earth is filled with violence because of them. I am surely going to destroy both, them and the earth."

[6:14] "So make yourself an ark of cypress wood; make rooms in it and coat it with pitch inside and out."

[6:15] "This is how you are to build it: The ark is to be three hundred cubits long, fifty cubits wide and thirty cubits high."

[6:16] "Make a roof for it, leaving below the roof an opening one cubit[e] high all around. Put a door in the side of the ark and make lower, middle and upper decks."

[6:17] "I am going to bring floodwaters on the earth to destroy all life under the heavens, every creature that has the breath of life in it. Everything on earth will perish."

[6:18] "But I will establish my covenant with you, and you will enter the ark"

[6:19] "You are to bring into the ark two of all living creatures, male and female, to keep them alive with you."

[6:20] "Two of every kind of bird, of every kind of animal and of every kind of creature that moves along the ground will come to you to be kept alive."

[6:21] "You are to take every kind of food that is to be eaten and store it away as food for you and for them."

Bible claims in Chapter Genesis 8:4 Noah's Ark landed on Mount Ararat of Turkey. So in the past century, dozens of expeditions have claimed of locating the ark in several places of Mount Ararat.

Location 1: During the first Ark seeker's expedition (1908) claimed to have traced on the north east side of Mount Ararat. They were probing over there for a century. But could not prove the existence of ark. They closed the effort of their expedition.

Location 2: On finding a large structure protruding out of ice and snow they started the expedition and on 2003 they released a satellite image showing an elongated structure with the similar dimensions of the ark. But their research was not aproved.

Location 3: The Turky Hong Kong (NAMI) expedition containing a team of evangelical Christians, found 7 large wooden planks. They asserted that they were 99.99% sure about the ark. But that particular area being a frequently flooded area, from which one cannot expect a preserved structure like an ark. They declared that "We do not make a claim that we have found Noah's ark. We will let you draw your own conclusions".

Location 4: BASE Institute with its CEO, Robert Cornuke was working near Mount Suleiman, located at Elburz mountain range in Iran. They had discovered beam like rocks. Those details are not matching with Biblical description of ark. It may be due to geological formation.

Location 5: In Mount Ararat, Turkey, Ron Wyatt in 1980 was probing on this "ark shaped" formation. Christian archeologist and geologist rejected this claim, on the ground that these formations are caused by the depositions of mud around eroded crops. Untill now they are continuing their expedition with modern equipment hoping to prove the existence of the real ark. A picture of ark like structure, was released by them.

In the Holy Quran it is quoted that ship's final hault was on the mount Judi. This place is located 100 kms from south-east peak of the Mount Ararat; which at present is called as Cudi or Kurdish mount. [الله اعلم !]

Future has to answer about the real resting place of the ark. Allah knows best!

الحمدلله

8. "Verily, that was a clear trial. And We ransomed him with a great sacrifice. And We left for him (a goodly remembrance) among the later generations." (37:106 to 108). What is the trial? Who underwent that trial?

Answer: Ibrahim (AS), sacrificing the only son born by prayers at his old age.

Allah سبحانه وتعالى miraculously protected Ibrahim (AS) from the punishment of the huge fire. The tyrant King of His time considered himself as God, disputed again with Ibrahim (AS). With the reply of Ibrahim (AS) the King became tongue-tied.

The information of his miraculous escape from the blazing fire along with his spell bound reply to the arrogant King, spread throughout the kingdom. He was continuously calling people to believe in Allah. But out of fear of the tyrant King, nobody listened and followed Ibrahim (AS).

Only two believed and followed Ibrahim (AS); his nephew Lut (AS) and a woman named Sara. Ibrahim (AS) married Sara, leaving his family, his society and the city along with his two believers by assuring: "Verily, I am going to my Lord. He will guide me!" (37:99)

First, those three proceeded to the city Ur, then to Haran and then to Palestine and finally arrived at Egypt. Ibrahim (AS) prayed to Allah: "O my Lord! Bestow upon me the gift of [a son who shall be] one of the righteous!" (37:100). Whereupon Allah gave him the glad tiding of a boy possessing forbearance. (37:101). During their stay in Egypt, the ruler king tried to misbehave with his wife Bibi Sara. But Allah protected her by paralyzing his hands. The king begged her to pray. She prayed and he became normal. Again he tried to misbehave. On second request, Bibi Sara prayed again and he was cured. So he gifted her a maid servant called Hajar. Bibi Sara being childless, married Hajar to Ibrahim (AS). Very soon Hajar delivered a son, named Ismail (AS).

Allah [عَزَّ وَجَلَّ] conveyed His messages through dreams to Ibrahim (AS). When Ismail (AS) was still nursing, by Allah's order in the dream, he took his wife Hajar and her son for a long journey. Ibrahim (AS) left his wife and infant with little water and food in a dry place, near Arafath mountain valley, where now present Makkah is located. His wife enquired as: "Are you leaving us in this barren valley?" He was silent. She being a Prophet's wife, asked again: "Did Allah ﷺ command you to do so?" Saying "Yes" he walked away. As her trust in Allah Subhanahuthala was strong, she assured herself: "We are not going to be lost, since Allah is with us".

Allahu Akbar! As she said 'The Best Planner' Allah was with them. After a struggle of running to and fro from Mount Safa and Marwa for water the Almighty Allah had blessed her, her child and the barren valley. Allah [سبحانه وتعالى] sent Jibreel (AS) there, to gush with the Zam Zam water from which she earned and lived.

Years passed! When Ibrahim (AS) was in Palestine with Bibi Sara, he had another dream consequently for three days, in which he was sacrificing his only son Ismail (AS). Understanding the message of Allah, he went to the valley again to meet his son and wife. By this time "his son was old enough to walk with him". Ibrahim (AS) explained his dream to his son: "O my son! I have seen in a dream that I am slaughtering you (offer you in sacrifice to Allah), so look what you think!" His son replied: "O my father! Do that which you are commanded, In-sha-Allah, you shall find me of As-Sabirin (the patient one)." (37:102). A prophet's son, a nine-year-old one, to reply in such matured manner; was a sign of his becoming a prophet in future.

It also indicated the way he was brought up by pious and patient mother and the way he had learned by experience, while he was left alone in the barren valley.

Then, with the permission of his wife Ibrahim (AS) took his son near Mount Arafath. Shaitan appeared to him at the Masa and raced with him, but Ibrahim (AS) got there first. Then Jibreel (AS) took him to Jamrat Al-Aqabah and the Shaitan appeared and required him to disobey Allah's command. Thereupon, Ibrahim (AS) stoned him with seven pebbles as per the instructions of Jibreel (AS). Then Shaitan appeared again at Al-Jamrah Al-Wus-ta and was stoned with seven pebbles until he disappeared. Then again when he appeared in Jamrathul Kubra and Ibrahim (AS) pelted him with seven pebbles.

"When they both (father and son) had submitted themselves (to the Will of Allah), and he had laid him prostrate on his forehead for slaughtering" (37:103). And We called out to him: "O Ibrahim! You have fulfilled the dream!" "And thus Ibrahim (AS) fulfilled what Allah ordered him to do so" (53:37). "Verily! Thus We do reward the Muhsinun (good-doers) " (37:104 and 105). Allah says in Quran-e-Majeedh, "Verily, this was a clear test for Ibrahim (AS) (37:106). And We ransomed him with a great sacrifice" (37:107). Angels replaced a ram from Paradise in the place of Ismail (AS). It was clearly a test when he was commanded to sacrifice his son, which, he hastened to do in submission to the command of Allah. Ibrahim (AS) fulfilled all that Allah had ordered.

Yes, Subhanallah! "Whoever submits his face to Allah and he is a good-doer, then his reward is with Allah, on such shall be no fear, nor shall they grieve." (2:112). Allah Subhanahuthala made it a tradition till the Day of Resurrecction to all believers to perform animal sacrifice and sa'ee during Hajj and Umra. Allah ﷻ referred this as, "We left for him (a goodly remembrance) among the later generations." (37:108). "Peace be upon Ibrahim! (37:109)." We, Muslims remember Ibrahim (AS) daily in all our Salah along with our Prophet Mohammad ﷺ.

Opinions of Jews and Christians about this incidence:

The Jews and Christians claim that it was Ishaq (AS), whom Ibrahim (AS) sacrificed. Reports of Ibn Kathir assert without any doubt, it was Ismail (AS) and not Ishaq (AS). Ibn Jarir narrated that Ibn Abbas said, "The one who was ransomed was Ismail (AS). The Jews claimed that it was Ishaq (AS), but it is untrue."

Muhammad bin Ka`b (RA) said, "I was with Umar bin Abd Al-Aziz (RA). He sent for a man who was with him in Syria, a Jew, who had become a Muslim and was committed to Islam, and he thought that he had been one of their scholars." Umar (AS) asked him, `Which of the two sons of Ibrahim (AS) commanded to be sacrificed?' He answered "Ismail (AS). By Allah, O Commander of the faithful! The Jews know this, but they were jealous of you Arabs because it was your (Fore) father about whom Allah issued this command and the virtue that Allah mentioned was because of his patience in obeying the command. So they denied that and claimed that it was Ishaq (AS), because he is their (Fore) father."

It was narrated by Ali; Ibn Umar; Abu Hurayrah; Abu At-Tufayl; Sa`id bin Al-Musayyib; Sa`id bin Jubayr; Al-Hasan; Mujahid; Ash-Sha`bi; Muhammad bin Ka`b Al-Qurazi; Abu Ja`far Muhammad bin Ali and Abu Salih, (Allah be pleased with them all), that the one who was to be sacrificed was Ismail (AS).

الحمدلله

9. "I am going to send it down unto you, but if any of you after that disbelieves, then I will punish him with a torment such as I have not inflicted on anyone among the 'Alamin (mankind and jinns)." (5:115) "You" refers to which Prophet?

Answer: Isa ibn Marium (AS).

When the Hawariyyun said: "O `Isa, (AS) son of Marium! Can your Lord send down to us a Maidah from heaven" Isa (AS) son of Marium, claimed: "Have Taqwa of Allah, if you are indeed believers." They insisted: "We wish to eat thereof and to be stronger in faith, and to know that you have indeed told us the truth and that we ourselves be its witnesses." (5:112 and 113)

Imam Qurtubi has elaborated upon the disciple's request explaining that they continued to ask even after being objected by Isa (AS), son of Marium, for the following four reasons:

- To fulfill their hunger due to poverty or fasting for many days or possibly to gain blessings from heavenly food.

- To strengthen their faith.

- To satisfy their hearts to accept Isa (AS) as a Prophet; to satisfy their hearts that Allah ﷻ accepted them and to satisfy themselves that Allah had chosen and given them to eat the food from heaven.

- The fourth and final reason is that they could bear witness to the miracle/sign of Allahuthala, through His Prophet Isa (AS), the son of Marium.

Isa (AS), son of Marium, said: "O Allah, our Lord! Send us from heaven a table spread (with food) that there may be for us -- for the first and the last of us -- a festival and a sign from You; and provide us sustenance, for You are the Best of sustainers.'" (5:114). As-Suddi commented that it means, "We will take that day as a day of celebration, that we and those who come after us would consider sacred." Sufyan Ath-Thawri said that it means, "A day of prayer."

Allah [عَزَّ وَجَلَّ] ordained: "I am going to send it down unto you, but if any of you after that disbelieves, then I will punish him with a torment such as I have not inflicted on anyone among the `Alamin." (5:115). Allahuthala bestowed him so many signs and miracles. Those people were not still satisfied with them.

Ibn Abi Hatim recorded that Ibn Abbas had said, "So the angels brought the table down containing seven fish and seven pieces of bread and placed it before them. So the last group of people ate as the first group did." Ibn Jarir recorded that Ishaq bin Abdullah said that the table was sent down to Isa (AS) son of Marium having seven pieces of bread and seven fish, and they ate from it as much as they wished. But when some of them stole food from it, saying, "It might not come down tomorrow," the table ascended. These statements testify that the table was sent down to the Children of Israel during his time, as a result of Allah's accepting supplication from Isa (AS).

Imam Qurtubi has narrated that the majority of the scholars believe that the table was actually sent down. Qurtubi has supported this view by observing, "The correct view is that the table did descend." He gives description of this incident as follows: "A red table between two clouds, one above and one beneath it descended. Whilst the people were staring in wonder upon it, he was praying to his Lord, "O Allah! Make it a source of Mercy and not a trial, 'You' are my Lord to whom I ask for a miracle, so You give." The table landed in front of Isa (AS), who prostrated immediately and so did the disciples with him."

The Qur'an has not mentioned the type of food that decended down. Ammar ibn Yasir referring a hadhees in Tirmidhi claimed that "Maidah did come from the heavens which included bread and meat." It also appears in this hadhees that some of those people committed a breach of trust, and put it off for the next day as well. As a result, they were transformed into monkeys and swines. (May Allah keep us protected from His wrath). This very hadhees also tells us that they ate from it. However, storing it for future use was prohibited. (Mayan al-Qur'an).

And Allah ﷻ said in Quran, "I am sending it down to you. But whoever among you denies afterwards will be subjected to a torment I have never inflicted on anyone of My creations." (5:115). And the entire surah is named as "Maidah". Above two references are the proof, to accept that "Maidah" desended down! [!الله اعلم]

Only Allah [سبحانه وتعالىٰ] knows as to what, when and how it happened!

Ibn Jarir referred that Abdullah bin Amr claimed, "Those who will receive the severest torment on the Day of Resurrection are three":

1. The hypocrites, "Verily, the hypocrites will be in the lowest depths of the Fire." (4:145)

2. "Those from the people of Al-Ma'idah who disbelieved in it." (5:115).

3. The people of Firaun. "And on the Day when the Hour will be established (it will be said to angels): "Cause Fir'aun's people to enter the severest torment!" (40:46).

الحمدلله

10. "And it is He Who feeds me and gives me to drink. And when I am ill, it is He who cures me." Which Prophet said these words about Allah?

Answer: Ibrahim (AS). [As Shura, 26: 79 and 80]

Ibrahim (AS) was born to a well-known idol sculpturer Aazar, in the kingdom of Babylon. He used to watch his father making idols. (Some people say that he lost his father during childhood and he called his uncle as father). When his father and his people were worshipping those idols, he used to raise many questions.

He questioned his father and his people, "What are these images, to which you are devoted?" (21:52). "Do you observe that which you have been worshipping" (26:75). They replied that "We found our fathers worshipping them." (21:53) and continued "We worship idols, and to them we are ever devoted." (26:71). Ibrahim (AS) responded: "Indeed you and your fathers have been in manifest error." (21:54).

Ibrahim (AS) wished to know:

"Do they hear you, when you call (on them)? (26:72). "Or do they benefit you or do they harm (you)?" (26:73). They said: "Nay, but we found our fathers doing so." (26:74). He enquired: "You and your ancient fathers? Verily! They are enemies to me, save the Lord of the Alamin" (26:76 and 77).

They exclaimed: "Have you brought us the truth, or are you one of those who play about?" He replied: "Nay, your Lord is the Lord of the heavens and the earth, 'Who' created them and of that I am one of the witnesses. And by Allah, I shall plot a plan (to destroy) your idols after you have gone away and turned your backs." (21: 55 – 58)

He personally discussed with his father affectionately and patiently:

He enquired with his father, while he was alone, "O my father! Why do you worship that which hears not, sees not and cannot avail you in anything? O my father! Verily, there has come to me of knowledge that which came not unto you. So follow me. I will guide you to a Straight Path. O my father! Worship not Shaitan. Verily! Shaitan has been a rebel against the Most Beneficent (Allah). O my father! Verily! I fear lest a torment from the Most Beneficent (Allah) overtake you, so that you become a companion of Shaitan (in the Hell-fire)." (19:42 to 45).

His father warned him:

His father threatened: "Do you reject my gods, O Ibrahim? If you stop not this, I will indeed stone you. So get away from me safely before I punish you." (19:46)

Ibrahim (AS) responded:

"Peace be on you! I will ask Forgiveness of my Lord for you. Verily! He is unto me, Ever Most Gracious" (19:47). "And I shall turn away from you and from those whom you invoke besides Allah. And I shall call on my Lord; and I hope that I shall not be unblest in my invocation to my Lord." (19:48)

Allah ﷻ refers about Ibrahim (AS) in Quran:

"Indeed there has been an excellent example for you in Ibrahim (AS) and those with him, when they said to their people: Verily, we are free from you and whatever you worship besides Allah, we have rejected you, and there has started between us and you, hostility and hatred for ever, until you believe in Allah Alone," (60:4).

Ibrahim (AS) was neither a Jew nor a Christian, but he was a true Muslim Hanifa (Islamic Monotheism – to worship none but Allah Alone) and he was not of Al-Mushrikun (an idol worshipper) (3:67). "It is those who believe (in the Oneness of Allah and worship none but Him Alone) and confuse not their belief with wrong for them (only) there is security and they are the guided. And that was Our proof which

'We' gave Ibrahim (AS) against his people. We raise whom We will in degrees. Certainly your Lord is All-Wise, All-Knowing." (6:82, 83)

He supplicated to Allahuthala:

He then prayed to His Almighty, "Who has created me, and it is He Who guides me; And it is He Who feeds me and gives me to drink. And when I am ill, it is He who cures me; And Who will cause me to die, and then will bring me to life (again); And Who, I hope will forgive me my faults on the Day of Recompense." (26:78-82).

"My Lord! Bestow Hukman (religious knowledge, right judgement of the affairs and Prophet hood) on me, and join me with the righteous; And grant me an honorable mention in later generations; And make me one of the inheritors of the Paradise of Delight; And forgive my father, verily he is of the erring; And disgrace me not on the Day when (all the creatures) will be resurrected; The Day whereon neither wealth nor sons will avail, Except him who brings to Allah a clean heart [clean from Shirk (polytheism) and Nifaq (hypocrisy)]". (26:83 to 89)

Then Allah [عَزَّ وَجَلَّ] describes as to what happens on the Day of judgement: "And Paradise will be brought near to the pious. And the (Hell) Fire will be placed in full view of the erring. And it will be said to them: "Where are those (the false gods whom you used to set up as rivals with Allah) that you used to worship instead of Allah? Can they help you or (even) help themselves?" Then they will be thrown on their faces into the (Fire), They and the Ghawun (devils, and those who were in error). And the whole hosts of Iblis together. They will say while contending therein. By Allah, we were truly in a manifest error." (26:90 to 97)

Follow as to how Allah [سبحانه وتعالى] answered all his prayers, except one:

His Lord accepted all his prayers.

• Allah [ٱلْمُجِيبُ] was provided him with the religious knowledge,

• Allahuthala granted Prophet hood to him; to his sons and to his offspring,

• Ummath of Prophet Mohammad ﷺ in their Salah, refer honorably to his name,

• Just as we were born naked, we will be resurrected naked and Allah [SWT] will adorn Ibrahim first, on the Day of Resurrection,

- And placed him in the Paradise, located at the seventh heaven, near Him (Allah ﷻ is over and above the seventh heaven)
- Allah ﷻ has treated him as His Best friend (Khaleel).

But his Lord never accepted his prayer about his father, because his father was an idol worshipper.

الحمدلله

بِسْمِ ٱللَّهِ ٱلرَّحْمَٰنِ ٱلرَّحِيمِ

9. Persons other than prophets mentioned in Quran

1. "Then they found one of Our slaves, unto whom We had bestowed mercy from Us, and whom We had taught knowledge from Us." (Surah Al Kahaf, 18:65) Who is the slave mentioned by Allah?

Answer: Khidr (AS)

Ubayy bin Ka'b referred to the narration of the Messenger of Allah ﷺ, "Musa (AS) got up to deliver a speech before the Children of Israel and he was asked, 'Who is the most learned person among the people?' Musa (AS) replied, 'I am'. Allah ﷻ rebuked him as he failed to attribute the knowledge to Allah [SWT]. So Allahuthala revealed the following to him: 'At the junction of the two seas there is a servant of Ours who is more learned than you.' Musa (AS) asked, 'O my Lord! How can I meet him?' Allah Subhanahuthala said, 'Take a fish and put it in a vessel and then set out, and where you lose the fish, you will find him.'

Musa (AS) travelled a long distance as directed:

Thereupon, Musa (AS) carried a fish in a vessel and set out, along with his boy-servant Yusha bin Nun. Allahuthala narrated this incident in Quran as: "Musa (AS) said to his boy-servant: 'I will not give up (travelling) until I reach the junction of the two seas or (until) I spend years and years in travelling.' (18:60). But when they reached the junction of the two seas, they forgot their fish, and it took its way through the sea as in a tunnel. So when they had passed further on (beyond that fixed place), Musa (AS) said to his boy-servant: 'Bring us our morning meal; truly, we have suffered much fatigue in our journey.' He said: 'Do you remember when we betook ourselves to the rock? I indeed forgot the fish, none but Shaitan made me forget it. It took its course into the sea in a strange (way)!' [Musa (AS)] said: 'That is what we have been seeking.' So they went back retracing their footsteps." (18:61 to 64). Hence they travelled back a long distance, until they reached the tunnel made by the fish.

There, they found a man called Khidr (AS):

In surah Kahaf Allah [SWT] says, "Then they found one of Our slaves, unto whom We had bestowed mercy from Us, and whom We had taught knowledge from Us." (18:65). Musa (AS) greeted him and introduced himself as, "I am Musa." He said, "Are you the Musa of the Children of Israel?" Musa (AS) said, "Yes".

Musa (AS) enquired with Khidr (AS) "May I follow you so that you teach me something of that knowledge (guidance and true path) which you have been taught (by Allahuthala)?" Khidr (AS) said: "Verily! You will not be able to have patience with me! And how can you have patience about a thing which you know not?"

Musa (AS) responded: "If Allah [عَزَّ وَ جَلَّ] wills, you will find me patient, and I will not disobey you in aught." Khidr (AS) said: "Then, if you follow me, ask me not about anything till I myself mention it to you." (18:66 to 70).

The knowledge learnt from Khidr (AS):

As they were proceeding Kidhar (AS) performed three acts which apparently looked not so good and merciful. In the first case, he holed the boat and damaged it. Musa (AS) had forgotten his promise and asked "Why did he do like that?" Then they saw a bird, sitting on the edge of the boat, dipping its beak in the sea. Al-Khidr made a comment over it, "My knowledge and your knowledge, in comparison to {The All-Knowing ٱلۡعَلِيمُ} Allah's knowledge, is like what this bird has taken out of the sea."

Then he killed a boy on the way and built a wall in a city whose people had denied food for them. When Musa (AS) asked him, "Why cannot you ask them to dine?" He said: "This is the parting between me and you, I will tell you the interpretation of (those) things over which you were unable to hold patience." (18:78). So he explained the reason for his deeds and told that he did it not of his own accord (18:82) but in accordance with the Almighty Allah's Command.

Khidr (AS) with Allahuthala's Mercy and Knowledge; is considered as mysterious and supernatural Nabi. He has not been mentioned in Quran by his name; even though there are more than twenty verses about his deeds. By Allah's command he can help those who are in trouble, while travelling.

The details about Khidr (AS):

- He is not an angel.
- He is still alive, as young adult with a long white beard.

- Since he drank water from Ayanul Hayath (Fountain of life), he is bestowed with long life.

- His job is to guide others or help those in distress, with Allah's [الْهَادِي - the Guide] command.

- He had been meeting Iliyas (AS) at Jerusalam, at every Ramzan.

- He also had been in touch with Dhulkarnine.

- He is capable of appearing at any time or for all times, anywhere or everywhere.

- Some say he is the grandchild of Adam (AS) or son of a King. [الله اعلم !]

Aahadhees about him:

★ "He was called Al-Khidr (AS), because he sat on a barren land and it turned green (Khadra) beneath him." [Imam Ahmad]

★ Al-Khiḍr's appearance at Prophet's Muhammad ﷺ funeral is related as follows: "A powerful looking, fine-featured, handsome man with a white beard came leaping over the backs of the people till he reached where the sacred body lay. Weeping bitterly, he turned toward the companions and paid his condolences. Abu Bakr (RA) and Ali (RA) said that he was Khiḍr (AS)." (Ibn al-Jazari 1994, p. 228.)

★ The Dajjal will kill a person once and then bring him back to life, then he will ask him, 'Do you believe that I am God?' That person will reply, 'No! I am convinced that you are the Dajjal of which the Prophet Mohammad ﷺ informed us.' Dajjal will throw him in his fire, which in reality will be Paradise. The narrator of this hadith is Abu Ishaq who said: 'It is commonly known that this person would be Khidr (AS)" [As told by Abu Sa'id al-Khudri].

الحمدلله

2. The third surah in the Quran is named as A'la-Imran. Who is this 'Imran'?

Answer: The father of Bibi Marium.

The following ayaath provides the clue with regard to Imran being the father of Bibi Marium:

"When the wife of Imran said: "O my Lord! I have vowed to you what is in my womb to be dedicated for your services, so accept this from me. Verily, you are the All-

Hearer, the All knower." (3:35). Then when she gave birth to her (child Marium), she said: "O my Lord! I have given birth to a female child" - and Allah knew better what she brought forth, - "And the male is not like the female and I have named her Marium, and I seek refuge with you for her and for her offspring from Shaitan, the outcast" (3:36).

{Follow the manner in which she prayed for her daughter and grandson! Even though Bibi Marium underwent a big trial, there is no claim or proof that the Shaitan approached her and her son, like he [Shaithan] causing hindrance to Ibrahim (AS) or Musa (AS) or Yusuf (AS) or Ayyub (AS)}.

"And Marium, the daughter of 'Imran who guarded her chastity; and We breathed into through Our Ruh [i.e. Jibreel (AS)], and she testified to the truth of the Words of her Lord [i.e. believed in the Words of Allah] "Be!" and he was; that is Isa (AS) - son of Bibi Marium; as a Messenger of Allah] and (also believed in) His Scriptures and she was of the 'Qanitin' (i.e. obedient to Allah)." (At-Tahrim, 66:12). Allah has selected Bibi Marium to show His Creative Power and mentioned her in Quran as "الْقَانِتِينَ" (Qanitin) and witnessed her as the best example among the believing women.

Allah refers in Al Quran that He has selected the family of Imran above the Alamin:

"Allah chose Adam (AS), Nuh (AS), the family of Ibrahim (AS) and the family of Imran above the Alamin." (3:33).

Another opinion:

Some claim that "Imran" is the name of the father of Musa (AS) and Harun (AS). They support this view from Quran and hadhees. Quran records that the people lived at the time of Bibi Marium calling her as "Sister of Harun!" (19:28).

Evidence from hadhees: "The Prophet ﷺ asked his Lord Allah, "Who is this?" He said, "This is your brother Musa, son of `Imran (موسى بن عمران), and those who followed him among the Children of Israel." I said, "O Lord! Where is my Ummah" Allah said, "Look to your right on the hill," and I looked and saw faces of men. Allah enquired, "Are you pleased?" and I stated, "I am pleased O Lord!" Allah proclaimed, "Look to the horizon to your left" and I saw faces of men. He again enquired, "Are you pleased?" and I said, "I am pleased, O Lord!" He said, "And with them are seventy-thousand who will enter Paradise without reckoning." Allah knows best! [الله اعلم !]

الحمدلله

3. "Say: Tell me! If this (Quran) is from Allah, and you deny it, and a witness from among the Children of Israel testifies that this Quran is from Allah so he believed while you are too proud." (46:10) Who is that witness from among the Children of Israel?

Answer: "A witness from among the Children of Israel" is Abdullah bin Salam (RA).

Al-Husayn ibn Salam was a Rabbi of Madhina. He was born in Jewish tribe of Banu Qaynuqa. He was rich and much respected because of his knowledge in Taurath. He led a disciplined life, by reading, preaching Taurath and working in his date palm garden.

He referred that "When I heard of the appearance of the Messenger of Allah ﷺ, I began to make enquiries about his name, his genealogy, his characteristics, his time and place and I began to compare this information with what is contained in our books. From these enquiries, I became convinced about the authenticity of his prophet hood and I affirmed the truth of his mission. However, I concealed my conclusions from the Jews. I held my tongue..." He was very eager to meet him.

When 'Al-Husayn bin Salam (RA) heard the arrival of the Prophet ﷺ at Madhina, he was working on the top of the palm tree at his orchard. His aunt named, Khalidah bint Al-Harith, was sitting under the tree. On hearing the news, he exclaimed loudly: "Allahu Akbar! Allahu Akbar!"

His aunt was surprised and said, "By God, if you had heard that Moses was coming, you would not have been so excited." He replied, "By God he is really, the 'brother' of Moses and follows his religion. He was sent with the same mission as Moses."

He rushed to meet the Prophet ﷺ and after reaching his assembly, found him as the man of traits defined in their text. He was overwhelmed with joy. It was narrated that 'Abdullah bin Salam (RA) said: "When the Messenger of Allah ﷺ came to Al-Madinah, the people rushed towards him and it was asserted that: 'The Messenger of Allah ﷺ has come!' I came along with the people to see him, and when I looked at the face of the Messenger of Allah ﷺ, I realized that his face was not the face of a liar.

The first message the Prophet ﷺ conveyed at Madhina was: "O people! Spread (the greeting of) Salam, offer food to people and pray at night when people are sleeping, you will enter Paradise in peace." As he stood by the Prophet ﷺ, he converted to Islam by reciting Shahadha. Prophet Muhammad ﷺ gave recognition to Al-Husayn by deliberately turning towards him and enquired his name. The Prophet ﷺ conveyed to him that he will be called thereafter as Abdullah ibn Salam (RA). Because 'Husayn means' "Horse foal".

In Sahih Bhukhari, vol. 4, hadhees number 546, it is recorded that Anas (RA) narrated about him: " Abdullah ibn Salam (RA) came to the Prophet ﷺ and exclaimed, "I am going to ask you about three things, which nobody knows except a prophet".

1. What is the first portent of the Hour?

2. What will be the first meal taken by the people of Paradise?

3. Why does a boy child resemble his father and why does he resemble his maternal uncle?"

Allah's Messenger ﷺ responded, "Jibreel (AS) has just now told me of their answers." Abdullah ibn Salam (RA) said, "He, from amongst all angels, is the enemy of the Jews."

Allah's Apostle ﷺ replied as,

1. The first portent of the Hour will be a fire that will bring together the people from the east to the west;

2. The first meal of the people of Paradise will be Extra-lobe (caudate lobe) of fish-liver.

3. As for the resemblance of the child to its parents: If a man has sexual intercourse with his wife and gets discharge first, the child will resemble the father, and if the woman gets discharge first, the child will resemble her." On that 'Abdullah bin Salam (RA) said, "I testify that you are the Apostle of Allah ﷺ."

He went home and introduced Islam to his family, including his aunt, Khalidah. They all willingly accepted their new faith and agreed to be cautious around the other Jews who might not be accepting the new religion.

Abdullah bin Salam (RA) further said, "O Allah's Apostle ﷺ! The Jews are liars and if they should come to know about my conversion to Islam before you ask them (about me), they would tell a lie about me."

The Jews came to Allah's Apostle ﷺ then Abdullah bin Salam (RA) went inside the house. Allah's Apostle ﷺ asked the Jews, "What kind of man is Abdullah bin Salam amongst you?" They replied, "He is the most learned person amongst us, and the best amongst us, and the son of the best amongst us." Allah's Apostle ﷺ said, "What do you think if he embraces Islam (will you do as he does)?" The Jews said, "May Allah save him from it." Then Abdullah bin Salam (RA) came out in front of them saying, "I testify that none has the right to be worshipped but Allah; and that Muhammad ﷺ is the Apostle of Allah." There upon they said, He is the evilest among us, and the son of the evilest amongst us and continued talking badly of him."

That is why Allah said in this ayath to the Jews,".......he (Abdullah bin Salam) believed while you are (other Jews) too proud (to believe)." (46:10).

Once, when the Messenger of Allah ﷺ enquired the Jews about the verses of stoning as a punishment for adultery, they concealed those verses from Taurath. But Abdullah bin Salam revealed in person, to the Prophet ﷺ, the lies of those Jews.

When the rebels were plotting the assassination of Uthman (RA) Abdullah bin Salam (RA) arrived to at the door where he stood and required the rebels, not to kill Uthman (RA) by saying: "O People! Do not draw the sword of God up your heads. By God! If you draw the sword you will never find an opportunity to put it back into its sheath; conflict and discord among the Muslims shall never end. Pay heed! Today, the government [punishes criminals] by the whip but if you kill this man, then the State will not be able to maintain order without the sword. Keep in mind that the angels are the guardians of Madhina at this time; if you kill him, the angels will desert Madhina." But the rebels never heeded his advice. Instead they rebuked him.

Abdullah ibn Salaam (RA) was known among the Sahabah as a man from "Ahl-al-Jannah"- (the people of Paradise). This was because of his determination on the advice of the Prophet ﷺ to hold steadfastly to the "most trust-worthy handhold" that is belief in and total submission to Allah.

Zayd bin Umayra narrates: "When Muadh was in his deathbed, he is asked, 'O Abu Abdur-Rahman! Will you give us advice?' They make Muadh sit up upon his request. He says, 'Ilm and belief are in their places. Learn ilm from four people: Abu-Darda (RA), Salman al-Farisi (RA), Abdullah bin Masud (RA) and Abdullah bin Salam (RA). For, I heard the Messenger of Allah ﷺ say, "Abdullah bin Salam (RA) is the tenth person of the ten people in Paradise."

Abdullah ibn Salam (RA) participated in the conquest of Syria and Palestine and visited Jabia with Caliph Umar (RA). He died in 43 AH, in Madhina.

الحمدلله

4. "It is only a human being who teaches him (Muhammad ﷺ). The tongue of the man is foreign, while the Quran is a clear Arabic tongue." (16:103). To which person, this ayath refers to?

Answer: Jabar/Yasar.

During the pre-islamic era:

Arabs were not very wealthy. They earned through trading. Their long journeys through deserts brought them closer to the nature. They were specific and meticulous in communicating finer thoughts in the finest form. Poetry was their passion. They competed each other in fluency and eloquence. Their literature was elegant, of high quality, exaggerated and boastful; but not in written form; passed through several generations, orally. They maintained prolific memory of thousands of quotes, anecdotes and poems. They were proud of their oratory, diction, eloquence and considered themselves to be the masters of their language. They treated the non-Arabs as 'Ajums', persons with speech impediment.

Specialties of Quran:

The Arabs, when they heard the Quran through an unlettered (Ummi Nabi) Prophet ﷺ, they were awe-struck, amazed, mesmerized and stunned. They were captivated with its style, eloquence, nobility, its sublime, solemn nature, its perfect grammar, concise, accurate use of words, its charm, poetic beauty and rhythmical prose. They realized its convincing power which created deeper impression on its listener, its accuracy and precision, with a standing testimony of truth and the plain facts expressed with clear parables without any exaggeration. This is true with earlier Mekkan surahs. Many were humbled and subdued by the words of the Quran and embraced Islam, immediately on listening it.

Even enemies of Muslims like Abu Jahal, Abu Sufyan and Al-Akhnas secretly listened to Prophet's ﷺ recitation of Quran during his night prayers at his house. Al- Walid ibn al-Mughirah, after hearing the Prophet's ﷺ recitation of Quran, said: "I have just heard Muhammad's ﷺ words, which for sure are neither a human's nor a jinn's. They are euphonious and relaxing, like a tree full of reachable fruits. They are of the highest quality and cannot be out-perfected."

Muhammad M. Pickthall, an English Muslim translator of Quran, describes as: "........ the Glorious Quran, that inimitable symphony, the very sounds of which move men to tears and ecstasy."

Even though their inner instincts made them realize that it is not written by any human but it was a divine diction. Their arrogance, leadership and pride made them blind. They called the Prophet ﷺ a sorcerer, forger, liar, madman, magician and the one who separates the members from their families. Even though they called him earlier as Al-Ameen, they were doubting about his message.

The disbelievers of Makkah insulted the Prophet ﷺ by alleging that his teachings were taught by a human. The Prophet ﷺ used to spend some of his time with the said 'human being'. So they claimed that from him, the Prophet ﷺ derived information. Knowingly they spread false statements claiming that it was an 'atypical book of linguistic excellence'.

Opinions about the person, who was suspected to be the informant of Quran, to Muhammad ﷺ:

Tanwîr al-Miqbas min Tafsir of ibn Abbas said: 'Jabr and Yasar teacheth him the Quran'.

Jalal-Al-Jalalayn said: 'They were Christian blacksmiths whom the Prophet ﷺ used to frequent.'

Maududi - Sayyid Abul Ala Maududi - Tafhim al-Qur'an claimed in this connection: "...traditions mention the names of several persons, one of whom was Jabar, the servant of some of the clans of Quraish and who used to sell goods by As-Safa."

"Abd Allah ibn Muslim narrated that 'We owned two Christian youths from the people of Ayn Tamr, one called Yasar and the other Jabar. Their trade was making swords but they also could read the Scriptures in their own tongue. The Messenger of Allah ﷺ used to pass by them and listen to their reading.' As a result, the idolaters used to say: He is being taught by them!"

Allah ﷻ answers such disbelievers in Quran, "But the man they refer, speaks a foreign language, where-as this 'Quran-e-Masjeedh' is in eloquent Arabic." He further asserts, "Surely those who do not believe in Allah's revelations will never be guided by Allah and they will suffer a painful punishment." (16:104). "No one fabricates lies except those who disbelieve in Allah's revelations, and it is they who are the 'true' liars." (16:105).

Such disbelievers will be condemned by Allah ﷻ and suffer a tremendous punishment. This is because they prefer the life of this world over the Hereafter.

Surely Allah never guides those who 'choose to' disbelieve. They are the ones whose hearts, ears, and eyes are sealed by Allah, and it is they who are 'truly' heed-less. (16:107 and 108).

Allahuthala assures that Quran-e-Pak is a clear message of a noble Messenger ﷺ:

"We did not give Prophet Muhammad ﷺ, knowledge of poetry" (36: 69). "And it is not the word of a poet......Nor the word of a soothsayer.... [It is] a revelation from the Lord of the worlds." (69: 40-43) "…And indeed it is a Book of exalted power. No falsehood can approach it from before or behind it: It is sent down by One, Full of Wisdom, Worthy of all Praise." (41:41-42).

To such disbelievers Allah [SWT] has challenges to:

Bring a book similar to Quran:

"Say: If the whole of mankind and Jinns were to gather together to produce the like of this Quran, they could not produce the like thereof, even if they backed up each other with help and support" (17: 88).

Bring something identical:

Or do they say, 'He fabricated the Message?' Nay, they have no faith! Let them then produce a recital like unto it - If it be they speak the Truth" (Al-Tur, 52:33).

Bring ten such surahs:

"Or they say, He (Prophet Muhammad ﷺ) forged it (the Quran). Say: Bring you then ten forged Surah (chapters) like unto it, and call whomsoever you can, other than Allah (to your help), if you speak the truth!" (11: 13);

Atleast bring One surah:

"Or do they say: He (Prophet Muhammad ﷺ) has forged it? Say: Bring then a Surah (chapter) like unto it, and call upon whomso ever you can besides Allah, if you are truthful!" (10: 38).

Allah [عَزَّ وَجَلَّ] also says in the Quran-al-Kithab that no one will be able to meet the above - mentioned challenge: "And if you are in doubt about what We have sent down upon Our Servant (Prophet Muhammad ﷺ), then produce a surah the like thereof and call upon your witnesses other than Allah, if you should be truthful. But if you do not - and you will never be able to - then fear the Fire, whose fuel is men and stones, prepared for the disbelievers" (2: 23-24)

They will never be able to do it:

And the fact is that no one could respond to it either at that time or ever since.

Allah [سبحانه وتعالى] swears:

"By the star when it vanishes" and assures to the Quraish, "Your companion (Muhammad ﷺ) has neither gone astray nor has erred. Nor does he speak of (his own) desire. It is only an Inspiration that is inspired. He has been taught (this Quran) by one mighty in power [Jibreel (AS)]." (53:1 - 5)

الحمدلله

5. "It was said to him: 'Enter Paradise.' He said 'Would that my people knew! That my Lord (Allah) has forgiven me, and made me of the honoured ones!" (Yasin, 36:25 and 26). Clarify as to who is "He".

Answer: A man called Habib an-Najjar, a single believer of three Messengers, in a town of idol worshippers

The object of this ayath is to warn the stubborn Quraish, denying the truth about our Prophet ﷺ. Allah [SWT] provides the example of the people of a town, who were punished for disobeying their Messengers.

The episode of a single believer:

It proceeds as: "When Allah Subhanahuthala sent to these idol worshippers (36:13) two Messengers, they belied them both. So Allah strengthened them with a third, and they said: "Verily! We have been sent to you as Messengers." (36:14).

"The people of the town asserted: "You are only human beings like ourselves and Allah has revealed nothing, you are only telling lies." (36:15). The Messengers responded: "Our Lord knows that we have been sent as Messengers to you. And our duty is only to convey the Message" (36:16 and 17).

"The people warned: "For us, we see an evil omen from you, if you cease not, we will surely stone you and a painful torment will touch you from us." (36:18). The Messengers held out: "Your evil omens be with you, because you are admonished? Nay, but you are a people transgressing all the limits." (36:19).

"From the farthest part of the town, a man came running and saying: "O my people! Obey the Messengers; obey those who ask no wages from of you and who are rightly guided." (36:20 and 21). "And why should I not worship Allah Alone, 'Who' has created me and to Whom we shall be returned." (36:22).

"Shall I take besides Him gods, if the Most Beneficent Allah intends me any harm, those god's intercession will be of no use for me whatsoever, nor can they save me." "Then verily, I should be in plain error." (36:23 and 24).

"Then the disbelievers killed him by striking him very badly. It was said to him: 'Enter Paradise.' He said: 'Would that my people knew! That my Lord Allah has forgiven me, and made me of the honoured ones!" (36: 25 to 27).

"And Allah sent not against this people after his death no angels from heaven, nor do 'We' send (such a thing)." (36:28). It was but one shout. Lo! They were all silenced, dead and destroyed.

This episode provides following lessons:

☆ Inspite of sending three Messengers, those people stood stubbern in idol worshipping, in denying as well as warning of stoning, if they continue their preaching.

☆ Those three Messengers could influence only a single man; that too from the outskirts of the town.

☆ Habib an-Najjar was knowledgable and God fearing, who came running to warn the punishment that will decend on them shortly.

☆ He was courageous enough to declare his faith; even though he was aware that his life was in immenant danger.

☆ Even after he became a Shaheed, he expressed concern for his people. He desired that his people could become aware of his supreme success!

☆ Allahuthala was impressed by this single believer than the three messengers.

☆ Almighty honoured him in his Hereafter!

☆ "Those who were killed for Allah ﷻ's sake are not dead. No! They are alive. But you do not perceive it." (2:154).

☆ "Allah ﷻ will never destroy a community without sending messengers nor destroy its inhabitants unless they are evil" (28:59).

الحمدلله

6. "And let not those among you who are blessed with graces and wealth swear not to give (any sort of help) to their kinsmen, Al-Masakin (the poor), and those who left their homes for Allah's Cause. Let them pardon and forgive. Do you not love that Allah should forgive you? And Allah is Oft-Forgiving, Most Merciful." (An-Noor, 24:22). To which of the companion of Prophet ﷺ, this ayath indirectly points out?

Answer: This ayath refers to Abu Bakr Siddiq (RA). It was revealed along with verses that proved the innocence of his daughter, the Mother of believers, who was the beloved wife of Prophet ﷺ, Ayesha (RA).

After returning from the battle of Bani al-Mustaliq the leader of the hypocrites, Abdullah bin Ubayy bin Salul, fabricated a false story against Ayesha (RA) and spread it to others. It was the subject of every gathering, the matter of discussion in every household in Madhina.

Some Muslims also took part in the spreading of this false story. Among them is Mistah bin Uthatha (RA), the son of the paternal aunt of Abu Bakr (RA). He was very poor, Muhazir (migrant from Makkah), being supported by Abu Bakr (RA) regularly with money. Mistah's role in spreading the slander, added more weight to it.

Though most of the sincere Muslims were confident of the innocence of Ayesha (RA), they maintained silence. The Prophet ﷺ was also quiet, waiting for Allah [SWT]'s indication. This rumour remained unchanged, for almost a month, until Allahuthala revealed the verses from 11 to 21, of Surae An-Noor.

In view of Mistah's behavior, Abu Bakr (RA) took an oath that he will never spend on Mistah again. Then Allah [عَزَّ وَ جَلَّ] revealed the ayath 24:22.

Abu Bakr (RA), despite his anguish coupled with hurt feelings, immediately responded by exclaiming, "By Allah, I would love it that Allah forgives me!" He promptly adopted his previous habit and sweared that he will never cease spending on Mistah (RA). This approves his title "As Siddiq".

As narrated by Abdullah bin Amr: Abu Bakr As-Siddiq said to the Prophet ﷺ "O Allah's Messenger ﷺ! Teach me an invocation with which I may invoke Allah in my prayers." The Prophet ﷺ said, "Say: O Allah! I have wronged my soul very much (oppressed myself), and none forgives the sins but You; so please bestow Your Forgiveness upon me. No doubt, 'You' are the Oft-Forgiving, Most Merciful."

[اللَّهُمَّ إِنِّي ظَلَمْتُ نَفْسِي ظُلْمًا كَثِيرًا، وَلاَ يَغْفِرُ الذُّنُوبَ إِلاَّ أَنْتَ، فَاغْفِرْ لِي مِنْ عِنْدِكَ مَغْفِرَةً، إِنَّكَ أَنْتَ الْغَفُورُ الرَّحِيمُ]

Source: Sahih al-Bukhari 7387, Sahih Muslim 2705.

This was the mercy and forgiveness that 'Al-Furqan' [Al-Quran] teaches us. This is the type of the mercy and ties of kinship that Allahuthala is pleased to see in His servants.

الحمدلله

7. On hearing which surah, recited in his sister's house, made Umar bin Kathab to embrace islam?

Answer: Surah Thaha.

Umar bin Khattab (RA) once speaking about his experience of embracing Islam conveyed, how Islam entered first in his heart.

While visiting the Haram, Umar (RA) saw the Prophet ﷺ praying. Prophet ﷺ was reciting the Surah Haqqah (the Reality) in his Salath. Hearing those verses, he thought, "By Allah, this is poetry as the Quraish have said." During that time the Prophet ﷺ continued: "That this is verily the word of an honoured Messenger. It is not the word of a poet, little is that you believe!" (69:40-41). Surprised on hearing those verses, Umar (RA) thought, "He must be a soothsayer." The Prophet ﷺ recited the next verses: "Nor is it the word of a soothsayer, little is that you remember! This is the Revelation sent down from the Lord of the Alamin" (69: 42-43). His heart was slightly inclined towards Islam.

Umar (RA), was a man of determination. His hatred towards the new religion was very strong. He just decided to kill the Messenger of Allah ﷺ. On his way he met Naim ibn Abdullah (RA), who saw him in fury and enquired Umar (RA) as to where was he going? Umar (RA) replied, "Muhammad (ﷺ) has forsaken our religion, shattered the unity of the Quraish; ridiculed them and vilified their gods. Today I will settle the matter once and for all by slaying him."

Naim informed Umar (RA) that his sister Fathima (RA) and her husband had embraced Islam. He advised him to put his own house in order, before thinking of killing the Prophet ﷺ. On hearing about this, Umar (RA) became more furious. He changed his direction and rushed to his sister's house. When he came near her house, he heard Khabbab (RA) was reciting the Surah Tha Ha (20th Chapter of the Quran); to the couple.

On hearing the foot-steps of Umar (RA), Khabbab (RA) hid himself inside a small room; whereas Fatima instantly concealed the manuscript. On entering the house, he demanded, "What was this non-sense murmur that I heard?' "Nothing," both answered, but "What have you heard?" "Yes! I accidentally discovered," continued Umar (RA) angrily. "I know that both of you have joined the path of Muhammad (ﷺ)." With these words, Umar threw himself upon his brother-in-law. Fatima rushed in to save her husband but Umar struck her hard and wounded her. Both husband and wife boldly and openly asserted: "Yes! We are Muslims; we believed in Allah and His Prophet ﷺ. Do whatever you will."

Upon seeing blood of her sister from the wound, he felt guilty. He apologized to them and requested to show the words of the Quran which they were reciting. First she hesitated and on seeing the change in his tone, she said "You are unclean. I cannot allow you to touch the words of Allah. So wash and come." After washing, Umar (RA) read the first few verses of Surah Thaha; "Verily! I am Allah! La ilaha illa (none has the right to be worshipped but I), so worship Me, and perform As-Salath (Iqamat-as-Salat) for My Remembrance." (20:14). Islam started entering his heart! He told in amazement, "How noble and sublime is this speech!"

Thereupon Khabbab (RA) came out of his hiding and exclaimed, "O Umar (RA), by God, I hope that Allahuthala would bless you with His Prophet's ﷺ call; for I heard him just last night imploring earnestly; "O Allah, strengthen Islam by either Abu Jahl or Umar Ibn al-Khattab. Now, Umar (RA) started fearing Allah." Umar (RA) asked Khabbab (RA) to lead him to the Prophet ﷺ.

Meanwhile Naim ibn Abdullah went straight to the Prophet ﷺ and warned him and his companions about Umar's earlier intention.

When Umar (RA) knocked at the door indicated by Khabbab (RA), one of the companions viewed through a chink in the door, to be sure of the person. Seeing Umar (RA) with his sword on, he hurried back to report Prophet ﷺ, "Umar bin Khattab is here armed with his sword." Hamza (RA) intervened to say, "Let him in. If he comes with a peaceful intent, then it is alright, but if not, therewith we will kill him with his own sword." The Prophet ﷺ, ordered his companions to hide.

As Umar (RA) entered the door, the Prophet ﷺ went forth to meet him. He seized Umar (RA)'s cloak, pulling it rather firmly enquired, "What for have you come, O son of Khattab? By Allah, I see that some calamity is to befall you before you have the final summons."

But Umar (RA) replied submissively, "O Messenger of Allah ﷺ, I have come to attest my faith in Allah and His Prophet ﷺ and what he has brought from Allah Subhanahuthala." The Prophet ﷺ raised the cry of 'Allahu-Akbar' so loudly that all the companions present in the house came to know that Umar (RA), had just accepted Islam (Ibn Hisham, Vol. I, pp. 342-46). The Muslims who were hiding began yelling "الله أكبر" [Allah is Great].

Umar (RA) proclaimed his faith publicly in front of Kabah. His conversion was a turning point to Muslims. This convertion made such a stir among Quraish, including his uncle Abu Jahl. They did not dare put up a clash with Umar (RA), even though they attempted at it. After his conversion the Muslims prayed openly in front of Haram Sherief! He really strengthened Islam!

الحمدلله

8. "O Prophet! Say to the captives that are in your hands: 'If Allah knows any good in your hearts, He will give you something better than what has been taken from you, and He will forgive you', and Allah is Oft-Forgiving, Most Merciful." (8:70). To whom it refers to?

Answer: Abbas bin Abdul Muthalib (RA)

Abbas bin Abdul Muthalib (RA) was the uncle of our Prophet ﷺ. He was about two and a half years elder than him. He loved his nephew very much. While building Kabah, Muhammad (ﷺ), as a boy carried the stones on his shoulders along with other boys. On carrying the stones for several times, his shoulder was bruised. Watching that, his uncle Abbas (RA) took off his own loin-cloth put it on the shoulder of his nephew, as a pad.

During one Hajj season in the valley of Mina, the Prophet ﷺ secretly met seventy men from Madhina who requested him to migrate to Madhina. Abbas (RA) was also present at that secret meeting and enquired: "You know that Muhammad ﷺ is highly respected and revered in our family. We have always protected him against the enemies. Now he wants to accompany you. If you can stand by his side till death, I do not object; otherwise you should not take the risk?" They assured their sincere and wholesome support. Abbas (RA) was satisfied. Muhammad ﷺ made hijrath to Madhina after few days, but Abbas (RA) stayed in Makkah.

Before the battle of Badr, while assembing the army at Makkah, Quraish declared: "Whoever does not come with us, his house will be destroyed." Abbas bin Abdul Muttalib, Naufal the son of Harith bin Abdul Muttalib and Aqeel bin Abu Talib, were forced to join the army.

The Prophet ﷺ knew fully well the position of these Quraish and had issued instructions to his companions as: "I have come to know that some people from Bani Hashim and others were forced to accompany the pagans, although they had no desire to fight us. Therefore, whoever meets any of Bani Hashim, do not kill them. Whoever meets Abu Al-Bukhtari bin Hisham, Abbas bin Abdul Muttalib, let they not be killed, for they were forced to come with the pagan army"

While fighting against Muslims, Abbas (RA), a huge man, was captured by Abul Yasar Ansari, who was small and brought him to the Prophet ﷺ. Abbas (RA) asserted that; "He has not captured me, my nephew Ali (RA) has taken me as a prisoner."

According to another report, it is narrated from Abu Yaseer that he says: "I saw Abbas and Aqeel being taken as prisoners by a man on a piebald horse and he brought and handed them to Ali ibn Abi Talib (RA) saying: "Take your uncle and brother, because you are more deserving of them."

The Holy Prophet ﷺ said: "My uncle is right, it was a huge angel who had come in the form of Ali (RA) and all the angels that our Almighty Allah has sent to help me, were sent in the form of Ali (RA) so that his awe may increase in the hearts of the enemies." and added: "He was Jibreel (AS)."

Ibn Abbas said, "On the eve after Badr, the Prophet ﷺ spent the first part of the night awake, while the prisoners were bound. His companions said to him, "O Allah's Messenger ﷺ! Why do you not sleep" He said to them, "I heard the cries of pain from my uncle Al-Abbas (RA), because of his shackles, so untie him." When his uncle stopped crying from pain, the Prophet ﷺ went to sleep.

After the battle, the Muslims returned to Madhina. Some seventy prisoners were taken as captives and are noted to have been treated in a fair manner. Most of the prisoners were released upon payment of ransom and those who were literate were released on the condition that they teach ten persons how to read and write which teaching was to count as their ransom.

Some men from Al-Ansar requested the Prophet ﷺ, "O Allah's Messenger ﷺ! Give us permission and we will set free our maternal cousin Al-Abbas without taking ransom from him." He said, "No, by Allah! Do not leave any Dirham of it."

Al-Abbas claimed, 'O Allah's Messenger ﷺ! I became a Muslim before.' Allah's Messenger ﷺ said, "Allah knows if you are Muslim! If what you are claiming is true, then Allah will compensate you. As for your outward appearance, it was against us. Therefore, ransom yourself, as well as, your nephews Naufal bin Al-Harith and Aqeel bin Abu Talib, and also your ally Utbah bin Amr, from Bani Al-Harith bin Fihr."

Abbas (RA) replied, 'I do not have that much (money), O Allah's Messenger ﷺ!' The Messenger ﷺ demanded to know, "What about the wealth that you and your wife Umm Al-Fadl buried, and you said to her, `If I am killed in this battle, then this money that I buried is for my children Al-Fadl, Abdullah and Quthm."

Al-Abbas said, 'By Allah, O Allah's Messenger ﷺ! I know that you are Allah's Messenger ﷺ, for this is a thing that none except Umm Al-Fadl and I knew. However, O Prophet ﷺ! Could you count towards my ransom the twenty Uwqiyah that you took from me (in the battle)' The Prophet ﷺ said, "No, for that was the money that Allah made as war spoils for us from you".

So Al-Abbas (RA) ransomed himself, his two nephews and an ally, and Allah revealed the verse 8:70. Abbas (RA) commented, "After I became Muslim, Allah gave me twenty servants in place of the twenty Uwqiyah I lost. And I hope for Allah's forgiveness."

Sharing the sorrows and joys of the Prophet ﷺ, Abbas (RA) not exposing of his conversion while staying in Makkah, conveyed important news to the Prophet ﷺ at Madhina. He helped many poor Muslims to migrate to Madhina.

Whenever Abbas (RA) thought of migrating to Madhina, the Prophet ﷺ prevented him and expressed that: "It is better, if you stay in Makkah. Just as I am the last of the line of Prophets, you shall be the last person to migrate from Makkah"

Shortly before the conquest of Makkah, he was granted the permission to migrate to Madhina. So he took his wife and children with him and reached Al Madhina. A wave of joy and happiness spread among Muslims, on his publicly proclaiming that he had embraced Islam.

Abbas (RA)'s faith towards Islam remained firm and strong. To earn the pleasure of Allah he was prepared to do anything, at any risk. He was loyal to Islam with his words, wealth and deeds.

The Prophet ﷺ granted him a piece of land on the south side of the Prophet's ﷺ Mosque. Abbas (RA) built a house on it. Later on he donated that house for the extention of the Mosque of Madhina-e-Munawara.

Even today you can visit and see that place at Madhina.

الحمدلله

9. "Would you kill a man because he asserts that 'My Lord is Allah, and he has come to you with clear signs (proofs) from your Lord? (40:28)". Whose statement is this to whom?

Answer: It was a believing man of Firaun's family, who hid his faith from Firaun.

As-Suddi said, he was a cousin of Firaun, by being a son of his paternal uncle. He was a member of the royal family of Pharaoh. He was one of the high-ranking official, most influential and most powerful person in the court of Pharaoh. When Firaun claimed "Leave me to kill Musa". This man was seized with anger. He defended Musa (AS) in a very wise and effective manner. There is no greater example of Jihadh than his act of speaking a just word before an unjust ruler. This believer of Pharaoh's people, named Hizqil, taught a powerful dawah process. It creates sympathy even if the opponents are as tyrannical as Pharaoh.

First thing he said is not to kill Musa (AS):

[40:28] "A believing man from Pharaoh's people, who was hiding his faith, argued, "Will you kill a man only for saying: 'My Lord is Allah,' [أَتَقْتُلُونَ رَجُلًا أَن يَقُولَ رَبِّيَ اللَّهُ] while he has in fact come to you with clear proofs from your Lord? If he is a liar, it will be to his own loss. But if he is truthful, then you will be afflicted with some of what he is threatening you with. Surely Allah does not guide whoever is a transgressor, a total liar."

[40:29] "O my people! Authority belongs to you today, reigning supreme in the land. But who would help us against the torment of Allah, if it were to befall us?" Pharaoh assured his people, "I am telling you only what I believe, and I am leading you only to the way of guidance."

Follow how Firaun has answered after his Dhawa.

He asked Firaun to fear Allahuthala's punishment on the Last Day, giving examples:

[40:30] And the man who believed cautioned, "O my people! I truly fear for you the doom of earlier enemy forces"

[40:31] "like the fate of the people of Noah, Aad, Thamud, and those after them. For Allah would never will to wrong His servants."

[40:32] "And, O my people! Verily! I fear for you the Day when there will be mutual calling (between the people of Hell and of Paradise)."

[40:33] "A Day when you will turn your backs and flee having no protector from Allah, and whomsoever Allah sends astray, for him there is no guide."

[40:34] "And indeed Yusuf (AS) did come to you, in times gone by, with clear signs, but you ceased not to doubt in that which he did bring to you, till when he died you said: "No Messenger will Allah send after him." Thus Allah leaves astray him who is a Musrif (a polytheist, oppressor, a criminal, sinner who commits great sins) and a Murtab" (one who doubts Allah's Warning and His Oneness).

[40:35] "Those who dispute about the ayath of Allah, without any authority that has come to them, it is greatly hateful and disgusting to Allah and to those who believe. Thus does Allah seal up the heart of every arrogant, tyrant. (So they cannot guide themselves to the Right Path)."

But the arrogant king never accepted his guidance and tried to plan another plot:

[40:36] And Firaun said: "O Haman! Build me a tower that I may arrive at the ways, the ways of the heavens, and I may look upon the *Ilah* (God) of Musa (AS) but verily, I think him to be a liar."

[40:37] "Thus it was made fair-seeming, in Firaun's eyes, the evil of his deeds, and he was hindered from the (Right) Path, and the plot of Firaun led to nothing but loss and destruction (for him)."

Still the true believer tried his best to propagate the truth, to his people:

[40:38] "And the man who believed said: "O my people! Follow me, I will guide you to the way of right conduct.

[40:39] "O my people! Truly, this life of the world is nothing but a (quick passing) enjoyment, and verily, the Hereafter that is the home that will remain forever."

[40:40] "Whosoever does an evil deed, will not be requited except the like thereof, and whosoever does a righteous deed, whether male or female and is a true believer (in the Oneness of Allah), such will enter Paradise, where they will be provided therein (with all things in abundance) without limit. "And O my people! How is it that I call you to salvation while you call me to the Fire!" [40:41]

[40:42] "You invite me to disbelieve in Allah (and in His Oneness), and to join partners in worship with Him; of which I have no knowledge, and I invite you to the All-Mighty, the Oft-Forgiving!"

There on he expressed his belief:

[40:43] "No doubt you call me to (worship) one who cannot grant (me) my request (or respond to my invocation) in this world or in the Hereafter. And our return will be to Allah, and *Al-Musrifun* (i.e. polytheists and arrogants, those who commit great sins, the transgressors of Allah's set limits) They shall be the dwellers of the Fire!

[40:44] "And you will remember what I am telling you, and my affair I leave it to Allah. Verily, Allah is the All-Seer of (His) slaves." So Allah saved him from the evils that they plotted (against him), while an evil torment encompassed Firaun's people. [40:45]

Allah records in Quran how Firaun and his people suffer punishment:

[40:46] The Fire; they [Firaun's people] are exposed to it, morning and afternoon, and on the Day when the Hour will be established (it will be said to the angels): "Cause Firaun's people to enter the severest torment!" And, when they will dispute in the Fire, the weak will say to those who were arrogant, "Verily! We followed you, can you then take from us some portion of the Fire?" [40:47]. Those who were arrogant will say: "We are all (together) in this (Fire)! Verily Allah has judged between (His) slaves!" [40:48]. And those in the Fire will say to the keepers (angels) of Hell: "Call upon your Lord to lighten for us the torment for a day!" [40:49]. They will say: "Did there not come to you, your Messengers with (clear) evidences and signs? They will say: "Yes." They will reply: "Then call (as you like)! And the invocation of the disbelievers is nothing but in error!" [40:50]

الحمدلله

10. Which is the only Companion of the Prophet ﷺ mentioned by name in Quran?

Answer: Zaid ibn Harith (RA).

Quran has referred to many incidences of good deeds as well as the mistakes committed by the Prophet's ﷺ companions. But their names have not been mentioned. In fact, during the revelation of Quran all the companions feared that Allahuthala may reveal their misdeeds and mistakes.

Zaid ibn Harithah (RA), is one of the most beloved companions of the Prophet ﷺ and the only companion to have been mentioned in the Quran by his name (33:37).

The story of Zaid (RA):

Zaid bin Harithah (RA) was an Arab, born to Harithah and Sudah. They were not from Makkah. Once Ziad's mother was travelling to meet her family with her son, on their way, they were attacked by their enemy tribe. They captured the boy and sold in the market of Ukaadh. A nephew of Bibi Khathija (RA) named Hakim ibn Huzaam bought him. While visiting his aunt in Makkah, he gifted this young boy to her.

Zaid (AS) was gifted to the Prophet by Bibi Khadija (RA):

When Bibi Khathija got married to the Prophet ﷺ she gifted Zaid (RA) to him. He treated Zaid (RA) not as a slave but as his own son. He freed him from slavery. Both of them were always together and he exhibited such an affection and he was called as the "beloved (habibi) of the Mohammad ﷺ". He was the first youth to become Muslim, when revelation came to the Prophet ﷺ.

There was a twist in the story of Zaid (RA):

Zaid's father Harithah was searching for his son. During one annual pilgrimage, the people of his tribe recognized Zaid (RA) in Makkah and informed his father about his existence there. Hence, Harithah came to Makkah with his brother. They met Muhammad ﷺ and required him to return his son, for a ransom. Prophet ﷺ told them that that he will consult Zaid (RA) and respond. If Zaid (RA) wished to go along with his father, he will be sent without ransom. However, if he desired to stay with him, then Harithah must allow him to do so. On Zaid (RA) being called for he recognized his father and his uncle. But he asserted firmly, "I would never leave Muhammad ﷺ for anything in this world."

Prophet ﷺ adopted him as a son:

On hearing this Harithah, the real father was shocked and surprised. Prophet ﷺ took Zaid (RA) to Kabah and publicly proclaimed that he had adopted Zaid (RA) as his son and as an heir. He should be called as Zaid ibn Muhammad. Harithah was satisfied that his son was with the honorable family of the Quraish.

Allah commanded people to call adopted son's name along with their own father's name:

"Nor has He made your adopted sons your real sons. That is but your saying with your mouths. But Allah says the truth, and He guides to the (Right) Path." (Al-Ahzab, 33:4). "Call them (adopted sons) by (the names of) their fathers; this is more equitable with Allah; but if you do not know their fathers, then they are your brethren in faith and your friends; and there is no blame on you concerning that in which you made a mistake, but (concerning) that which your hearts do purposely (blame may rest on you), and Allah is Forgiving, Merciful." (33:5).

Zaid (RA) was from then onwards known by his real name as Zaid ibn Harithah (RA)

Zaid's (RA) marriage with Zaynub (RA):

The Messenger of Allah ﷺ married him to the daughter of his paternal aunt, Zaynab bint Jahsh Al-Asadiyyah (RA), whose mother was Umaymah bint Abd Al-Muttalib. Muqatil bin Hayyan said, "The Prophet ﷺ on behalf of Zaid (RA), provided ten Dinars, sixty Dirhams, a veil, a cloak and a shirt, fifty Mudds of food and ten Mudds of dates, as mahar." Zaid (RA) lived with her for a year. Zaid (RA) was short, shy and dark skinned. He was a freed slave. Whereas Zaynab (RA) was from the noble family of Prophet ﷺ. Thereupon problems arose between them. Therefore, Zaid (RA) was often complaining about her to the Messenger of Allah ﷺ.

Meanwhile the Prophet ﷺ received information from Allah that Zaynab (RA) should be married to him. So for two reasons, he advised Zaid (RA), "Stay with your wife and have Taqwa of Allah." The first reason is even though the divorce is permissible, Allah dislikes it. Second reason is - if he marries the wife of his adopted son, Arabs with their custom of the Jahiliyyah, would embark on unkind, harsh, intentional, annoying remarks.

Allahuthala emphasized in the Holy Quran, "And (remember) when you said to him on whom Allah has bestowed grace and you have done a favor: "Keep your wife to yourself, and have Taqwa of Allah." But you did hide in yourself that which Allah will make manifest, you did fear the people whereas Allah had a better right that you should fear Him." (33:37).

Ibn Jarir narrated that Ayesha (RA) said, "If Muhammad ﷺ were to have concealed anything that was revealed to him of the Book of Allah, he would have concealed this Ayah" Allahuthala continued the same ayath as, "So when Zaid (RA) totally lost interest in keeping his wife, 'We' gave her to you in marriage, so that there would be no blame on the believers for marrying the ex-wives of their adopted sons after their divorce. And Allah's command is totally binding." (33:37).

Prophet sent marriage proposal through Zaid (RA):

According to the tafsir of Ibn Khathir, the Prophet ﷺ said to Zaid bin Harithah (RA), [اذْهَبْ فَاذْكُرْهَا عَلَيَّ] ("Go to her and tell her about me (that I want to marry her)". So, he went to her and found her kneading dough. Zaid (RA) said, `When I saw her I felt such respect for her that I could not even look at her and tell her what the Messenger of Allah ﷺ had said, so I turned my back to her and stepped aside, and said, `O Zaynab (RA)! Rejoice, for the Messenger of Allah ﷺ has sent me to propose marriage to you on his behalf.' She said, `I will not do anything until I pray to my Lord, may He be glorified.' So she went to the place where she usually prayed. Then the following ayath was revealed to the Prophet ﷺ:

To fulfill Allah's command, the Prophet ﷺ married her after her Iddath. He married her without any Wali, contractual agreement, mahar or witnesses among mankind. This was one of the breakthroughs and it abrogated the previous customs of adoption in pagan Arabs.

His remarkable achivements:

Zaid (RA) remained in the service of the Prophet ﷺ. He stood by his side through all thick and thin till the end of his life. He was the one who accompanied him to Taif. He was the one who fought many battles and in each battle was chosen by the Prophet ﷺ as the commander of his army. Ayesha (RA) said, "The Prophet never sent Zaid (RA) on an expedition but as a commander."

It was in the battle of Mutah that this "Habibi of Rasoolulallah ﷺ" was martyred in 8 A.H., with a smile on his lips. He was buried where the present day Jordan is located.

الحمدلله

بِسْمِ ٱللَّهِ ٱلرَّحْمَٰنِ ٱلرَّحِيمِ

10. Angels

1. Man is not alone. He is surrounded by the angels all the time. How many angels Allahuthala has spared for a single person?

Answer: For each day for each person, there are 8 angels in succession, 4 in the day and 4 at night. Two guardian angels for protection, one in front, another behind. Two watcher/recording angels {Kiraman Katibin}, one on the right side, recording the person's good deeds and the other on the left, recording his bad deeds.

Angels are creations of Allahuthala:

The angels are created by light and travel like a beam of a light. These winged creations of Allah ﷺ, worship Him tirelessly in the Universe and obey His Command. They are invisible to human beings. "All the praises and thanks be to Allah, the (only) Originator [or the (only) Creator] of the heavens and the earth, 'Who' made the angels messengers with wings, - two or three or four."

On the command of Allah [SWT], they provide all that is needed to the human beings. Allahuthala asserts in Quran-e-Kareem that these angels, "distribute (provisions, rain, and other blessings) by (Allah's) Command" {Adh-Dhariyat, 51:4}. {Fatir, 35:1}

Belief in angels, makes one's faith complete:

[2:177] "Al-Birr is (the quality of) the one who believes in Allah, the Last Day, the Angels, the Book, the Prophets."

[2:285] "Each believer, believes in Allah, His Angels, His Books, and His Messengers."

[4:136] "Whosoever disbelieves in Allah, His Angels, His Books, His Messengers, and the Last Day, then indeed he has strayed far away."

[42:5] "The angels seeing the deeds of mankind sincerely pray for us: "the angels glorify the praises of their Lord, and ask for forgiveness for those on the earth"

Thus, believing the angels makes one's faith complete; and disbelieving them makes a person go astray, away from Allah.

Quran refers about the angels surrounding a person:

[13:11] "For each (person), there are angels in succession, before and behind him. They guard him by the command of Allah"

[86:4] "There is no human being but has a protector over him (or her)"

[6:61] "He is the Irresistible, Supreme over His slaves, and He sends guardians over you, until when death approaches one of you"

[82:10 -12] "But verily, over you to watch you. Kiraman Katibin (honourable scribes) writing down (your deeds). They know all that you do." (The names of tha two angels are Raqib and Atid)

[50:16 to 18] "And indeed We have created man, and We know what his ownself whispers to him. And We are nearer to him than his jugular vein (vein of neck). (Remember!) that the two receivers (recording angels) receive, one sitting on the right and one on the left (to note his or her actions). Not a word does he (or she) utter, but there is a watcher by him ready (to record it)."

[10:21] "Our Messengers (angels) record all of that which you plot."

[43:80] "Or do they think that We hear not their secrets and their private counsel? (Yes We do) and Our Messengers (appointed angels in charge of mankind) are by them, to record."

[45:29] "This Our Record speaks about you with truth. Verily, 'We' were recording what you used to do (i.e. Our angels used to record your deeds)."

Every Mulim should know this Grace of Merciful Allahuthala:

The Prophet ﷺ asserted, "Truly the Angel on the left [of a person] withholds from recording the sinful deed committed by the Muslim servant who sinned for a period six 'hours'. If the servant regrets committing the sin and asks Allah for forgiveness, the Angel does not write down his sin. Otherwise, the angel records it as one bad deed." [Tabarani, Mu`jam al-Kabir]. Even after the sin has been recorded, it can be rubbed off as "repentance completely wipes away the sin and its traces." Therfore realize a bad deed as a 'sin' after its commitment and repent immediately to Allah ﷻ.

Angels pray on behalf of human beings and seek forgiveness for the believers:

"Those (angels) who bear the Throne (of Allah [ﷻ], The King) and those around it, glorifies the praise of their Lord, and believe in Him, and ask forgiveness for those who believe: "Our Lord! You comprehend all things in mercy and knowledge, so forgive those who repent and follow Your Way, and save them from the torment of the blazing Fire! Our Lord! And make them enter the Adn (Eden) Paradise (everlasting Gardens) which you have promised them, and to the righteous among their fathers, their wives, and their offspring! Verily, 'You' are the All-Mighty, the All-Wise. And save them from (the punishment, because of what they did of) the sins, and whomsoever You save from (the punishment, because of what they did of) the sins (i.e. excuse them) that Day, him verily, 'You' have taken into mercy. And that is the supreme success." {Ghafir, 40:7 - 9}

Allah [سبحانه وتعالى] commanded that His angels who are close to Him should pray for the believers in their absence, so it is a part of the angels' nature that they say 'Ameen' when a believer prays for his brother in his absence. Therefore, make a habit of praying for others!

الحمدلله

2. Name the three angels, who visited the house of Ibrahim (AS) to convey the good news of the birth of his son Ishaq (AS).

Answer: The honoured angel guests, of Ibrahim (AS) are Jibreel (AS), Mikaeel (AS) and Israfeel (AS). (Source: Ibn Khathir tafsir). But these names are not mentioned in the Quran.

Allah ﷻ directs the Prophet ﷺ to convey the news of Ibrahim (AS)'s guests (15:51) to his people:

"They came in the image of young handsome graceful men. They said: "Salaman!" He answered: "Salamun." a better reply in return for their greeting. (11: 70). Ibrahim (AS) then responded, "You are a people unknown to me." (11:69).

Then he required his family to bring food for them:

"Then he turned aside to his family secretly and brought a fat (roasted) calf (51:26) the best of his menu to entertain them." (11:69). "Brought it close to them, saying politely and kindly "What! Will you not eat." (51:27)

Ibrahim (AS) developed fear:

"But when he saw their hands went not towards it, he mistrusts them and conceived fear of them." (11:70). As per the Arab tradition, if some strangers refuse hospitality, it is assumed that they had come as enemies. But sooner, he understood that their refusal was due to their being angels. But he developed a fear as he knew that usually angels come to finish the affairs; bring punishment/test by Allah's command.

The angels conveyed good news to Ibrahim (AS) and his wife Bibi Sara

They confirmed: "Be not afraid, surely we give you the good news of a boy, possessing knowledge." (15:53)

"Ibrahim (AS) exclaimed: Do you give me good news (of a son) when old age has come upon me? Of what then do you give me good news!" (15:54). "They asserted: We give you good news with truth, therefore be not of the despairing." (15:55)

Ibrahim (AS) replied: "And who despairs of the mercy of his Lord but the erring ones?" (15:56). "Then the angels delivered the good news to Bibi Sara, of a knowledgeable son, Ishaq (AS) and to him Yaqub (AS) both of them were going to be Prophets." (11:71).

"Then his wife came up in great grief, and she struck her face" (51:29) and she said: "Woe unto me! Shall I bear a child while I am an old woman, and here is my husband an old man. Verily, this is a strange thing!" (11:72)

The angels continued, "Do you wonder at the decree of Allah! The mercy of Allah and His blessings be on you, O family of the Ibrahim (AS)! Allah is All-Praise worthy, All Glorious!" (11:73)

The other object of their visit:

Ibrahim (AS) exclaimed: "Then for what purpose you have come, O messengers?". They explained: "We have been sent against the people of Lut (AS)." (11:70); "who are criminals. To send down upon them stones of clay, marked by your Lord for transgressors." (51:32 to 34).

Bi bi Sara felt glad that the people of Lut (AS) would be destroyed on account of their rebellious and transgressive acts against Allah, the Exalted.

"So when Ibrahim's fear has been gone and his heart was filled with joy, because of the good news of a child, he began to dispute with the angels concerning the people of Lut (AS)." (11:74). "For he was tender hearted and merciful and always turned to Us." (11:75).

The angels responded, "O Ibrahim (AS), desist from this now that your Lord's decree has been issued and the scourge which cannot be averted by anyone shall overtake them." "They then went to the people of Lut (AS)." (11:76).

الحمدلله

3. Which angel will blow the trumpet; before Qiyamath?

Answer: Angel Israfeel (AS).

Quran reminds to the blowing of the trumpet, in several places. When the trumpet will be blown:

[69:14] "The earth and the mountains shall be crushed with a single crushing".

[39:68] "On the second blowing, from the graves men will come out quickly to their Lord." and "they shall stand up awaiting." (36:51)

[27:87 and 39:68] "the dwellers of heavens and earth shall be terrified except the ones Allah please, and all shall come together."

[18:99] "Allah will gather man-kind all together"

[23:101] "There shall be no ties of relationship between men nor shall they ask of each other."

[50:20 and 21] "Every soul shall come, with it a driver and a witness."

[6:73] "His is the kingdom on that day "

Even though the act of Israfeel (AS) is mentioned in the Quran, his name was never mentioned.

There are several ahadhees about Israfeel (AS):

When the Prophet ﷺ went to Isra, he saw Israfeel (AS) and he informed his companions about him. "Israfeel (AS) is holding the trumpet and waiting ready to blow it upon the order of Allah." (Tabari, Jamiul- Bayan, VII, 211; Ibn Kathir, Tafsirul-Quranil-Azim, Egypt, n.d. III, 276).

In Mustadrak al-Haakim it is narrated that Abu Hurayrah (RA) referred: The Messenger of Allah ﷺ claimed: "Since the time when the one who will blow the Trumpet was appointed, his eyes are ever ready, looking towards the Throne, fearing lest the command be issued before he blinks, as if his eyes are two brilliant stars."

Narrated by Abdullah ibn Abbas, the Messenger of Allah ﷺ said, "Allah created Israfeel (AS) who has been keeping his feet in line from the day he was created, and not raising his glance. Between him and the Lord Who is Blessed and Exalted, there are seventy lights, not one of which he could approach without being burned." (Al-Tirmidhi Hadith, 5731)

Once the Prophet ﷺ was enquired by his wife why he was praying so hard, he answered: "How can I feel happy when the Angel Israfeel (AS) has put his lips to the trumpet, waiting to hear the order to blow the trumpet?" [Narrated by Abu Sa'id al-Khudri (RA)]. This statement, very much distressed his companions, hence, he told them to seek comfort through reciting, [حَسْبُنَا اللَّهُ وَنِعْمَ الْوَكِيلُ] - "Sufficient for us is Allah, and an excellent Guardian is He" (3:173) (Al-Tirmidhi Hadith 409).

Prophet ﷺ used to pray, "O Allah, the Lord of Jibreel (AS), Michaeel (AS), and Israfeel (AS) grant me refuge from the heat of fire and the punishment of grave." (Sunan an-Nasa'i, 5519).

Abu Salamah bin Abdur-Rahman said: "I asked Ayesha (RA): 'With what did the Prophet ﷺ start his voluntary prayers?' She said, "O Allah, the Lord of Jibreel (AS), Michaeel (AS), and Israfeel (AS), Originator of the heavens and the earth, Knower of the unseen and the seen, you judge between your servants in that over which they differ. Guide me, by your will, in what they differ over regarding the truth. Verily, you guide whomever you will to the straight path." [Sahih Muslim, 770, Sunan an-Nasa'i 1625]

According to ahadhees, an important task of Israfeel (AS) is to blow the Trumpet, while the other tasks have also been attributed to him. They are:

- ❖ Guarding the great book Al-Lawh al-Mahfooz, The Preserved Tablet.
- ❖ Carry Allah's Throne.
- ❖ He was one amongst the three angels conveying Ibrahim (AS) the good news of the birth of his son Ishaq (AS) and destroying Lut's people.

Allah knows best! [الله اعلم !]

الحمدلله

4. Who is (مَالِك) Maalik? Who will call him, crying?

Answer: Maalik is the angel who guards the Hell. The dwellers of Hell will call him crying!

And they (the dwellers of the Hell) will cry: "O Maalik (Keeper of Hell)! Let your Lord make an end of us." (وَنَادَوْا يَا مَالِكُ لِيَقْضِ عَلَيْنَا رَبُّكَ قَالَ إِنَّكُم مَّاكِثُونَ) He will say: "Verily you shall abide forever." (Az-Zukhruf, 43:77). Prophet Muhammad ﷺ during his night journey to heavens, met the angel Maalik. Jibreel (AS) affirmed that Maalik never smiled, after the creation of the Hell-fire.

Maalik was assisted by 19 angels as wardens of Fire (74:30). Allah refers in another place of Quran-e-Paak that these angels are stern and severe and always obeying the command of Almighty Allah! "A fire whose fuel is men and stones, over which are [appointed] angels stern and severe, who flinch not [from executing] the commands they receive from Allah, but do [precisely] what they are commanded." (66:6).

Therfore, Allahuthala calls all the believers and warns: "O you who believe! Save yourselves and your families from that fire" (66:6). Because Hell is a very hard place to stay which is prepared for the disbelievers (3:131) and transgressors.

Allah [SWT] has provided enough warning about Hell, through His Messengers. It is asserted in surah Al Ghafir that even if they call Allah to lighten the suffering, Allah will not come and rescue. "And those in the Fire will say to the keepers (angels) of Hell: "Call upon your Lord to lighten for us the torment for a day!" The angels will exclaim: "Did there not come to you, your Messengers with (clear) evidences (and signs)? They will say: "Yes." The angels will reply: "Then call (as you like)! And the invocation of the disbelievers is nothing but in vain (as it will not be answered by Allah)!" (40: 49-50).

Samurah (RA) narrated that the Prophet ﷺ said: "Last night I saw [in a dream] two men along with Jibreel (AS), coming to me. One of them said, 'The one who lights the fire is Maalik, the gatekeeper of Hell; I am Jibreel (AS), and this is Michaeel (AS).'" [Sahih al-Bukhari]

Ibn Abbas (RA) related: "The Prophet ﷺ said, 'On the night of my ascent to Heaven. I saw Musa (AS) (who was a tall, brown, curly-haired man) as if he was one of the men of the Shan'awah tribe. Then I saw Isa ibn Marium (AS), a man of medium height, of moderate complexion inclined to the red and white colors, and of lank hair. I also saw Maalik, the gatekeeper of the Hell-fire.'" [Muslim]

When you hear or read the word 'Malik', you at once think of Allah Subhanahuthala. One of the beautiful names of Allah is Malik meaning "King". But the spelling in Arabic is different.

Observe the following ayaath:

"Then High above all be Allah, the True King." (Taha, 20:114). (فَتَعَٰلَى ٱللَّهُ ٱلْمَلِكُ ٱلْحَقُّ)

In a seat of truth (i.e. Paradise), near the Omnipotent King (فِى مَقْعَدِ صِدْقٍ عِندَ مَلِيكٍ مُّقْتَدِرٍ) (Al-Qamar, 54:55).

He is Allah than Whom there is none has the right to be worshipped but He, the King, the Holy, the One Free from all defects and the Giver of security, (هُوَ ٱللَّهُ ٱلَّذِى لَآ إِلَٰهَ إِلَّا هُوَ) (ٱلْمَلِكُ ٱلْقُدُّوسُ) (Al-Hashr, 59:23).

Whatsoever is in the heavens and whatsoever is on the earth glorifies Allah, the King, the Holy, the All-Mighty, the All-Wise. (يُسَبِّحُ لِلَّهِ مَا فِى ٱلسَّمَٰوَٰتِ وَمَا فِى ٱلْأَرْضِ ٱلْمَلِكِ ٱلْقُدُّوسِ ٱلْعَزِيزِ ٱلْحَكِيمِ) (Al-Jumma, 62:1).

The King of mankind, (مَلِكِ ٱلنَّاسِ) (An-Nas, 2).

In surah Fathiha in the fourth aya Malik is mentioned as (مَالِكِ يَوْمِ ٱلدِّينِ) and here it means the Only "Owner" of the Day of Recompense (1:4).

Allahuthala knows best! [الله اعلم !]

الحمدلله

5. During the revelation of which surah, Jibreel (AS) came along with large number of angels?

Answer: Surathul An'aam

Filling the whole horizon, 70,000 angels came along with Jibreel (AS) Glorifying and Praising Allah, (سبحانه وتعالى) when this surah was revealed. Ibn 'Abbass narrated that the whole Surah was revealed at Makkah, for the first time, at one sitting.

Asma-u-bint Yazid (RA), the first cousin of Muaz bin Jabal, the great companion of the Prophet ﷺ had reported: "During the revelation of this Surah, the Prophet ﷺ was riding on a she-camel and I was holding her nose string. The she-camel began to feel the weight bearing heavily that it seemed as if her bones would break under it." It sat down.

Allah ﷻ has been praised 70 times in this surah. This was revealed when the Prophet ﷺ and Muslims faced hard trials and suffering before Hijrah. Its central theme is Thaweheed.

Allahuthala says, each soul has to believe Allah ﷻ, His angels, His Book and His Messengers [Al Baqara, 2: 285].

The angels are referred as "malayak" in Arabic. It means "to assist and help". Unlike human beings they are obedient, always worship Allahuthala and immediately carry out His commands. Angels prefer hearing Quran as they cannot read it. So whenever Quran is recited, recite loudly.

الحمدلله

6. Who is (رُوح الْقُدُس) Ruh-ul-Qudus?

Answer: The angel Jibreel (AS) (2:87; 2:253; 5:110; 16:102; and 26:193).

Meaning of the name Jibreel:

"Jibr", "Mik" and "Israf" all mean, worshipper, while "eel" means, Allah". Ibn 'Abbas (RA) says that "jabr" means "Abd/slave"and also "Slave of Allah". Here the Allah's name Al-Quddus is selected to denote the holiness. It means the One who is beyond the comprehension of the human's understanding of purity, perfection and holiness.

Jibreel (AS) is also mentioned as (الرُّوحُ الْأَمِينُ) Ruhul-Ameen, "The Faithful Spirit" (26: 193). It is translated in the holy Quran as the 'Holy Spirit'.

Jibreel (AS) was the "first being (in the form of angel) to be created". When Jibreel (AS) was brought into existence, this first soul, said: (لَا حَوْلَ وَلَا قُوَّةَ إِلَّا بِاللهِ).

Allah having created Heaven and Hell, required him to see both. This we learn from the following hadhees Qudsi:

On the authority of Abu Hurayrah (RA), it is affirmed that the Messenger of Allah ﷺ quoted:

"When Allah created Paradise and Hell-fire, He sent Jibreel (AS) to Paradise, saying: "Look at it and at what I have prepared therein for its inhabitants." The Prophet ﷺ said that Jibreel (AS) came to it and looked at it as to what Allah had prepared therein for its inhabitants. So Jibreel (AS) returned to Allah and said: 'By your glory, no one hears of it without entering it.' So Allah ordered that it be encompassed by forms of hardship and difficulties and He said: "Return to it and look at what I have prepared therein for its inhabitants." The Prophet ﷺ said: So Jibreel (AS) returned to it and found that it was encompassed by forms of hardship and difficulties. Then he returned to Allah and said: 'By Your glory, I fear that no one will enter it.' He said:

"Go to Hell-fire and look at it and what I have prepared therein for its inhabitants, and he found that it was in layers, one above the other. Then he returned to Him and said: 'By Your glory, no one who hears of it will enter it.' So He ordered that it be encompassed by lust. Then He said: Return to it. And he returned to it and said: "By Your glory, I am frightened that no one will escape from entering it." It was recorded by Tirmidhi, who said that it was a good and a sound hadhees (Recorded also by Abu Dawud and an-Nasa'i).

Original form of Jibreel (AS):

Imam Ahmad had recorded that Abdullah bin Masud said, "The Messenger of Allah ﷺ saw, Jibreel in his original shape having six hundred wings, each wing filling the side of the horizon, with a colorful array, and pearls and rubies falling from each wing as much as only Allah knows."

"And certainly he saw him (Jibreel [AS]) in another descent, at the farthest lote-tree; Near which is the Garden, the place to be resorted to." (An-Najm, 53: 13 - 15)

When he appears as an angel, he will be invisible to others while visible and audible to the Prophet ﷺ alone. At times he will appear in human form, resembling the most handsome Sahaba, named Dahya ibn Kalbi (RA).

Umar (RA) said: "One day we were all sitting with Rasuloollah ﷺ. A man with extremely white clothing and with extra black hair came and sat in front of Nabi ﷺ touching his laps questioning him and the Prophet ﷺ was responding. Then that man left. Nabi ﷺ enquired: "Do you know who he is? He is Jibreel (AS), who came to teach me about Islam, Eeman and Ehisaan" (Saheeh Bukhari, 48; Muslim, 9)

His character, strength and status:

Jibreel (AS) is a mighty angel, with a magnificient strength and adorable actions. His status is very high; his task is great and he occupies a high rank among all the creations. He is honorable, noble and trustworthy, full of radiance. He was respected and obeyed by the highest gathering of angels.

Description of Jibreel (AS) in Quran by Allah:

Surah An- Najm describes that "He has been taught by one angel of mighty power and great perfection, who once rose to his true form. While on the highest point above the horizon, then he approached the Prophet ﷺ, coming so close that he was only two arms-lengths away or even less. Then Allah revealed to His servant what He revealed through Jibreel (AS). The Prophet's ﷺ heart did not doubt what he saw." (53:5 to 11)

Surah At-Takwir describes that "Indeed, this 'Quran' is the Word of Allah delivered by Jibreel (AS), a noble messenger-angel, full of power, held in honour by the Lord of the Throne, obeyed there 'in heaven' and trustworthy." (81: 19 to 21)

He is a Messenger to all the Messengers:

Jibreel (AS) was sent as Messenger from Allah, to the Messengers of this world commencing from Adam (AS) to our Prophet ﷺ.

He consoled Adam (AS) after he was expelled from Paradise. He took Idris (AS) to fourth heaven, just to seek the post-poning of his death. But the angel of death came there and by Allah's command Idris (AS)'s soul was taken away.

He went to Ibrahim (AS) before he was thrown into the furnace, enquiring whether he could help him. But Ibrahim (AS) said to him "حسبنا الله ونعم الوكيل" - "Sufficient for us is Allah, and [He is] the best Disposer of affairs." But by Allah's command Jibreel (AS) cooled down the fire.

When Bibi Hajar was running in panic, up and down the Safa and Marva hills, seeking water leaving her crying baby [Ismail (AS)]; Jibreel (AS) was there, to create a flow of Zam-zam by tapping his feet.

He protected Yusuf (AS) when his brothers threw him into the well.

He brought glad tidings of child birth to Bibi Marium, Zakariya, Ibrahim (AS) and Bibi Sara.

Jibreel (AS) appeared before Bibi Marium as a perfectly formed man (19:17) and when she was afraid he told "I am only a messenger from your Lord, sent to bless you with a pure son." (19:19) and Allah breathed into her of His inspiration and made her and her son as a sign for the Nations." (21: 91 and 66:12).

"Allah gave clear miracles to Isa (AS) son of Marium, and strengthened him with the Holy Spirit." (2:253 & 5: 110). He supported Isa ibn Marium (AS) to carryout all his miracles.

He came in human form with two other angels to destroy Lut's (AS) people. He turned the whole city upside down, with the tip of one of his wings.

He opened the Prophet Muhammad's ﷺ chest and washed it with Zam-Zam water twice. Once, during his childhood and for the second time, when he was taken to the heavens.

The Prophet ﷺ said, "While I was at Makkha, the roof of my house was opened and Jibreel (AS) descended, opened my chest and washed it with Zam-Zam water. Then he brought a golden tray full of wisdom and faith and having poured its content into my chest and he closed it. Then he took my hand and ascended with me to the nearest Heaven."

He taught Quran, Salath and Sunnah to our Prophet ﷺ. Narrated Ibn Shihab: "…………….Don't you know that once Jibreel (AS) came and offered the prayer (Fajr prayer) and Allah's Apostle ﷺ prayed too, then he prayed again (Zuhr prayer) and so did Allah's Apostle ﷺ and again he prayed ('Asr prayers) and Allah's Apostle ﷺ did the same; again he prayed (Maghrib-prayer) and so did Allah's Apostle ﷺ and again prayed ('Isha prayer) and so did Allah's Apostle ﷺ and (Jibreel [AS]) said, 'I was ordered to do so (to demonstrate the prayers prescribed to you)?"………[Sahih Bukhari 1:10:500].

Allah [SWT] appointed Michael (AS) and Jibreel (AS) to be his viziers or personal advisers.

Jibreel (AS) was also involved in teaching, helping, protecting, advising and guiding Mohammad ﷺ throughout his Prophet hood. During battles, he came along with thousands of angels and helped and protected the Muslim army from enemies.

Narrated Ayesha (RA): "When Allah's Apostle ﷺ returned on the day (of the battle) of Al-Khandaq he put down his arms and took a bath. Then Jibreel (AS) whose head was covered with dust, came to him saying, 'You have put down your arms! By Allah, I have not put down my arms yet.' Allah's Apostle ﷺ said, 'Where (to go now)?' Jibreel (AS) said, 'This way,' pointing towards the tribe of Bani Quraiza. Therefore, Allah's Apostle ﷺ went out towards them." (Sahih Bukhari 4:52:68).

Allah ﷻ revealed the Quran through Jibreel (AS):

The hadhees says, "The angel came to him and asked him 'to read'. The Prophet ﷺ replied, 'I do not know how to read.' The Prophet ﷺ added, 'The angel caught me (forcefully) and pressed me so hard that I could not bear it any more. He then released me and again asked me to read and I replied, 'I do not know how to read.' Thereupon he caught me again and pressed me a second time till I could not bear it any more. He then released me and again asked me to read but again I replied, 'I do not know how to read (or what shall I read)?' Thereupon he caught me for the third time and pressed me, and then released me and said, 'Read in the name of your Lord, who has created (all that exists) has created man from a clot. Read! And your Lord is the Most Generous." (96:1 to 3)

The following verses of Quran are a witness to this:

[16:102] "Say: The 'Holy spirit' has revealed it from your Lord with the truth, that it may establish those who believe and as a guidance and good news for those who submit."

[26:193] "The Faithful Spirit (الرُّوحُ الأَمِينُ) has descended with it."

[26:192-195] "And truly this is a revelation from the Lord of the Worlds, which the trustworthy spirit (Jibreel [AS]) has brought down to your heart, in order that you may be from the warner's, in plain Arabic language"

[16:102] "Say, the 'Holy Spirit' (Jibreel [AS]) has brought the revelation from your Lord in Truth, in order to strengthen those who, believe, and as a Guide and Glad Tidings to Muslims"

[53:2 -11] "Your companion (Mohammad ﷺ) has neither gone astray nor has erred. Nor does he spoke of his own desire. It is only a Revelation revealed. He has been taught by one mighty in power. One free from any defect in body and mind then he rose and became stable. Then he approached and came closer and was at a distance of two bows length nearer. So revealed to his slave whatever He revealed."

Those who consider Jibreel (AS) as their enemy are enemies of Allah:

It is revealed from the following verse: "Whoever is an enemy to Allah and His angels and His messengers – Jibreel (AS) and Michaeel (AS) – then indeed, Allah is an enemy to the disbelievers." (Quran 2:98).

Death of Angel Jibreel (AS)?

There is an opinion that angels do not die as they have no body and soul like human beings.

But there is a long (more than twenty pages), weak but popular hadhees narrating that angels also die. Allah only knows the truth. The Prophet ﷺ said, "On the Day of Judgement when everything in the earth perishes, Allah will ask, "Who remains?".

The Angel of Death replies, "O Allah Your noble face! You are here, me and the angels Israfeel (AS), Michaeel (AS) and Jibreel (AS). Then Allah will ask to take the soul of Israfeel (AS), then the soul of Michaeel (AS) and then lastly the soul of Jibreel (AS); who will fall on his face; spread out his wings and die in Thasbi, Subhanallah! Then Allah will take the soul of Izraeel (AS). Allah asserts, "Every single person perishes and only the noble face of your Lord remains" (55:26, 28:88).

Further Allah questions, "To whom belongs the Dominian today?" Nobody will be there to answer Him. He Himself will say, "To Allah, the One Subduer". Then Allah will Resurrect everybody including the angels, Jinn and Men." [الله اعلم !]

Allah knows best!

الحمدلله

7. What opinion angels developed, on Allah informing them that He is to create human beings?

Allahuthala intended to create human beings as the Khalifah on earth:

This is clear from the following verses of Quran: 'Your Lord said to the angels: "I am going to place a successive human authority [Khalifah] on earth." (2:30). It is also mentioned in two other places, "And it is He Who has made you [Khalaif] generations coming after generations, replacing each other on the earth." (6:165). "And makes you inheritors of the earth, (Khulafa') generations after generations." (27:62).

Before creating Adam, Allah informed angels about this:

'Khalifah' means vicegerent. He is the one who exercises the authority on behalf of his Creator. He, the vicegerent, shall submit to Him, serve Him, obey and act according to the guidance sent down by Him. Allah has the power over his life and death.

While informing about his creation to angels, Allah سبحانه وتعالى did neither consult the angels nor seek their help. Ibn Khathir says by creating mankind, "Allah's generosity and bounteousness, became apparent."

On hearing about his creation, angels wished to know from Allahuthala:

The angels were curious about this and wished to know from Allah, "Will You place in it someone who will spread corruption there and shed blood while we glorify Your praises and proclaim Your holiness?" (2:30). They expressed what they thought, without disputing with Allah's intention. They did not become envious of the human beings. They did not demand vicegerency. They ever glorified His praise. They have been keeping the heaven and earth, clean and holy. His orders were always carried out fully with obedience, in earnestness and faithfulness. They required to know why 'Their Lord' intented creating a new species? They were unable to understand the need for a vicegerent.

How angels knew that this creation would commit mischief on earth?

As recorded by al-Qurtubi and Ibn Kathir: The Angels wished to know: 'What are the qualities and nature of that vicegerent?' Allahuthala said: "His offspring will cause mischief on earth, envy and kill one another". For such a reason the angels intend knowing: 'Will you place on earth those who will cause mischief?'

The word Khalifa means a reformer, one who gives up corruption; opts to establish justice and who prevents prohibited actions. When the angels heard the word Khalifa, on the contrary, they concluded that offspring of Adam will cause mischief.

Ibn Abbas and Abu al-Aliyah reported that Al-Qurtubi and other scholars narrated that the angels witnessed, before the creation of Adam, the mischief and bloodshed caused by the Jinn, on earth. Thus, Allah sent the Iblis and his followers prior to their becoming disbelievers, to confront the Jinn.

Allah [SWT] responded to the angels, by furnishing the reason for creating Adam:

Allahuthala clarified, "I know what you do not know." (2:30). "You cannot understand the need and wisdom of the appointment of a vicegerent as I do. Your services do not suffice for the purpose that I have in view. I want something more than the services you have mentioned. That is why I am going to create a being on the Earth and endow him with some powers." He, the Knower of unseen continued: "I am not giving Adam only authority but also knowledge. The question you asked about his appointment is only one aspect of the matter. Its good aspect is weightier and valuable than its evil aspect. Because of a lesser evil, I do not want to give up a greater good." He, the Most Powerful in creation assured, "I will create among them Prophets and send Messengers. I will also create among them truthful, martyrs, righteous believers, worshippers, the modest, the pious, the scholars who implement their knowledge, humble people and those who love Allah and follow His Messengers."

Finally, He promised that "they are enveloped in My pardon and veiled in My mercy."

Allah, the All-Wise [الْحَكِيمُ] taught Adam all names and required him to inform the Angels:

"He taught Adam the names of all things, then He presented them to the angels and said, 'Tell Me the names of these, if what you say is true?" (2:31). The angels replied, "Glory be to You! We have no knowledge except what You have taught us. You are truly the All-Knowing, All-Wise." (2:32) Allah said, "O Adam! Inform them of their names." Then when Adam did, Allah said, "Did I not tell you that I know the secrets of the heavens and the earth, and I know what you reveal and what you conceal?" (2:33)

Allah [SWT] had warned the mankind that if they indulge in evil deeds He will destroy them and replace the earth by angels: "And if it were Our will, 'We' would have (destroyed you (mankind all, and) made angels to replace you (Yakhlufun) on the earth." (43:60)

Abu Harayrah (RA) narrated that the Prophet ﷺ said:

Allah (glorified and exalted be He) has supernumerary angels who prove about seeking out gatherings in which Allah's name is being invoked: they sit with them and fold their wings round each other, filling that which is between them and between the lowest heaven. When [the people in the gathering] depart, [the angels] ascend and rise up to heaven. He (the Prophet ﷺ) said: Then Allah (mighty and sublime be He) asks them - [though] He is most knowing about them: "From where have you come?" And they say: "We have come from some servants of Yours on Earth: they were glorifying You (Subhanallah), exalting you (Allahu akbar), witnessing that there is no god but You (La ilaha illa llah), praising You (Al-Hamdulillah), and asking [favours] of You." He says: "And what do they ask of Me?" They say: "They ask of You, Your Paradise!" He says: "And have they seen My Paradise?" They say: "No, O Lord." He says: "And how would it be were they to have seen My Paradise!" They say: "And they ask protection of You." He asks, "From what do they ask protection of Me?" They say: "From Your Hell-fire, O Lord." He says: "And have they seen My Hell-fire?" They say: "No!" He says:" And how would it be were they to have seen My Hell-fire?" They say: "And they ask for Your forgiveness." He (the Prophet ﷺ) said: "Then He says: I have forgiven them and I have bestowed upon them what they have asked for and I have granted them sanctuary from that from which they asked protection." He (the Prophet ﷺ) said: They say: "O Lord, among them is So-and-so, a much sinning servant, who was merely passing by and sat down with them." He (the Prophet ﷺ) said: And "He says: And to him [too] I have given forgiveness: he who sits with such people shall not suffer." (It was related by Muslim, al-Bukhari, at-Tirmidhi, and an-Nasa'i).

Abu Hurairah (RA) reported: The Messenger of Allah ﷺ said, "There are angels who take turns in visiting you by night and by day, and they all assemble at the dawn (Fajr) and the afternoon (Asr) prayers. Those who have spent the night with you, ascend to the heaven and their Rubb, 'Who' knows better about them, asks: `In what condition did you leave My slaves?' They reply: `We left them while they were performing Salath and we went to them while they were performing Salath." [Al-Bukhari and Muslim].

Thus Allah showed to angels that some of His vicegerents are nearly equal in prayers to angels. And Allah's attributes like Mercy and Forgiveness have been revealed only by the creation of Adam. Allah knows best! [الله اعلم !]

الحمدلله

8. How angels remove the soul of a believer and a disbeliever?

Death is certain and it is written in the womb itself:

We come from Him and will return to Him. Allahuthala says in Quran about death like this. "Every soul shall taste death" (3:185) "And the stupor of death will come in truth" (50:19). And "Wheresoever you may be, death will overtake you even if you are in fortresses built up strong and high!" (4:78) "He (Allah) who created death and life, so that He may test you as to which of you is better in deeds." (67:2).

"Narrated `Abdullah bin Mus'ud, the Allah's Messenger (ﷺ), the true and truly inspired stated, "(The matter of the Creation of) a human being is put together in the womb of the mother in forty days, and then he becomes a clot of thick blood for a similar period, and then a piece of flesh for a similar period. Then Allah sends an angel who is ordered to write four things. He is ordered to write down his (i.e. the new creature's) deeds, his livelihood, his (date of) death, and whether he will be blessed or wretched (in religion). Then the soul is breathed into him." (Sahih al-Bukhari 3208 and Sahih Muslim, Book 33, Number 6390).

Who removes the soul?

It is Allah Subhanahuthala, who removes the soul. Allah has assigned Izraeel (AS) as the angel of death. This angel has many helpers and assistants.

The following verses prove this statement:

Allah [ٱلْمُمِيتُ] removes the soul: [39:42] "It is Allah Who takes away the souls at the time of their death, and those that die not during their sleep. He keeps those (souls) for which He has ordained death and sends the rest for a term appointed. Verily, in this are signs for a people who think deeply."

The angel of death [مَلَكُ ٱلْمَوْتِ] removes the soul: [32:11] "Say, the angel of death who has been entrusted with you will take you. Then to your Lord you will be returned."

Group of angels remove the soul: [6:61] "When death comes to any of you, our angels take their soul, never neglecting this duty."

Those who remove the soul of a believer:

[16:32] Those whose lives, the angels take while they are in a pious state (i.e. pure from all evil, and worshipping none but Allah Alone) saying (to them): "Salamun Alaikum" enter you Paradise, because of (the good) which you used to do (in the world)." [79:2] "By those (وَٱلنَّٰشِطَٰتِ - angels) who gently take out (the souls of the believers)." [41:30] "Surely those who say, "Our Lord is Allah," and then remain steadfast, the angels descend upon them, saying, "Do not fear, nor grieve. Rather, rejoice in the good news of Paradise, which you have been promised!"

Those who remove the soul of a disbeliever:

[8:50] "And if you could but see when the angels take the souls of those who disbelieved. They are striking their faces and their backs and [saying], "Taste the punishment of the Burning Fire."

[47:27] "Then how [will it be] when the angels take them in death, striking their faces and their backs?"

[4:97] "Verily! As for those whom the angels take (in death) while they are wronging themselves (as they stayed among the disbelievers even though emigration was obligatory for them), they (angels) say (to them): "In what (condition) were you?" They will say, "We were oppressed in the land." They [the angels] will say, "Was not the earth of Allāh spacious [enough] for you to emigrate therein?" For those, their refuge is Hell - and evil it is as a destination."

[79:1] 'By those (وَٱلنَّٰزِعَٰتِ - angels) who pull out (the souls of the disbelievers and the wicked) with great violence.'

[6:93] "And if you could but see when the Zalimun (polytheists and wrong-doers, etc.) are in the agonies of death, while the angels are stretching forth their hands (saying): "Deliver your souls! This day you shall be recompensed with the torment of degradation because of what you used to utter against Allah other than the truth. And you used to reject His Ayat (proofs, evidences, verses, lessons, signs, revelations, etc.) with disrespect! "

[16:28] "Those whose lives, the angels take while they are doing wrong to themselves (by disbelief and by associating partners in worship with Allah and by committing all kinds of crimes and evil deeds)." Then, they will make (false) submission"

What happens to the soul after death and before resurrection?

Allah [عَزَّ وَجَلَّ] states in Quran, "And they ask you about the soul. Say: The soul is one of the commands of my Lord, and you are not given aught of knowledge but a little." (17:85). After death, when people bury him, the body remains in the ground, while the soul is in the state of Barzakh (human being do not know what happens). The body and soul can be connected by Allah's Will. It also dependent on a person's deeds in this world. The bliss or punishment of the Barzakh is not the same as that of the Hereafter. The body slowly disintegrates in earth and will be resurrected on the blowing of second trumpet.

Ahadhees about the death of believers:

Abu Huraira (RA) reported: The Prophet ﷺ, said, "When death approaches the believer, angels of mercy come to him with white silk, saying: 'Come out satisfied and well-pleasing to the rest and comfort of Allah and to a Lord who is not angry!' So it comes out like the best fragrance of musk until they pass him between themselves and reach the gate of heaven, saying: 'How pleasant is this fragrance you have brought from the earth!' The souls of believers come to Him more joyful than one of you whose loved ones return home." [Sunan al-Nasai,1832].

Al-Bara ibn Azib reported: The Prophet ﷺ, said, "Verily, when the believer is ready to depart the world and is facing the Hereafter, angels from heaven descend with bright faces, as if their faces were the sun, with them are the shrouds and perfumes of Paradise, until they sit from him a distance as far as the eye can see. Then, the angel of death, upon him be peace, comes until he sits by his head and he says: 'O pure soul! Come out to the forgiveness of Allah and His pleasure!' He takes it out like a drop from a water-skin and holds it, never to leave his hand for the blink of an eye until he places it in that shroud and perfume. The scent coming from it is more pleasant than any musk you would find on the face of the earth. He ascends and passes by no gathering of angels but that they say: 'What a pure spirit!' They say he is this person, son of this person, calling him by the best names by which he was known in the world, until he stops at the lowest heaven and seeks entry and it will be opened for him. The company of each heaven brings him closer to the heaven following it until he stops at the seventh heaven. Allah Almighty will say: 'Write the record of My servant in the righteous register ('Illiyyeen,) and return him to the earth, for from it I created them, to it I return them, and from it I will take them out once again.' His spirit will be returned to his body and two angels will come to sit by him, saying to him: 'Who is your Lord?' He will say: 'My Lord is Allah.' They will ask: 'What is your religion?' He will say: 'My religion is Islam.' They will enquire: 'Who is the one who has sent you?' He will say: He is the Messenger of Allah ﷺ. They will say: 'How did you know?.'He will say: 'I read the Book of Allah, had faith in it, and believed in it.' A heavenly announcement will be made: 'My servant has spoken the truth! Spread out carpets for him in Paradise, clothe him for Paradise, and open a gate for him to Paradise!' Its comforts and fragrances will come to him and his grave will become spacious as far as his eye can see. A handsome man, with fine clothes and wonderful fragrance, will come and say: 'Glad tidings of what pleases you, for this was your Day you were promised!' He (believer) will say: 'Who are you with such a handsome face?' He will say: 'I am your righteous deeds!' He will say: 'O Lord, begin the Hour that I may return to my family and property!' [Musnad Ahamad, 18534]"

It is narrated in Muslim that Abu Hurayrah (RA) said: "A good soul that has come from the earth; may Allah bless you and the body in which you used to dwell." He also said: "Then they take it up to its Lord, may He be glorified and exalted." Then Allah states, "Roam with it until the end of the world."

Ahadhees about the death of disbelievers:

Abu Huraira (RA) reported that the Prophet ﷺ, said, "Verily, when death approaches the unbeliever, angels of punishment come to him with sackcloth, saying: 'Come out displeased and displeasing to the punishment of Allah Almighty!' So the soul of the disbeliever comes out like the foulest stench of a corpse until they take it to the gate of the earth, saying how foul is this stench until the souls of unbelievers are brought to him." [Sunan al-Nasai, 1832]

The Prophet ﷺ continued, "Verily, when the unbeliever is ready to depart the world and is facing the Hereafter, angels descend from heaven with darkened faces and with them sack-cloth. They will sit away from him as far as the eye can see. Then, the angel of death approaches and he sits by his head and he says: 'O filthy soul, come out to the displeasure of Allah and His wrath!' He will be separated from his body like the tearing of skewers from wet wool and the angel holds it in his hand, never to leave it for the blink of an eye, until he places it in this sack-cloth. The smell coming from it is like the foulest corpse found upon the face of the earth. They will ascend with him and not pass by a gathering of angels who would say: 'What a filthy spirit! They say he is this person, son of this person, calling him by the ugliest names by which he was known in the world, until he stops at the lowest heaven. They will request it to be opened for him; but it will not open.' Then, the Prophet ﷺ recited the verse, "The gates of heaven will never open for the disbeliever, nor will they enter Paradise, until the camel goes through the eye of the needle," (7:40). The Prophet ﷺ said, "Allah Almighty will say: Write his record in the wicked register (Sijjin) at the lowest earth. His spirit will be thrown down," then the Prophet ﷺ recited the verse, "It is as though he had fallen from the sky and was snatched by the birds or the wind carried him down into a remote place," (22:31). The Prophet ﷺ said, "His spirit will return to his body and two angels will come to sit by him, saying to him: 'Who is your Lord?' He will say: 'Uh, uh, I do not know!' They will say: 'What is your religion?' He will say: 'Uh, uh, I do not know!' They will say: 'Who is the one who has sent you?' He will say: 'Uh, uh, I do not know!' A heavenly announcement will be made: 'He has lied! Spread carpets for him in Hell-fire and open a gate for him to Hell-fire! It's heat and it's flames will approach him and he will be squeezed in his grave until his ribs press together.' An ugly man, with hideous clothing and a foul stench, will approach him and say: 'Glad tidings of what despairs you, for this is your Day you were promised!' He will say: 'Who are you with the evil face?' He will reply: 'I am your wicked deeds!' He will beg: 'O Lord, do not begin the Hour' (Musnad Ahamad, 18534)"

Abu Hurayrah (RA) said: "The people of heaven say, 'An evil soul that has come from earth,' then it is said, 'Roam with it until the end of the world.' But if it was an evil man, they say, 'Come forth, O' evil soul which was in an evil body. Come forth blameworthy and receive the tidings of a boiling fluid and dirty wound discharges and other torments of similar kind, all together!" (Surah Saad, 38:57-58)

Therefore, O believers do as Allah commands:

"Allah never delays a soul when its appointed time comes." [63:11]. So, "O believers! Be mindful of Allah and let every soul look to what deeds it has sent forth for tomorrow. And fear Allah, for certainly Allah is All-Aware of what you do." [59:18] "And spend [in the way of Allah] from what We have provided you before death approaches one of you" [63:10]. Prepare yourself for death and Aqeera!

الحمدلله

بِسْمِ ٱللَّهِ ٱلرَّحْمَٰنِ ٱلرَّحِيمِ

11. Communities

1. "O Allah! if this is the truth from Thee, then rain upon us stones from heaven or inflict on us a painful punishment." (8:32). Which Prophet's community prayed like this?

Answer: The community of Prophet Mohammed ﷺ in Makkah.

The Makkan Quraish uttered these words as a challenge rather than a prayer to Allah. In spite of their refusal to heed, neither the rain of stones nor any other punishment was inflicted upon them. Therefore, they argued that the message of the Prophet ﷺ, is neither true nor from Allah.

Allah responded by sending down the following verse:

"And Allah would not punish them while you (Muhammad ﷺ) are amongst them, nor will He punish them while they seek (Allah's) Forgiveness." (8:33). The Prophet ﷺ was not exhausted in conveying his messages in spite of his community causing him much torture! He was, relentlessly and patiently inviting the people of Makkah to the truth! When they plotted to kill him, Allah commanded him to depart from that land.

Good number of people in Makkah, sought Allah's forgiveness and strived to reform themselves. How can Allah punish them? Allah repeatedly warns and reminds of the punishment to the disbelievers, of ancient times. They rejected the truth even after receiving it with clear signs. Instead of believing it, they demanded to witness the punishment with their own eyes, of which they were warned.

They demanded from their Prophets:

- "So cause a piece of the heaven to fall on us, if you are of the truthful!" (26:187)
- "So bring us that wherewith you have threatened us if you are of the truthful." (7:70)

- "Bring about your threats if you are indeed one of the Messengers (of Allah)." (7:77).
- "Bring Allah's torment upon us if you are one of the truthful." (29:29).

Even the Quraish wished to know from their Prophet ﷺ:

"Why do you not bring angels to us if you are of the truthful ones?" (15:5) "O you to whom the Reminder has been sent down! Verily, you are a mad man! Why do you not bring angels to us if you are of the truthful" (15:7).

They demanded: "Or you have a garden of date-palms and grapes, and cause rivers to gush forth in their midst abundantly. Or you cause the heaven to fall upon us in pieces, as you have pretended, or you bring Allah and the angels before (us) face to face; Or you have a house of adornable materials (like silver and pure gold, etc.), or you ascend up into the sky, and even then we will put no faith in your ascension until you bring down for us a Book that we would read." (17: 91 to 93).

Then Allah required His Prophet ﷺ to respond:

"Say (O Muhammad ﷺ) Glorified (and Exalted), be my Lord (Allah) above all that evil they (polytheists) associate with Him! Am I anything but a man, sent as a Messenger?"

"And even if We opened to them a gate from the heaven and they were to continue ascending thereto, they would surely say: 'Our eyes have been (as if) dazzled. Nay, we are a people bewitched." (15:15 and 16). They made fun of the proof, evidence, signs and miracles sent through the Messengers, to warn them. It was the worst type of disbelief.

Finally, Allah has answered them:

"And who does more wrong than he who is reminded of the ayath of his Lord, but turns away from them forgetting what his hands have sent forth. Truly, 'We' have set veils over their hearts, lest they should understand this (the Quran), and on their ears deafness. And if you call them to guidance, even then they will never be guided." (18:57). "And your Lord is Most Forgiving, Owner of Mercy. Were He to call them to account for what they have earned, then surely, He would have hastened their punishment. But they have their appointed time, beyond which they will find no escape." (18:58).

الحمدلله

2. "Was there any town (community) that believed (after seeing the punishment) and its faith (at that moment) saved it (from the punishment)?" (10:98) This question refers to which Prophet's community?

Answer: Communityof Yunus (AS).

When Yunus (AS) told his people in Nineveh town to worship Allah [SWT], they ignored him. He warned them that if they kept on with their idolatery, Allah's punishment would soon follow! Instead of fearing Allah [عَزَّ وَ جَلَّ], they told him they were not afraid of his threat. "Let it happen." Yunus (AS) was very angry, "in that case, I will leave you to your misery!" So saying he left Nineveh fearing that Allah's punishment will come soon.

On his departing from the city, the people of Nineveh found the skies turning red like fire. As the threat was approaching, they were engulfed with fear. They recollected the wrath of Allah; His severe punishment destroying the community of Aad, Thamud and Nuh (AS). Was such a situation similar and whether they ignored the reminders of their Prophet Yunus (AS). They started realizing their foolishness! With such a fear, all gathered on the mountain. With sincere faith and belief in their hearts they started seeking forgiveness and mercy of Allah, the Almighty. The mountains also echoed their prayers.

Accepting their sincere repentance, Allah Subhanahuthala removed His punishment and showered His blessings on the people of Nineveh. With the threatened punishment turning into Allah's Mercy, the community of Yunus (AS) became thankful and started praying for the return of their Prophet.

After three days of continuous glorification and repentance, Yunus (AS) came out from the stomach of the fish, being weak and feeble. After having a bath, he prostrated and thanked Allahuthala. After regaining his strength, he slowly walked towards his hometown. All of them gathered instrength and welcomed him. He was surprised to see the change in his community. Together, they thanked Allah [سبحانه وتعالى] for His Mercy. The community of Yunus (AS) is the only exceptional community that turned Allah's Wrath into Mercy, by their sincere repentance!

Thus Allah ﷻ continues: "........ except the people of Jonah; when they believed, removed from them the torment of disgrace in the life of the present world and permitted them to enjoy for a while" (10:98).

الحمدلله

3. "............in place of their two gardens We gave to them two gardens yielding bitter fruit and tamarisk and a few lote-trees." At which area did Allah Subhanahuthala replace, these gardens?

Answer: At a place called Saba (Saba,34:16)

Allahuthala blessed the people of Saba with two gardens:

Saba, is a land where people dwell near a dam known as Marab. It was located between the two mountains. The place was provided with two gardens on its right and on it's left, with lots of sweet fruits. People were living very happily there. Allah required them to eat the provisions available and be grateful to their Lord.

Quran says:

[34:15] "Indeed there was for Saba, a sign in their dwelling place, – two gardens on the right hand and on the left (and it was said to them) "Eat of the provision of your Lord, and be grateful to Him, a fair land and an Oft-Forgiving Lord."

They became disobedient and ungrateful:

Later they turned away from Allah, became disobedient and ungrateful. Thereafter Allah sent rats which destroyed the base of the dam, as a result the stored water flooded their dwellings.

Allahuthala replaced their garden of sweet fruits with trees of bitter fruits:

The flood destroyed their two fruit bearing gardens. As a result, the trees of bitter fruits like tamarisks and lote trees grew up in those gardens. Never Allah punishes in such a way, unless the community is disbelieving and ungrateful. Allah says in surah Saba:

[34:16] "But they turned away (from the obedience of Allah), so We sent against them flood released from the dam, and We converted their two gardens into gardens producing bitter bad fruits, tamarisks and lote-trees."

[34:17] "Like this We requited them because they were ungrateful disbelievers. And never do We requit in such a way except those who are ungrateful, (disbelievers)."

Allahuthala favoured their path, for an easy travel:

Allahuthala further continues by mentioning His favours to those people by placing the blessed towns one after the other in stages, so that it is easy for them to travel.

[34:18] "And We placed between them and the towns which We had blessed, towns easy to be seen, and We made the stages (of journey) between them easy (saying): "Travel in them safely both by night and day."

But they desired their journey to be longer:

[34:19] "But they said: "Our Lord! Make the stages between our journey longer," and they wronged themselves, so We made them as tales (in the land), and We dispersed them all, totally. Verily, in this are indeed signs for every steadfast grateful (person)."

They were following Iblis:

Excepting the true believers Iblis influenced the rest, who followed him. Iblis had no authority over the believers expecting while the Almighty tests them. Allah is a Hafiz of everything. All-Knower of everything i.e. He keeps record of each and every person, as regards their deeds and then He will reward them.

[34:20] "And indeed Iblis did prove true his thought about them, and they followed him, all except a group of true believers."

[34:21] "And he (Iblis) had no authority over them, except that We might test him, who believes in the Hereafter from him who is in doubt about it. And your Lord is a Hafiz over everything."

Lessons to be learnt:

- Must be obedient to Allah.
- Must not be ungrateful.
- Must be satisfied with the favours provided by Allah.
- Allah's punishment is always severe.
- Nobody can help when Allah punishes.
- Do not follow Shaitan's foot-steps.

- If you are strong in faith, Shaitan cannot influence, when Allah tests you.
- Allah is our Protector. Therefore, submit yourself to Him.

الحمدلله

4. "But Allah's (Torment) reached them from a place whereof they expected it not, and He cast terror into their hearts, so that they destroyed their own dwellings with their own hands and the hands of the believers." Who were those who destroyed their own dwellings?

Answer: Jewish tribe of Bani An-Nadir, the residents of Madhina (Al-Hashr, 59:2)

When the Nabi ﷺ migrated to Al-Madhina, he entered into a peace treaty with the Jews of Madhina. Part of the agreement was that they would not help anyone, against Muslims. If an enemy were to attack Muslims, they agreed to protect and help the Muslims.

The Muslims and Jews maintained good relations and mutual respect. Their friendly relations continued until the Quraish brain washed some of the Jews. As a result, Banu Nadir developed friendly relations with the enemies of Muslims. They provided some geographical information of Madhina to Quraish, during the battle of Uhad. Besides this, when the Prophet ﷺ sought for the blood money for killing two Muslim brothers, they agreed to pay it and invited the Prophet ﷺ for a feast with his companions.

While Prophet ﷺ and his companions were waiting near the wall of one of their houses; it was their plan to assassinate the Prophet ﷺ by rolling a huge stone from above. Allah Subhanahuthala commanded the Prophet ﷺ, through Jibreel (AS), to leave from that place immediately; thereupon he stood up and walked to Madhina without informing anybody.

In his book of Seerah, Muhammad bin Ishaq bin Yasar said: "When the companions learnt that the Messenger of Allah ﷺ was absent for a long time, they went in search of him and they saw a man coming from Al-Madhina. They enquired with him and he replied that he saw the Prophet ﷺ entering Al-Madhina. The Messenger's companions left the place, went to the Prophet ﷺ and on enquiry they were informed about the news of the betrayal plot of the Jews.

He ordered them to prepare for war and march forth towards Bani An-Nadir. The Prophet ﷺ himself gathered his forces and marched to the area of Bani An-Nadir, who had taken refuge in their fortified fortress. The Messenger of Allah ﷺ ordered their date trees be cut down and burnt. The Jews heralded at the Prophet ﷺ, `O Muhammad (ﷺ)! You used to forbid mischief on the earth and blame those who did it. Why is it that you had the date trees cut down and burnt?'

Meanwhile, Abdullah bin Ubayy bin Salul, Wadiah, Malik bin Abi Qawqal, Suwayd, Dais and several others who all belonged to the tribe of Al-Khazraj bin Bani Awf, sent a message to Bani An-Nadir saying, 'Be firm and strong. We will never abandon you. If you are attacked, we will fight along with you and if you are forced to leave Al-Madinah, we will accompany you.' The Jews waited for this claim of support, but the hypocrites did not act. Allah cast terror in the hearts of the Jews.

They asked the Messenger ﷺ to allow them a safe passage out of Al-Madhina and to spare their lives. In return, they would only take what their camels could carry, except for weapons. The Prophet ﷺ agreed. The Jews collected all the wealth, their camels could transport. One of the Jews demolished his own house around its door, so that he could carry the door on the back of his camel."

Allahuthala refers this incidence in the Holy Quran as:

"He it is Who drove out the disbelievers among the people of the Scripture (i.e. the Jews of the tribe of Bani An-Nadir) from their homes at the first gathering. You did not think that they would get out. And they thought that their fortresses would defend them from Allah! But Allah cast terror into their hearts. Allah's punishment reached them from a place where they expected it not. They destroyed their own dwellings with their own hands and the hands of the believers. Then take admonition, O you with eyes (to see)." (59:2).

Allahuthala continues in Holy Quran: "And had it not been that Allah had decreed exile for them, He would certainly have punished them in this world, and in the Hereafter their's shall be the torment of the Fire." (59:3). "That is because they opposed Allah and His Messenger (Muhammad ﷺ). And whosoever opposes Allah, then verily, Allah is Severe in punishment." (59:4). "What you (O Muslims) cut down of the palm-trees (of the enemy), or you left them standing on their stems, it was by Leave of Allah, and in order that He might disgrace the Fasiqun (rebellious, disobedient to Allah)." (59:5).

الحمدلله

5. Who are the people of Tubba?

Answer: The people of Tubba were Himyarotes, the branch of Sabaeans (fire-worshippers), who lived in Saba (present Yemen).

They were Arab descendants of Qahtan. They had a luxurious life by carrying on agriculture and commerce. They lived in prosperity and splendor.

Allahuthala quoted them in Surah Ad-Dhukhan and Surah Qaf:

"Verily, these (Quraish) people are saying: 'There is nothing but our first death, and we shall not be resurrected. Then bring back our fore-fathers, if you speak the truth!' Are they better or the people of Tubba and those before them? We destroyed them because they were indeed Mujrimun." (Ad-Dukhan, 44:34- 37).

"And the dwellers of the Wood, and the people of Tubba; every one of them denied their Messengers, so My Threat took effect." (Qaf, 14).

The Quraish idolaters, who denied the resurrection were compared to people of Tubba and Allahuthala threatened and warned them with the irresistible punishment, which they underwent.

Tubba was the title of the kings of Himyarotes like the title of Khosroes, Caesar, Paraoh, Negus etc. One amongst the Tubba, whose name was Asad Abu Kurayb, left Yemen with the aim of expanding his kingdom and domain. He passed through Al-Madhina during the days of Jahiliyyah. He fought its inhabitants who resisted him. They fought him during day and supplied with food by night, feeling ashamed he refrained from harming them. He was accompanied by two Jewish Rabbis, who advised him and told him that he would never capture this city, for it would be the place to which a Prophet would migrate towards the end of time.

So he retreated and took the two Rabbis with him to Yemen. When he passed by Makkah, he wanted to destroy the Kabah, but they told him not to do that either. They told him about the significance of that House, that it had been built by Ibrahim (AS); and that it would gain importance through the Prophet who would be sent towards the end of time.

Thereof he respected it, performed Tawaf around it, gave sacrifices and covered the Kabah for the first time with a fine cloth (Kiswa). After returning to Yemen he invited its people to follow the religion of guidance, along with him. At that time, the religion of Musa (AS) was the religion followed by those who were guided prior to the coming of the Isa (AS). So the people of Yemen accepted the religion of guidance along with him. Among the Himyarite Kings, he ruled for the longest period extending for about 326 years.

After his death, the people of Tubba faced the Divine wrath and were destroyed with the flood from the dam. Their two gardens were replaced with bitter fruits and they were scattered here and there throughout the land, as mentioned in Surah Saba

الحمدلله

6. Who can change the state of goodness of a community, whether by themself or by the Prophets or by Allah? What Quran says about this?

Answer: They themselves.

The Holy Quran says in Surah Rad, (13:11) "Verily! Allah will not change the good condition of people as long as they do not change their state of goodness themselves."

This is an important verse which indicates that Allah, may He Be Blessed and Exalted, in His perfect justice and wisdom, states that the man is responsible for his own life.

Allah [سبحانه وتعالى] created man in the best of stature (95:4). He was impatient (70:19), hasty (21:37), weak (4:28) and in toil while Allah has created him. (90:4) He gave him intelligence and knowledge. He showed him right and wrong by sending the Messengers then and there with guiding Scripters. He bestowed him with all sorts of favours; grace; mercy and always protects him through angels against evil and harm; forgives him when he repents.

Allahuthala has ordained:

And certainly, 'We' shall test you with something of fear, hunger, loss of wealth, lives and fruits (2:155). And that Allah may test the believers (3:166) by a fair trial from Him (8:17) and tests the hypocrites (3:167) and destroys the disbelievers. (3:141).

We are ever putting (men) to the test (23:30) so as to know to which of them are best in deeds (18:7 and 67:2); and to prove who is willing to stand up for Him and His messengers without seeing Him; (57:25) to know who are true, and who are liars; (29:3) and to know who strive hard and the patient ones (47: 31).

Thus, Allah Subhanahuthala does not change the condition of the people from good to bad or bad to good, ease to hardship or hardship to ease.

But a nation/a community/a person can change conditions from:

★ disbelief to belief;

★ false to truth;

★ bad to goodness;

★ defending evil with good;

★ disobedience to obedience;

★ cruelty to kindness;

★ impatience to patience;

★ arrogant to submissiveness;

★ proud to humble;

★ fithna/war, to peace;

★ stingness to generous;

★ ungrateful to grateful;

★ ignorance to knowledgeable;

★ forgetting Allah to fearing Allah;

★ bad intensions to good intensions;

★ indulging in sin to regret sin;

★ committing sin to repenting;

★ distrust to trust;

★ turning away from Allah to reverting towards Allah;

★ follow his own will to follow Allah's Will, that is, in short from Zalimun to Muttaqun.

If a nation/community/a person changes the attitude around them, it will bring Kindness and Mercy of Allah; that tends to change the hearts, trails, favours, punishment, hardships, environment, poverty, diseases, calamity, drought, famine, war etc.

Allah ﷻ confirms: "And your Lord is not at all unjust to (His) slaves" [41:46]. "He is All-Sufficient for His creatures' needs." (2:247, 3:73) "He is Ever All-Sufficient as a

Disposer of affairs" (4:81 and 171). "Allah will never change a grace which He has bestowed on people until they change what is in their own selves" [8:53]. Or He may give them respite and give them time so that they might turn to the right path, but if they do not then they will be seized unexpectedly: "Consider not that Allah is unaware of that which the Zalimun do, but He gives them respite up to a Day when the eyes will stare in horror" [14:42],

"So, when they forgot with which they had been reminded, 'We' opened for them the gates of everything, until in the midst of their enjoyment in that which they were given, all of a sudden, 'We' took them and lo! They were plunged into destruction with deep regrets and sorrows" [6:44]

"For those who answered their Lord's Call will be rewarded with finest (i.e. Paradise). But those who answered not His Call ...... For them there will be the terrible reckoning." (13:18)."

الحمدلله

7. "Did you (O Muhammad ﷺ) not think of those who went forth from their homes in thousands, fearing death? Allah said to them, "Die". And then He restored them to life. Truly, Allah is full of Bounty to mankind, but most men thank not." (2:243). What is the story behind?

Answer: Ibn Abu Hatim related that Ibn Abbas said that these people mentioned herein, were the residents of a village called Dawardan. Ali bin Asim said that they were from Dawardan, a village several miles away from Wasit (in Iraq).

Allah سبحانه وتعالى narrated this incidence when people were to be called for Jihadh. Death is certain. No caution averts death. There is no refuge from Allah, through death in this world we go to Allah Himself.

About four thousand persons left their land fearing death, due to plague. They were from the Children of Israel. First they went to a forest and later to a fertile valley, where they lived a long and happy life. They led a luxurious life, with the favours provided by Allah. But forgot their past and were not thankful for the favours of Allah.

On their becoming ungrateful, Allah commanded them "To die". He sent two angels, one from above and another from below the valley; who raised a single shout. All the people died instantaneously. Their bodies became rotten and disintegrated. Their bones were scattered. Then a Prophet from the Children of Israel, came there and on watching their destruction, prayed to Allah to bring them back to life. Allah accepted his prayer and commanded the bones to come together, then to cover it with flesh and skin; lastly He commanded the souls to return to their body. Allah had brought them back to their life after a long time. Allah proved His capacity of resurrection, a great sign and a clear evidence.

Thus Allah mentioned this incident as an example for learning a lesson from it.

Hadhees about plague:

Imam Ahmad reported that Abdullah bin Abbas (RA) said that once Umar bin Al-Khattab (RA) went to Ash-Sham (Syria) he was informed in a place called Sargh, that plague had broken out in Ash-Sham. Abdur-Rahman bin Awf informed; "I have knowledge regarding this matter. I heard Allah's Messenger ﷺ say: 'If the plague breaks out in a land that you are in, do not leave that land to escape from it. If you hear about it in a land, do not enter it.' Umar (RA) thanked Allah and then went back.

الحمدلله

8. "Cursed were the people of the ditch" (85:4). Why they were cursed?

Quran asserts:

"Cursed were the People of the Ditch. Of fire fed with fuel. When they sat by it. And they witnessed what they were doing against the believers. And they had no fault except that they believed in Allah, the Almighty, Worthy of all praise! To Whom belongs the dominion of the heavens and the earth! And Allah is Witness over everything." (85:4-9).

The above mentioned event occurred at Al-Ukhdud, a place located 5 km south of Najran city in Saudi Arabia. Through courage, patient, wisdom, strong faith and great sacrifice, a boy converted the majority of his people to the right religion. Muhammad bin Ishaq referred in his book of Seerah that Dhu Nuwas named as Zurah, the last Himyarite King killed those twenty thousand people during one morning in the Ditch of fire.

The episode of the Boy and the King:

This episode is narrated as a long hadhees in, "The Book of Zuhd and Softening of Hearts, 55, Chapter 17 and Hadhees 93"

Suhaib reported that Allah's Messenger ﷺ stated: "There lived a king before you and he had a (court) magician. As he (the magician) grew old, he said to the king: I have grown old, send some young boy to me so that I should teach him magic. He (the king) sent to him a young man so that he should train him (in magic). And on his way (to the magician) he (the young man) found a monk sitting there. He (the young man) listened to his (the monk's) talk and was impressed by it. It became his habit that on his way to the magician he met the monk and sat there and he came to the magician (late). He (the magician) beat him because of delay. He made a complaint of that to the monk and he said to him: When you feel afraid of the magician, say: 'Members of my family had detained me. And when you feel afraid of your family you should say: The magician had detained me.'

It so happened that there came a huge beast (of prey) and it blocked the way of the people, and he (the young boy) said: 'I will come to know today whether the magician is superior or the monk is superior.' He picked up a stone and said: 'O Allah, if the affair of the monk is dearer to Thee than the affair of the magician, cause death to this animal so that the people should be able to move about freely.' He threw that stone towards it and killed it and the people began to move about (on the path freely). He (the young man) then came to that monk and informed him and the monk said: 'Sonny, today you are superior to me. Your affair has come to a stage where I find that you would be soon put to a trial, and in case you are put to a trial don't give my clue.'

The boy started curing various diseases:

That young man began to treat the blind and those suffering from leprosy and he in fact began to cure people from (all kinds) of illness. When a companion of the king who had gone blind heard about him, he came to him with numerous gifts and said: 'If you cure me all these things collected together here would be yours.' He said: 'I myself do not cure anyone. It is Allah Who cures and if you affirm faith in Allah, I shall also supplicate Allah to cure you.' He affirmed his faith in Allah and Allah cured him and he came to the king and sat by his side as he used to sit before. The king enquired him: 'Who restored your eyesight?' He asserted: 'My Lord'. Thereupon the king proclaimed: 'It means that your Lord is One besides me?'. He assured: 'My Lord and your Lord is Allah', so the king took hold of him and tormented him till he gave a clue of that boy. The young man was thus summoned and the king said to him: 'O boy, it has been conveyed to me that you have become so much proficient in your magic that you cure the blind and those suffering from leprosy and you do such and such things.' Thereupon he said: 'I do not cure anyone; it is Allah Who cures' and the king took hold of him and began to torment him. So he gave a clue of the monk.

The king killed the monk:

The monk was thus summoned and it was said to him: 'You should turn back from your religion'. He, however, refused to do so. He (ordered) for a saw to be brought (and when it was done) he (the king) placed it in the middle of his head and tore it into parts till a part fell down. Then the courtier of the king was brought and it was said to him: 'Turn back from your religion'. Arid he refused to do so, and the saw was placed in the midst of his head and it was torn till a part fell down.

The king tried to kill the boy through various means but he escaped every time:

Then that young boy was brought and it was said to him: 'Turn back from your religion'. He refused to do so and he was handed over to a group of his courtiers. And he 'said to them: Take him to such and such mountain; make him climb up that mountain and when you reach its top (ask him to renounce his faith) but if he refuses to do so, then throw him (down the mountain). So they took him and made him climb up the mountain and he said: 'O Allah, save me from them (in any way) Thou likest and the mountain began to quake and they all fell down' and that person came walking to the king. The king enquired to him: 'What has happened to your companions?' He said: 'Allah has saved me from them'. He again handed him to some of his courtiers and said: 'Take him and carry him in a small boat and when you reach the middle of the ocean (ask him to renounce) his religion, but if he does not renounce his religion throw him (into the water)'. So they took him and he said: 'O Allah, save me from them and what they want to do'. It was quite soon that the boat turned over and they were drowned and he came walking to the king and the king said to him: 'What has happened to your companions?' He said: 'Allah has saved me from them.'

Then the boy informed the way by which he has to be killed:

He said to the king: 'You cannot kill me until you do what I ask you to do'. And he said: 'What is that?' He said: 'You should gather people in a plain and hang me by the trunk (of a tree). Then take hold of an arrow from the quiver and say: In the name of Allah, the Lord of the young boy; then shoot an arrow and if you do that then you would be able to kill me'. So he (the king) called the people in an open plain and tied him (the boy) to the trunk of a tree, then he took hold of an arrow from his quiver and then placed the arrow in the bow and then said: 'In the name of Allah, the Lord of the young boy'; he then shot an arrow and it bit his temple. He (the boy) placed his hands upon the temple where the arrow had bit him and he died and the people said: 'We affirm our faith in the Lord of this young man, we affirm our faith in the Lord of this young man, we affirm our faith in the Lord of this young man.'

Many followed the religion of the boy and the king killed all of them in the fire of the ditch:

The courtiers came to the king and it was said to him: 'Do you see that Allah has actually done what you aimed at averting. They (the people) have affirmed their faith in the Lord'. He (the king) commanded ditches to be dug at important points in the path. When these ditches were dug, and the fire was lit in them it was said (to the people): He who would not turn back from his (boy's) religion would be thrown in the fire or it would be said to them to jump in that. (The people courted death but did not renounce religion) till a woman came with her child and she felt hesitant in jumping into the fire and the child said to her: 'O mother, endure (this ordeal) for it is the Truth.' [Sahih Muslim, 3005].

Few scholars claimed that this incident was repeated more than once:

- ❖ Ibn Abu Hatim has recorded: "the incident of the ditch took place in the Yemen during the lifetime of Tubba"
- ❖ In Constantinople, during his lifetime, Constantine threw the Christians in fire.
- ❖ In Iraq at Babylon, during the lifetime of Bikhtinassar, same fate faced by three Christians.

Allah conveys the following message along with this story in Surah Brooj:

"Those who persecute the believing men and women and then do not repent will certainly suffer the punishment of Hell and the torment of burning. Surely those who believe and do good will have Gardens under which rivers flow. That is the greatest triumph. Indeed, the crushing grip of your Lord is severe. For He is certainly the One Who originates and resurrects all. And He is the All-Forgiving, All-Loving. Lord of the Throne, the All-Glorious, Doer of whatever He wills." (85:10 - 16)

الحمدلله

بِسْمِ ٱللَّهِ ٱلرَّحْمَٰنِ ٱلرَّحِيمِ

12. Quranic verses

1. What are the verses of Quran that will guard those who recite them, against the Dajjal?

Answer: Abu Darda (RA) reported: The Prophet ﷺ said, "If anyone learns by heart the first ten verses of the Surah al-Kahf, he will be protected from the Dajjal." [Sahih Muslim 809a, Book 6, Hadith 311] Another narration, attributed that the Prophet ﷺ said, "Also by memorizing from the last ten verses of Surah Al-Kahf." [Sahih Muslim, 809]

Let us check the first 10 verses of surah Kahf:

[18:1] "All the praises and thanks be to Allah, 'Who' has sent down to His slave (Muhammad ﷺ) the Book (the Quran), and has not placed therein any crookedness. (He has made it)"

[18:2] "Straight to give warning (to the disbelievers) of a severe punishment from Him, and to give glad tidings to the believers, who work at righteous deeds, they shall have a fair reward. (i.e. Paradise)."

[18:3] "They shall abide therein forever."

[18:4] "And to warn those (Jews, Christians, and pagans) who say, "Allah has begotten a son.""

[18:5] "No knowledge have they of such a thing, nor had their fathers. Mighty is the word that comes out of their mouth [i.e. He begot (took) sons and daughters]. They utter nothing but a lie."

[18:6] "Perhaps, you, would kill yourself (O Muhammad ﷺ) in grief, over their footsteps (for their turning away from you), because they believe not in this narration."

[18:7] "Verily! We have made that which is on earth as an adornment for it, in order that We may test them (mankind) as to which of them are best in deeds."

[18:8] "And verily! We shall make all that is on it (the earth) a bare dry soil."

[18:9] "Do you think that the people of the Cave and the Inscription were a wonder among Our Signs?"

[18:10] "(Remember) when the young men fled for refuge (from their disbelieving folk) to the Cave, they said: "Our Lord! Bestow on us mercy from Yourself, and facilitate for us our affair in the right way!"

Do you know why Allah asked to memorise (not just to recite, because it has to enter deep in one's heart) these ten verses for those who will be present at the appearance of Dajjal? It may not be possible to read Quran in his presence.

The core message of the Prophet ﷺ and that of Quran is:

★ Allah is ever praise worthy.

★ Allah is Wahid (One).

★ He has no offspring.

★ Those who assign/propose, partners to Allah, are destined to go to Hell.

★ Life of this world is full of attractions, trails, tests and transitary.

★ Those who believe the above and perform righteous deeds; will be rewarded with Paradise.

★ The disbelievers, the arrogant and wrong doers will be sent to Hell.

This core message is revealed in the first ten verses of Surae Kahf, along with another message:

Seek the Mercy of Allah and His Will, at the time of trials to follow the right path; like the faith of the companians of the cave. Due to His Will and Mercy, a person is directed towards the straight path, otherwise he may be easily deceived by Dajjal/Shaithan.

And in the last ten ayaath the same core theme is reminded again. Allah poses two questions and provides answers to them.

1."Do then those who disbelieve, think that they can consider My slaves [i.e., the angels, Allah's Messengers, 'Isa (AS) the son of Marium or any thing/body and Dajjal etc.] as Auliya (lords, gods, protectors, etc.) besides Me? (18:102).

2. "Shall we inform you of who will lose the most deeds?" (18:103)

He answers those question as:

"They are those whose efforts are in vain in this worldly life, while they think they are doing good! It is they who reject the signs of their Lord and their meeting with Him, rendering their deeds void, so We will not give their deeds any weight on Judgment Day. That is their reward: Hell, for their disbelief and mockery of My signs and messengers." (18:104 – 106). If you consider the angels, Allah's Messengers, 'Isa (AS) the son of Marium, or any object and Dajjal etc., as your god, you lose all your good deeds and then your place will be Hell.

Allah the Great, whose praise cannot be penned by any means, guides the Yahoodh (Jews), Nasara (Christians) and Kafir (idolaters) from the Prophet's time (You know that Sura Kahf was revealed as an answer to three questions which the Jews raised before our Prophet ﷺ in the presence of Quraish) till Dajjal's time, by advising: "So whoever hopes for the Meeting with his Lord, let him work righteousness and associate none as a partner in the worship of his Lord." (18:110). These verses are applicable to all the people for all times. This is the miracle of Quran!

[Kindly open your Quran translation in your mother tongue and read and understand the first and last 10 ayaath of Quran. May Allah always keep you in special care!] Aameen!

الحمدلله

2. "And among mankind is he who worships Allah as it were, upon the very edge; if good befalls him, he is content therewith; but if a trial befalls him, he turns back on his face..." (22:11) What Allah says about him in Quran?

Answer: Allah ﷻ asserts, "He loses both this world and the Hereafter. That is the evident loss for him."

One who lacks strong faith in Allah, stands on the edge between kufr and Islam. If all is favourable, with an easy life, with the fulfilling of all his wishes he will be pleased to remain in Islam.

On any calamity striking or any mishappening taking place or on encountering hardship, or losing anything – one will become the slave of himself, due to his weak faith. On one's faith over Allah ﷻ becomes wavering, forgetting Him and on turning away from Him; he easily falls into kufr (disbelief). He becomes a victim of false deities. Such a person, a victim of wavering belief, is a loser both in this world as well as in the Hereafter. He is worse than the disbeliever. A disbeliever neither fears God; nor about accountability; nor about the punishment in the Hereafter even though his life in this world will be a pleasing for him. But Muslims, after believing in Allah; turn away from Him and embark on a disbelief Allah will never forgive them; as per the verse: "Allah will not forgive them, nor guide them on the (Right) Way." (4:137).

This ayath was revealed referring to the Banu'l-Hallaf, the hypocrites of the Banu Asad and Ghatafan of Madhina. There are various interpretations by the commentators, with regard to this ayath.

One of the commentators of the Quran refers that: "This verse was revealed about those Bedouins, who used to travel from the desert to Madhina, to meet the Messenger of Allah ﷺ, if one of them had, during such visits, good health, or his mare gave birth to seemly foals or his wife delivered a boy, with his wealth and cattle multiplying - he would be pleased and well contended. He would say: 'Since I embraced this religion, I have not seen anything but good'. If, on the other hand, he fell ill, during such visits, or his wife delivered a girl, or his foals were stillborn, or he loses his wealth, or if the payment of alms to him was delayed - the Shaitan would come to him and whisper: 'Since you embraced this religion you have not gained anything but evil'. Being misguided, he would renounce his religion." Allah, exalted, therefore revealed this ayath.

Atiyyah reported that Abu Said al-Khudri said: "A Jewish man who had embraced Islam lost his sight, wealth and children. He thought that Islam was ill-omened and so he went to the Prophet ﷺ, and said: 'Discharge me!' The Prophet ﷺ said: 'You do not get discharged from Islam'. The man said: 'I did not gain any good from this religion of mine!' The Prophet ﷺ said: 'O Jew, Islam melts men as fire melts the dross of iron, silver and gold'. Therefore, such a verse was revealed.

The most frequent prayer of the Prophet ﷺ is "Oh turner of the hearts (Allah, the Highest), keep our hearts firm on your religion ".

Once the wife of the Prophet ﷺ, Umma Salamah (RA) enquired him, "Why you offer this dua so frequently?" In response he replied: "O Umm Salamah (RA), there is no human but that his heart is between the fingers of Allah. Whoever He wills, is made steadfast and whoever He wills, is deviated."

Allah requires us to pray as follows: "Our Lord! Let not our hearts deviate after You have guided us, and grant us mercy from You. Truly, 'You' are the Bestower." (3:8). Aameen!

الحمدلله

3. "Therefore, treat not the orphan with oppression and not repulse the beggar; And proclaim the Grace of your Lord." (Ad-Dhuha: 9 to 11). Why Allah سبحانه وتعالى commanded the Prophet ﷺ to follow the above mentioned deeds?

Answer: Prophet ﷺ was himself an orphan in need and therefore Allah commanded him as well his Umma, not to oppress any orphan; and not to repulse the beggars but be grateful for His favours.

Al-Awfi reported from Ibn Abbas, "Jibreel (AS) delayed his visit on one occasion to the Messenger of Allah ﷺ, for a number of days/weeks/months. He felt very much both physically and psychologically weak; developing a doubt as to whether Allah was angry with him; forgot and rejected him as Prophet. He was disturbed, depressed and his worship was affected and he became ill."

Then Abu Lahab's wife, a neighbor of the Prophet ﷺ commented sarcastically, `O Muhammad (ﷺ)! I think that your devil has finally left you.' Even the idolaters of Makkah were making fun of him saying, "Muhammad's Lord has abandoned and hates him" So Allah سبحانه وتعالى revealed, the following verse: - 'By the forenoon. By the night when it darkens. Your Lord has neither forsaken you nor hates you.' (93:1-3).

Allahuthala consoled the Nabi ﷺ personally. He swears by forenoon which gives freshness, hope and another chance of a new life. And swears by the stillness of night - an appropriate time for talking with the Lord. (93:1 and 2). Through this ayaath Allah provided peace, hope, positivity and also rejuvenates his faith. He provides an assurance as: "And indeed the Hereafter is better for you than the present life." (93:4).

Allah سبحانه وتعالى continues his message by remiding the Prophet ﷺ: "Did He not find you an orphan and give you shelter? (93: 6) And find you lost (that is, unrecognized by men) and guided (you)? (93:7). He found you poor, and made you rich and self-sufficient? (93:8)"

Yes! Muhammad ﷺ lost his father before he was born. Lost his mother at the age of six. Lost his loving care taker grandfather at eight and was left to be cared by Abu Thalib, his paternal uncle. His uncle provided protection and strong support when he was ordained as a Prophet ﷺ; by also suffering along with the Prophet ﷺ during the boycott.

His father left behind for his family, only a girl servant and a she-camel. He earned his living as a Shepard during his childhood and carried on trade while he was young. He married Bibi Khatheeja (RA), a wealthy lady, who willingly spent all her wealth for the sake of Islam. With his sincerity and effort in trade and commerce, he became self-sufficient.

Hence Allahuthala commanded him. "Therefore, as for the orphan, do not oppress (him). And as for the beggar, do not repulse (him)." (93:9 and 10). We should help those in need, if not try to excuse them politely.

Prior to his attaining Prophet hood, his society used to call him as "Al-Ameen" (the trust worthy). His society was known for ignorance, idol worshiping forgetting their fore-father Ibrahim's religion. He used to medidate in the cave Heera all alone, in pursuit of truth, peace and faith. Allah ﷻ enlightened and guided him, with His revelations. His society took efforts to prevent the spread of his religion and also attempted to kill or execute him!

Thereupon Allah, the Almighty had commanded him to be thankful for the numerous blessings He had showered on him. "And as for the favor of your Lord, do proclaim (it)." (93:11). The same command applies to us also!

Then Allah [SWT] consoled His Prophet ﷺ that he will win over his enemies and Islam will spread all over the world! And in the next world, He will be granted the greatest reward. Allah says, "And soon your Lord will grant you, and you shall be pleased". (93:5)

This surah asserts the love and care Allah has been showering on us, by making our present conditions better than the previous ones. Therefore, remember; glorify Him and thank Him! Spread positivity. Be thankful to the favours that Allah has bestowed on you!

الحمدلله

4. "God does not forbid you, with regard to those who did not fight you because of your faith nor drove you out of your homes, from dealing kindly and justly with them. God loves those who are just." (60:8). When, why and where this ayath was revealed?

Allah the Exalted, states to the believers:

"You have in Ibrahim (AS) as well as in the prophets and friends of Allah good role models, regarding their declaration of enmity towards their relatives who were idolaters, which should be emulated". (60:6)

Prior to the revealing of this verse, the believers declared that their relatives who were idolaters, as their enemies. They exhibited their enmity on them and absolved themselves of all their actions.

Allahuthala knew that this was hard on the believers and so He revealed: "It may be that Allah will ordain love between you and those of them with whom you are at enmity" [60:7].

According to the tafsir and hadhees, the verse 60:8 was revealed in the context of Abu Bakr's daughter, Asma (RA)'s refusal to let her mother in her house, because she was a disbeliever.

One of the wives of Abu Bakr, was Qutaylah bint Abdul Uzza. She was a disbeliever, remaining behind in Makkah even after the hijarath. Asma (RA) was born to her. After the peace treaty of Hudaibiyah, when the traffic opened between Makkah and Madinah, she came to Al-Madhina to see her daughter and also brought some gifts.

Imam Ahmad recorded that Asma bint Abu Bakr has stated, "During the period of the peace treaty of Quraish with Allah's Messenger (ﷺ), my mother, accompanied by her father, came to visit me, and she was a pagan. I consulted Allah's Messenger (ﷺ), "O Allah's Messenger (ﷺ)! My mother has come to me and she desires to receive a reward from me, shall I keep good relation with her?" He said, "Yes, keep good relation with her." [Sahih al-Bukhari 3183; Book 58, Hadith 25]

Imam Ahmad recorded that Abdullah bin Zubayr said, "Qutaylah came visiting her daughter, Asma bint Abu Bakr (RA), with some gifts, such as Dibab, cheese and butter. She was an idolatress at that time. Asma refused to accept her mother's gifts and did not let her enter her house. Ayesha (RA) asked the Prophet ﷺ about his verdict and Allah sent down this Ayath (60:8) Asma (RA) then let her mother into her house and accepted her gifts".

Therefore, the believers must distinguish the disbelievers as to whether they are hostile or not. If the disbelievers are fighting or driving the believers out or treating tyrannically on account of their faith in Allah, then Allah commands them against establishing friendly ties with the disbelievers: "It is only as regards to those who fought against you on account of religion, and have driven you out of your homes, and helped to drive you out, that Allah forbids you to befriend them. And whosoever will befriend them, then such are the Zalimun " (60:9). The Muslims can deal justly with the disbelievers who do not cause any harm to them on account of accepting Islam.

Allah loves who are just (5:42) and dislike people who are friendly with the tyrannical disbelievers.

الحمدلله

5. For what reason, the following aayaths have been revealed stage by stage, with intervals?

1. 2:219

2. 4:43

3. 5:90 and 91.

Answer: For the gradual prohibition of alcohol. (Khamr الْخَمْرُ/intoxicant)

Just like other evils prevalent during the pre-islamic days, the Arabian society was addicted to alcohol.

Allah revealed an ayath [16:67] in Surah Naml, which related to alcohol:

"And of the fruits of the palms and the grapes - you obtain from them intoxication and goodly provision; most surely there is a sign in this for a people who ponder." (16:67). The fruits are the good provisions as food from Allah. They also obtain the drink (alcohol) from that. It is one of the favours of Allah! Prophet Muhammad ﷺ and some of his companions, since inception desisted from consuming alcohol at Makkah, while most of the others were addicted.

When the Prophet ﷺ migrated to Madhina, a city known for dates, he found that its residents, in spite of its evil and harmful effects were cherishing the wine and alcohol produced from it. As alcohol and gambling destroys man's wealth and intellect, Umar bin Kattab (RA), Maaz Ibn Jaba (RA) and some of the other companions approached Prophet ﷺ and required a solution to prevent the use of alcohol.

Once, Uthmaan Ibn Maalik invited a few companions for a meal. As per custom, liquor was served after the meal. Thereafter, they used to get involved in another Arab custom of self-praising of their family and clan, in the form of poetry; continued to tease and belittle others who did not belong to their group. During this gathering, Saad Ibn Abi Waqqas (RA) criticized and belittled the Ansars of Madhina. Enraged at this, an Ansari youth threw a bone at him, which inflicted a severe wound on the head of Saad ibn Waqqas (RA). He then complained against the youngster to the Prophet ﷺ, after which he prayed to Allah: "O Allah! Grant us a clear cut directive regarding alcohol."

Imam Ahmad recorded that Abu Maysarah (RA) had said that "Umar (RA) pleaded, O Allah! Give us a clear ruling regarding Al-Khamr!" Therafter, Allah [SWT] sent down the Ayath 219 of Surah Al-Baqarah.

1) This Ayah [2:219] was the first stage of prohibiting Khamr:

"They ask you about intoxicants and games of chance. Say: In both of them there is a great sin and means of profit for men, and their sin is greater than their profit." (2:219). Yet, Umar (RA) still prayed, "O Allah! Give us a clear ruling regarding Khamr." On the contrary, some of the companions presumed that this verse did not prohibit alcohol so they declared that consuming moderate amount would not be harmful. However, shortly an incident occurred which brought about the next stage of revelation from Allah Subhanahuthala!

Ali bin Abi Talib (RA) informed that "Abdur-Rahman bin Awf prepared some food and invited us. After consuming food, alcohol was served. When all became intoxicated, the time for prayer arrived and one of them was required to lead the prayer. The one who led the prayer, recited surha Khafiroon in a wrong manner. Then, the ayath 43 in Surah An-Nisa was revealed."

2) [4:43] Second stage of Prohibition of Khamr:

"O you who believe! Do not approach Salath while you are in a drunken state until you know what you are saying" (4:43). Umar (RA) was summoned by Prophet ﷺ and the ayath was recited to him. Not being convinced, he still pleaded, "O Allah! Give us a clear ruling regarding Al-Khamr."

At the time of prayer, the Messenger of Allah ﷺ directed someone to proclaim; "Let not anyone who is drunk, approach the prayer." After this warning majority of the companions who gave priority to Salath, refrained totally from drinking. Exceptionally, few others consumed alcohol during the intervening periods of prayers.

3) [5:90 and 91] A final and clear prohibition of Khamr in Surah Al-Maidah:

"O you who believe! Intoxicants and games of chance and (sacrificing to) stones set up and (dividing by) arrows are abomination of the Shaitan's work; So avoid that in order that you may be successful." (5:90). "The Shaitan only desires to cause enmity and hatred to spring in your midst by means of intoxicants and games of chance, and to keep you off from the remembrance of Allah and from prayer. "So, will you not then abstain (cease)?" (5:91) On the ayath (5:90) in Surah Al-Ma'idah being revealed, Umar (RA) was again summoned and the ayath was recited to him. When he reached during recitation: "So, will you not then abstain? he said, "We shall abstain, we shall abstain."

This is also the narration collected by Abu Dawud Book 20, Number 3662 and also in At-Tirmidhi and An-Nasai.

Ahadhees about Prohibition of Khamr (Intoxicants):

As for Al-Khamr, Umar bin Khattab (RA), the Leader of the faithful, used to say, "It includes all what intoxicates the mind."

Imam Ahmad recorded that Abu Hurayrah (RA) narrated: "There were three stages of prohibiting Khamr (intoxicants). When the Messeger of Allah ﷺ migrated to Al-Madinah, the people were consuming alcohol and also gambling, so they enquired the Messenger of Allah ﷺ about these aspects, for which Allah revealed the verse 2:219. The people proclaimed that alcohol and gambling were not prohibited for them. Allah only said, "In them is a great sin, and some benefit for men.' So they went on drinking Khamr until one day, one of the emigrants lead his companions in the Maghrib prayer and mixed up the ayath during his recitation. Thereafter Allah sent down a tougher statement 4:43. Then, the people used to drink before the time of the prayer so that they would attend the prayer while sober. A firmer ayath 5:90 and 91 was later revealed." Abu Dawud, At-Tirmidhi, and An-Nasa'i recorded this Hadith.

Imam Ahmad recorded that Anas (RA) said, "I once was giving an alcoholic beverage to Abu Ubaydah bin Al-Jarrah, Ubayy bin Kab, Suhayl bin Bayda and several of their friends, meeting at Abu Talhah's house. When they were almost intoxicated, some Muslims came and said, "Did you not know that the Khamr has been prohibited?" They said, `We'll wait and ask.' They then said, `O Anas! Spill the remaining alcohol out of your container.' By Allah! They never drank it again. This is also recorded in the Two Sahihs.

On that day the streets of Madina were flooded with alcohol.

In another narration by Anas (RA), a man asked, `O Allah's Messenger ﷺ! What about those who died drinking it?' `Some people were killed and wine was still in their stomachs.' Allah sent down the following verse, "Those who believe and do righteous good deeds, there is no sin on them for what they ate (in the past), if they fear Allah (by keeping away from His forbidden things), and believe and do righteous good deeds, and again fear Allah and believe, and once again fear Allah and do good deeds with Ihsan (perfection). And Allah loves the good doers. (5:93)"

The Messenger of Allah ﷺ said: "Whoever drinks alcohol amongst my Umma, his prayer will not be accepted for forty days"

The Messenger of Allah ﷺ said, "Whoever drinks Khamr in the life of this world and does not repent for it, will be deprived of it in the Hereafter" (Muslim - 3736 and Al-Bukhari -5147)

"Every intoxicant is Khamr, and every intoxicant is unlawful."

"Alcohol is the mother of all evils and it is the most shameful of evils." (Sunan Ibn-I-Majah, Vol. 3, Book of Intoxicants, Chapter 30, Hadith, 3371)

"Anything which intoxicates in a large quantity, is prohibited even in a small quantity." (Sunan Ibn-I- Majah Vol. 3, Book of Intoxicants, Chapter 30, Hadhees, 3392) Thus there is no excuse for a nip or a tot.

Al-Tirmidhi, Hadith – 4477, Narrated by Jabir ibn Abdullah – The Prophet ﷺ said, "He who believes in Allah and the Last Day must not sit at a table/gathering, where wine is being circulated."

According to Sunan Ibn-I- Majah Vol. 3, Book of Intoxicants, Chapter 30, Hadhees, 3380, it was reported by Anas (RA) that the Prophet ﷺ said:

Allah's curse falls on ten groups of people who are involved with alcohol.

1. The one who drink it,
2. the one who serve it,
3. the one who sell it,
4. the one who carry it,
5. the one to whom it has been carried,
6. the one who brew it,

7. the one who helps to brew it,
8. the one who buys it,
9. the one who buys it for someone else,
10. the one who utilizes the income from it"

May Allah protect all the Muslim Umma from this evil! Aameen!

الحمدلله

6. "And the three left till for them the earth, vast as it is, was straitened and their ownselves were straitened to them, and they perceived that there is no fleeing from Allah, and no refuge but with Him." (9:118). For what sin these three were punished and for which they repented to Allah?

Answer: As those three stayed back in Madhina, without accompanying Thabuk expedition, with no reliable reason.

The three are:

"Kaab bin Malik, Hilal bin Umayyah and Murarah bin Ar-Rabi, all of them were Ansar." The last two participated in the battle of Badr. That itself proves that they were highly faithful. Kaab did not participate in the battle of Badr, but accompanied the Holy Prophet ﷺ in every other expedition.

Participating in any battle for the sake of religion, was considered as Jihadh. Allah has ordained in Quran, "Fight in the way of Allah against those who fight against you, and do not exceed the limits" (2:190). At the time of the Prophet ﷺ all Muslims (except the hypocrates), eagerly participated in order to avail very high status in the Hereafter. When all the Muslims were commanded to go for Tabuk expedition, the above referred three persons, stayed with no reliable reasons.

Punishment:

When the Holy Prophet ﷺ came back from Tabuk, he met all those who did not praticipate (about eighty persons). Most of them furnished fictitious reasons for not coming. But those three spoke the truth.

In spite of their partipation in previous battles, they were severely punished for their non-participation in the Tabuk Expedition. The Prophet ﷺ ordered the Muslims not to converse with them to the extent of not responding, even to their greetings. So the earth shrinked for them. Their soul became a destitute. They realized that they cannot flee from Allah and can seek refuge only with Him. The most merciful one, made them to turn to him; by accepting their repentance and forgave them.

After a boycott of fifty days, this verse (9:118) decended from Allah:

"Then, He accepted their repentance, that they might repent. Verily, Allah is the One Who accepts repentance, Most Merciful." [9:118]. The details are given in the following hadhees narrated by Kaab bin Malik. As he became old and blind, he himself conveyed this to his care taker, his son Abdullah.

The hadhees narrated in detail by Kaab bin Malik: [Sahih Muslim, The Book of Repentance 2769 a, b]

Kaab bin Malik proclaimed: "I never remained behind Allah's Messenger ﷺ from any expedition which he undertook except the Battle of Tabuk and the Battle of Badr. So far as the Battle of Badr is concerned, nobody was blamed for remaining behind, as Allah's Messenger and the Muslims did not set out for attack but for waylaying the caravan of the Quraish, but it was Allah Who made them confront their enemies without their intention (to do so).

I had the honour to be with Allah's Messenger ﷺ on the night of Aqaba when we pledged our allegiance to Islam and it was more dear to me than my participation in the Battle of Badr, although Badr was more popular amongst people as compared with that (Battle of Tabuk). And this is my story of remaining back from Allah's Messenger ﷺ on the occasion of the Battle of Tabuk.

Never did I possess means enough and (my circumstances) more favourable than at the occasion of this expedition. And, by Allah, I had never before this expedition simultaneously had in my possession two rides.

Allah's Messenger ﷺ set out for this expedition in an extremely hot season; the journey was long and the land (which he and his army had to cover) was waterless and he had to confront a large army, so he informed the Muslims about the actual situation (they had to face), so that they should adequately equip themselves for this expedition, and he also told them the destination where he intended to go. And the Muslims, who accompanied Allah's Messenger ﷺ at that time were large in number but there was no proper record about them. Kaab (further) said: Few were the persons who wanted to absent themselves and were under the impression that they could easily conceal themselves (and thus remain undetected) until revelations from Allah, the Exalted and Glorious (descended about them). And Allah's Messenger ﷺ set out on an expedition, when the fruits were ripe and their shadows had been lengthened. I had weakness for them and it was during this season that Allah's Messenger ﷺ made preparations and the Muslims too along with him. I also set out in the morning so that I should make preparations along with them but I came back and did nothing but said to myself: I've means enough (to make preparations) as soon as I like. And I went on delaying (postponing my preparations) until the people were about to depart and it was in the morning that Allah's Messenger ﷺ set out with the Muslims too along with him, but I made no preparations. I went early in the morning and came back, but I made no decision. I continued to do so until they (the Muslims) hastened and covered a good deal of distance.

I also made up my mind to march on to meet them. Would that I had done that but perhaps it was not destined for me. After the departure of Allah's Messenger ﷺ, as I went out amongst people I was shocked to find that I did not see anyone like me but people who were labelled as hypocrites or the people whom Allah granted exemption because of their incapacity and Allah's Messenger ﷺ took no notice of me until he reached Tabuk. (One day as he was sitting amongst the people in Tabuk) he exclaimed: 'What has happened to Kaab bin Malik?' A person from Banu' Salama said to Allah's Messenger ﷺ: 'the (beauty) of his cloak and his appreciation of his sides have allured him and he was thus detained.' Muadh bin Jabal said: 'Woe be upon that what you contend. Allah's Messenger ﷺ, by Allah, we know nothing about him but good.' Allah's Messenger ﷺ however, kept quiet. It was during that time that he (the Holy Prophet ﷺ) saw a person (dressed in all white (garment) shattering the illusion of eye (mirage). Thereupon Allah's Messenger ﷺ said: May he be Abu Khaithama and lo, it was Abu Khaithama al-Ansari and he was that person who contributed a sa' of dates and was scoffed at by the hypocrites. Kabb bin Malik further said: When this news reached me that Allah's Messenger ﷺ was on his way back from Tabuk, I was greatly perturbed. I thought of fabricating false stories and asked myself how I would save myself from his anger on the following day. In this connection, I sought the help of every prudent man from amongst the members of my family and when it was said to me that Allah's Messenger ﷺ was about to arrive, all the false ideas vanished (from my mind) and I came to the conclusion that nothing could save me but the telling of truth. Therefore, I decided to speak the truth and it was in the morning that Allah's Messenger ﷺ arrived (in Madhina). And it was his habit that as he came back from a journey, he first went to the mosque and prayed two Rakaths of nafil (as a mark of gratitude) and then sat amongst people.

And as he did that, those who had remained behind him began to put forward their excuses and take an oath before him and they were more than eighty persons. Allah's Messenger ﷺ accepted their excuses on the very face of them and accepted their allegiance and sought forgiveness for them and left their secret (intentions) to Allah, until I presented myself to him. I greeted him, he smiled and there was a tinge of anger in that. He then me: "Come forward." I went forward until I sat in front of him. He said to me: "What kept you back? Could you not afford to go in for a ride?" I said: "Allah's Messenger ﷺ, by Allah, if I were to sit in the presence of anybody else from amongst the worldly people, I would have definitely saved myself from his anger on one pretext (or the other) and I have also the knack of falling into argumentation, but, by Allah, I am fully aware of the fact that if I were to put forward before you a false excuse to please you, Allah would definitely provoke your wrath upon me, and if I speak the truth you may be annoyed with me, but I hope that Allah would make its end well and, by Allah, there is no valid excuse for me. By Allah, I never possessed so good means, and I never had such favorable conditions for me as I had when I stayed behind you (failed to join the expedition)." Thereupon, Allah's Messenger ﷺ said: "This man told the truth, so get up until Allah gives a decision in your case."

I stood up and some people of Banu Salama followed me in hot haste, and they said to me: "By Allah, we do not know about you that you committed a sin prior to this. You, however, showed inability to put forward an excuse before Allah's Messenger ﷺ as those who stayed behind, have put forward excuses. It would have been enough for the forgiveness of your sin that Allah's Messenger ﷺ would have sought forgiveness for you. By Allah, they continued to incite me until I thought of going back to Allah's Messenger ﷺ and contradict myself. Then I said to them: "Has anyone else also met the same fate?" They said: "Yes, two persons have met the same fate as has fallen to you and they have made the same statement as you have made, and the same verdict has been delivered in their case as it has been delivered in your case." I said: 'Who are they?' They said: 'Murara bin ar-Rabia Amiri and Hilal bin Umayya al-Waqafi.'

They made a mention of these two pious persons to me who had participated in the Battle of Badr and there was an example for me in them. I went away when they named these two persons. Allah's Messenger ﷺ forbade the Muslims to talk with three of us from amongst those (persons) who had stayed behind him. The people began to avoid us and their attitude towards us underwent a change and it seemed as if the whole atmosphere had turned (hostile) against us and it was in fact the same atmosphere at which I was fully aware and in which I had lived (for a fairly long time). We spent fifty nights in this very state and my two friends confined themselves within their houses and spent (most of the) time in weeping, but as I was young and strong amongst them I got (out of my house), participated in congregational prayers, moved about in the bazar; but none spoke to me. I came to Allah's Messenger ﷺ as he sat amongst people after the prayer, greeted him and asked myself whether his lips stirred in response to my greetings (or not). Then I observed prayer beside him and looked at him with stealing glances and when I attended to my prayer, he looked at me and when I cast a glance at him he turned away his eyes from me. And when the harsh treatment of the Muslims towards me extended to a (considerable) length of time, I walked until I climbed upon the wall of the garden of Abu Qatada who was my cousin, and I had the greatest love for him. I greeted him but, by Allah, he did not respond to my greetings. I said to him: "Abu Qatada, I adjure you by Allah, arn't you well aware of the fact that I love Allah and His Messenger ﷺ the most. He kept quiet. I again repeated saying: "I adjure you by Allah. Arn't you well aware of the fact that I love Allah and His Messenger ﷺ the most. He kept quiet. I again adjured him, whereupon he said: "Allah and the Messenger ﷺ are best aware of it." My eyes began to shed tears and I came back climbing down from the wall and as I was walking in the bazar of Madhina, a Nabatean from amongst the Nabateans of Syria, who had come to sell food grains in Madhina asked people to direct him to Kaab bin Malik. People gave him the indication by pointing towards me. He came to me and delivered to me a letter of the King of Ghassan and as I was a scribe I read that letter and it was written as follows: "Coming to my point, it has been conveyed to us that your friend (the Holy Prophet ﷺ) is subjecting you to cruelty and Allah has not created you for a place where you are to be degraded and where you cannot find your right place, so you come to us that we should accord you honour." As I read that letter and I said: 'This is also a calamity, so I burnt it in the oven.'

When out of the fifty days, forty days had passed and Allah's Messenger ﷺ received no revelation, there came the messenger of Prophet ﷺ to me and said: "Verily, Allah's Messenger ﷺ has commanded you to remain separate from your wife. I said: "Should I divorce her or what (else) should I do? He said: "No, but only remain separate from her and don't have sexual contact with her." The same message was sent to my companions. So I said to my wife: "You better go to your parents and stay there with them until Allah gives the decision in my case."

The wife of Hilal bin Umayya came to Allah's Messenger ﷺ and enquired: "O Allah's Messenger, Hilal bin Umayya is a senile person, he has no servant. Do you disapprove of my serving him?" He said: "No, but don't go near him." She said: "By Allah, he has no such instinct in him. By Allah, he spends his time in weeping from that day to this day."

Some of the members of my family said to me: "Were you to seek permission from Allah's Messenger ﷺ in regard to your wife as he has granted permission to the wife of Hilal bin Umayya to serve him." I said: "I would not seek permission from Allah's Messenger ﷺ for I cannot say what Allah's Apostle ﷺ may say in response to my seeking permission. Moreover, I am a young man."

It was in this state, that I spent ten more nights and thus fifty nights had passed that (people) had observed boycott with us. It was on the morning of the fiftieth night that I observed my dawn prayer and was sitting on one of the roofs of our houses. And I was in fact sitting in that very state which Allah, the Exalted and Glorious, has described about us in these words: "Life had become hard for myself and the earth had compressed despite its vastness." I heard the announcer from the peak of the hill of Sal saying at the top of his voice: "Kaab bin Malik, there is glad tidings for you!" I fell down in prostration and came to realize that there was (a message of) relief for me. Allah's Messenger ﷺ had informed the people of the acceptance of our repentance by Allah as he offered the dawn prayer. So the people went on to give us glad tidings while some of them went to my friends in order to give them the glad tidings. A person galloped his horse and came from the tribe of Aslam and his horse reached me more quickly than his voice. And when he came to me whose sound I heard, he gave me the glad tidings. I took off my clothes and clothed him with them because of his bringing good news to me and, by Allah, I possessed nothing else (in the form of clothes) than these two on that occasion. I requested one to lend me two clothes and dressed myself with them. I came to Allah's Messenger ﷺ and on my way I met groups of people who greeted me because of (the acceptance of) repentance and they said: 'Here is a greeting for you for your repentance being accepted by Allah.' (I moved on) until I came to the mosque and Allah's Messenger ﷺ had been sitting there amongst persons. Talha bin Ubaidullah got up and rushed towards me; shook hands with me; greeted me; and by Allah, no person stood up (to greet me) from amongst the emigrants except him. Kaab said that he never forgot (this good gesture of) Talha.

Kaab further said: "I greeted Allah's Messenger ﷺ with 'Assalamu Alaikam' and his face was glistening because of delight, and he said: "Let there be glad tidings and blessings for you, the like of which (you have neither found nor you will find, as you find today) since your mother gave your birth." I asked: Allah's Messenger ﷺ "Is this acceptance of repentance from you or from Allah?" He said: "No, (it is not from me), it is from Allah," and it was common with Allah's Messenger ﷺ that as he was happy his face brightened up and it looked like a part of the moon and it was from this that we recognised it (his delight)."

As I sat before him, I said: "Allah's Messenger ﷺ, am I allowed to give in charity my wealth for Allah's sake and for the sake of His Messenger ﷺ. There upon Allah's Messenger ﷺ said: "Keep some property with you, as it is better for you." I said: 'I shall keep with me that part (of my property) which fell to my lot (on the occasion of the expedition of) Khaibar.' I told the Allah's Messenger ﷺ, verily, Allah has granted me salvation because of truth and, therefore, (I think) that repentance implies that I should not speak anything but truth as long as I live." He said: "By Allah, I do not know whether anyone amongst the Muslims was put to more severe trial than I, by Allah because of telling the truth. And since I made a mention of this to Allah's Messenger ﷺ up to this day I have not told any lie and by Allah, I have decided not to tell a lie and I hope that Allah would save me (from trials) for the rest of my life. Allah, the Exalted and Glorious, revealed these verses:

"Certainly, Allah has turned in Mercy to the Prophet ﷺ and the emigrants and the helpers who followed him in the hour of hardship after the hearts of a part of them were about to deviate; then He turned to them in mercy. Surely, to them He is Compassionate, Merciful and (He turned in Mercy) to the three who were left behind until the earth despite its vastness became strait for them and their souls were also straitened to them."

Kaab said: 'By Allah, since Allah directed me to Islam there has been no blessing more significant for me than this truth of mine which I spoke to Allah's Messenger ﷺ and if I were to tell a lie, I would have been ruined like those who were ruined by telling lies, for in regard to those who told lies Allah used harshest words used for anyone as He descended revelation."

Allah warns the believers in the next ayath, "O you who believe! Be afraid of Allah, and be with those who are true (in words and deeds)." (9:119). The ayath requires one to always adhere to the truth in his words and action. Seek refuge with Allah. He will show you a path and save from destruction.

Narrated Abdullah (RA) The Prophet ﷺ said, "Truthfulness leads to Al-Birr (righteousness) and Al-Birr leads to Paradise. And a man keeps on telling the truth until he becomes a truthful person. Falsehood leads to Al-Fujur (wickedness – evil doing) and Al-Fujur leads to the (Hell) Fire. And a man keeps on telling lies until he is written as a liar before Allah." [Sahih Al-Bukhari, 6094; Book 78, Hadith 121]

الحمدلله

7. "If you desire the life of this world, and its glitter, then come! I will make a provision for you and set you free in a handsome manner." [33: 28]. In this ayath of Quran to whom "you" and "I" are referred to?

Answer: In this verse "you" refers to the wives of Prophet ﷺ and "I" to the Prophet Mohammad ﷺ.

On facing very many difficulties during the battle of Trench at Madhina and also after the raid of Bani Quraizah, Prophet's ﷺ economic conditions became worse. His mammoth responsibility of propagating Islam, was making inroads in his earnings and livelihood for his family. During that occasions, he had four wives: Saudah (RA), Ayesha (RA), Hafsah (RA) and Umm Salama (RA).

One day Abu Bakr (RA) and Umar (RA) went to see the Prophet ﷺ, for whom the permission was granted; thereupon they entered his house. The Prophet ﷺ was sitting by being surrounded by all his wives, observing silence. The visiting companians understood that they were involved in a serious family discussion. They also sat quietly. The Prophet ﷺ informed them that "They were demanding money for household expenditure."

As fathers of his two wives they questioned their daughters, "Why do you embarrass and demand from him, what he does not have?" Being his closest companions they fully knew the condition of the Prophet ﷺ.

Allah ﷻ being aware of His Messenger's economic hardship, physical strain and mental peace, revealed the aayath of surah Al-Ahazab from verse 28 to 34:

[33:28] "O Prophet (Muhammad ﷺ)! Say to your wives: If you desire the life of this world, and its glitter, then come! I will make a provision for you and set you free in a handsome manner (divorce)."

[33:29] "But if you desire Allah and His Messenger, and the home of the Hereafter, then verily, Allah has prepared for the good-doers amongst you an enormous reward."

[33:30] "O wives of the Prophet ﷺ! Whoever of you commits an open illegal sexual intercourse, the torment for her will be doubled, and that is ever easy for Allah."

[33:31] "And whosoever of you is obedient to Allah and His Messenger ﷺ, and does righteous good deeds, 'We' shall give her, her reward twice over, and 'We' have prepared for her Paradise."

[33:32] "O wives of the Prophet ﷺ! You are not like any other women. If you keep your duty (to Allah), then be not soft in speech, lest he in whose heart is a disease should be moved with desire, but speak in an honourable manner."

[33:33] "And stay in your houses, and do not display your-selves like that of the times of ignorance and perform As-Salath and give Zakath and obey Allah and His Messenger ﷺ. Allah wishes only to remove evil and sins, etc. from you, O members of the family of the Prophet ﷺ, and to purify you with a thorough purification."

[33:34] "And remember (O you the members of the Prophet's ﷺ family, the Graces of your Lord), that which is recited in your houses of the Verses of Allah and Al-Hikmah. Verily, Allah is Ever Most Courteous, Well Acquainted with all things."

Through these aayath Allah سبحانه وتعالى made them realise the responsibilities of Ummul Momineen. They were not ordinary women. They were considered as the models for the whole Umma. Allah desired ro remove all the impurities from them. On observing all the five duties of Islam; reciting Quran; adhering to Islamic manners; adopting righteousness; piety etc. they will be granted double the reward in the Hereafter.

After receiving this revelation [If you desire the life of this world, and its glitter, then come! I will make a provision for you and set you free in a handsome manner], he first to consulted with Ayesha (RA) and enquired: "I ask you a thing; do not be hasty in answering; consult with your parents then decide." She responded as: "Should I consult my parents about this? I seek Allah and His Messenger ﷺ and the Hereafter." He raised the same questions to all his wives and they also offered the same reply. This process of seeking the opinion of a wife; allowing her to decide to stay or not in marriage bond, is called 'takhyir.'

Once Islam was established with victory after the battle of Trench and the raid by the tribes of Banu Quraizah in Madhina, initial steps were commenced towards the social reforms in Islam, with their being enforced from the house of Prophet ﷺ himself. His wives were required to avoid the practice of preislamic days of ignorance.

Similarly, in another situation Allah, forgave the wives of the Prophet ﷺ and when they committed a wrong he corrected it (66:4 and 5).

Even though these verses have been revealed to the wives of Prophet ﷺ it is also a guidance to all the wives of Muslims. When a husband's income is less, she can budget her livelihood according to it. She is entitled to encourage her husband to earn more, but should not demand beyond his capacity. She should be obedient to Allah, fulfill all her religious duties, purify herself with isthigfar, also to be soft in speech by adhering to honourable manners.

The wives of the Prophet ﷺ should never be ignorant of Quran and Sunna. They must always recite Quran; follow it by adhering to Sunnah. Guide the other women about its real meaning and thier benefits.

During the period of revelation of the Quran, the companions; the family members of Prophet ﷺ and other Muslims had developed great fear of Allah. They were very careful in their acts and deeds, fearing that verses will be sent down by Allahuthala to point out their mistakes. May Allah provide such fear to us also, so that we also achieve HIGH RANK AND A DOUBLE REWARD. Aameen!

الحمدلله

8. Which are the verses of Al Quran proved the innocence of Ayesha (RA), the mother of the believers, after the slander against her?

Answer: In Surah An-Noor, verses 11 to 23.

[24:11] "Verily! Those who brought forth the slander (against Ayesha (RA) the wife of the Prophet ﷺ) are a group among you. Consider it not a bad thing for you. Nay, it is good for you. [This is to the house hold of Ayesha (RA)]. Unto every man among them will be paid that which he had earned of the sin and as for him among them who had the greater share therein, his will be a great torment." [This part of ayath was revealed pointing out towards Abdullah bin Ubayy and his followers and also to those who spread the slander].

[24:12] "Why then, did not the believers, men and women, when you heard it (the slander) think good of their own people and say: "This (charge) is an obvious lie?"

[24:13] "Why did they not produce four witnesses? Since they (the slanderers) have not produced witnesses! Then with Allah they are the liars."

[24:14] "Had it not been for the Grace of Allah and His Mercy unto you in this world and in the Hereafter, a great torment would have touched you for that whereof you had spoken."

[24:15] "When you were propagating it with your tongues, and uttering with your mouths, that whereof you had no knowledge, you counted it a little thing, while with Allah it was very great."

[24:16] "And why did you not, when you heard it, say: It does not beseem us that we should talk of it; glory be to Thee! this is a great calumny?"

[24:17] "Allah forbids you from it and warns you not to repeat the like of it forever, if you are believers."

[24:18] "And Allah makes the ayath plain to you, and Allah is All-Knowing, All-Wise."

[24:19] "Verily, those who like that (the crime of) illegal sexual intercourse should be propagated among those who believe, they will have a painful torment in this world and in the Hereafter. And Allah knows and you know not." [The above ayaath were revealed to those who spread the slander].

[24:20] "And had it not been for the Grace of Allah and His Mercy on you, (Allah would have hastened the punishment upon you). And that Allah is full of kindness, Most Merciful!"

[24:21["O you who believe! Follow not the footsteps of Shaitan. And whosoever follows the footsteps of Shaitan, then, verily he commands Al-Fahsha' [i.e. to commit indecency (illegal sexual intercourse, etc.)], and Al-Munkar [disbelief and polytheism (i.e. to do evil and wicked deeds; to speak or to do what is forbidden in Islam, etc.)]. And had it not been for the Grace of Allah and His Mercy on you, not one of you would ever have been pure from sins. But Allah purifies (guides to Islam) whom He wills, and Allah is All-Hearer, All-Knower."

[24:22] "And let not those among you who are blessed with graces and wealth swear not to give (any sort of help) to their kinsmen, Al-Masakin (the poor), and those who left their homes for Allah's Cause. Let them pardon and forgive. Do you not love that Allah should forgive you? And Allah is Oft-Forgiving, Most Merciful." [This ayath refers to Abu Bakr (RA)].

[24:23]. "Verily, those who accuse chaste women, who never even think of anything touching their chastity and are good believers, are cursed in this life and in the Hereafter, and for them will be a great torment."

The slander/ the episode of [إفك] ifk:

The people who spread slander, raised their accusations against Ayesha (RA), the mother of the believers. These people were not two or three, but a group. Nowhere, either in the Seerah or in the ahadhees, it had been explained as to what that slander was.

When and why this happened?

While the Prophet ﷺ and his Companions were returning from the expedition of Bani Mustaliq, Sura thul-Munafiqun (Hypocrites) was revealed. The reason for revealing this Surah is due to a small dispute between the companions and Abdullah bin Ubay bin Salul, the chief of the hypocrites. Allah exposed the intention of the hypocrites. It was in the very same return journey Abdullah bin Ubay bin Salul focused his attack directly on Prophet ﷺ, by accusing his beloved wife Ayesha (RA) and spreading the slander, in Madhina.

About Abdullah bin Ubayy bin Salul:

Abdullah ibn Ubayy ibn Salul was the chief of Banu Khazraj, an Arab tribe and also one of the leaders of Madhina. Upon the arrival of the Prophet Muhammad ﷺ, Abdullah Ibn Ubayy became a Muslim, not because he was attracted towards the religion but to retain his leadership. His followers also converted to Islam. Joining with them, he repeatedly disputed, conflicted with and betrayed the Prophet ﷺ. Thereafter, he was labelled as "leader of the Munafiqun". He was waiting for an oppurtunity to attack the Prophet ﷺ personally, as he felt that after the arrival of Prophet ﷺ at Madhina, he had lost the chances of kingship.

Even Muslims were involved in the spread of slander:

Some of the Muslims started believing it, while others thought it might be possible and discussed about it. Zaid bin Rifaah, Mistah bin Uthathah and Hassan bin Thabit are the three muslims, who were actively involved in the spreading of slander. This slander continued for almost a month, until a wahi was revealed.

Prophet's ﷺ response:

As a religious leader and husband, the Prophet ﷺ consulted this problem with Ali (RA), Usaka bin Zaid (RA), his other wives, Ayesha's servant personally and the other muslims openly, after his sermon. Finally, he directly advised Ayesha (RA) to repent, if she had really committed sin.

Ayesha (RA) in her own words described this situation in a long hadhees: [Sahih al-Bukhari, 2661; Book 52, Hadith 25]

Ayesha (RA) narrated: "Whenever Allah's Messenger ﷺ intended to go on a journey, he would draw lots amongst his wives and would take with him the one upon whom the lot fell. During a Ghazwa of his, he drew lots amongst us and the lot fell upon me, there upon I proceeded with him after Allah had decreed the use of the veil by women. I was carried in a Howdah (on the camel) and dismounted while still inside. When Allah's Messenger ﷺ was through with his Ghazwa and returned home, we approached the city of Madhina, Allah's Messenger ordered us to proceed at night. When the order of setting off was given, I walked till I was past the army to answer the call of nature. Then I came back to my howdah. Then I put my hand to my chest and noticed that a necklace of mine that was made of onyx and cornelian was lost. There upon I went back and searched for it, and was delayed.

In the mean-time, the people who used to lift my howdah onto my camel came along and put it on the camel, thinking that I was inside. In those times women were slenderer and not so heavy, they only ate mouthful of food. Hence, the people did not think anything of the howdah being so light when they lifted it up, as I was a young woman. They set off, and I found my necklace after the army had moved on.

Then I came back to the place where we had stopped, and I saw no one to respond. I remind at that place, thinking that the people would miss me and come back for me. While I was sitting there, I fell asleep. Safwan bin Al-Muattal As-Sulami Adh-Dhakwani had availed rest during the night, behind the army. Then he set out just before daybreak and reached the place where I slept and saw the outline of a person sleeping.

He came and recognized me, as he had seen me before Hijab was made obligatory. When he saw me and said ` "Inna lil-lah-wa inn a ilaihi rajiun" (Truly, to Allah we belong, and truly, to Him we shall return) I woke up, and covered my face with my outer garment. By Allah, he did not speak a word to me and I did not hear him say anything except `Truly, to Allah we belong, and truly, to Him we shall return,' until he brought his camel and made it kneel so that I could ride upon it. Then he set out leading the camel until we caught up with the army at Zuhr.

There are people who were doomed because of what happened to me, and the one who had the greater share therein was Abdullah bin Ubayy bin Salul.

When we came back to Al-Madhina, I was ill for a month, and the people were talking about what the people of the slander were saying, and I knew nothing about it. What upset me when I was ill was that I did not see the kindness I used to see on the part of the Messenger of Allah ﷺ.

When I was ill; he would just come in and say, "How is that lady?" That is what upset me! I did not feel that there was anything wrong until I went out after I felt better, and Umm Mistah went out with me, walking towards Al-Manasi and I came back towards my house.

Umm Mistah stumbled over her apron and said, `May Mistah be ruined!' I said to her, `What a bad thing you have said! Are you abusing a man who was present at Badr? She said, `Good grief, have you not heard what he said' I said, `What did he say?' So she told me what the people of the slander were saying, which made me even more ill.

When I returned home, the Messenger of Allah ﷺ came in to me and greeted me, then he said, "How is that lady?" I said to him, `Will you give me permission to go to my parents'

At that time, I wanted to confirm the news by hearing it from them. The Messenger of Allah ﷺ gave me permission, so I went to my parents and asked my mother, `O my mother, what are the people talking about. My mother said, `Calm down, for by Allah, there is no beautiful woman who is loved by her husband and has co-wives but those co-wives would find fault with her.' I said, `Subhan Allah! Are the people really talking about that? I wept throughout the whole night until morning. My tears never ceased and I did not sleep at all, and morning came while I was still weeping. Because the revelation had ceased, the Messenger of Allah ﷺ called `Ali bin Abi Talib and Usamah bin Zaid, and consulted them.

Usaka bin Zaid said what he knew of the good reputation of the Prophet's ﷺ wives and added, 'O Allah's Messenger ﷺ! Keep your wife, for, by Allah, we know nothing about her but good.' `Ali bin Abu Talib said, 'O Allah's Messenger ﷺ Allah has not imposed restrictions on you, and there are many women other than she, yet you may ask the woman-servant who will tell you the truth.'

On that Allah's Messenger ﷺ called Barirah and said, 'O Barirah. Did you ever see anything which roused your suspicions about her?' Barirah said, 'No, by Allah Who has sent you with the Truth, I have never seen in her anything faulty, except that she is a girl of immature age, who sometimes sleeps and leaves the dough for the goats to eat.'

On that day Allah's Messenger ﷺ ascended the pulpit and requested that somebody support him in punishing Abdullah bin Ubayy bin Salul. Allah's Apostle ﷺ said, 'Who will support me to punish that person (`Abdullah bin Ubayy bin Salul) who has hurt me by slandering the reputation of my family? By Allah, I know nothing about my family but good, and they have accused a person about whom I know nothing except good, and he never entered my house except in my company.'

Sad bin Muadh got up and said, 'O Allah's Messenger ﷺ! By Allah, I will relieve you from him. If that man is from the tribe of the Aus, then we will chop his head off and if he is from our brothers, the Khazraj, then order us and we will fulfill your order.' On that Sad bin Ubada, the chief of the Khazraj and before this incident, he had been a pious man, got up, motivated by his zeal for his tribe and said, 'By Allah, you have told a lie; you cannot kill him, and you will never be able to kill him.' On that Usaid bin Al-Hadir got up and said (to Sad bin Ubada), 'By Allah! you are a liar. By Allah, we will kill him; and you are a hypocrite, defending the hypocrites.' On this the two tribes of Aus and Khazraj got excited and were about to fight each other, while Allah's Messenger ﷺ was standing on the pulpit. He got down and calmed them till they became silent and he kept quiet.

On that day I kept on weeping so much so that neither did my tears stop, nor could I sleep. In the morning my parents were with me and I had wept for two nights and a day, till I thought my liver would burst from weeping. While they were sitting with me and I was weeping, an Ansari woman asked my permission to enter, and I allowed her to come in. She sat down and started weeping with me. While we were in this state, Allah's Messenger ﷺ came and sat down and he had never sat with me since the day they forged the accusation. No revelation regarding my case came to him for a month. He recited Tashah-hud (i.e. None has the right to be worshipped but Allah and Muhammad is His Apostle) and then said, 'O `Ayesha! I have been informed such-and-such about you; if you are innocent, then Allah will soon reveal your innocence, and if you have committed a sin, then repent to Allah and ask Him to forgive you, for when a person confesses his sin and asks Allah for forgiveness, Allah accepts his repentance.' When Allah's Messenger ﷺ finished his speech my tears ceased completely and there remained not even a single drop of it.

I requested my father to reply to Allah's Messenger ﷺ on my behalf. My father said, 'By Allah, I do not know what to say to Allah's Messenger ﷺ. I said to my mother, 'Talk to Allah's Messenger ﷺ on my behalf.' She said, 'By Allah, I do not know what to say to Allah's Apostle ﷺ.'

So even though I was just a young girl who had not memorized much of the Quran, I said: `By Allah, I know that you have heard so much of this story that it has become planted in your minds and you believe it. So now if I tell you that I am innocent -- and Allah knows that I am innocent -- you will not believe me; but if I admit something to you -- and Allah knows that I am innocent -- you will believe me. By Allah, I cannot find any example to give you except for that which the Prophet Yusuf's father said, "So (for me) patience is most fitting. And it is Allah Whose help can be sought against that (lie) which you describe"

Then I turned my face away and lay down on my bed. By Allah, at that point I knew I was innocent and that Allah would prove my innocence, because I was innocent, but by Allah, I did not think that Allah would reveal the ayaath of Quran that would be forever recited concerning my situation, because I thought of myself as too insignificant for Allah, to reveal anything concerning me. But I hoped that the Messenger of Allah ﷺ would see a dream in which Allah would prove my innocence. By Allah, the Messenger of Allah ﷺ did not move from where he was sitting and no one left the house before Allah sent down revelation to His Prophet ﷺ. After the revelation, the Messenger of Allah ﷺ was smiling -- the first thing he said was, "Be glad O Ayesha! Allah has declared your innocence."

My mother said to me, `Get up and go to him.' I said, `By Allah, I will not go to him and I will not give praise to anyone except Allah, may He be glorified, for He is the One Who has proven my innocence!'

Abu Bakr, (RA) who used to spend on Mistah bin Uthathah because he was a close relative and being poor, said, `By Allah, I will never spend anything on him again after what he has said about Ayesha (RA). Then Allah revealed, "And let not those among you who are blessed with graces and wealth swear not to give to their kinsmen until His saying: "Do you not love that Allah should forgive you. And Allah is Oft-Forgiving, Most Merciful."

Therefore, Abu Bakr (RA) said, `By Allah, certainly I love that Allah should forgive me.' So he resumed spending on Mistah as he had spent on him before, and he said, `By Allah, I shall never stop spending on him.'

The Messenger of Allah asked Zaynab bint Jahsh (RA) about my situation, and said, "O Zaynab (RA)! What do you know and what have you seen" She said, `O Messenger of Allah, may Allah protect my hearing and my sight. By Allah, I know nothing but good.' She is the one who used to compete with me among the wives of the Prophet ﷺ, but Allah protected her (from telling lies) because of her piety. But her sister Hamnah bint Jahsh kept on fighting on her behalf, so she was doomed along with those who were doomed. [Also recorded in Sahih Muslim 2770a; Book 50, Hadith 65]

Lessons learnt from this episode:

★ The Prophet ﷺ had no knowledge of the unseen, unless Allah announce it to him.

★ Even though Prophet ﷺ was grieving for a month and patiently waiting; no revelation came for about a month.

★ He felt very much for the pious Safwan.

★ He, himself investigated the matter with Usama, Ali ibn Abu Thalib and the servant maid of Ayesha (RA).

★ Prophet ﷺ as a religious leader, exhibited communal responsibility and sought opinion from others privately and publicly.

★ Ayesha (RA) was calm and cool while being alone, thinking that on finding her absence, someone will come to pick her up. Therefore, she slept without any fear.

★ Safwān (RA) woke up the Mother of the Believers, with the most honourable of addresses. He never talked more than that. He walked silently all the way while Ayesha (RA) was riding his camel.

★ Nobody (servants, parents, husband and relatives) informed Ayesha (RA) about this slander, as she was ill for about a month.

★ The slanderer's own mother on the enquiry by Ayesha (RA) informed her about the slander.

★ Even Ayesha (RA) enquired as to how could she blame such a reputed Badari in such a manner.

★ When she heard about the slander, she sought her husband's permission to go to her parent's house. She never discussed anything with her husband about it.

★ Her parents consoled her in a soft manner, without blaming anyone who spread the slander.

★ She wept silently for two days, not knowing what to do.

★ Not getting any wahi for a month, the Prophet ﷺ dealt this matter directly with his wife suggesting her to either defend or repent to Allah.

★ Ayesha (RA) at this time sought the support of her parents, but both out of love and respect to the Prophet ﷺ, never enquired anything regarding this with their son-in-law.

★ Ayesha (RA) just 15 years old, as a wife of the Prophet ﷺ, then had to defend herself and referred the example of the father of Yusuf (AS), who adhered to beautiful patience. Thereafter she never cried.

★ She never even thought for a moment that Allah will send any revelation to prove her innocence, but thought that the truth will be revealed to Prophet ﷺ through some dream or anything similar.

★ But Allah who tested the Prophet ﷺ, the family of Abu Bakr (RA) and the people of whole Madhina, both Muslims and hypocrites with such a slander, put an end to it by revealing the ayaath in surah Noor.

★ After such a revelation, Abu Bakr (RA) sought forgiveness of Allah and continued in helping his relative Mistah.

★ Rasoolullah ﷺ forgave Abdullah bin Ubayy and on his death, as per the request of his son and much against the advice of Umar bin Khathab (RA), handed his shirt to shroud the dead body and offered the Janaza prayer.

★ After his death, thousands embrased Islam on watching this kind act of Rasoolullah ﷺ.

As Allah mentioned this incident which turned to be good for the family of Ayesha (RA).

الحمدلله

9. This ayath has been often repeated in Qura-e-Masjeedh -"There shall be no fear on them, nor shall they grieve." (و)(ف) لَا خَوْفٌ عَلَيْهِمْ وَلَا هُمْ يَحْزَنُونَ) To whom does it refer?

★ **To those who believe in Allah ﷺ and the Last Day.**

[2:62 and 5:69] "Verily! Those who believe and those who are Jews and Christians, and Sabians, whoever believes in Allah and the Last Day and do righteous good deeds shall have their reward with their Lord, there shall be no fear on them, nor shall they grieve."

★ **Those who say "Our Lord is Allah" and remain firm.**

[46:13] "Verily those who say, 'Our Lord is Allah,' and remain firm (on that Path), on them shall be no fear, nor shall they grieve."

★ **Those who believe, perform righteous good deeds, observe Salath and offer Zakath.**

[41:30] "In the case of those who say, 'Our Lord is Allah', and further, stand straight and steadfast, the angels descend on them (from time to time): Fear ye not! Nor grieve!"

[6:48] "..........whosoever believes and does righteous good deeds, there shall be no fear on them, nor shall they grieve.'

[2:277] "Truly those who believe and do deeds of righteousness and perform As-Salath, and give Zakath, they will have their reward with their Lord. There shall be no fear on them, nor shall they grieve."

★ **One who submits himself to Allah Subhanahuthala**

[2:112] "Whoever submits his face (himself) to Allah and he is a good-doer and in accordance with Sunnah of Allah's Messenger Muhammad ﷺ then his reward is with his Lord, there shall be no fear on them, nor shall they grieve."

★ **Those who follow Allah's Guidance**

[2:38] "......whoever follows My Guidance, there shall be no fear on them, nor shall they grieve."

★ **Those who spend their wealth, in the cause of Allah [عَزَّ وَ جَلَّ]**

{2:262} 'Those who spend their wealth in the Cause of Allah, and do not follow up their gifts with reminders of their generosity or with injury, their reward is with their Lord. There shall be no fear on them, nor shall they grieve.'

[2:274] 'Those who spend their wealth (in Allah's Cause) by night and day, in secret and in public, they shall have their reward with their Lord. There shall be no fear on them, nor shall they grieve.'

★ **Those who are pious, righteous and worshipping Allah** ﷻ

[7:35] "Whosoever becomes pious and righteous, there shall be no fear on them, nor shall they grieve."

[43:68] "My worshippers! No fear shall be on you this Day, nor shall you grieve."

★ **Those who are close to Allah [SWT]**

[10:62] "Oh, verily, they who are close to Allah there shall be no fear on them, nor shall they grieve."

★ **The martyrs are entitled to enter Paradise**

[3:17] "They (martyred) rejoice in what Allah has bestowed upon them of His Bounty, rejoicing for the sake of those who have not yet joined them, but are left behind (not yet martyred) that there shall be no fear on them, nor shall they grieve."

[7:49] "Enter Paradise there shall be no fear on them, nor shall they grieve."

الحمدلله

بِسْمِ ٱللَّهِ ٱلرَّحْمَٰنِ ٱلرَّحِيمِ

13. Enemies

1. Allahuthala mentions at several places in Quran "an open enemy to you." Who is that open enemy?

Answer: Shaitan is our open enemy (2:168 and 208, 6: 142, 12:5, 17:53, and 43: 62). Therefore, you also take him as an enemy. (35:6).

Iblis was one of the jinn. (18:50). Allahuthala created the jinn earlier from smokeless hot fire. (15: 27, 7:12 and 55:15). The Prophet ﷺ said, "No human being is there without an accompanying jinn". Every person is accompanied with four angels along with one jinn.

★ Why shaitan become an enemy of mankind?

From the hadhees, we were informed that when Allahuthala created Adam (AS), Iblis took much interest and observed it keenly. He learnt that

1. Allah [سبحانه وتعالى] created him with clay.
2. Adam (AS) appeared to be hasty.

Allah ﷻ created Adam (AS) and then provided a shape of a human being. Then He commanded the angels, "Prostrate before Adam" and they obeyed, except Iblis. (7:11). Thus he disobeyed the command of his Lord (18:50). Allah [SWT] questioned: "O Iblis! What prevents you from prostrating yourself to one whom I have created with Both My Hands. Are you too proud (to prostrate to Adam) or are you one of the high exalted?" Iblis said: "I am better than he, 'You' created me from fire, and 'You' created him from clay." (38:75 and 7:12). "He was proud and was one of the disbelievers." (2:34 and 38:74). (Allahuthala) said: "(O Iblis) get down from this (Paradise), it is not for you to be arrogant here. Get out, for you are of those humiliated and disgraced." (7:13). Since then, Iblis became the enemy of Adam (AS).

★ **Shaithan whispered to Adam (AS) and his wife, to disobey the command of Allahuthala:**

When Adam (AS) and his wife were in Paradise, Allah commanded them not to go near a particular tree and forbid them from eating the fruit of that tree. But Shaitan swore by Allah [SWT] to them both, saying: "Verily, I am one of the sincere well-wishers for you both." (Al-Araf, 7:21) and also whispered: ""Your Lord has forbidden this tree to you only to prevent you from becoming angels or immortals." (Al-Araf, 7:20). "O Adam! Shall I lead you to the Tree of Eternity and to a kingdom that will never waste away?" (Taha, 20:120). "So they both ate from the tree and then their nakedness was exposed to them, prompting them to cover themselves with leaves from Paradise. So Adam disobeyed his Lord, and so lost his way." (Taha, 20: 121).

"Then their Lord called out to them saying: Did I not forbid you that tree and tell you verily, Shaitan is an open enemy unto you?" (Al-Araf, 7:22). And ordered: "Get down, one of you an enemy to the other. On earth will be a dwelling-place for you and an enjoyment, for a time." (Al-Araf, 7:24). He said: "Therein you shall live, and therein you shall die, and from it you shall be brought out (i.e. resurrected)." (7:25). They said: "Our Lord! We have wronged ourselves. If You forgive us not, and bestow not upon us Your Mercy, we shall certainly be of the losers." (7:23). Allah forgave Adam (AS) and his wife.

★ **Allah [عَزَّ وَ جَلَّ] cursed Shaitan:**

"(Allah) said to Shaitan: Then get out from here, for verily, you are outcast. And verily! My Curse is on you till the Day of Recompense." (38:78). "Get out from this (Paradise) disgraced and expelled. Whoever of them (mankind) will follow you, then surely I will fill Hell with you all." (7:18 and 38:85)

★ **Shaitan sought respite till the Day of Resurrection:**

Iblis pleaded to Allah ﷻ: "Allow me respite till the Day they are raised up (i.e. the Day of resurrection)."

(Allahuthala) responded: "You are of those allowed respite." (Iblis) asserted: "Because You have sent me astray, surely I will sit in wait against them (human beings) on Your Straight Path." (7:14 - 16 and 38:79 and 80). "Then I will come to them from before them and behind them, from their right and from their left, and You will not find most of them as thankful ones (i.e. they will not be dutiful to You)." (7:17).

★ **Shaitan promised that he will lead men astray**:

Iblis said: "O my Lord! Because you misled me, I shall indeed adorn the path of error for them (mankind) on the earth, and I shall mislead them all." (15:39). "Except Your chosen, (guided) slaves among them." (15:40). "Verily, I will mislead them, and surely, I will arouse in them false desires; and certainly, I will order them to slit the ears of cattle, and indeed I will order them to change the nature created by Allah." And whoever takes Shaitan as a protector instead of Allahuthala, has surely suffered a manifest loss. "He [Shaitan] makes promises to them, and arouses in them false desires; and promises of Shaitan are nothing but deceptions." (4:119 and 120). Allah said, "Certainly, you shall have no authority over My slaves, except those who follow you. And surely, Hell is the promised place for them all." (15:42 and 43)

★ **Shaitan is a plain enemy of humanity. He**

- is ever ungrateful to his Lord. (17:27)
- is always a rebel against the Most Beneficent Allah. (19:44)
- misguides humans to: "Disbelieve in Allah" (59:16)
- threatens man of poverty and encourages him to commit evil deeds. (2:268)
- attracts the disbelievers with false hopes (47:25)
- deviates man from the right religion (43:62)
- present their deeds as seemingly fair (6:43).
- induces enmity and hatered amongst human being (5:91).
- turns away from Allahuthala's remembrance (43:14 and 58:19)
- offers promises and arouses in them false desires; which is nothing but deception. (4:121)
- spreads disagreement amongst humanity (Al-Isra, 53)
- encourages humanity to become spendthrifts (17:27)
- encourages the use of intoxicants, gambling, Al-Ansab, and Al-Azlam (using arrows to seek luck or decisions). (5:90)
- invites his followers to become the dwellers of blazing Fire (Fatir, 6); for tasting the torment of Fire. (31:21)

Allah Subhanahuthala ordains in Quran, "O Children of Adam! Let not Shaitan deceive you, as he got your parents [Adam and Hawwa] out of Paradise, stripping them of their raiments, to show them their private parts. Verily, he and his soldiers see you from where you cannot see them. Verily, 'We' made the Shayatin protectors and helpers for those who believe us not." (7:27)

★ He misled many of the Prophets, their family members and their people:

"Never did We send a Messenger or a Prophet before you, but; when he did recite the revelation or narrated or spoke, Shaitan threw (some falsehood) in it. But Allah abolishes that which Shaitan throws in. Then Allah establishes His Revelations. And Allah is All-Knower, All-Wise" (22:52).

"That He (Allah ﷻ) may make what is thrown in by Shaitan a trial for those in whose hearts is a disease (of hypocrisy and disbelief) and whose hearts are hardened. And certainly, the wrong doers are in an opposition far-off (from the truth against Allah's Messenger and the believers)." (22:53)

"Shaitan, when he says to man: "Disbelieve in Allah." But when (man) disbelieves in Allah, Shaitan says: "I am free of you, I fear Allah, the Lord of the Alamin (mankind, jinns and all that exists)!" (59:16)

"Aad and Thamud (people)! And indeed (their destruction) is clearly apparent to you from their (ruined) dwellings. Shaitan made their deeds fair-seeming to them, and turned them away from the (Right) Path, though they were intelligent." (29:38).

Ibrahim (AS) warned his idolater father, "O my father! Verily! I fear lest a torment from the Most Beneficent (Allah) overtake you, so that you become a companion of Shaitan. So worship not Shaitan." (Marium, 19:45)

Because of Shaitan's misdeeds, Ayyub (AS) suffered for 18 years. He said: "Verily! Shaitan has touched me with distress and torment!" (38:41). He created enmity between the brothers of Yusuf (AS) whose punishment was extended in the prison due to the forgetfulness of the co-prisoner.

Shaitan caused Musa (AS) to kill a man. (Al-Qasas, 15) Musa's servant forgot the fish because of him, while they were travelling. (18:63).

"The queen of Saba and her people worshipping the sun instead of Allah, and Shaitan has made their deeds fair-seeming to them, and has barred them from (Allah's) Way, so they have no guidance," (27:24).

Shaitan said to Quraish during the Battle of Badr, "No one of man-kind can overcome you this Day and verily, I am your neighbour (for each and every help)." But when the two forces came in sight of each other, he ran away and said "Verily, I have nothing to do with you. Verily! I see what you see not. Verily! I fear Allah, for Allah is Severe in punishment." (8:48).

★ **Allah [عَزَّ وَجَلَّ] has warned about Shaitan in several parts of the Holy Quran:**

"Did I not ordain for you, O Children of Adam, that you should not worship Shaitan. Verily, he is a plain enemy to you." (36:60). "And whoever takes Shaitan as a protector instead of Allah, has surely suffered a manifest loss." (4: 119).

"So follow not the footsteps of Shaithan, surely he is to you an open enemy." (6:142). "Follow not the footsteps of Shaitan. And whosoever follows the footsteps of Shaitan, then, verily he commands to commit indecency, and disbelief and polytheism. And had it not been for the Grace of Allah and His Mercy on you, not one of you would ever have been pure from sins." (24:21).

"Surely, Shaitan is an enemy to you, so treat him as an enemy. He only invites his followers that they may become the dwellers of the blazing Fire." (35:6). "Do not take him as an intimate friend. Indeed, his plot is feeble." (4:76). "Worship not Shaitan. Verily! Shaitan has been a rebel against the Most Beneficent." (19:44). "Shaitan threatens you with poverty and orders you to commit evil deeds, whereas Allah promises you Forgiveness from Himself and Bounty, and Allah is All-Sufficient for His creatures' needs, All-Knower." (2:268).

"Secret counsels are only from Shaitan, in order that he may cause grief to the believers. But he cannot harm them in the least, except as Allah permits, and in Allah let the believers put their trust" (58:10). "And We have guarded nearest heaven from every outcast Shaitan so that he will not hear anything from there." (37:7)

"Whoever disbelieves in Taghut and believes in Allah, then he has grasped the most trustworthy handhold that will never break." (2:256). "Had it not been for the Grace and Mercy of Allah upon you, you would have followed Shaitan, save a few of you." (4:83).

"Enter perfectly in Islam (by obeying all the rules and regulations of the Islamic religion) and follow not the footsteps of Shaitan. Verily! He is to you a plain enemy." (2:208). "Those who disputes concerning Allah, without knowledge, will follow every rebellious Shaitan." (Al-Hajj, 22:3).

"Shaitan made their deeds fair-seeming for the people of every nation when the Messengers were sent. So he is their helper to go them astray." (16:63)

★ **How Shaitan guided people to become astray:**

¶ He commands mankind towards evil and indecency so that they speak against Allah, what they do not know. (2:169).

¶ He only desires to lead them farther away (4: 60)

¶ He persistently plunge their human associates deeper into wickedness, sparing no effort (7:202)

¶ He leads men out of the light into darkness (2:257)

¶ He causes fear. (3:175).

¶ He descends upon every lying and sinful one (26:222)

¶ At last, he abandons his followers on the Day of judgement.

"When the matter has been decided on the Day of Judgement he will say: Verily, Allah promised you a promise of truth. And I too promised you, but I betrayed you. I had no authority over you except that I called you, so you responded to me. So blame me not, but blame yourselves. I cannot help you, nor can you help me. I deny your former act in associating me as a partner with Allah (by obeying me in the life of the world). (Ibrahim, 22).

★ **Allah ﷻ commands us to seek refuge from Shaitan:**

- "Verily, those who are the pious, when an evil thought comes to them from Shaitan, they remember (Allah), and (indeed) they then see (aright)." (7:201).
- "I seek refuge with (Allah) the Lord of mankind, the King of mankind, the God of mankind. From the evil of the whisperer (Shaitan) who withdraws, who whispers in the hearts of mankind, from among of jinn and mankind." (114:1-6).
- "When you want to recite the Quran, seek refuge with Allah [سبحانه وتعالى] from Shaitan, the outcast." (16: 98).
- "And if an evil whisper from Shaitan tries to turn you away (O Muhammad ﷺ) (from doing good, etc.), then seek refuge in Allah." (41:36)
- Bibi Marium's mother prayed to Allah ﷻ, "I seek refuge with Allah for her and for her offspring from Shaitan, the outcast." (3:36)

الحمدلله

2. " We gave him treasures, that of which the keys would have been a burden to a body of strong men. .... We caused the earth to swallow him and his dwelling place ". (28:76) To whom this refers to?

Answer: Qaroon.

Qaroon was the cousin (the son of paternal uncle) of Musa (AS). He was a rich man, a proud, disbeliever and the one among the Children of Israel. He was very arrogant and also a mischief maker. Initially he used to read Taurath with his sweet voice, but later turned into a jealous cousin of Musa (AS) and Harun (AS). He used to inform everything about them to Firaun.

He kept all his treasures of gold and silver in separate rooms, which were locked with huge keys. The keys alone had to be carried by sixty mules. He used to drag his garments on the ground, out of pride and arrogance. Allah described him in Quran as: "Verily, Qaroon (Korah) was of Musa (AS)'s people, but he behaved arrogantly towards them. And We gave him of the treasures, that of which the keys would have been a burden to a body of strong men." (Al-Qasas, 28:76).

His own people advised him not to be proud, because of his wealth and not to be ungrateful. For being benefitted with a Hereafter, he should share his wealth with the poor. They also requested him not to be a mischief maker. "Do not be prideful! Surely Allah does not like the prideful." (28:76).

"But seek, with his wealth which Allah has given on you, the home of the Hereafter, and forget not your portion of legal enjoyment in this world, and do good as Allah has been good to you, and seek not mischief in the land. Verily, Allah likes not the Mufsidun." (28:77). For which he replied that, "This has been given to me only because of my knowledge." (28:78).

Allah [SWT] provided his reply, which is the message to all, through Qaroon: "Did he not know that Allah had already destroyed some from the generations before him who were far superior to him in power and greater in accumulating wealth? There will be no need for the wicked to be asked about their sins." (28:78).

One day, "He went forth before his people, in such a pomp. Those who were desirous of the life of the world, said: "Ah, would that we had the like of what Qaroon has been given? Verily! He is the owner of a great fortune." (28:79). "But those who had been given religious knowledge said to them, the believers who are patient through their righteous deeds, can get a reward better than him. They said: "Woe to you! The

Reward of Allah (in the Hereafter) is better for those who believe and do righteous good deeds, and this none shall attain except those who are patient (in following the truth)." (28:80).

Allah [عَزَّ وَ جَلَّ] punished him in this world, in the presence of his people. "So We caused the earth to swallow him and his dwelling place. Then he had no group or party to help him against Allah, nor was he one of those who could save themselves." (28:81).

Of course, "Those who had desired (for a position like) his position the day before, they learned the lesson and said: 'Know you not that it is Allah Who enlarges the provision or restricts it to whom so ever He pleases of His slaves. Had it not been that Allah was Gracious to us, He could have caused the earth to swallow us up (also)!" (28:82). Allah always stresses this point to man-kind, repeatedly informing that the disbelievers will never be successful!

Allah [SWT] mentioned this event again in Surah Al-Ankaboot as to how He destroyed the arrogant sinners like Qaroon, Haman, Firaun, the community of Salih (AS), Lut (AS) and Nuh (AS), (29: 39 and 40), who ignored the Messengers, bringing clear signs from Allah. They called their Prophets "A sorcerer, a liar!" (40:24). Hence, they could not win Allah. They were punished in a unique manner in this world; so also another severe punishment will be awaiting them in the Hereafter.

The lesson learnt from the punishment, faced by Qaroon:

★ Allah [عَزَّ وَ جَلَّ] enlarges the provision to whom so ever He pleases.

★ Excess of wealth or poverty, is a test by Allah in this world.

★ Wealth brings pomp, pride, disobedience and haughtiness amongst some humans.

★ Allah [SWT] dislikes those who enjoy wealth, with ungratefulness.

★ Seek the abode of the Hereafter with the wealth that Allahuthala has provided in this world.

★ Be good, as Allah Subhanahuthala is always good to you.

★ Desist from mischief. Allah ﷻ dislikes the mischief makers.

★ Sinners will not be questioned on the Day of Judgement. They will be directed towards Hell.

★ The real knowledge about Allah ﷻ draws man towards piety and righteous deeds

★ Believers who are patient and perform righteous deeds will get a great reward.

★ Disbelievers will never be successful.

★ If the sinners are punished by Allah Subhanahuthala, none will come to their rescue.

★ Fear Allah [SWT]! Thank Him for His favours.

الحمدلله

3."Have you seen the one who prevents a slave when he prays? (96:9 and 10). In this verse who is the "one who" prevents? Who is referred as the "slave"?

Answer: The one who prevents is "Abu Jahl" and the slave referred is "Prophet Mohammad ﷺ"

Abu Jahl's real name was Amr ibn Hisham. Because of his intelligence, eloquence and wisdom he was called as Abu al-Hakam (Father of Wisdom). He belonged to a different clan of Quarish, the Banu Makhzum. He is the uncle of Umar bin Khattab (RA).

Abu Jahl (Father of Ignorance/folly) was the nick name given by Muslims. He was the polytheist, most powerful and a great tyrant of Makkah. He was very arrogant, heartless, transgressor, most ungrateful and a strong opposer of Islam. He developed unflinching enmity and hatered towards Islam and Allah's Rasool ﷺ.

As a man of wisdom, Abu Jahl was mesmerized and touched by the eloquence of Quran. Under the cover of darkness, he preferred to overhear to the recitation of Quran by the Prophet ﷺ during his Tahajjud prayers. Though he realized the truth about Islam, his prestige and tribal pride prevented him from becoming a believer.

The Banu Makhzum (Abu Jahl's clan) always competed with the Banu Hashim (the Prophet's ﷺ clan). Abu Jahl once told, "We competed with Banu Abd Manaf (Banu Hashim) in everything to attain status and nobility. They fed people, so we also fed people. They offered charity, so we also offered charity. They looked after people; so did we. We acted so, until we became equals. And now they say, 'A Prophet has come from Banu Hashim, who receives revelations from the heaven' How can we possibly compete with this? By Allah, we will never believe in him and we will never accept his message!"

Prophet ﷺ prayed that either of the two i.e. Amr (Abu Jahl) or Umar, should embrace Islam. In response to the prayer Umar bin Kattab (RA) accepted Islam, where as Amr died as a kafir.

Abu Jahl not only rejected the message of the Prophet ﷺ but also exhibited strong opposition by joining hands with the leaders of other clans:

1. All the opposition leaders complained to Abu Thalib, a respectable chieftain of Banu Hashim that his nephew was cursing their idols, by raising wild allagations. Even small matters were blown to big propotions.

2. Bargained with Abu Thalib, offering to exchange the Prophet ﷺ for a beautiful young man they chose. But he never accepted such a deal.

3. Required banning the recitation of Quran, in public.

4. Boycotted and tortured the Muslims without supplying any of their daily necessities.

4. Ridiculed, rebuked, humiliated publicly the Prophet ﷺ, the believers and also tortured the converted slaves.

5. Indulged in false accusations against the Prophet ﷺ and referred him as a liar, a madman, a fortune teller, a sorcerer, a magician and also as one who was a victim of magic.

6. Required him to bring about miracles like - turning Makkah into a garden of grapes and dates; to spurt out a spring from earth; to convert Safa mountain into gold; to split the moon; to make an angel decend from heaven; to allow a small piece of sky fall over them; to convert the house of the Prophet ﷺ as one of gold and silver; and to bring Allah Subhanahuthala himself in their front.

7. Attemted negotiation of a deal with him whereby he should worship their gods on one day and his Allah, on another day.

8. Warned and prevented the pilgrims against meeting him, alleging that he was mad; and that he will mesmerize the people thereby separate them from their families.

9. Planned to assassinate him and gathered each one from every clan to kill him as and when he comes out of the house.

Al-Bukhari (240) and Muslim (1794) narrated that Abd-Allah ibn Masood (RA) said: "Whilst the Messenger of Allah ﷺ was praying at the Kabah, Abu Jahl and his companions were sitting nearby. They had slaughtered a camel the previous day, and Abu Jahl proclaimed: "Which of you will go and get the abdominal contents of the camel and place it on the back of Muhammad ﷺ when he prostrates?"

The worst of the people went and fetched it and when the Prophet ﷺ prostrated, it was placed inbetween his shoulders. They started laughing, leaning against one another. "I was standing there watching, and if I had had any power, I would have lifted it from the back of the Messenger of Allah ﷺ. The Prophet ﷺ remained in prostration, not lifting his head, until someone went and told his daughter Fatimah (RA). She came with Juwayriyah (RA), and removed it from him"

Ahmad, At-Tirmidhi, An-Nasa'i and Ibn Jarir, all recorded it from Ibn Abbas with the following wording: "The Messenger of Allah ﷺ was praying at the Maqam-e-Ibrahim when Abu Jahl bin Hisham passed by him and said, `O Muhammad (ﷺ)! Haven't I prevented you from this?' He threatened the Prophet ﷺ and thus, the Messenger of Allah ﷺ became angry with him and reprimanded him. Then he said, `O Muhammad (ﷺ)! What can you threaten me with, "By Allah, I have the most kinsmen of this valley with me in the large." Then Allah revealed, "Then let him call upon his council. We will call out the guards of Hell!"

Ibn `Abbas then said, "If he had called his people, the angels of torment would have seized him at that very instant." Ibn Jarir recorded from Abu Hurayrah that Abu Jahl said, "Does Muhammad (ﷺ) cover his face with dust (i.e., from prostration) while he is among you all" They (the people) replied, "Yes." Then he said, "By Al-Lat and Al-`Uzza, if I see him praying like this, I will stomp on his neck, and I will certainly put his face in the dust." So the Messenger of Allah ﷺ came and he began praying, which made it possible for Abu Jahl to stomp on his neck. Then the people became surprised at him (Abu Jahl) because he began retreating on his heels and covering himself with his hands. Then it was said to him, "What's the matter with you?" He replied, "Verily, between me and him is a ditch of fire, monsters and wings." Then the Messenger of Allah ﷺ said, "If he had come near me, the angels would have snatched him limb by limb."

He was stamped as a liar by Allah (96:6-19):

[96:6] "Nay! Verily, man does transgress all bounds (in disbelief and evil deed etc.).

[96:7] Because he considers himself self-sufficient.

[96:8] Surely! Unto your Lord is the return.

[96:9] Have you (O Muhammad ﷺ) seen him (i.e. Abu Jahl) who prevents;

[96:10] A slave (Muhammad ﷺ) when he prays?

[96:11] Tell me, if he (Muhammad ﷺ) is on the guidance (of Allah)?

[96:12] Or enjoins piety?

[96:13] Tell me if he (Abu Jahl) denies (the truth) and turns away?

[96:14] Knows he not that Allah does see (what he does)?

[96:15] Nay! If he (Abu Jahl) ceases not, 'We' will catch him by the forelock;

[96:16] A lying, sinful fore-lock!

[96:17] Then, let him call upon his council (of helpers),

[96:18] We will call the guards of Hell (to deal with him)!

[96:19] Nay! (O Muhammad ﷺ) Do not obey him (Abu Jahl). Fall, prostrate and draw near to Allah!"

On, another occasion Abu Jahl proclaimed, "O Allah! If this (Quran) is indeed the Truth from You, then rain down on us a shower of stones from the sky or bring on us a painful torment" (8:32). So Allah revealed "And Allah would not punish them (Quraish) while you (Prophet ﷺ) were amongst them, nor He will punish them while they seek (Allah's) forgiveness" (8:33).

"A man from Irash brought some camels of his to Makkah and Abu Jahl bought them from him. He kept back the money, so the man came to the assembly of Quraish when the apostle was sitting at the side of the mosque and said: 'Who among you will help me to get what is due to me from Abul-Hakam b. Hisham? I am astranger, a wayfarer, and he will not pay his debt.' They said: 'Do you see that man sitting there?' pointing to the apostle ﷺ. (In fact they were making game of him for they knew quite well of the enmity between him and Abu Jahh) 'Go to him. He'll help you to your right.' So the man went and stood over the apostle ﷺ and said, 'O Servant of God, Abul-Hakam b. Hisham has withheld the money he owes me. I am a stranger, a wayfarer, and I asked these men to tell me of someone who would help me to my right and they pointed to you, so get my money from him, God bless you.' The apostle got up and went with him. When they saw this, the men said to one of their member, 'Follow him.' The apostle went to his house and knocked on the door, and when he asked who was there he said, 'Muhammad (ﷺ)! Come out to me.' He came out to him pale with agitation, and the apostle said, 'Pay this man his due.' 'One moment until I give him his money,' he said, and went indoors and came out again with the amount he owed and paid it to the man. The apostle went away saying, 'Go about your business.' The Irashite went back to the gathering and said, 'May God reward him, for he has got me my due.'

Then the man they had sent after them came back and reported what he had seen. 'It was extraordinary,' he said: 'he had hardly knocked on the door when out he came breathless with agitation,' and he related what had been said. Hardly had he done so when Abu Jahl himself came up and they said: 'Whatever has happened, man? We've never seen anything like what you've done.' 'Confound you,' he said; 'By God as soon as he knocked on my door and I heard his voice I was filled with terror. And when I went out to him there was a camel stallion towering above his head. I've never seen such a head and shoulders and such teeth on a stallion before. By God, if I'd refused to pay up it would have eaten me.' (From The Life of Mohammad, Guillaume's English translation of the Sira of ibn Ishaq, pp. 178)"

His death:

He was killed by two Ansari boys, at the Battle of Badr. Even prior to his death, he was enquiring about the status of the battle and hearing that the Prophet ﷺ had won, he proclaimed, "You have climbed high, you little shepard." Then they took off his head to show it to the Prophet ﷺ. By thanking Allah, he proclaimed, "This is the Firaun of this Ummah."

As Allah's words in surah At-Teen "We have certainly created man in the best of stature; Then We turn him to the lowest of the low" (95:4-5). Abu Jahl was moulded perfectly in physic, intellectually and provided with nobility but his arrogance, pride, disbelief and oppression, brought him down to the lowest level.

الحمدلله

4. "Then go away! And verily, your (punishment) in this life will be that you will say: "Touch me not; and verily, you have a promise that will not fail........" Who was awarded this punishment?

Answer: Samiri, a mischief maker from Bani Israil, who made a golden calf and asked them to worship.

Allah Subhanahuthala commanded Musa (AS) to fast for thirty days and then come to Mount Sinai to get the divine guidance. Allah required him to fast again for ten more days and revisit Sinai.

Quran declares: "We appointed thirty nights and added to the period ten more and he completed the term appointed by his Lord." And he claimed to his brother Harun (AS): "Replace me among my people, act in the Right way and follow not the way of mischief makers." (7:142).

After forty days Musa (AS) hastened to Mount Sinai to meet Allah. (20:83) He exclaimed: "They are close on my footsteps, and I hastened to You, O my Lord, that You might be pleased." (20:84) Allah proclaimed: "Verily! We have tried your people in your absence, and As-Samiri has led them astray." (20:85)

Then Musa (AS) returned to his people in a state of anger and sorrow. He said: "O my people! Did not your Lord promise you a fair promise? Did then the promise seem to you long in coming? Or did you desire that wrath should descend from your Lord on you, so you broke your promise to me by disbelieving in Allah and worshipping the calf." (20:86)

They said: "We broke not the promise to you, of our own will, but we were made to carry the weight of the ornaments of the Firaun's people, then we cast them into the fire, and that was what As-Samiri suggested." (20:87)

"Then he took out from the fire for them, a statue of a calf which made the sound of a calf. They said: "This is your ilah (god), and the ilah of Musa, but Musa (AS) has forgotten this." (20:88). "They know that the statue of the calf could not answer them a word, and that it had no power either to harm or do good to them?" (20:89).

And Harun (AS) forewarned them beforehand: "O my people! You are being tried in this, and verily, your Lord is Allah the Most Beneficent, so follow me and obey my order." (20:90) "They said: We will not stop worshipping the calf, until Musa (AS) returns to us." (20:91).

Musa (AS) said: "O Harun (AS)! What stopped you when you saw them going astray; (20:92). "That you followed me not (according to my advice to you)? Have you then disobeyed my order?" (20:93).

Harun (AS) said: "O son of my mother! Seize (me) not by my beard, nor by my head! Verily, I feared lest you should say: 'You have caused a division among the Children of Israel, and you have not respected my word!' "(20:94).

Then Musa (AS) proclaimed: "And what is the matter with you. O Samiri! (20:95) Why did you do so?"

Samiri said: "I saw what they saw not, so I took a handful of dust from the hoof print of the messenger [Jibreel (AS)'s horse] and threw it into the fire in which were put the ornaments of the Firaun's people. Thus my inner-self suggested to me." (20:96)

Musa (AS) exclaimed: "Then go away! And verily, your punishment in this life will be that you will say: "Touch me not (i.e. you will live alone exiled away from mankind); and verily (for a future torment), you have a promise that will not fail. And look at your ilah, to which you have been devoted. We will certainly burn it, and scatter its particles in the sea." (20:97)

Thus mischief makers are sure to receive punishment in both the worlds.

الحمدلله

5. "Leave Me Alone (to deal) with whom I created Alone. And then granted him resources in abundance. And children to be by his side! And made life smooth and comfortable for him!" (Al- Muddathir, 74:11 to14). About whom was this stated?

Answer: Quraish named Walid bin Mughirah.

Walid bin al-Mughirah was a rich, eminent and famous poet of Quraish. He had ten or twelve sons of whom Khalid bin Walid, who popularly called as "Sword of Allah". Walid was one of the five major opponent of Muhammad ﷺ. Walid has been indirectly mentioned in several verses of Quran.

1. After realizing that Abu Talib would not give up protection of Prophet ﷺ on any account, the Quraish leaders went to Abu Talib with Walid's son Umara, and said, 'O AbuTalib, this is Umara bin Walid, the strongest and most handsome young man among Quraish, so take him. You will have the benefit of his intelligence and support. Adopt him as a son and give up to us, your nephew who has opposed your religion and the religion of your fathers, disrupted the unity of your people and mocked our way of life, therefore, we must kill him. That will be man for man.' But Abu Talib refused this offer.

2. Walid ibn al-Mughira, along with Utba ibn Rabiah, Shayba offered the Prophet ﷺ "in exchange to be their King and marry as many beautiful women he liked, therby he abandons his mission of preaching Islam." To this offer, Muhammad ﷺ replied,

"By Allah, if they put the sun in my right hand and the moon in my left, I would not abandon it."

3. Walid bin Mughirah came to the Prophet ﷺ to listen what has been revealed to him. The messenger of Allah ﷺ recited the Surah Fussilath to him. Being the best and elequent in Arabic language the very first word "Ha--meem" influenced him very much! After listening to the whole surah he was much impressed by the style, words chosen, its melody, truth, the guidance, the past events, the descriptions, its miraculous words and its supernatural quality. His heart became softened.

"And what can I possibly say? There is not a single man who is more knowledgeable of poetry or prose than I, or even that of the Jinn, and by Allah, what he says bears no resemblance to these things. I swear by Allah that it is not poetry, nor magic, nor the prattling of insanity. Verily, his speech is from the Words of Allah!" "By Allah, what he says has a sweetness in it, a charm upon it; the highest part of it is fruitful and the lowest part of it gushing forth with bounty; it dominates and cannot be dominated, and it crushes all that is under it." "Verily it is truly elegant. Verily, it is exalted and it is not overcome."

4. When tha Quraish learnt about this they gathered and claimed, `By Allah, if Walid is converted (to Islam) all of the Quraish will be converted.' When Abu Jahl heard this he proclaimed, `By Allah, I will deal with him for you.' So he went to Walid's house and said: "Don't you see that your people are collecting charity for you?" Walid questioned: "Why is that?" Abu Jahl replied: "So that they can give it to you, as they see that you went to Muhammad ﷺ to get some of his food."

Walid said: "Quraish knows that I am of the wealthiest of its sons." Abu Jahl said, if he was afraid of the punishment of the Hereafter, he should pay him a certain amount of money and he would take the responsibility to suffer the punishment on his behalf. Walid accepted the offer. Then he paid only a little of the amount that he had promised to his polytheist friend and withheld the rest.

Allah revealed in Surah Najm, "Did you (O Muhammad ﷺ) observe him who turned away from Islam. And gave a little, then stopped (giving)? Is with him the knowledge of the unseen so that he sees? Or is he not informed with what is in the pages of Musa (AS). And of Ibrahim (AS) who fulfilled all that what Allah ordered him to do. That no burdened person shall bear the burden of another." (An-Najm, 33- 38).

5. Abu Jahl further said: "So, say to Muhammad ﷺ some-thing that would convince your people that you were opposing him." Walid was fully convinced of the truth of

Muhammad ﷺ and the Quran, but he did not wish to leave his leadership and position among Quraish. He said to Abu Jahl "Leave me alone" for sometime. Allah described in Quran in Al Muddathir [Surah 74 verses 11-25], in such a way, so as to bring in our mind the picture of how he thought alone in his house;

[74:11] "Leave Me Alone (to deal) with whom I created Alone (without any means, i.e. Al-Walid bin Al-Mughirah Al-Makhzumi)!

[74:12] And then granted him resources in abundance.

[74:13] And children to be by his side!

[74:14] And made life smooth and comfortable for him!

[74:15] After all that he desires, I should give more;

[74:16] Nay! Verily, he has been stubborn and opposing Our Ayath

[74:17] I shall oblige him to (climb a slippery mountain in the Hell-fire called As-Saud, or to) face a severe torment!

[74:18] Verily, he thought and plotted;

[74:19] So let him be cursed! How he plotted!

[74:20] And once more let him be cursed, how he plotted!

[74:21] Then he thought;

[74:22] Then he frowned and he looked in a bad tempered way;

[74:23] Then he turned back and was proud;

[74:24] Then he said: "This is nothing but magic from that of old;

[74:25] This is nothing but the word of a human being!"

As per his advice, Quraish called Muhammad ﷺ a sorcerer, who had brought a message by which he separated a man from his father, brother, wife and family. The Quraish accordingly warned the people attending trade fair and prevented them from converting to Islam. Allah cursed him twice! And mentioned also the severe punishment he is going to get in the Hell!

6. When Walid said: "Does Allah send down revelations to Muhammad ﷺ and ignore me, the greatest chief of Quraish, to say nothing of Abu Masud Amr ibn Umayr al-Thaqafi, the chief of Taif, we being the great ones of Ṭaif and Makkah?" The response

to this question was: And they say: "Why is not this Quran sent down to some great man of the two towns (Makkah and Taif)? And when the truth came to them, they said, this is magic, and we disbelieve therein." [Sura 43: 30 and 31] (From The Life of Mohammad, Guillaume's English translation of the Sira of ibn Ishaq, pp. 164)

7. "One day as Muhammad ﷺ was going around the Kabah, Walīd approached him along with al-Aswad ibn al-Muṭṭalib ibn Asad ibn Abdul-Uzza, Umayya ibn Khalaf and al-Aṣ ibn Wail to offer him a proposition. They proclaimed: 'Muhammad ﷺ, let us worship what you worship and you worship what we worship. If what you worship is better than what we worship we will take a share of it, and if what we worship is better than what you worship, you can take a share of that.' The response to this proposition from Allah was: 'Say, O disbelievers, I do not worship what you worship, and you do not worship what I worship, and I do not worship what you worship, and you do not worship what I worship; You have your code of life (Deen) and I have mine.' [Sura Al- Kafiroon, 109]." (From The Life of Mohammad, Guillaume's English translation of the Sira of ibn Ishaq, pp. 165)

8. "Walid was having a long conversation with Muhammad ﷺ, who greatly desired to convert Walid to Islam. Then Ibn Umm Maktum, a blind man, passed by and began to ask Muhammad ﷺ doubts about Quran. Muhammad ﷺ "found this hard to bear and it annoyed him," because Ibn Umm Maktum was diverting him from Walid and spoiling the chance of his conversion. When the man became "importunate", Muhammad ﷺ went off frowning and left him. The verse revealed on this occasion, was from Sura 80, Abasa, 1 to 11." (From The Life of Mohammad, Guillaume's English translation of the Sira of ibn Ishaq, pp. 167)

9. One day Muhammad ﷺ passed by Walid, Umayya ibn Khalaf and Abu Jahl ibn Hisham. They reviled and mocked him, which caused the Prophet ﷺ distress. The Quran addressed this situation: "Apostles have been mocked before thee, but that which they mocked at hemmed them in." (Surah 6:10)

10. In another incident when Walid and his group insulted Muhammad ﷺ, Allah revealed in Surah Qalam,

[68:10] "And obey not everyone who swears much, and is considered worthless,

[68:11] A slanderer, going about with calumnies,

[68:12] Hinderer of the good, transgressor, sinful,

[68:13] Cruel, after all that base-born (of illegitimate birth),

[68:14] (He was so) because he had wealth and children.

[68:15] When Our Verses (of the Quran) are recited to him, he says: "Tales of the men of old!"

[68:16] We shall brand him over the nose!"

The verse, "Cruel, after all that base-born" exposed Walid ibn Mughirah's illegitimate birth. Later he verified with his mother and 'found to be true'. [الله اعلم !]

11. When Walid and his friends persisted in constant mockery of Muhammad ﷺ, this verse was recited: "Proclaim what you have been ordered and turn away from the polytheists. We will surely protect you against the mockers who put another god beside Allah. In the end they will know." (Sura 15:94)

12. "One day Muhammad ﷺ was sitting and discussing with Walid and other Quraish near the Kabah. Al-Naḍr ibn Al-Harith joined them. Al-Naḍr interrupted, the Prophet ﷺ's speech. Muhammad ﷺ did not respond until Al-Naḍr became silent. Then he recited the verses: "Verily you and what you serve other than Allah is the fuel of Hell. You will come to it. If these had been gods they would not have come to it, but all will be in it everlastingly. There is wailing and there they will not hear." (21:98 to 100). After that he left the group silently.

After that Abdullah ibn al-Zibara al-Sahmi arrived and sat with the gathering. Walid conveyed to him the Prophet's words and said: "By Allah, al-Naḍr could not stand up to Muhammad (ﷺ) just now, and he alleged that we and our gods are fuel for Hell." Abdullah proudly replied, "If I had found him, I would have refuted him. Ask Muhammad ﷺ, 'Is everything that is worshipped besides God, in Hell with those who worship it?' We worship the angels; the Jews worship Uzayr; and the Christians worship Jesus Son of Mary." Those who were listening to his words thought that he said convincingly.

When Muhammad ﷺ was told of this, he proclaimed: "Everyone who wishes to be worshipped to the exclusion of God, will be with those who worship him. They worship only Shaitan and those they have ordered to be worshipped." Then this verse of the Quran was revealed: "Those who have received kindness from us in the past will be removed far from it and will not hear its sound and they abide eternally in their heart's desire." [Sura 21:101-102] (From The Life of Mohammad, Guillaume's English translation of the Sira of ibn Ishaq, pp. 163)

13. "Walid provided protection to the Muslim Uthman ibn Maẓun. When Uthman saw the misery in which the apostle's companions were living while he lived night and day under Walid's protection, he declared, 'It is more than I can bear that I should be perfectly safe under the protection of a polytheist, while my friends are afflicted for Allah's sake.' So he went to Walid and renounced his protection. Walid asked him to renounce his protection publicly as he had given it publicly. So Uthman declred in public, 'I have found him loyal and honorable in his protection, but I don't want to ask anyone but Allah for protection; so I give him back his promise!" (From The Life of Mohammad, Guillaume's English translation of the Sira of ibn Ishaq, pp. 169)

14. When the five of Prophet ﷺ's mockers were present near Kabah, Jibreel (AS) the stood near the Prophet ﷺ and informed about their fate, as they passed one by one. When Al-Walid passed by Jibreel (AS) stated, "He had an old scar of a wound on the bottom of his ankle. Some years earlier as he was trailing his gown when he passed by a Khuza'i who was feathering an arrow, and the arrowhead caught in his wrapper and scratched his foot – a mere nothing. But the wound opened again and he died of it." (From The Life of Mohammad, Guillaume's English translation of the Sira of ibn Ishaq, pp. 187)

15. As Allah said in surah Al-Muddathir he will get severe punishment (74:17) in the Hell. He further says:

[74:26] "I will cast him into Hell-fire.

[74:27] And what will make you know exactly what Hell-fire is?

[74:28] It spares not (any sinner), nor does it leave (anything unburnt)!

[74:29] Burning the skins!

[74:30] Over it are nineteen (angels as guardians and keepers of Hell). And also [68:16] We shall brand him over the nose!"

الحمدلله

6. Name the only person amongst the enemies of Islam, who was cursed by Allahuthala in the Holy Quran?

Answer: Abu Lahab ibn Abdul Muttalib

He was an uncle of the Holy Prophet. His original name was Abdul Uzza. Lahab means "flames" and hence they nicknamed him so because of the radiant look on his face. But Muslims called him as 'father of the flames.'

Before Islam:

On the birth of Prophet Mohammed ﷺ, at Makkah, Abu Lahab freed a slave. He deputed his maid Thawbiyah to nurse the child. He was affectionate with his orphan nephew, like a father. Later on, two of his sons were married with the two daughters of the Holy Prophet ﷺ, Ruqayya and Umm Kulthum. Being minors, they were staying with the Prohet ﷺ. Abu Lahab was a neighbour of the Prophet ﷺ.

While declaring the Prophet hood:

By the command of Allah, the Prophet ﷺ went out to the premises of Kabah, climbed the Mount Saffa and invited the people of Makkah, in a loud voice. Puzzled Makkans gathered with great curiosity and enquired "O Muhammad, why did you gather us here? What are you going to announce?"

"O Banu Abd Al-Muttalib, O Banu Fihr, O Banu Luay; would you believe me if I say that there is an enemy at the foot of this mountain behind, ready to launch an attack on you" They replied: "Yes. You are Al-Ameen (trustworthy) and Al-Sadiq (truthful) and we have never heard you speak lies."

"In that case, I inform you of a great punishment that is ahead. God the Exalted has commanded me to warn my closest kin of the punishment in the hereafter. I invite you to say, "Allah is One, there is no God. I am His servant and Messenger." If you accept what I have said, then I guarantee that you will enter heaven. Also know that I cannot be of service to you in this world nor in the hereafter unless you say, "Allah is One, there is no other God but He."

After hearing this, the gathering dispersed silently by whispering and conversing among themselves. But Abu Lahab, who always loved his nephew Mohammed ﷺ, took a stone and threw it straight towards Prophet ﷺ and cried, "'May you perish for this! Is this what you have gathered us here for?" "Even if what my nephew says is true, I will save myself from the painful torment on the Day of Judgment with my wealth and my children."

Blood was flowing down the face of the Holy Prophet ﷺ, which caused him great pain. It was a great shock to the Prophet ﷺ on the first day of the declaration of

Prophet hood and his invitation towards the true religion of Islam. Abu Lahab was the first to exihibit his enmity against this message and opposed vehemently above all.

Abu Lahab received the curse of Allah:

Due to the violent hostility, lasting grudge and hate of Abu Lahab exihibited against the beloved Prophet ﷺ, Almighty Allah sealed Abu Lahab's fate and later on revealed Surah 111 in the Holy Quran:

1. "Perish the two hands of Abu Lahab, and perish he!

2. His wealth and his children (etc.) will not benefit him!

3. He will be burnt in a Fire of blazing flames!" (111:1-3)

On such a revelation, he became furious. Being his neighbour, he and his wife made the life of the Prophet ﷺ miserable. He instructed two of his sons to divorce the two daughters of the Prophet ﷺ.

The curse extended to Abu Lahab's family:

Abu Lahab did not restrict himself in torturing his nephew, but included his family members. His wife, Arwa bint Harb, nicknamed Umm Jameel, was the sister of Abu Sufyan, who discretely spread thorny bushes or filth in front of the Prophet's ﷺ house. He influenced his son, Utaiba to harass Holy Prophet ﷺ. Utaiba went to the Prophet ﷺ, while he was reciting Surah an-Najm. Utaiba said loudly, "I swear by the Lord of an-najm (the star) that I denounce your prophet hood" and proudly spat toward the direction of Prophet ﷺ, who prayed: "O my Lord! Subject him to the power of a dog from among Your dogs." So scared was Abu Lahab with the Prophet's ﷺ words that while on a journey, he placed his son in the middle of the people out of fear! However, a lion came by midnight, killed him while he was sleeping. And his wife, died miserably as per the words of Allah in Surah Masad, with twisted palm-fiber in her neck.

During the period of Prophet's ﷺ stay at Makkah:

When the Prophet ﷺ commenced preaching at Makkah, Abu Lahab continued to insult him. Prophet ﷺ was neither cared nor was shaken by the insinuating allegations made against him. His approach was dignified against his opposers.

Rabiah ibn Abbad, recalls: "When I was young, I once watched along with my father, Allah's Messenger ﷺ, preaching Islam to the Arab tribes, by proclaiming: "O people! Say 'La Ilaha Illallah' so that you can save yourselves." A cross-eyed, bright-faced man, who used to be behind him, would repeat after Prophet's ﷺ call: 'O sons of…, this man wants you to forsake al-Laat and al-`Uzza (two idols worshiped by the pagan Arabs) and your allies, the jinn, the children of Malik ibn Aqmas and to substitute them with these innovations and non-sense he has come forward with. Neither listen to him, nor follow what he preaches.' I asked my father who was that man and he informed me that it was Abu Lahab, the Prophet's uncle." He did this during every Hajj season or at Ukaz Fair by proclaiming openly, "O people! He is my nephew; he is lying to you, stay away from him."

Once Abu Lahab asked Muhammad ﷺ: "If I were to accept your religion, what would I get?" The Prophet ﷺ replied: "You would get what the other believers would get." Abu Lahab responded: "Is there no preference or distinction for me?" In which Muhammad ﷺ replied, "What else do you want?" Abu Lahab responded: "May such religion perish in which I and all other people should be equal and alike!"

He created confusion amongst the people who met the Prophet ﷺ. It was told, "When Abu Lahab saw his nephew speaking to a stranger, he would wait until they parted and he would go to the stranger and ask him, "What did he tell you? Did he say, 'Black?' Well, then it's white. Did he say 'morning?' Well, then it's night." He faithfully used to declare the exact opposite of whatever he heard from Muhammad ﷺ and the Muslims.

Once the opposing Quraish imposed a complete social and business boycott on the clan of Banu Hashim, forced starvation on them, with a threat to hand over the Prophet ﷺ to them. Ignoring this threat, the other members of Banu Hashim took an oath to protect the Prophet ﷺ, where as Abu Lahab was the only member of their clan, to join non-Muslim Quraish. He supported the pagans, by signing the document of boycott. His aim was to cause hardship to the Prophet ﷺ and Muslims, with regard to their living conditions.

The Quraish humiliated, insulted, degraded and even planned to kill the Prophet Muhammad ﷺ. Traditionally, Arabs always supported their clan when any injustice was caused. Abu Lahab joined the Quraish of other clans, to abuse his nephew. Abu Lahab from amongst Banu Hashim, volunteered to surround the house of Prophet ﷺ, along with other clan members, to kill him.

For ten years, Abu Lahab continued to claim that, "I heard that it has been revealed to Muhammad (ﷺ) that I will never change; that I will never become a Muslim and will enter the Hellfire." Even during that period, he never accepted Islam and never sympathized with Muslims.

After the Hijra:

Abu Lahab did not participate in the Battle of Badr against the Prophet ﷺ. He sent Aas bin Hisham bin Mughira' to the battle in his place, in exchange of 4,000 Dirhams due from Aas bin Hisham. Abu Lahab was anxiously awaiting the result of the the battle.

Abu Sufyan bin Harith passed on the news about the battle, "The fact is that the Quraish met our enemy and turned their backs. The Muslims forced us to escape, taking available prisoners as they pleased. I cannot blame our tribesmen because they had to face not only Muslims but men wearing white robes riding piebald horses, who were between heaven and earth. They spared nothing and no one had a chance." On hearing this, Abu Rafi, a slave of Abbas bin Abd al-Muttalib, a Muslim, happily proclaimed: "They were angels!".

On hearing this, Abu Lahab, knocked him to the ground and beat him. Umm al-Fadl, al-Abbas's wife, defended Abu Rafi. She took a stick and hit on Abu Lahab's head, shouting: "Do you think that you can abuse him just because Abbas is away?" It left a deep wound on Abu Lahab's head.

Abu Lahab's death:

Abu Lahab died seven days after this incident. He developed sepsis caused by the wound. His skin started developing pustules. On his death, his family fearing infection, were hesitant to touch and bury him. Thereafter, departed leaving the dead body in the house itself. The neighbors scolded his sons alleging, "It is disgraceful. You should be ashamed of leaving your father to rot in his house." So they stayed away and hired slaves to wash his body. They then, using long poles shuffled the body into the pit. They filled the pit with stones, thrown from a distance.

He was one of the four richest men of the Quraish. Even his own wife and the children, did not save him from the punishment of this world. He has been always boasting about his wealth, his position and children; but all abandoned him during his death.

Abu Lahab's elder son, Utba, and his daughter Durrah embraced Islam after the conquest of Makkah. By leading an exemplary life, Utba earned the honorable title of Sahabi.

الحمدلله

7. "Build for him a building (like a furnace) and throw him into the blazing fire!" (37:97). Who said this?

Answer: Namrud, the King of Babylone.

Allah refers about this king, in Surah Baqara:

Through the 258th verse of Surah Baqara, the debate between Prophet Ibrahim (AS) and the arrogant King of Babylon in Iraq named Namrud, has been revealed. He was a tyrant and a disbeliever. He used to designate himself as "Lord of everything". Ibrahim (AS) was born in Babylon, during the rule of Namrud and his father was an idol maker.

Ibrahim (AS) and his people:

Ibrahim (AS)'s people maintained a huge temple, full of idols in the middle of which there was a biggest statue. As a child, he used to visit the temple with his father. He watched his people bowing down, begging and seeking help to remove their troubles. He was aware that those statues could neither see nor hear nor understand their request.

He assured himself, "And by Allah, I shall plot a plan (to destroy) your idols after you have gone away and turn your backs." Once a great celebration was arranged outside the city by the King. According to his command the whole city had to attend the celebration. Ibrahim (AS) excused himself, claiming that "Verily, I am sick." (37:89) and stayed behind. "So they turned away from him, and departed" (37:90). He played this trick to remain home and not to accompany them to the pagan's feast.

He damaged the idols in their temple:

Ibrahim (AS) was waiting for such an occasion. On rushing to the temple, he found the streets empty, while the temple was deserted. On entering the temple, he found lots of food items, placed in front of the statues. "Then he turned to their aliha (gods) and claimed: "Will you not eat (of the offering before you)? What is the matter with you that you speak not? Then he turned upon them, striking (them) with (his) right hand." (37:91 to 93). He destroyed all the statues except the big one. He wanted to show his people, a practical proof of their foolishness in worshipping something other than Allah. He left the temple.

On returning to the city, the people after entering the temple, were shocked to see the broken pieces of their so called gods lying scattered all over. They proclaimed: "Who has done this to our aliha (gods)? He must indeed be one of the wrong-doers." Then they recalled: "We heard a young man talking (against) them who is called Ibrahim (Abraham)." They said: "Then bring him before the eyes of the people, that they may testify." (21:59 to 61).

Then the worshippers of idols came towards him, hastening (37:94). "They said: 'Are you the one who has done this to our gods, O Abraham?' [Ibrahim (AS)] said: 'Nay, this one, the biggest of them (idols) did it. Ask them, if they can speak!' So they turned to themselves and said: 'Verily, you are the wrong-doer.' (their first thought and said): 'Indeed you [Ibrahim (AS)] know well that these (idols) speak not!' [Ibrahim (AS)] said: 'Worship you that which you (yourselves) carve? While Allah has created you and what you make!" (37:95 and 96) "Do you then worship besides Allah, things that can neither profit you, nor harm you? "Fie upon you, and upon that which you worship besides Allah! Have you then no sense?" (21:62 to 67).

They threw Ibrahim (AS) in fire:

Even after knowing their foolishness, they were so arrogant to accept the real truth. They were boiling with anger in their hearts. They proclaimed: "Burn him and help your aliha (gods), if you will be doing." (21:68) "Build for him a building (it is said that the building was like a furnace) and throw him into the blazing fire!" (37:97). The king commanded to all the citizens to bring as much as wood as possible. They prepared a huge furnace and collected fire wood for several days. They ignited it. All were watching the fire from a distance. The heat was affecting their faces. They brought Ibrahim (AS) there. Angel Jibreel (AS) came and enquired as to whether he needed any help. But Ibrahim (AS) told "Allah is Sufficient for me! He is the great Protector and Helper" Finally he was thrown into the fire.

Allah Subhanahuthala rescued him from fire:

A miracle happened! Allahuthala asserted, "So they plotted a plot against him, but We made them the lowest." (37:98) "We (Allah) said: "O fire! Be 'you' coolness and safety for Ibrahim (AS)!" And they wanted to harm him, but 'We' made them the worst losers. "And 'We' rescued him ...... to the land which 'We' have blessed for the Alamin" (21: 69 to 71). The raging fire had become cool. Ibrahim (AS) came out of fire unharmed. This miracle shamed the tyrant and his people, but it did not cool the flame of anger in their hearts.

Allah ﷻ sends Messengers to people ruled by an arrogant King or leaders. If they humble themselves, turn to Him and became grateful, He increase His favors. If they still remain arrogant, He punishes them in the manner they could not even imagine! History informs us that Namrud died later because of a small insect that entered inside his skull.

الحمدلله

8. Whose wife is mentioned as "the carrier of fire-wood", in Quran?

Answer: The wife of Abu Lahab.

It is asserted in Surah Masad:

"May the hands of Abu Lahab be ruined, and ruined is he. His wealth will not avail him or that which he gained. He will burn in a Fire of flame. And his wife – the carrier of fire-wood. Around her neck is a rope of fibre. (Al Masad,111:1-5)

The wife of Abu Lahab caused trouble to the Prophet ﷺ:

Abu Lahab, the uncle and the main enemy of Allah and His messenger ﷺ, was living along with his wife as a neighbour of the Prophet ﷺ. His wife Arwa, was the sister of Abu Sufyan. Because of her beauty she was known as "Umm Jameel". She was a highly influential woman of the Quraish. She joined with her husband and brother, in exhibiting her enmity and disbelief against the Prophet ﷺ. Deciding to inflict harm to Holy Prophet's ﷺ while he comes out for fazar prayer; she used to spread thorny bushes or filth in front of his door, during night.

Her reaction to the revelation of Surah Masad:

Ibn Kathir in his tafsir explains:

Abu Bakr's (RA) daughter Asma (RA) had narrated: "When this Surah was revealed, Umm Jameel heard it. She went out in search of the Prophet ﷺ with anger. She carried a handful of stones and she was uttering "He criticizes our father, and his religion is our scorn, and his command is to disobey us." She stumbled because of her waist gown, while she was making circuits around the House (the Kabah) and she said, `Cursed be the reviler.'

The Prophet ﷺ was sitting with Abu Bakr (RA), near Kabah. His companion said: "O Messenger of Allah ﷺ there she comes and I fear that she should say something critical and disrespectful words against you." The Prophet ﷺ replied: "She will not see me." Then he recited some of the verses of Quran as a protection for himself. This is, as Allah says, "And when you recite the Quran, 'We' put between you and those who believe not in the Hereafter, an invisible veil." (17:45).

She came nearer to Abu Baker (RA). As the Prophet ﷺ claimed, he became invisible to her though he was sitting next to Abu Baker (RA). Thinking that he is sitting alone she said to Abu Bakr (RA): "I have been told that he is satirizing me, and by God, if I had found him I would have smashed his mouth [with this, pointing out to a stone pestle in her hand]. By God, I am a poet.' Then she said:

> "We reject the reprobate,
> His words we repudiate,
> His religion we loathe and hate."

(From The Life of Mohammad, Guillaume's English translation of the Sira of ibn Ishaq, pp. 161). She further said, "I hear that your companion has mocked me." Abu Bakr (RA) replied: "No, by the Lord of this House, he has not mocked you." What Abu Bakr meant was she was not mocked by the Prophet ﷺ, but by Allah Himself.

Allah gave her the title "carrier of the wood":

The words حَمَّالَةَ الْحَطَبِ literally mean: "carrier of the wood". The commentators have provided several meanings:

◆ She has been described as "tale-bearer", as she used to carry evil tales and slander and create hatred among people.

◆ The one who carries 'the sin' as a burden.

◆ She will be supplying wood to the fire; in which Abu Lahab would be burning in the Hereafter.

The word جِيد means a neck decorated by a necklace. Wearing a valuable necklace, she used to claim: "By Lat and Uzza, (names of her idols) I will sell away this necklace and expend the price to satisfy my enmity against Muhammad ﷺ." In the Hell she would have a rope of "مَسَدٍ" round her neck instead of that necklace because of her vengeance, pride and arrogance.

Different meanings are attributed to the word "مَسَدٍ" by various commentators:

- a tightly twisted rope;
- rope made from palm-fibre;
- rope made from camel-skin, or camel-hair.
- a cable made by twisted iron strands.

Her death took place as predicted by Allah Subhanahuthala.

In spite of the threat destined to her, she never changed her attitude:

It is true that this Surah openly curses Abu Lahab and his wife, because of their attitude, behaviour and deeds; and those people with similar qualities will meet the same punishment. It is one of the predictions of the Holy Quran. Even with the open curse of Allah, both Abu Lahab and his wife, neither changed nor feared! Their hearts had been already sealed by Allah.

الحمدلله

بِسْمِ ٱللَّهِ ٱلرَّحْمَٰنِ ٱلرَّحِيمِ

14. About Resurrection and the Day of Resurrection

1. He Wished to know: "Oh! How will Allah ever bring it to life after its death?" [2:259]. Who is he? How did he realize the power of Allah, to resurrect?

Answer: He is Uzayr, whom Allahuthala resurrected 100 years, after his death. His donkey was also resurrected from its bones, in his presence.

Ibn Khathir in his tafsir, explains this incident as follows:

"Mujahid bin Jabir claimed that the person referred in the ayath 2:259 is Uzayr. He is from the Children of Israel. Nebuchadnezzar destroyed Jerusalem and also killed its people, thereupon it became deserted. The roofs and walls of the houses in the city, were erased to the ground. Uzayr was shocked to see the fate of the city, which had developed a great civilization. With surprise he exclaimed, "Oh! How will Allah ever bring it to life after its death." [2:259]. On watching its utter destruction, he wondered how will it return to its former state.

Thereafter, Allahuthala caused him to remain dead for a hundred years and then resurrected him. When Allah [SWT] resurrected Uzayr, the first organ restored were his eyes, to enable him to watch as to what Allah does while bringing back life to his body. After resurrection, Allah ﷻ enquired him, through the angel as to how long did he remain dead. Uzayr responded: "Perhaps I remained dead for a day or part of a day." The scholars explained that since the man died in the early part of the day and Allahuthala resurrected him in the latter part of the day, when he saw that the sun was still apparent, he thought that it was the sun of that very day. Therefore, he had said, "Or part of a day."

Allah Subhanahuthala informed him: "Nay, you have remained dead for a hundred years, look at your food and your drink, they show no change." He had grapes, figs and juice and he found them as he left them. Neither did the juice was spoiled nor the figs had become bitter nor the grapes were rotten. "And look at your donkey! How

Allah brings it back to life while you are watching. And thus We have made you a sign for the people that Resurrection occurs." (2:259).

As Suddi narrated, "Uzayr observed the bones of his donkey, which were scattered all around him to his right and left, and Allah [عَزَّ وَجَلَّ] sent a wind that collected the bones from all over the area. Allah then brought every bone to its place, until they formed a full donkey made of fleshless bones. Allah then covered these bones with flesh, nerves, veins and skin. Allah sent an angel who blew life in the donkey's nostrils and the donkey started to bray by Allah's Leave." All this occurred while Uzayr was watching and this is when he proclaimed, "I know that I did witness it with my own eyes. Therefore, I am the most knowledgeable in this matter among the people of my time."

The real purpose in mentioning this event is for proving as to how Allah [سبحانه وتعالى] chose the believer with strong faith. Uzayr could have been a Prophet. The restoration of Uzayr to life, is a living testimony.

Jerusalem was rebuilt 70 years after Uzayr's natural death, thereafter its inhabitants increased and the Children of Israel also moved back to it.

Uzayr is mentioned in the Quran: "And the Jews say: 'Uzayr (Ezra) is the son of Allah', and the Christians say: 'Messiah is the son of Allah'. That is a saying from their mouth. They imitate the saying of the disbelievers of old. Allah's curse be on them, how they are deluded away from the truth!" (At-Taubah, 9:30)

الحمدلله

2. How Ibrahim (AS) witnessed the act of resurrection, by Allah Subhanahuthala?

Answer: Al Baqara, 2:260.

Ibrahim (AS) - Khaleelullah prayed to Almighty, "My Lord show me how You give life to the dead" (Al Baqara, 260). Allah asserted: "Do you not believe?" Ibrahim (AS) said: "Yes (I believe)! But to be stronger in Faith."

Ibn Khathir, in his explanations mentions that the scholars are of opinion that the reason behind Ibrahim (AS) enquiring with Allah is: 'the statement made by his King Namrud'. Ibrahim (AS) refers about Allah to Namrud, "My Lord is He, who gives life and causes to die" for that the arrogant King replied proudly, "I give life and cause death." Ibrahim (AS) said, "Verily! Allah causes the sun to rise from the east; then cause it to rise from the west." So the disbeliever was utterly defeated. And Allah guides not the people, who are Zalimun." (2:258).

Answer by Allah to Ibrahim (AS):

Then Allah [سبحانه وتعالى] commanded, "Take four birds, then cause them to incline towards you, then slaughter them and put a portion of them on every hill and call them they will come to you in haste." (2:260).

Ibn Khathir's explanation to this ayath:

Ibrahim (AS) trained the four birds in such a way that they came to him on his call. Then he slaughtered, removed their feathers, cut them into pieces, mixed the pieces of the birds and placed them on four or seven hills. Ibn Abbas narrated, "Ibrahim (AS) held the heads of these birds in his hand. Next, Allah commanded Ibrahim to call the birds to him and he followed the Allah's command. Ibrahim witnessed the feathers, blood and flesh of these birds fly at each other and the parts flew to their bodies, until every bird came back to life and came walking at a fast pace towards Ibrahim (AS). Thus the example that Ibrahim (AS) having witnessed it, became more impressive. Each bird came to collect its head from Ibrahim's hand and on offering another head, the bird refused to accept it. When Ibrahim (AS) offered each bird its own head, the head was placed on its body by Allah's leave and power."

Allahthala being the Creator of everything (The Qaliqh), proved to Ibrahim (AS) how he resurrected the dead, as He is the Originator (Basith). He creates for the first time and also resurrects the same; an act which is easy for Him. He is All powerful (Qadeer). To create anything, He will say, "Be!" (Qun). It will become (fayakoon).

الحمدلله

3. "But you were seized with a thunderbolt (lightning) while you were looking. Then We raised you up after your death, so that you might be grateful." (2:55 and 56). Who were the objects of such resurrection?

Answer: The Children of Israel, during the time of Musa (AS).

Allahuthala refers in Surah Baqara, about the list of favours, the Children of Israel had received:

"O Children of Israel! Remember My Favour which I bestowed upon you and that I preferred you to the 'Alamin (of your time period, in the past)." (2:47). "We delivered you from Firaun's people, who were afflicting you with a horrible torment, killing your sons and sparing your women," (2:49). "We separated the sea for you and saved you and drowned Firaun's people while you were looking." (2:50). "When We appointed for Musa (AS) forty nights, and (in his absence) you took the calf (for worship), and you were Zalimun (polytheists and wrong-doers, etc.). We forgave you so that you might be grateful." (2:51 and 52). "We gave Musa (AS) the Scripture [the Taurath] and the criterion (of right and wrong) so that you may be guided aright." (2:53). "And We shaded you with clouds and sent down on you Al-Manna and the quails." (2: 57)

When Musa (AS) required water for his people, 'We' said: "Strike the stone with your stick." Then gushed forth therefrom twelve springs. Each (group of) people knew its own place for water. "Eat and drink of that which Allah has provided and do not act corruptly, making mischief on the earth." (2:60).

And (O Children of Israel, remember) when We took your covenant and We raised above you the Mount (saying): "Hold fast to that which We have given you, and remember that which is therein so that you may become Al-Muttaqun (the pious). (2:63). Then after that you turned away." (2:64).

The Children of Israel desired to see Allah ﷻ, directly:

Inspite of all these favours, the Children of Israel had been always mistrusting Musa (AS). Abdur-Rahman bin Zayd bin Aslam described the following event, "Musa (AS) returned from meeting with his Lord carrying the Tablets on which He wrote the Taurath. He found that they had worshipped the calf in his absence. Consequently, he commanded them to kill themselves and they complied therefore Allah forgave them. Musa (AS) declared to them, 'These Tablets have Allah's Book, containing what He commanded you and what He forbade for you.' They said, 'Should we believe this statement because you said it. By Allah, we will not believe until we see Allah in the open, until He shows us Himself and says: This is My Book, therefore, adhere to it. Why does He not talk to us as He talked to you, O, Musa'"

On their demanding to see Allah [عَزَّ وَجَلَّ] directly, they were seized with a lightning. As-Suddi commented, "They died with a bolt of lightning," Musa (AS) feared that the Children of Israel would suspect him of having taken the men to a solitary place and got them slaughtered. He stood up crying and supplicating to Allah, `O Lord! What should I say to the Children of Israel when I go back to them after 'You' destroyed the best of them. If it had been Your will, 'You' could have destroyed them and me before; would 'You' destroy us for the deeds of the foolish ones among us"

Allahuthala accepted his prayer, and gave those, a new life. Allah revealed to Musa (AS) that these seventy men were among those who worshipped the calf. Afterwards, Allah brought them back to life one man at a time, while the rest of them were watching how Allah was bringing them back to life.

الحمدلله

4. "Strike him (the dead man) with a piece of it (the cow)." Thus Allah brings the dead to life and shows you His Ayat (proofs, evidences, verses, lessons, signs, revelations, etc.) so that you may understand." (2:73). Do you know the back ground of this incident?

The incident of a killed Israelite:

Allahuthala reminded the incident of the Children of Israel killing a man and falling into dispute, as to who was the murderer. Allah ﷻ revealed that which they were hiding. (2:72). During the time of Musa (AS), among the Bani Israel, there was a rich man who had no family. His only relative, was his nephew. The said nephew, being selfish and greedy desired to inherit wealth from his uncle, without delay. Thereupon, during the darkness of night, he killed his uncle and placed the dead body on the door steps of some other house. The next morning, came out of his house crying that somebody killed his uncle. The children of Israel kept blaming one another, disputing and fighting. Someone advised them to approach Musa (AS), who will correctly identify the murderer.

They met Musa (AS). Reported everything that took place and required him to seek the help of his Lord. Musa (AS) declared to the people, as instructed by Allah [SWT], "Verily, Allah commands you that you slaughter a cow." They said, "Do you make fun of us?" He said, "I take Allah's Refuge from being among the foolish." (2:67).

The Children of Israel were ever stubborn and disobedient. They mistrusted Musa (AS) and always used to question him. They said, "Call upon your Lord for us that He may make plain to us what type of cow it is!" Musa (AS) said, "Allah [عَزَّ وَ جَلَّ] says, 'Verily, it is a cow neither too old nor too young, but (it is) between the two conditions', so do what you are commanded." (2:68). If they had obeyed Allah ﷻ's command immediately, their affair would have been made simple.

They said, "Call upon your Lord for us, to make plain to us its colour." He said that "Allah says, 'It is a yellow cow, bright in its colour, pleasing to the beholders.' (2:69). They said, "Call upon your Lord for us to make plain to us what it is. Verily to us all cows are alike, and surely, if Allah wills, we will be guided." (2:70). Then Musa (AS)] said, "He says, 'It is a cow neither trained to till the soil nor water the fields, without blemish, having no other colour except bright yellow.' They said, "Now you have brought the truth." Therfore, they slaughtered it though they were near to not doing it. (2:71).

The incident of the yellow cow:

The Chidren of Israel, went out in search of such a cow. They found a cow with the orphan boy, with all requirements. This boy's father was a very pious man. On his death bed, the man said, "O Allah, I place my wife, my little son, and my only possession, a calf, in Your care." He asked his wife to leave the cow into the nearby forest. He desired to protect his only property, from the selfish and greedy fellow men.

When the Bani Israel found the appropriate cow, in the custody of the orphan boy, they required to know its price. He replied that after enquiring from his mother about its price and then sell it. But they bargained twice, offering a very low price. This, irritated the boy who declared, "I will not sell the cow without my mother's approval, even if you offer me its skin filled with gold!" Upon hearing this, his mother smiled and said, "Let that be the price: Its skin filled with gold." With the advice of his mother he was able to earn a good amount, for his cow. The Children of Israel paid a heavy amount for the cow that fulfilled their requirements. They agreed and bought the cow, by paying its skin full of gold.

With the part of the slaughtered cow, they struck on the dead man. The dead man at once, resurrected by Allah ﷻ's command and revealed that his nephew was the murderer. Immediately he died again.

The lessons derived from this incident are the following:

- Have strong faith in Allahuthal and submit to His Will,
- Obey His commands and orders, as He is the All-Knower.
- By following the above, Allah [SWT] makes life easy.

- Piety and truthful earning, will make Allah ﷻ look after one's family, even in his absence.
- Consult all family matters with elders, as they will provide better advice on the basis of their experience.
- On the right time, Allah [عَزَّ وَ جَلَّ] will pay the reward.
- Allah Subhanahuthala will bring out the truth, even if it is hidden tactfully.
- Do not irritate others, especially Allahuthala, with unwanted questions which will make matters complicated.
- Do not earn the anger and wrath of Allah [SWT].

الحمدلله

5. What will be the question that Allahuthala will raise at Isa (AS), son of Bi Bi Marium, on the Day of Resurrection, as referred in Quran?

Answer: "O Isa (AS), the son of Marium! Did you say unto men: 'Worship me and my mother as two gods besides Allah?" (5:116).

The Christians apart from adhering to the Trinity concept; they even worshipped the mother of Jesus, Mary, with all faith. The Bible does not claim Mary to be divine. During the first three centuries after Messiah, the practice of worshipping Mary, was not adopted in Christianity. Towards the end of the third century of the Christian era, Mary being considered divine and the practice of 'Mariolatry' [idolatrous worship of the Virgin Mary] commenced amongst Christians. But their church did not accept such practice till 431 A.C. Subsequetly, they started using the term, 'Mother of God' to notify Mary. Roman Catholics still follow 'Mariolatry', one way or the other. During the revelation of Quran, Mary was considered as deity. Statues of Mary were considered as important, not only in churches but also in notable places. People started worshiping, supplicating and seeking help from her. After several centuries, the Protestants strongly opposed 'Mariolatry' and brought about a reformation.

The conversation between Allah [SWT] and Isa (AS), expected to takeplace on the Day of Resurrection, in front of his followers:

Allah will exclaim, "O Isa (AS), the son of Marium! Did you say unto men: 'Worship me and my mother as two gods besides Allah?" He will answer: "Glory be to You! It was not for me to say what I had no right. Had I said such a thing, 'You' would surely have known it. You know what is in my inner-self though I do not know what is in

Yours, truly, You, only You, are the All-Knower of all that is hidden and unseen." (5:116).

"Never did I say to them aught except what You (Allah) did command me to say: 'Worship Allah, my Lord and your Lord.' And I was a witness over them while I dwelt amongst them, but when 'You' took me up, 'You' were the Watcher over them, and 'You' are a Witness to all things." (5:117).

After him, the preachings and teachings of Isa (AS), changed. He very well knew that he cannot intercede on behalf of his followers. Thereupon, "Then, Isa (AS), the son of Marium, will say, "If You punish them, they are, 'Your' slaves, and if 'You' forgive them, verily 'You', only You are the All-Mighty, the All-Wise." (5:118).

This is an admonition and warning to the Christians of the whole world.

Allah will declare:

"This is a Day on which the truthful will profit from their truth: theirs are Gardens under which rivers flow (in Paradise) – they shall abide therein forever. Allah is pleased with them and they with Him. That is the great success (Paradise). (5:119). "To Allah belongs the dominion of the heavens and the earth and all that is therein, and He is Able to do all things." (5:120).

الحمدلله

6. Which ayath of the Quran that affirms 'waking up from sleep' is similar to resurrection?

Answer: "'It is Allah Who calls back the souls of people upon their death as well as the souls of the living during their sleep. Then He keeps those for whom He has ordained death, and releases the others until their appointed time. Surely in this are signs for people who reflect." (39:42).

Allah created night for relaxing, resting and sleeping. The following three verses of Quran prove this:

1. 'And He it is Who made the night a garment for you, and the sleep a rest, and He made the day to rise up again.' (25:47).

2. "By the night when it covers" (92:1)

3. "We have made your sleep as a repose and made the night as a cover," (78:9).

Here, Allah describes the darkness of night as a garment, which covers everything.

Allah rhythmically provided sleep to all living beings during night, which is a divine gift. It is essential and compulsory for all, except nocturnal beings. It is equal, simultaneous and free for all. During nights, with calmness and silence prevailing, all creations will sleep while the body is rejuvenated, revived and refreshed. Day and night are favours granted by Allah. "It is out of His mercy that He has made for you the night and the day that you may rest therein and that you may seek of His bounty… (28:73) Therefore, Allah expects us to thank Him!

Ibn Khathir recorded in his Tafsir that Allah causes man to "die a lesser death" during his sleep. When the angels extract his soul, man experiances a "greater death". At the time of his sleeping, even though the 'ruh' of a person is removed from his body, still it is connected with his body (man is unaware of its connection), then, it returns immediately on his waking up.

The following ayaath explains this, as a sign of Allah:

- "It is He, 'Who' takes your souls by night (when you are asleep), and has knowledge of all that you have done by day, then he raises (wakes) you up again that a term appointed (your life period) be fulfilled, then in the end unto Him will be your return. Then He will inform you what you used to do." (6:60)

Every person should realize that waking up from sleep, is equal to resurrection after death. One's life and death are entirely in Allah's hand. No one knows whether he will certainly wake up alive or not, in the morning. He is foolish in turning away from Allah, to whom he has to return. At present, the night is used either to work or spend in entertainment; thereafter sleep during the most of the day. Adhering to such an act, "man is at a loss." (103:2).

Before sleeping, remember Allah, His Grace, His powers and thank Him and seek forgiveness and recite any one of these supplications or all.

Prayer:

Abu Hurayrah, (RA), said that the Messenger of Allah ﷺ stated: "When anyone of you goes to bed, let him brush down the bed with his garment, for he does not know what has come on his bed since he left it. Then let him say,

Dua 1: "In Your name my Lord, I lie down and in Your name I rise, so if You should take my soul then have mercy upon it, and if You should return my soul then protect it in the manner You do so with Your righteous servants. " (Al-Bukhari and Muslim)

بِاسْمِكَ رَبِّي وَضَعْتُ جَنْبِي، وَبِكَ أَرْفَعُهُ، فَإِنْ أَمْسَكْتَ نَفْسِي فَارْحَمْهَا، وَإِنْ أَرْسَلْتَهَا فَاحْفَظْهَا، بِمَا تَحْفَظُ بِهِ عِبَادَكَ االصَّالِحِينَ

Dua 2: "In Your Name, O Allah, I live and die." اللَّهُمَّ بِاسْمِكَ أَمُوتُ وَأَحْيَا

Dua 3: "O Allah! Save me from Your punishment the day Your servants are resurrected." اللَّهُمَّ قِنِي عَذَابَكَ يَوْمَ تَبْعَثُ عِبَادَكَ

Dua 4: "O Allah, I submit my soul unto You, and I entrust my affair unto You, and I turn my face towards You, and I totally rely on You, in hope and fear of You. Verily there is neither refuge nor safe haven from You except with You. I believe in Your Book which You have revealed and in Your Prophet whom You have sent."

اللَّهُمَّ أَسْلَمْتُ نَفْسِي إِلَيْكَ، وَفَوَّضْتُ أَمْرِي إِلَيْكَ، وَوَجَّهْتُ وَجْهِي إِلَيْكَ، وَأَلْجَأْتُ ظَهْرِي إِلَيْكَ، رَغْبَةً وَرَهْبَةً إِلَيْكَ، لَا مَلْجَأَ وَلَا مَنْجَا مِنْكَ إِلَّا إِلَيْكَ، آمَنْتُ بِكِتَابِكَ وَبِنَبِيِّكَ الَّذِي أَرْسَلْتَ

Dua while waking up:

الحَمْدُ لِلَّهِ الَّذِي أَحْيَانَا بَعْدَ مَا أَمَاتَنَا وَإِلَيْهِ النُّشُورُ

Imam Muhammad al-Baqir also states: "When you wake up from sleep claim, All Praise is for Allah who has returned my soul so I Praise Him and worship Him."

الحمدلله

7. In Surah Booruj, Allah swears by "the Promised Day." What is that Promised Day?

Answer: The Promised Day is "The Day of Resurrection"

We are reminded, again and again of this reality of the Last Day by Allah, the Exalted, in the Quran.

Verses of Quran about "the Promised Day":

• Allah states, "And the disbelievers swear by Allah with the most energetic of their oaths: Allah will not raise up him who dies. Yes, indeed! by a promise which He has willed upon Himself; but most people know it not." (16:38).

• "Surely, the Hour is coming, there is no doubt about it, and certainly, Allah will resurrect those who are in the graves." [22:7].

- "Surely, He will gather you together on the Day of Resurrection about which there is no doubt. And who is truer in statement than Allah?" [4:87].

- "…they will be resurrected (for reckoning), on a Great Day, the Day when (all) mankind will stand before the Lord of the Alamin" [84:4 to 6].

- "He will gather you together on Resurrection Day, which is beyond all doubt - but most human beings understand it not." (45:26)

- "Allah [alone] can raise them from the dead, whereupon unto Him they shall return" (6:36)

- "Verily, judgment is bound to come!" (51:6)

- "Unto Him you shall be resurrected." (67:15)

- "…and then, if it be His will, He shall raise him again to life," [80:22]

- "Say: 'Yes, by my Sustainer! Most surely will you be raised from the dead, and then, most surely, will you be made to understand what you did [in life]! For, easy is this for God!" (64:7)

- "And [know, O man] that the Last Hour is bound to come, beyond any doubt, and that God will resurrect all who are in their graves" (22:7).

- "God's promise [of resurrection] is true, and that there can be no doubt as to [the coming of] the Last Hour." (18:21).

- "Do they not know that they are bound to be raised from the dead" (83:4).

Allah warns about that Day:

- "for he who denies God, and His angels, and His revelations, and His apostles, and the Last Day, has indeed gone far astray." (4:136)

- "let every person look to what he has sent forth for tomorrow (for the great day), and fear Allah." (59:18)

- "On the Day of Resurrection, 'We' shall make him taste the torment of burning (Fire)." (22: 9)

- "Those are they who have bought the life of this world at the price of the Hereafter. Their torment shall not be lightened nor shall they be helped." (2:85)

- "Your Ilah (God) is One Ilah. But for those who believe not in the Hereafter, their hearts deny (the faith in the Oneness of Allah), and they are proud." (16:22)

- "And warn of the Day of Assembling, of which there is no doubt, when a party will be in Paradise and a party in the blazing Fire (Hell)." (42:7)
- "You' assembly of jinns and mankind! "Did not there come to .... warning of the meeting of this Day of yours." (6:130)
- "But [on the Day of Judgment] We shall most certainly give those who were bent on denying the truth full understanding of all that they ever did, and shall most certainly give them [thereby] a taste of suffering severe." (41:50)

The claim of those, who deny resurrection:

- "That is but our first death, and we shall not be raised to life again." (44:35).
- "There is no life beyond our life in this world: we die and we live [but once], and we shall never be raised from the dead!" (23:37)
- "They say: "What! After we have died and become mere dust and bones, shall we, forsooth, be raised from the dead?" (23:62, 37:16, 56:47)
- "And [thus, too,] they say, 'After we will have become bones and dust, shall we, forsooth, be raised from the dead in a new act of creation?" (17:49, 17:98)
- "Who could give life to bones that have crumbled to dust?" (36:78)
- "They who are bent on denying the truth claim that they will never be raised from the dead!" (64:7)
- "On the Day when God will raise them all from the dead, they will swear before Him as they [now] swear before you, thinking that they are on firm ground [in their assumptions]. Oh, verily, it is they, who are the [greatest] liars!" (58:18)

The disbelievers question as to when will be the day of resurrection?

The disbelievers of all the time exclaim "When is this promise [of resurrection] to be fulfilled?" (36:48).

"They [mockingly] ask, "When is that Day of Judgment to be?" (51:12)

Allah replies:

"For that [resurrection which they deride] will be [upon them of a sudden, as if it were] but a single accusing cry and then, lo! they will begin to see [the truth]" (37:19)

"Verily, with God alone rests the knowledge of when the Last Hour will come" (31:34 and 41:47)

"Allah's [alone] is the knowledge of the hidden reality of the heavens and the earth. And so, the advent of the Last Hour will but manifest itself [in a single moment,] like the twinkling of an eye, or closer still: for, behold, Allah has the power to will anything." (16:77)

Allah describes the happenings of that day:

Peoples' hearts will be pounding, not knowing their fate. Even the believers convinced of the truth; will be severely worried.

Trumpet will be blown:

- Allah, the Exalted, informs us: "And the Trumpet will be blown, and all who are in the heavens and all who are on the earth will swoon away, except him whom Allah wills." (39:68)

- "And the Trumpet will be blown (again) and behold! From the graves they will come out quickly to their Lord." (36:51). His will be the dominion on the Day when the trumpet [of resurrection] is blown. (6:73)

- When the Trumpet will be blown with one blowing (the first one), And the earth and the mountains shall be removed from their places, and crushed with a single crushing, then on that Day shall the (Great) Event befall, And the heaven will split asunder, for that Day it (the heaven will be frail (weak), and torn up, And the angels will be on its sides, and eight angels will, that Day, bear the Throne of your Lord above them. That Day shall you be brought to Judgement, not a secret of you will be hidden. (69:13 to 18)

- "They have not recognized the worth of Allah as his worth should be recognized. On the Day of Resurrection, the whole earth shall be in His grasp and all the heavens shall be rolled up in His right hand. Glory be to Him! Exalted be He above what they associate with Him." (39:67)

- "The sun wound round and lost its light and is overthrown. And the stars shall fall; And the mountains shall have made to pass away; when the pregnant she-camels shall be neglected; And the wild beasts shall be gathered together; And the seas shall become as blazing Fire or shall overflow; And the souls shall be joined with their bodies" (81:1 to 7)

- "On the Day when the earth is riven asunder all around them as they hasten forth: that gathering will be easy for Us [to encompass]. (50:44)

Horrors of the Day:

"On the Day you see it every nursing mother will be distracted from that [child] she was nursing, and every pregnant woman will abort her pregnancy, and you will see the people [appearing] intoxicated while they are not intoxicated; but the punishment of Allah is severe." (22:2).

"And every person will come forth along with an (angel) to drive (him), and an (angel) to bear witness."(50:21)

"The Day which shall turn the hair of children grey," (73:17)

"You shall see the eyes of the disbelievers fixedly stare in horror. (They will say): "Woe to us! We were indeed heedless of this; nay, but we were wrong doers." (21:97)

"When they will shrink in terror, with nowhere to escape - since they will have been seized from so close nearby. And they will say (in the Hereafter): "We do believe (now);" but how could they receive from a place so far off (i.e. to return to the worldly life again)." (34:51 and 52).

"Then, when there comes second blowing of Trumpet, That Day shall a man flee from his brother, And from his mother and his father, and from his wife and his children." (80:33 to 36).

"Some faces that Day, will be bright (true believers of Islamic Monotheism). Laughing, rejoicing at good news (of Paradise). And other faces, that Day, will be dust-stained; Darkness will cover them, such will be the disbelievers in Allah, the wicked evil doers." (80:38 to 42).

"So (O Muhammad ﷺ) withdraw from them. The Day that the caller will call (them) to a terrible thing. They will come forth, with humbled eyes from (their) graves as if they were locusts spread abroad, hastening towards the caller, the disbelievers will say: "This is a hard Day." On the Day when the Summoning Voice will summon [man] unto something that the mind cannot conceive." (54:6 to 8)

The occurance of resurrection:

- "Oh, woe unto us! Who has roused us from our sleep [death]?" (36:52).
- "You shall be raised from the dead on Resurrection Day." (21:16)

- But only, it will be a single shout (i.e., the second blowing of the Trumpet)]. When, behold, they find themselves over the earth alive after their death" (79:13 &14)
- "The Day when they shall come forth in haste from their graves, as if racing towards a goal-post" (70:43).
- "On the Day when Allah will raise them all from the dead and will make them truly understand all that they did [in life]: Allah will have taken [all of] it into account, even though they [themselves] may have forgotten it - for God is witness unto everything." (58:6)
- "On a Day when He will call you, and you will answer by praising Him, thinking all the while that you have tarried [on earth] but a little while." (17:52)

The Prophet ﷺ describes about such event. He proclaimed: "You will be gathered, bare-footed, naked, and uncircumcised." Quran quotes: "As We began the first creation, 'We' shall repeat it." (21:104) The first human being to be dressed on the Day of Resurrection will be Prophet Ibrahim (AS). Next will be our Prophet ﷺ." (Saheeh Al-Bukhari).

Duration of the Day:

The Prophet ﷺ declared: "That day will be 50,000 years long, after which a person will be admitted into Paradise or cast into Hell." (Abu Dawood)

Our deeds will be weighed, on this day:

- "But We shall set up just balance-scales on Resurrection Day, and no human being shall be wronged in the least: for though there be [in him but] the weight of a mustard-seed [of good or evil], We shall bring it forth; and none can take count as We do!" (21:47)
- "Allah will judge between you all on the Day of Resurrection" (4:141).
- "He will clear and judge the disputes what people differ." (given in several places of Quran).

The receiving of their records by the human beings:

After an agonizing wait, people's record of deeds will be provided.

- "And the Book will be placed and you will see the criminal sinners, fearful of that which is recorded therein. They will say: "Woe to us! What sort of Book is this that leaves neither small thing nor a big thing, but has recorded it with numbers!" (18:49)

- "Then as for he who is given his record in his right hand, he will be judged with an easy account and return to his people in happiness. But as for he who is given his record behind his back, he will cry out for destruction and [enter to] burn in a Blaze." (84:7-12)

- "And every human being's destiny have We tied to his neck; and on the Day of Resurrection We shall bring forth for him a record which he will find wide open;" (17:13)

- This is further clarified by Allah in the following verses: "So as for he who is given his record in his right hand, he will say, 'Here, read my record! Indeed, I was certain that I would be meeting my account.' So he will be in a pleasant life – In an elevated Garden, its [fruit] to be picked hanging near. [They will be told], 'Eat and drink in satisfaction for what you put forth in the days past.' (69:19-24)

- But as for he who is given his record in his left hand, he will say, 'Oh, I wish I had not been given my record and had not known what is my account. I wish it [i.e., my death] had been the decisive one. My wealth has not availed me. Gone from me is my authority.' [God will say], 'Seize him and shackle him. Then into Hellfire drive him. Then into a chain whose length is seventy cubits insert him.' Indeed, he did not used to believe in God, 'the Most Great', nor did he encourage the feeding of the poor. So there is not for him here this Day any devoted friend. Nor any food except from the discharge of wounds; none will eat it except the sinners." (69:25 - 37)

Nobody will come for intercession on that Day:

- "The Day when no friend shall be of the least avail to his friend, and when none shall be succored" (44:41)

- "When that Day comes, not a soul will speak. unless it be by His leave" (11:105)

- "On that Day, to every one of them will his own state be of sufficient concern" (80:37)

- "Oh, you might well argue in their behalf in the life of this world: but who will argue on their behalf with God on the Day of Resurrection, or who will be their defender?" (4:10

- "Neither your relatives nor your children will benefit you on the Day of Resurrection (against Allah). He will judge between you." (60:3)
- "On that Day a person shall not avail another, nor will intercession be accepted from him nor will compensation be taken from him nor will they be helped." (2:48).

Prophet Mohammed's ﷺ intercession, will be accepted on that day. No other Prophet is capable of offering intercession for their communities.

Condition of the sinners:
- "their suffering will be doubled on Resurrection Day: he shall abide in ignominy." (25:69)
- "the evildoers will be told: "Taste [now] what you have earned [in life]!" (39:24)
- "then, (for them) would be a return with loss!" (79:12)
- "their works are in vain, on the Day of Resurrection" (18:105)
- "Verily, on that Day they all will share in their common suffering." (37:33)
- They were told, "We have removed your covering, and sharp is your sight this Day!" (50:22).
- "On the Day when He shall call out to them, "Where, now, are those [alleged] partners of Mine?" - they will [surely] answer, "We confess unto Thee that none of us can bear witness [to anyone's having a share in Thy divinity]!" (41:47)
- "they would surely offer it as ransom from the awful suffering [that will befall them] on the Day of Resurrection" (39:47).
- "We shall raise him up blind." (20:124)
- "they shall bear the full weight of their own burdens, as well as some of the burdens of those ignorant ones whom they have led astray" (16:25).
- "Hence, warn men of the Day when this suffering may befall them, and when those who did wrong [in their lifetime] will exclaim: 'O our Sustainer! Grant us respite for a short while, so that we might respond to Thy call and follow the apostles!' [But God will answer:] 'Why - were you not aforetime wont to swear that no kind of resurrection and retribution awaited you" (14:44)

- "Allah will neither speak unto them nor look upon them on the Day of Resurrection, nor will He cleanse them of their sins; and grievous suffering awaits them." (3:77)

Status of the pious believers, with righteous deeds:

- "Verily, those who do righteous deeds-shall have their reward with their Sustainer; and no fear need they have, and neither shall they grieve." (2:62).
- "Those who are [especially] constant in prayer, and spend in charity, and all who believe in God and the Last Day - these it is unto whom We shall grant a mighty reward." (4:162)
- "He whom We have promised an excellent promise (Paradise), which he will find true." (28:61).
- "And Paradise will be brought near to the Muttaqun (pious) not far off. (It will be said): "This is what you were promised," (50:31)
- This is what you were promised, – (it is) for those oft-returning (to Allah) in sincere repentance, and those who preserve their covenant with Allah. Who feared the Most Beneficent (Allah) in the Ghaib (unseen):
- "Enter you therein in peace and security; this is a Day of eternal life!" (50:34)
- Those who brought into paradise will indeed have gained a triumph" (3:185)

Prayer:

The 'Lord of the Day of Judgment!' (1:4). 'Do not put me to shame on the Day when all will be raised from the dead.' (26:87). "Grant Thy forgiveness unto me, and my parents, and all the believers, on the Day on which the [last] reckoning will come to pass!" (14:41). Aameen!

الحمدلله

8. "On this day We shall seal up their mouths and their hands will speak to Us and their legs bear witness to what they used to earn." (36:65). Can you mention any other organ that will be a witness, against a Mujrimun (sinner), on the Day of Judgement?

The answer is: 1. Ears. 2. Eyes. 3. Tongue and 4. Skin.

On the Day of Resurrection, Allahuthala gathers all the sinners together, in front of Hell. Al Quran asserts: "And (remember) the Day that the enemies of Allah will be gathered to the Fire, so they will be collected there (the first and the last)." (41:19). The sinners of all the times, will be chased towards Hell.

Allah mentions about this in three places in Quran:

In this world, Allah has appointed two angels to record the deeds of every human being. On the Day of Resurrection, their deeds will be provided as a book of record. Allah declares: "And We have fastened every man's deeds to his neck, and on the Day of Resurrection, 'We' shall bring out for him a book which he will find wide open." (17:13). It will be announced: "Read your book. You, yourself are sufficient as a reckoner against you this Day." (17:14). On that Day, the stubborn disbelievers, on reading their book attempt at denying their bad deeds; claiming that they never committed any crime; and will further argue with their Lord that their witnesses are liars; apart from denying the truthfulness of their book of deeds. They will seek the mercy of Allah to be just with them. At that time Allah will seal their mouths and claim "their hands will speak to Us and their legs will bear witness to what they used to earn." (36:65).

In another part of the Holy Quran, Allah states, " ......when they reach the Hell-fire, their hearing (ears) and their eyes, and their skins will testify against them as to what they used to do." (Fussilath, 41:20). And the sinners will ask their organs, "Why do you testify against us?" They will reply: "Allah has caused us to speak, as He causes all things to speak, and He created you the first time, and to Him you are made to return." (Fussilath, 41:21). "And you have not been hiding against yourselves, lest your ears, and your eyes, and your skins testify against you, but you thought that Allah knew not much of what you were doing." (41:22). "And that thought of yours which you thought about your Lord, has brought you to destruction, and you have become (this Day) of those utterly lost! (41:23). Allah informs them at such circumstance, "......... the Fire will be a home for them, and if they beg for to be excused, yet they are not of those who will ever be excused." (41:24).

Surah Al-Qiyama also upholds that: "On that Day man will be informed of what he sent forward (of his evil or good deeds), and what he left behind (of his good or evil traditions). Nay! Man will be a witness against himself. "Though he may put forth his excuses (to cover his evil deeds)." (75: 13 and 15).

In another place it is observed, "On the Day when their tongues, their hands, and their legs or feet will bear witness against them as to what they used to do." (24:24). When the mouth of the sinner is sealed, the tongue which was uttering lies all along, will divulge the truth about him.

Two of the aahadhees refer to the same concept:

Hadhees 1:

Ibn Abi Hatim recorded in Muslim and An-Nasa'i, that Anas bin Malik, (RA) said, "We were once with the Prophet ﷺ and he smiled so broadly that his molar could be seen, then he exclaimed: "Do you know why I am smiling?" We replied, `Allah and His Messenger ﷺ knows the best.' He declared: "Because of the way a servant will argue with his Lord on the Day of Resurrection. He will say, "O Lord, will You not protect me from injustice?" Allah will say, "Of course!" The man will say, "I will not accept any witness against me except from myself." Allah will say, "Today you will be sufficient witness against yourself, and the honorable scribes will serve as witnesses against you." Then his mouth will be sealed, and it will be said to his faculties, "Speak!" So they will speak of what he did. Then he will be permitted to speak, and he will say, "May you be doomed! It was for you that I was fighting."

Hadhees 2:

Ibn Jarir narrated that Abu Musa Al-Ashari, (RA) said, "The believer will be called to account on the Day of Resurrection, and his Lord will show him his deeds, just between him and His Lord. He will admit it and will say, `Yes, O Lord, I did do that.' Then Allah will forgive him; his sins and conceal them and no creature on earth will see any of those sins, but his good deeds will be seen, and he want all the people to see them."

"Then the disbeliever/the hypocrite. will be brought to account and his Lord will show him his deeds and he will deny them, saying, `O Lord, by Your glory, this angel has written down things that I did not do.' The angel will say to him, `Did you not do such and such, on such a day and in such a place?' He will say, `No, by Your glory, I did not do that.' When he says this, Allah will seal his mouth.' Musa Al-Ashari, (RA) said, "I think that the first part of his body to speak will be his right thigh."

Allah has pre-warned mankind about the Day of Judgement:

"After our death Allah will question each one of us about hearing, sight and heart." (17: 36). On that occasion Allah will ask them this question: "O you the assembly of jinns and mankind! "Did not there come to you Messengers from amongst you, reciting unto you My Verses and warning you of the meeting of this Day of yours?" They will say: "We bear witness against ourselves." It was the life of this world that deceived them. And they will bear witness against themselves that they were disbelievers." (6:130).

Yes! Allah is Capable of everything, "إِنَّ اللَّهَ عَلَىٰ كُلِّ شَيْءٍ قَدِيرٌ" He is the one who made a stone, a born child and a tree to talk. He can make anything to speak and assert the Truth. That is easy for Him! Subhanallah!

الحمدلله

9 "Nay, it will be worse for them; the things which they withheld shall be tied to their necks like a collar on the Day of Resurrection." [3:180] Towards which action, Allah ﷻ will provide this punishment in the Hereafter?

Answer: Stinginess

Allah said, "And let not those who [greedily] withhold what Allāh has given them of His bounty ever think that it is better for them. Rather, it is worse for them. Their necks will be encircled by what they withheld on the Day of Resurrection. And to Allāh belongs the heritage of the heavens and the earth. And Allāh, of what you do, is [fully] Aware." (3:180). Therefore, Allah declares to those people, the punishment as, "the objects which they withheld without giving to others shall be tied to their necks like a collar on the Day of Resurrection."

Stinginess, is the worst evil trait. It is a worse disease. Such a conduct Allah سبحانه وتعالىٰ dislikes.

The similar ayaath in the Quran are:

- "Those who hord gold and silver and do not spend (anything out of it) for the cause of Allah ﷻ, should know that their recompense will be a painful torment on the Day of Judgment and that their treasures will be heated by the fire of hell and pressed against their foreheads, sides and back with this remark: 'These are your own treasures which you hoarded for yourselves. See for yourselves what they feel like.' (9:34-5)"
- "Shaitan threatens men with poverty and enjoins to be niggardly" (2:268).
- "In his love for wealth, man is very intense.' (100:8).

- "When evil afflicts them they become greatly grieved and niggardly when good befalls them." (70:20 and 21).
- "If you control the treasures of the mercy of the Lord, then you would withhold (them) from fear of spending, and man is niggardly." (17: 100).
- "Men's souls are swayed by stinginess." (4: 128).
- "When Allah عزّ وجل gave them wealth out of His Grace, they became niggardly of it and they turned back and they withdrew." (9:76).
- "They do this against their own soul" (47:38). "They go to the extreme of considering themselves free from the need of Allah." (92:8). "These stingy ones try to make others also stingy and they hide the favours that Allah has given on them." (4:37 and 57:24). "Because of this Allah will bring forth malice." (47:37).
- "Woe to every (kind of) scandal-monger and back biter, who pile up wealth and lay it by. He thinks that his wealth will make him immortal." (104:1-2).
- "Woe to those who do (good) to be seen, and withhold the necessaries of life." (107: 4, 6 and 7).

Several noble traits like Zakath, sadaqa, munificence, self-sacrifice and helping others are destained to disappear, when a person becomes stingy. It is for this reason that the Prophet ﷺ has warned: "No miser shall enter Paradise." "A miser is far from Jannat, far from people, and close to the fire" (Tirmidhi). "The people of the Hell are those who are rude, stingy and arrogant." (Bukhari, Adab 61; Ayman 9).

Aahadees about stinginess:

As per Abu Hurayrah (RA) the Prophet ﷺ had stated: "Whoever Allah makes wealthy and he does not pay the Zakath, then on the Day of Resurrection his wealth will be made in the likeness of a bald-headed poisonous male snake with two black spots over the eyes. The snake will encircle his neck and bite his cheeks and proclaim, 'I am your wealth, I am your treasure." (Sahih Bukhari, Vol.2, Book 24, Number 486)

Abu Dharr (RA) narrated: "Allah dislikes three groups of people............. the old adulterer, the stingy and the arrogant." (İbn Hıbban / Tergıb ve Terhib)

Ali (RA) narrated: "Allahuthala dislikes the one who is stingy in his lifetime but generous at the moment of death." (Hatib) He continued, 'The worst person is the Bakheel (miser), he is wretched in this world and is punished in the next world'. The Prophet ﷺ once picked up one of his grand-children, kissed him and then said, "The children are the flowers of Jannah, but they make a person Bakheel (stingy), coward and make him fear death"

"If mankind had two valleys full of property, he would desire for the third one. Only earth can satisfy him. Allah accepts the repentance of those who repent." (Muslim, Zakat 116).

To get rid of stinginess one has to purify, first the heart! "One who gives Zakat, who entertains his guest and who helps others in time of calamities; is saved from stinginess." (Bukhari, Mazalim, 8)

A hadhees states that: "Refrain from stinginess because stinginess destroyed those who lived before and tempted them to shed each other's blood and to consider harams to be halal…" (Muslim, Birr 56)

Narrated Abu Huraira (RA), the Prophet (ﷺ) stated, "Every day two angels come down from Heaven and one of them says, 'O Allah! Compensate every person who spends in Your Cause,' and the other (angel) says, 'O Allah! Destroy every miser." (Sahih al-Bukhari 1442)

The main cause of stinginess is:
- weakness in faith
- fear of poverty
- greediness
- desire to live in luxury
- fearing the future of their children
- forgetting that Allah provides everything
- ignoring the fact that everything belongs to Allah

Allah encourages spending wealth, for a good cause:

If a man shares his wealth to others, by way of Zakath and Sadaqa, Allahuthala will provide 10 to 700 times (or even more) replacement in this world or reward in the Hereafter! Allah declares, "Spend out of what He has made you to be successors" (57:7). "Whatever thing you spend, He exceeds it with reward, and He is the best of Sustainers. (34:39)"

"Know that your wealth and children are a temptation for you and that Allah has the greatest reward for the righteous ones." (8:28).

"Spending money for the cause of Allah is as the seed from which seven ears may grow, each bearing one hundred grains. Allah gives in multiples to those whom He wants. Allah is All-Sufficient and All-knowing." (2:261). Neither should there be intense love towards money; wealth and worldy gains nor should there be intense hatred towards these. Wealth becomes a blessing and mercy of Allah; if it is used timely, wisely and appropriately.

Allah records, "And let not your hand be tied (like a miser) to your neck, nor stretch it forth to its utmost reach (like a spendthrift), so that you become blameworthy and in severe poverty." (17:29)

Frequent prayers of Prophet ﷺ were: "I seek refuge with You from frightfulness and stinginess"

May Allah سبحانه وتعالٰى grant us the necessary ability to fight this distasteful disease and may He remove the thought of stinginess from our heart! Aameen!

الحمدلله

10. And remember when your Lord brought forth from the loins of the children of Adam their descendants and had them testify regarding themselves. Allah asked, "Am I not your Lord?" They replied, "Yes, 'You' are! We testify." He cautioned, "Now you have no right to say on Judgment Day, 'We were not aware of this." (7:172). What this covenant is called?

Answer: This is known as the covenant of Alusth (عهد ألَسْتُ) or Promise or the covenant of Eternity.

After creating Adam (AS), our Creator wiped the back of our father Adam (AS), all the descendants of Adam (AS); brought out of our fathers' loins. Allah stated that all the Children of Adam testified against themselves claiming Allah is their Lord and King; and that there is no deity worthy of worship except Him. Allah knows the weakness of the Children of Adam! On the day of resurrection, they cannot claim that they were unaware. Those who obey the covenant, enter paradise. Allah created all of them with this Fitrah (natural inclination). The following aayath of Quran, stands evidence for this:

- "And if you ask them who created them, they will surely say: 'Allah'" [Az-Zukhruf, 43:87].
- "So direct your face toward the religion, inclining to truth. [Adhere to] the fiṭrah of Allah upon which He has created [all] people. No change should there be in the creation of Allah. That is the correct religion, but most of the people do not know." (30:30).

There is a hadhees; which also mentions that Allah took Adam's children from his loins and divided them into those on the right and those on the left, as people deserving Paradise and the Hell. If the children of Adam fail to respect their covenant, Allah will also disregard His promise. Allah declares, "...and be faithful to (your) covenant with Me, I will fulfill (My) covenant with you." (2:40). If we Muslims fulfill the covenant of Allah, by obeying Him and His messenger, thereby, He will fulfill His promise of success and reward (Paradise) for us.

Several ahadhees are associated with this ayath:

Narrated Abu Huraira (RA): The Prophet ﷺ asserted, "Every child is born with a true faith of Islam (i.e. to worship none but Allah Alone) and his parents convert him to Judaism or Christianity or Magianism, as an animal delivers a perfect baby animal. Do you find it mutilated?" [Sahih al-Bukhari 1385].

Muslim recorded that `Iyad bin `Himar said that the Messenger of Allah ﷺ referred in the hadhees qudsi: "Allah said, `I created My servants Hunafa' (monotheists), but the devils came to them and deviated them from their religion, prohibiting what I allowed." (Sahih Muslim 2865).

Imam Ahmad recorded that Anas bin Malik (RA) said that the Prophet ﷺ stated, "It will be said to a man from the people of the Fire on the Day of Resurrection, `If you owned all that is on the earth, would you pay it as ransom' He will reply, `Yes.' Allah will say, `I ordered you with what is less than that, when you were still in Adam's loins, that is, 'associate none with Me (in worship)'. You insisted that you associate with Me (in worship)." (Sahih al-Bukhari 6557). This was recorded in the Two Sahihs commenting on this Ayah (7:172),

Jami at-Tirmidhi [3076] records that Abu Hurayrah (RA) narrated that the Messenger of Allah ﷺ said, "When Allah created Adam, He wiped Adam's back and every person that He will create from him until the Day of Resurrection fell out from his back. Allah placed a glimmering light between the eyes of each one of them. Allah showed them to Adam and Adam exclaimed, `O Lord! Who are they?' Allah replied, `These are your offspring.' Adam saw a man from among them whose light he liked. He wished to know, `O Lord! Who is this man?' Allah replied, `This is a man from the latter generations of your offspring! His name is Dawud.' Adam wished to know, `O Lord! How many years would he live?' Allah responded, `Sixty years.' Adam said, `O Lord! I have forfeited forty years from my life for him.' When Adam's life came to an end, the angel of death came to him (to take his soul). Adam said, `I still have forty years from my life term, don't I?' The angel exclaimed, `Have you not given it to your son Dawud?' Adam denied it so also his offspring followed suit (denying Allah's covenant). Adam forgot and his offspring forgot, Adam made a mistake and his offspring made the same mistake.)

Allah knows the best!

الحمدلله

بِسْمِ ٱللَّهِ ٱلرَّحْمَٰنِ ٱلرَّحِيمِ

15. About Surahs

1. Which surah is called As-Shifa?

Answer: Surah Al-Fathiha

As narrated by Abu Saeed (RA): "Some of the companions of the Prophet ﷺ went on a journey till they reached some of the Arab tribes (at night). They required the latter to treat them as their guests but they refused. The chief of that tribe was then bitten by a snake (or stung by a scorpion) and they tried their best to cure him but in vain. Some of them said (to the others), "Nothing has benefitted him, will you go to the people who resided here at night, it may be that some of them might possess something (as treatment)."

They went to the group of the companions and reported, "Our chief has been bitten by a snake (or stung by a scorpion) and we have tried everything but he has not benefitted. Have you got anything (useful)?" One of them replied, "Yes, by Allah! I can recite a Ruqya, but as you have refused to accept us as your guests, I will not recite the Ruqya for you unless you fix for us some wages for it." They agreed to pay them a flock of sheep. One of them then went and recited (Surah Al-Fathiha): "All the praises and thanks be to Allah, the Lord of the Alamin."

On being puffed over, the chief who became all right as if he was released from a chain; stood up and started walking, showing no signs of sickness. They paid them, what they agreed to pay. Some of the companions then suggested to divide their earnings among themselves, but the one who performed the recitation said, "Do not divide the sheep till we meet the Prophet ﷺ and narrate the whole story to him and await his order." Therefore, they went to Allah's Messenger ﷺ and narrated the incident. Allah's Messenger ﷺ enquired, "How did you come to know that Surat Al-Fathiha was recited as Ruqya?" After smiling he added, "You have done the right thing. Divide (what you have earned) and assign a share for me as well." {Sahih Bukhari, Hadith No:2276; Volume 3, Book 36, Number 476}

The surah is known by various names:

🌼 "Umm Al-Kitab" - because it is "the mother of the book". The Quran starts with this surah. It is the summary of the entire Quran.

🌼 "Al-Hamd" - It contains comprehensive veneration of the Almighty in the first half and great dua for His servant, in the second half. Allah, the Exalted, said, "A half of it is for Me and a half for My servant and My servant shall acquire what he asked for." [Muslim and An-Nasai]

🌼 "As-Salath" - because without reciting this surah the Salath, will be incomplete. The Prophet ﷺ repeated thrice, "Whoever performs any prayer in which he did not read Al-Hamd, then his prayer is incomplete."

🌼 "Ash-Shifa" because it is used as a cure for diseases.

🌼 "Ar-Ruqyah" because it is used as a remedy for snake and scorpian bite by companions.

🌼 "Seven Mathani" since it contains the seven verses repeatedly recited (15:87).

🌼 Asas-al-Quran - it is "the Basis of Quran." It contains the most essential fundamental teachings of Islam, i.e. Admiration of One - Allah Subhabahuthala who guides Whom He wishes. It is also called as Al Quranul Azeem, Al Khafiya.

"Bimillah hirrahaman nirraheem" is a part of Al-Fathihah. It should be recited aloud like the rest of Al-Fatihah.

Ahadhees about Surah Fathiha:

Our Prophet ﷺ asserted, "Allah [SWT] did favour to me by giving this Surah and making it equivalent to Holy Quran. It is one of the noblest treasures of Arsh".

Anas (RA) reported that the Prophet ﷺ as having said: "Should I not inform you of the most noble and excellent part of the Quran?" He then recited "Alhumdhulillahi Rabbil Alamin" (An Nasai)

Surah Al-Fathiha is the most outstanding part of Furqan-e-Hameed, indicating the best form of concise teaching, first praise Allah, then pray.

In one of the tradition, the Holy Prophet ﷺ said that reciting of sura Al-Hamd, is equivalent to the recitation of two-third of Holy Quran.

This surah was revealed on two occasions. Once, during Jibreel (AS) demonstrated Salath to the Prophet ﷺ. So also while our Prophet ﷺ went on a Night journey, Allahuthala revealed this surah through another Angel.

Abu Huraira reported: The Apostle of Allah ﷺ declared, "If anyone observes prayer in which he does not recite Umm al-Quran, it is deficient [he said this three times] and not complete. At times we are behind the Imam. He said: Recite it inwardly, for he had heard the Messenger of Allah ﷺ declare that Allah the Exalted had said: "The great Quran starts with the praising of Almighty Allah as "Alhumdhulillahi Rabbil Aalameen - All praise and thanks be to Allah, the Lord of Existence." When anybody refer to this: Allah says, `My servant has praised Me.' When the servant says, "The Most Gracious, the Most Merciful." Allah holds, `My servant has glorified Me.' When it is stated that "The Owner of the Day of Recompense." Allah says, `My servant has glorified Me,' or `My servant has related all matters to Me.' When it is said, "You (alone) we worship, and You (alone) we ask for help." Allah asserts, `This is between Me and My servant, and My servant shall acquire what he sought.' When it is pleaded, "Guide us to the straight path. The way of those on whom You have granted Your grace, not (the way) of those who earned Your anger, (like Jews) nor of those who went astray (like Christians)", Allah confirms, `This is for My servant, and My servant shall acquire what he asked for.' It is customary to say, `Aameen' after `Waladdallin', so that Allah will answer our supplication. [Sahih Muslim 395a and also by Malik, at-Tirmidhi, Abu-Dawud, an-Nasa'i and Ibn Majah].

الحمدلله

2. When and why Surah Yusuf was revealed?

The entire surah, with the exception of four verses, was revealed during the most difficult period of our Nabi ﷺ's life. It was revealed after boycott or during the Year of Sorrow, prior to Hijra, during which period the Quraish were planning to kill or exile or imprison him.

۞ It was at that time, the companions wanted to know the trials and tribulations of the Prophets of Allahuthala in the past.

۞ It was then, Jews through Quraish questioned him, "Why did the Israelites go to Egypt?"

In the midst of these trials and tribulations, Allah Subhanahuthala revealed this surah, to console, to uplift and to provide strength to His worshipping servant - the Prophet ﷺ.

Because of their faith in Allah ﷻ, Muslims were persecuted, with years of boycott and isolation. When Muslims returned to the city after boycott, the Prophet ﷺ lost his beloved wife Khadijah (RA), who was the first believer; friend; supporter and comforter. He also lost his uncle, a father-figure, a great protector, Abu Talib. With the loss of his two ardent supporters, the Prophet ﷺ went to the people of Ṭaif to seek support. They not only rejected his message but also chased him and stoned him. Thereupon, he literally ran towards Makkah with bleeding injuries. He sent word to many, seeking protection, who were unwilling. Finally, under the protection of Al-Mutim bin Adi, he returned to Makkah.

Arabs, did not know the history of the Israelites (the Children of Yaqub [AS]). The Jews thought that the Prophet ﷺ would not be able to give an answer about the Isralite's migration to Egypt. Allahuthala revealed the whole story of the Prophet Yusuf (AS) to the Prophet ﷺ, who recited it to the Quraish, on the spot.

This surah, with complete details was meant to comfort not only the Prophet ﷺ; but also intended to bring mental and emotional relief to the believers.

It is a proof of his Prophet hood. It was further proved that the sayings of the Prophet ﷺ, were not based on mere hearsay; but through the revelation from Allah [سبحانه وتعالى]. Quraish were ultimately informed in the ayath seven "Indeed there are signs in this story of Yusuf and his brothers for the inquirers (from among the Quraish)"

After two years of the revelation of surah Yusuf, the Quraish tried to kill the Prophet ﷺ, but he migrated to Madhina and soon acheived his objective. After the conquest of Makkah, like the brothers of Yusuf (AS), the Quraish stood meekly before the Prophet ﷺ, who enquired with them, "What treatment do you expect from me now?" They replied, "You are a generous brother and the son of a generous brother." On this response, he generously forgave them, stating, "I will give the same answer to your request that Yusuf (AS) stated to his brothers: "...today, no penalty shall be inflicted on you: you are forgiven."

Ya Allah! Make us also generous with everybody, like our leader the Prophet ﷺ. Aameen!

الحمدلله

3. Do you know which Surah of Quran begins with, "Allah has sent down and ordained its legal laws and revealed manifest ayaath that you remember?"

Answer: Surah An-Noor.

Following are the legal laws and manifest ayaath from Surathun-Noor:

About the punishment of zina:

[24:2] "The woman and the man guilty of illegal sex, flog each of them with a 100 stripes in front of party of the believers"

[24:3] "The adulterer or a Mushrik or a prostitute is forbidden to the believers and vice versa."

Punishment for those who accuse chaste woman:

[24:4] "And those who accuse chaste women, and produce not four witnesses, flog them with eighty stripes, and reject their testimony forever."

[24:6] "And for those who accuse their wives, with no witnesses except them-selves, take four testimonies, and the fifth invoking the Curse of Allah on him if he is a liar "

[24:7] And the fifth should be that the Wrath of Allah be upon her if her husband speaks the truth "

[24:8] "But it shall avert the punishment (of stoning to death) from her, if she bears witness four times by Allah, that he her husband is telling a lie.

[24:9] "And the fifth (testimony) should be that the Wrath of Allah be upon her if he (her husband) speaks the truth.

[24:19] "Verily, those who like that (the crime of) illegal sexual intercourse should be propagated among those who believe, they will have a painful torment in this world and in the Hereafter. "

Restrains us from following the footsteps of Shaitan:

[24:21] "Follow not the footsteps of Shaitan, he commands Al-Fahsha, and Al-Munkar. And had it not been for the Grace of Allah and His Mercy on you, not one of you would ever have been pure from sins. But Allah purifies (guides to Islam) whom He wills, and Allah is All-Hearer, All-Knower."

Pardon and forgive the kinsmen, for their mistakes:

[24:22] "And let not those among you who are blessed with graces and wealth swear not to give (help) to their kinsmen, the poor, and those who left their homes for Allah's Cause. Let them pardon and forgive."

Seek permission to enter others houses or the private parts of our house:

[24:27] "Enter not houses other than your own, until you have asked permission and greeted those in them "

[24:28] "And if you find no one therein, still, enter not until permission has been given. And if you are asked to go back, go back, for it is purer for you, "

[24:29] "There is no sin on you that you enter houses uninhabited "

[24:58] "Let your slaves and slave-girls, and those among you who have not come to the age of puberty ask your permission on 3 occasions; before Fajr prayer, and while you put off your clothes for the noonday, and after the 'Isha' prayer. "

[24:59] "So the children among you come to puberty, also ask for permission "

To lower the gaze:

[24:30] "Tell the believing men to lower their gaze, and protect their private parts. That is purer for them. "

[24:31] "And tell the believing women to lower their gaze, and protect their private parts and not to show off their adornment except only that which is apparent and to draw their veils all over Juyubihinna ... And let them not stamp their feet so as to reveal what they hide of their adornment."

[24:60] "And as for women past child-bearing who do not expect wed-lock, it is no sin on them if they discard their (outer) clothing... But to refrain is better for them. "

Recommend the marriage for those who are single:

[24:32] "And marry the unmarried among you and the righteous among your male slaves and female slaves. If they should be poor, Allah will enrich them from His bounty, and Allah is all-Encompassing and Knowing."

Obey Allah and His Messenger ﷺ:

[24:54] "Obey Allah and obey the Messenger ﷺ, but if you turn away, ... If you obey him, you shall be on the right guidance.

[24:52] And whosoever obeys Allah and His Messenger ﷺ, fears Allah, and keeps his duty (to Him), such are the successful ones.

Trading should not permit deviation, from the remembrance of Allah:

[24:37] "Men whom neither trade nor sale diverts them from the remembrance of Allah (with heart and tongue), nor from performing As-Salat (Iqamat-as-Salat), nor from giving the Zakat. They fear a Day when hearts and eyes will be overturned (from the horror of the torment of the Day of Resurrection).

Clarification with the regard to the houses, where one can eat:

[24:61] "There is no restriction on the blind, nor any restriction on the lame, nor any restriction on the sick, nor on yourselves, if you eat from your houses, or the houses of your fathers, or the houses of your mothers, or the houses of your brothers, or the houses of your sisters, or the houses of your father's brothers, or the houses of your father's sisters, or the houses of your mother's brothers, or the houses of your mother's sisters, or (from that) whereof you hold keys, or (from the house) of a friend. No sin on you whether you eat together or apart. But when you enter the houses, greet one another with a greeting from Allah (i.e. say: As-Salamu 'Alaikum – peace be on you) blessed and good. Thus Allah makes clear the Ayat (these Verses or your religious symbols and signs, etc.) to you that you may understand"

Finally, Allah asserts:

[24:64] Certainly, to Allah belongs all that is in the heavens and the earth. Surely, He knows your condition and (He knows) the Day when they will be brought back to Him, then He will inform them of what they did. And Allah is All-Knower of everything.

الحمدلله

4. In Surah 30 - Ar Room, Allah refers to seven signs, which commence in Arabic [وَمِنْ آيَاتِهِ] What are those seven signs?

Answer: Ar Room, 20 to 25 and 46.

1. He created man from dust:

"And among His Signs is this, that He created you (Adam [AS]) from dust, and then - behold you are human beings scattered!" (Ar-Room, 20).

2. He created for men, wives from among themselves:

"And among His Signs is this, that He created for you wives from among yourselves, that you may find repose in them, and He has put between you, affection and mercy. Verily, in that are indeed signs for a people who reflect." (30:21).

3. He created the heavens; the earth; and the difference in languages and colours:

"And among His Signs is the creation of the heavens and the earth, and the difference of your languages and colours. Verily, in that are indeed signs for men of sound knowledge" (30:22).

4. He created night for sleep and the day for work:

"And among His Signs is the sleep that you take by night and by day, and your seeking of His Bounty. Verily, in that are indeed signs for a people who listen." (30:23).

5. He created lightning and rains that revives plant life.

"And among His Signs is that He shows you the lightning, by way of fear and hope, and He sends down water (rain) from the sky, and therewith revives the earth after its death. Verily, in that are indeed, signs for a people who understand." (30:24)

6. Heaven and earth are under His command and He will call out men from their graves:

"And among His Signs is that the heaven and the earth stand by His Command, then afterwards when He will call you by single call, behold, you will come out from the earth (i.e. from your graves)" (30:25).

7. He created winds as glad tidings of His Mercy and for the sailing the ships:

"And among His Signs is this, that He sends the winds as glad tidings, giving you a taste of His Mercy (i.e. rain), that the ships may sail at His Command, and that you may seek of His Bounty, in order that you may be thankful." (30:46).

Adam (AS) was created by collecing clay from different regions of the earth. " Narrated Abu Musa Al-Ash'ari: that the Messenger of Allah ﷺ said: "Indeed Allah Most High created Adam from a handful that He took from all of the earth. So the children of Adam come in according with the earth, some of them come red, and white and black, and between that, and the thin, the thick, the filthy, and the clean." [Jami at-Tirmidhi 2955].

His wife was created from his rib. They lived together with affection and mercy. The children of Adam (AS) were spread over in different areas of the earth. They speak different languages.

Similarly, the change of the day and night is a great sign which no body realizes, imagining it to be a routine. He created day to work and night to sleep. But some out of the present generation, uses this in an opposite manner.

Heaven, earth and all that is in between them are under His Command. A single call will make all men resurrect from their graves. He provides wind, as glad tidings before rains. Sometimes it is so strong, creating fear whereas at times it provides hope of a healthy life. Ships sail over the sea by His command.

Allah through these signs requires us to listen, to acquire sound knowledge, to understand, to reflect and to be thankful for all His favours! Therefore, the believers must be thankful for all these bounties from Allah سبحانه وتعالى!

الحمدلله

5. When was the surah Ad-Dhuha, revealed?

Answer: On not receiving any wahi for a long time, this surah was revealed to the Prophet ﷺ.

Angel Jibreel (AS) did not visit him for a considerable duration. The idolaters started claiming, "Muhammad's [ﷺ] Lord had abandoned and hated him." Being disturbed, depressed and was sad the Prophet ﷺ wondered as to whether Allah was angry with him. He feared that he was abandoned, ignored and that he was not required to be a prophet!

Imam Ahmad recorded that Jundub (RA) had claimed, "The Prophet ﷺ became ill, so he did not attend the prayers for a night or two." [Sahih al-Bukhari 1124]. Narrated Jundab bin Abdullah (RA): Jibreel (AS) did not come to the Prophet ﷺ (for some time) and so one of the Quraish women said, "His Satan has deserted him." So came the Divine Revelation of surah Ad-Dhuha." [Sahih al-Bukhari 1125]

Allah revealed the said surah to infuse hope, positivity, assurance and peace, in him! Allah سبحانه وتعالى renewed the Prophet ﷺ's faith by proclaiming, "By the forenoon. (93:1). By the night when it darkens (93: 2). Your Lord has neither forsaken you nor hated you (93:3). And indeed the Hereafter is better for you than the present life (93:4) and surely your Lord will give so much to you that you will be pleased." (93:5). These words not only consoled our Prophet ﷺ but will also console those who recite them.

Allah ﷻ exclaims to the Messenger ﷺ, "Did He not find you, an orphan, O Muhammad ﷺ and gave you a refuge? (93:6) And He found you unaware and guided you? (93:7) And He found you, poor and made you rich and self-sufficient? " (93:8)

Indeed, Muhammed ﷺ was born a semi-orphan; lost his father before birth and also lost his mother at the age of six; his affectionate grandfather who was his care taker, at the age of eight. Thereafter, he was brought up by his paternal uncle Abu Thalib, who showered abundant affection and supported him throughout. His uncle, underwent hardship in protecting his nephew from enemies. Therupon, Allah commanded the Prophet ﷺ, not to treat the orphans unjustly or harshly. The Prophet ﷺ was aware of the pain of an orphan, therefore Allah commanded: "So do not oppress the orphan". (93:9)

His father had left only a she-camel and a slave girl, to be inherited. The Prophet ﷺ earned his living as a Shepard during his child hood and through trade in his youth. After marrying Bibi Khatheeja (RA), a wealthy lady, he became self-sufficient with his sincerity and hard work in trade and commerce. Thereupon, Allahuthala guided him to avoid chasing the needy. (93:10). With no provision available to help, one should excuse them politely.

Before attaining his Prophet hood, his society was totally ingnorant, worshiping idols, forgetting their fore-father Ibrahim's religion. He was in search of peace, truth and faith by retreating himself alone for days together, in the cave 'Heera'. It was there that Allah, 'the Most Merciful' guided and enlightened him with His revelation. Thereby, Allah the Almighty, had commanded him to be thankful for the numerous blessings provide to him, by guiding him towards the right path and for selecting him as a Messenger. The same command is applicable to his Ummath.

Allah asserted to the Prophet ﷺ that he will win over his enemies; thereafter Islam will spread all over the world; and in the Here-after will receive his greatest reward. Allah assures, "And soon your Lord will grant you, and you shall be pleased" (93:5).

This surah proves us the love and care of Allah, showered on the Prophet ﷺ and his followers by changing the prevailing conditions into better ones than the earlier ones in this world; and by promising them the best of the Hereafter (93:4). Therefore, the

Muslims are required to be kind to others and also to remember the Merciful Allah; glorify Him; and thank Him!

الحمدلله

6. Mention the name of the Surah, in which the following special verses are found:

1. Verse relating to loan [is also the longest verse in Quran].
2. Verse relating to abulation.
3. Verse relating to the change of the direction of Qibla.
4. Verses relating to Thayamum.
5. Verse relating to Divine Light.

1. Verse relating to loan is also the longest verse in Quran: (Al-Baqara, 2:282)

"O believers! When you contract a loan for a fixed period of time, commit it to writing. Let the scribe maintain justice between the parties. The scribe should not refuse to write as Allah has taught them to write. They will write what the debtor dictates, bearing Allah in mind and not defrauding the debt. If the debtor is incompetent, weak, or unable to dictate, let their guardian dictate for them with justice. Call upon two of your men to witness. If two men cannot be found, then one man and two women of your choice will witness—so if one of the women forgets the other may remind her. The witnesses must not refuse when they are summoned. You must not be against writing contracts for a fixed period—whether the sum is small or great. This is more just for you in the sight of Allah, and more convenient to establish evidence and remove doubts. However, if you conduct an immediate transaction among yourselves, then there is no need for you to record it, but call upon witnesses when a deal is finalized. Let no harm come to the scribe or witnesses. If you do, then you have gravely exceeded your limits. Be mindful of Allah, for Allah is the One Who teaches you. And Allah has perfect knowledge of all things." (2:282)

2. Verse relating to abulation (Maida, 5:6)

"O, you who believe! When you intend to offer As-Salath (the prayer), wash your faces and your hands (forearms) up to the elbows, rub (by passing wet hands over) your heads, and (wash) your feet up to ankles." (5:6)

3. Verse relating to the change of the direction of Qibla (Al-Baqara, 2:144).

"Indeed, 'We' see you, O Prophet ﷺ turning your face towards heaven. Now We will make you turn towards a direction of prayer that will please you. So turn your face towards the Sacred Mosque in Makkah — wherever you are, turn your faces towards it. Those who were given the Scripture certainly know this to be the truth from their Lord. And Allah is never unaware of what they do." (2:144).

4. Verses relating to thayamum: (An-Nisa, 4:43 and Al-Maida, 5:6)

"O believers! Do not approach prayer while intoxicated until you are aware of what you say, nor in a state of full impurity — unless you merely pass through the mosque — until you have bathed. But if you are ill, on a journey, or have relieved yourselves, or been intimate with your wives and cannot find water, then purify yourselves with clean earth, wiping your faces and hands. And Allah is Ever-Pardoning, All-Forgiving." (4:43)

"And if you are in a state of full impurity, then take a full bath. But if you are ill, on a journey, or have relieved yourselves, or have been intimate with your wives and cannot find water, then purify yourselves with clean earth by wiping your faces and hands. It is not Allah's Will to burden you, but to purify you and complete His favour upon you, so perhaps you will be grateful." (5:6)

5. Verse relating to Divine Light: (An-Noor, 24:36)

"Allah is the Light of the heavens and the earth. The parable of His Light is as (if there were) a niche and within it a lamp, the lamp is in glass, the glass as it were a brilliant star, lit from a blessed tree, an olive, neither of the east (i.e. neither it gets sun-rays only in the morning) nor of the west (i.e. nor it gets sun-rays only in the afternoon, but it is exposed to the sun all day long), whose oil would almost glow forth (of itself), though no fire touched it. Light upon Light! Allah guides to His Light whom He wills. And Allah sets forth parables for mankind, and Allah is All-Knower of everything."

الحمدلله

7. Similar to surah Ar-Rahaman, which are the two other surahs containing (more than four) repeated verses?

Answer: 77th Surah Al Mursalath and 26th Surah Ash-Shuara.

Allah سبحانه وتعالى revealed the Quran in Arabic language. Arabs were very proud of their poetic style and loved it. Surah Ash-Shuara, meaning "Poet"; lays emphasis to such a style by containing repeated verses. Similarly, surah Ar- Rahaman, surah Al Mursalath and surah Al Qiyama repeat the same verses, to draw the attention of the stubborn disbelievers.

Repetition of words and ayaath are meant for:

- ◆ eloquence
- ◆ emphasis
- ◆ to reflect good style of expression and
- ◆ to draw the attention of the stubborn disbelievers
- ◆ to embed the contents deeply in mind
- ◆ for memorizing and remembering the contents, with ease.

Repetition is found in the stories of Prophets and their people by also mentioning of Paradise and its dwellers; Hell with its horrors; the appearance of day and night; the life, death, Qiyamath and resurrection.

★ The verse which is repeated 31 times:

"Then which of the Blessings of your Lord will you both (jinn and men) deny?"

(Ar-Rahaman, 55:13,16,18, 21,23, 24, 28, 30, 32, 34, 36, 38, 40, 42, 45, 47, 49, 51, 53, 55, 57, 59, 61, 63, 65, 67, 69, 71, 73, 75 and 77).

★ The verse which is repeated 10 times:

"Woe that Day to the deniers (of the Day of Resurrection)!" (Al Mursalath, 77:15, 19, 24, 28, 34, 37, 40, 45, 47,49).

★ Each verse, that is repeated 8 times:

1. "And verily! Your Lord, He is indeed the All-Mighty, the Most Merciful." (As-Shuara, 26:9, 68, 104, 122, 140, 159, 175, 191).

2. "Verily! In this is indeed a sign (or a proof), yet most of them are not believers." (As-Shuara, 26:8, 67, 103, 121, 139, 158,174, 190)

3. "We reward the Muhsinun (good-doers)." (12:22, 28:14, 37:80, 105, 110, 121, 131, 77:44).

★ **Each verse, that is repeated is repeated 7 times:**

1. "So fear Allah, keep your duty to Him, and obey me." (As Shuara, 26:108, 126, 131, 144, 150, 163, 179)

2. "Ha, Meem." (40:1, 41:1, 42:1, 43:1, 44:1, 45:1, 46:1).

★ **The verse that is repeated 6 times:**

"Alif-Lam-Mim"-"الم" (2:1, 3:1, 29:1, 30:1, 31:1, 32:1).

★ **Each verse, that is repeated 5 times:**

1. "When their brother .... said to them: "Will you not fear Allah and obey Him?"

Only the words in the dashed line will change as Nuh (AS) [26:106] or Hud (AS) [26:124] or Salih (AS) [26:142] or Lut (AS) [26:161] or Shuiab (AS). [26:177]

2. "I am a trustworthy Messenger to you." (As Shuara, 26:107, 125, 143, 162, 179).

3. "Alif-Lam-Ra." (10:1, 11:1, 12:1, 14:1, 15:1).

4. "No reward do I ask of you for it, my reward is only from the Lord of the Alamin" (As Shuara, 26: 109, 127, 144, 164, 180)

5. "Is there any ilah (god) with Allah?" (27: 60 to 64)

★ **The verse that is repeated 4 times:**

"And We have indeed made the Quran easy to understand and remember, then is there any that will remember?" (54:17, 22, 32,40)

★ **Each verse, that is repeated 3 times:**

1. "They say: "When will this promise come to pass? If you are telling the truth." (21:38, 34:29, 67:25)

2." Verily, he was one of Our believing slaves." (37:81, 111 and 132)

3. "Then, how (terrible) was My Punishment and My Warnings?" (54: 16, 21 and 30)

★ **Each verse, that is repeated 2 times:**

More than 15 ayaaths are repeated twice either in the same surah or in different surahs. Few are referred here under:

1. "So glorify the Name of your Lord, the Greatest." (56:96, 69:52).

2. "The Lord of Musa (AS) and Harun (AS)." (7:177 and 26:48)

3. "Saying: "We believe in the Lord of the Alamin." (7:121 and 26:47).

4. "Then he followed another way." (18:89 and 92)

5. "These are Verses of the manifest Book." (26:2 and 28:2).

6. "They will abide therein (Hell). Neither will their torment be lightened, nor will it be delayed or postponed." (2:162 and 3:88).

7. Ta-Sin-Mim (26:1 and 28:1)

8. "By the manifest Book" (43:2 and 44:2).

9. "Or that the Ghaib (unseen) is in their hands, so that they can write it down?" (52:41 and 68:47)

10. "Except the chosen slaves of Allah" (37:74 and 128)

11. "The revelation of the Book (this Quran) is from Allah, the All-Mighty, the All-Wise." (39:1, 45:2).

الحمدلله

8. Which surah contains, in its last three ayaath, the maximum of the excellent names (الأسْمَاءُ الْحُسْنَىٰ) of Allah Subhanahuthala?

Answer: Al-Hashr, 59:22 to 24.

"He is Allah, other than whom there is no god, Knower of the unseen and the witnessed. He is the Entirely Merciful, the Especially Merciful."

"He is Allah, other than whom there is no god, the Sovereign, the Pure, the Perfection, the Grantor of Security, the Overseer, the Exalted in Might, the Compeller, the Superior. Exalted is Allah above whatever they associate with Him."

"He is Allah: The Creator, the Inventor, the Shaper. He alone has the Most Beautiful Names. Whatever is in the heavens and the earth constantly glorifies Him. And He is the Almighty, All-Wise." (Al-Hashr 59:22 to 24).

Being the most Supreme, Allah has innumerable attributes. Human mind is not capable of comprehending His attributes. Allah Himself records His ninty-nine names in the Holy Quran. These verses inherently make us feel that our "ila" is not an ordinary Creator, but "Almighty". He alone is worthy of worship, as there is no lord or god which exists, excepting Him. Each of His names are interconnected with His two or three attributes. Restricting one specific meaning to one name, is beyond human comprehention. It is impossible to translate many of His names, in an exact and appropriate manner, in any language.

He is Alimul Ghaib [عِلْمُ الْغَيْبِ]

He is aware of whatever is apparent and what all is not comprehendable, in this universe. Nothing escapes His knowledge, irrespective of its being material, thoughts or deeds.

He is Al-Shahadha [الشَّهَادَةِ]

He is the Witness. Everything is recorded in 'His great book' as to the past, the present and the future. He will be a true witness for every thing.

He is Ar-Rahamanur Raheem [الرَّحْمٰنُ الرَّحِيْمُ]

His mercy is limitless. "Allah divided mercy into one-hundred parts; He retained ninety-nine parts with Him; sent down one part to the earth and due to that part His creations are merciful, to each other"

He is Al-Malik [الْمَلِكُ]

He is of the Emperor of the entire universe; owning everything, all powerful with the authority, including command and control.

He is Al- Quddhoos [الْقُدُّوْسُ]

He is Pure, Holy, Perfect and free from all defects. He has guided us to keep our body, soul, mind and heart clean thereby commanded us to eat what is pure, through His book.

He is As-Salam [السَّلَامُ]

As-Salam means the flawless source of peace and Bestower of security. During Hijra, as soon as the Prophet ﷺ entered Madhina, he declared, "O people, spread peace, feed the hungry, pray at night when people are sleeping and you will enter Paradise, in peace."

He is Al-Mumin [الْمُؤْمِنُ]

Allah describes Himself as Al-Mumin, meaning, "The Infuser of Faith". The root word 'amn' in classical Arabic means the source of faith. He is the One who bestows the gifts of peace, security, and faith. Al-Mu'min removes fear, affirms His oneness, and is the Most Trustworthy!

He is Al-Muhaimin [الْمُهَيْمِنُ]

He is a Witness for His servant's deeds. He is ever watching, His creation's declarations and deeds. Nothing can be hidden from Him as He has knowledge of all. It refers to His supreme nature as being the guardian or the absolute authority.

He is Al-Aziz [الْعَزِيزُ]

Being Almighty, He is all strong and most powerful. Nobody can defeat nor defy Him. Those who recite or listen the Holy Quran are required to understand, think and ponder that Allah has mentioned a pair of His names together, always. For example عَزِيزٌ غَفُورٌ. Being all powerful, He can punish the wrong doers then and there. But, He is the Great Forgiver. Allah grants an oppurtunity to the guilty, to realise their mistakes and turn to Him in repentance, thereupon they can be forgiven.

He is Al-Jabbar [الْجَبَّارُ]

Allah is referred as Al-Jabbar which means, "The Compeller". According to His 'Desire' (or Decree) everything takes place. He reforms, resolves, restores and brings back to the normal state, any uncomfortable situation.

He is Al-Mutakabbir [الْمُتَكَبِّرُ]

He is the one who is 'All Supreme'. Pride is an attribute, which does not fit with anyone excepting Allah. Abu Hurayrah (RA) narrated that the Prophet ﷺ stated: "Allah the Most High, declares: "Pride is my cloak and majesty is my Izar (lower garment), and I will punish whoever contends with Me over either of them" (Sunan Abi Dawud, 4090)

He is As-Subhan [سُبْحَانَ]

Various meanings are furnished to this attribute of Allah. "Glory be to Allah" "Exhalted is Allah" "Allah is Perfect." High is He, above all with whom the disbeleivers associate, as being His partners. When any Muslim realizes Allah's bounty and glory; thereby he praises Him by exclaiming "Subhanallah". During testing times and on being subjected to weakness, every Muslim repeats "Subhanallah", thereby seeking help, restoring patience and faith. Prophet ﷺ said: "glorify Allah one hundred times. Thus, it will be recorded for him as one thousand good deeds, or one thousand bad deeds will be erased." (Sahih Muslim 2698).

Abu Huraira (RA) narrated that "Some poor people came to the Prophet ﷺ and enquired as to, "'The wealthy people will get higher grades and will have permanent enjoyment they pray like us and fast. They have more money by which they perform the hajj and Umra; fight and struggle in Allah's Cause and offer charity."

"The Prophet ﷺ said, 'Shall I not tell you a thing upon which you act, you would catch up with those who have surpassed you? Nobody would overtake you and you would be better than the people amongst whom you live except those who would do the same. Say Subhanallah, Alhamdulillah, and Allahu Akbar 33 times each, after every [compulsory] prayer.'" (Sahih al-Bukhari 843).

He is Al-Khaliq [الْخَـالِـق]

Means "The Creator". He creates something from nothing, from non-existence to existence. Nothing comes by itself nor by accident nor anyone else creates, excepting Allah. If He intends creating something, On His declaring "Be" it comes into existence, in the form that He wills.

He is Al-Baari [الْبَارِئُ]

Allah is "The Inventor of every thing." He brings into existence, any thing or a being, in a specific manner without any model, in perfect proportion without any defect.

He is Al-Musawwir [الْمُصَوِّرُ]

Being Al-Musawwir, He brings into existence anything which He wills in the shape and form He decides. Once He creates and produces in a desired manner, He fashions it in a unique way.

All that is in the heavens and the earth and in between Glorify His Best names, that is Al-Asma' Al-Husna. He is undoubtedly the All-Mighty, the All-Wise.

"Allah has the Most Beautiful Names. So call upon Him by them, and keep away from those who abuse His Names. They will be punished for what they used to do." (7:180). "Say, O Prophet [ﷺ], "Call upon Allah or call upon the Most Compassionate — which ever you call, He has the Most Beautiful Names." (17:110).

The ninety-nine names of Allah are:

No	Name	Meaning	No	Name	Meaning
1	الرَّحْمٰنُ	The Beneficent	34	الْغَفُورُ	The Great Forgiver
2	الرَّحِيمُ	The Merciful	35	الشَّكُورُ	The Most Appreciative
3	الْمَلِكُ	The King	36	الْعَلِيُّ	The Most High
4	الْقُدُّوسُ	The Most Sacred	37	الْكَبِيرُ	The Most Great
5	السَّلَامُ	The Source of Peace	38	الْحَفِيظُ	The Preserver
6	الْمُؤْمِنُ	The Infuser of Faith	39	الْمُقِيتُ	The Sustainer
7	الْمُهَيْمِنُ	The Preserver of Safety	40	الْحَسِيبُ	The Reckoner
8	الْعَزِيزُ	All Mighty	41	الْجَلِيلُ	The Majestic
9	الْجَبَّارُ	The Compeller	42	الْكَرِيمُ	The Most Generous
10	الْمُتَكَبِّرُ	The Supreme	43	الرَّقِيبُ	The Watchful
11	الْخَالِقُ	The Creator	44	الْمُجِيبُ	The Responsive One
12	الْبَارِئُ	The Evolver	45	الْوَاسِعُ	The All-Encompassing
13	الْمُصَوِّرُ	The Fashioner	46	الْحَكِيمُ	The All-Wise
14	الْغَفَّارُ	The Constant Forgiver	47	الْوَدُودُ	The Most Loving
15	الْقَهَّارُ	The All-Prevailing One	48	الْمَجِيدُ	The Glorious
16	الْوَهَّابُ	The Supreme Bestower	49	الْبَاعِثُ	The Infuser of New Life
17	الرَّزَّاقُ	The Provider	50	الشَّهِيدُ	The All Witnessing
18	الْفَتَّاحُ	The Supreme Solver	51	الْحَقُّ	The Absolute Truth
19	الْعَلِيمُ	The All-Knowing	52	الْوَكِيلُ	The Trustee
20	الْقَابِضُ	The Withholder	53	الْقَوِيُّ	The All-Strong
21	الْبَاسِطُ	The Extender	54	الْمَتِينُ	The Firm
22	الْخَافِضُ	The Reducer	55	الْوَلِيُّ	The Protecting Associate
23	الرَّافِعُ	The Exalter	56	الْحَمِيدُ	The Praiseworthy
24	الْمُعِزُّ	The Honourer	57	الْمُحْصِي	The All-Enumerating
25	الْمُذِلُّ	The Dishonourer	58	الْمُبْدِئُ	The Originator
26	السَّمِيعُ	The All-Hearing	59	الْمُعِيدُ	The Restorer,
27	الْبَصِيرُ	The All-Seeing	60	الْمُحْيِي	The Giver of Life
28	الْحَكَمُ	The Impartial Judge	61	الْمُمِيتُ	The Creator of Death
29	الْعَدْلُ	The Utterly Just	62	الْحَيُّ	The Ever-Living
30	اللَّطِيفُ	The Subtle One,	63	الْقَيُّومُ	The Sustainer
31	الْخَبِيرُ	The All-Aware	64	الْوَاجِدُ	The Perceiver
32	الْحَلِيمُ	The Most Forbearing	65	الْمَاجِدُ	The Illustrious
33	الْعَظِيمُ	The Magnificent	66	الْوَاحِدُ	The One

No	Name	Meaning	No	Name	Meaning
67	اَلْأَحَدُ	The Unique	84	مَالِكُ الْمُلْكِ	Owner of the Dominion
68	اَلصَّمَدُ	The Eternal	85	ذُوالْجَلَالِ وَالْإِكْرَامِ	Lord of Glory and Honour
69	اَلْقَادِرُ	The Omnipotent One	86	اَلْمُقْسِطُ	The Just One
70	اَلْمُقْتَدِرُ	The Powerful	87	اَلْجَامِعُ	The Gatherer
71	اَلْمُقَدِّمُ	The Promoter	88	اَلْغَنِيُّ	The Self-Sufficient
72	اَلْمُؤَخِّرُ	The Delayer	89	اَلْمُغْنِي	The Enricher
73	اَلْأَوَّلُ	The First	90	اَلْمَانِعُ	The Withholder
74	اَلْآخِرُ	The Last	91	اَلضَّارُّ	The Distresser
75	اَلظَّاهِرُ	The Manifest	92	اَلنَّافِعُ	The Propitious
76	اَلْبَاطِنُ	The Hidden One	93	اَلنُّورُ	The Light
77	اَلْوَالِي	The Sole Governor	94	اَلْهَادِي	The Guide
78	اَلْمُتَعَالِي	The Self Exalted	95	اَلْبَدِيعُ	The Incomparable Originator
79	اَلْبَرُّ	The Source of All Goodness	96	اَلْبَاقِي	The Everlasting
80	اَلتَّوَّابُ	The Ever-Pardoning	97	اَلْوَارِثُ	The Inheritor
81	اَلْمُنْتَقِمُ	The Avenger	98	اَلرَّشِيدُ	The Guide
82	اَلْعَفُوُّ	The Pardoner	99	اَلصَّبُورُ	The Patient
83	اَلرَّؤُوفُ	The Most Kind			

Allah records in the Holy Quran:

Allah has revealed His names repeatedly in the Holy Quran, primarily for us to understand as to who He is. Allah mentions at a time, two of His names in many places as: [اَلْعَلِيمُ ٱلْحَكِيمُ] [ٱلْعَزِيزُ ٱلْحَكِيمُ] Almighty, All-Wise; [غَفُورٌ رَّحِيمٌ] - All-Forgiving Merciful; -Most All-Knowing, All-Wise; [ٱلتَّوَّابُ ٱلرَّحِيمُ] - Accepter of Repentance, Most Merciful [وَٰسِعٌ عَلِيمٌ] - All-Encompassing, All-Knowing; [ٱلسَّمِيعُ ٱلْعَلِيمُ] - All-Hearing, All-Knowing and [رَءُوفٌ رَّحِيمٌ] - Ever Gracious and Most Merciful. There is nothing more sacred and blessed than understanding them.

The Two Sahihs recorded that Abu Hurayrah narrated that the Messenger of Allah ﷺ had declared, "Allah, the Exalted has ninety-nine Names, one hundred less one; whoever then preserves them, will enter Paradise. Allah is Witr (One) and He likes the Witr." Therefore, always remember Allah with His beautiful names, as Allah declares: "Surely Allah guides to Himself, those who turn to Him and those who believe and whose hearts find comfort in the remembrance of Allah. Surely in the remembrance of Allah do hearts find comfort." (13:27 and 28). Therefore, to receive His favours and to tread in the right path, fear Allah, remember Allah, praise Allah and be grateful to Allah.

الحمدلله

بِسْمِ ٱللَّهِ ٱلرَّحْمَٰنِ ٱلرَّحِيمِ

16. Miscellaneous

1. Are you a person who feels or laments, "I am the one suffering so much in my life, while others are enjoying " Do you know how Allah consoles, guides and also promises the reward for you, in return?

"Indeed, 'We' have created humankind in constant struggle": (90:4)

Each and every human being, in whatever position he is placed, is bound to face some sort of struggle at some stage of his life. Allah confirms that it, as a part of human legacy. None can escape from it. He is bound to avoid the whispers of Shaitan. At times, he may face struggle in an over-whelming manner.

Allah consoles mankind:

Allah consoles humanity by asserting that it is not the only one, which suffers but every creation of His, at different times. The struggle is not for ever, as He has assured, "Allah will grant after hardship, ease." (At-Talaq, 65:7)

Quran asserts that: "Allah has created death and life, that He may test you which of you is best in deed." (67:2) We should not consider the test of Allah, as a suffering. Even those favours of His, provided abundantly, are meant to test us!

He further consoles by declaring: "Allah burdens not a person beyond his scope." (2:286). And "So verily, with the hardship, there is relief. Verily, with the hardship, there is relief. So when you have finished (from your occupation), then stand up for Allah's worship (i.e. stand up for prayer). And to your Lord (Alone) turn (all your intentions and hopes and) your invocations. (94:5 - 8)." We should realize that humanity has been created to worship Him.

Allah exclaims at the believers, "Do people think that they will be left alone because they say: "We believe," and will not be tested?" (29:2). Narrated Abu Huraira (RA): Allah's Messenger ﷺ declared, "If Allah wants to do good to somebody, he afflicts him with trials" [Sahih al-Bukhari 5645]. Allah being [خَبِيرًا بَصِيرًا] the All knower and All Seer, is aware of your struggle.

Analyse your innerself and assess the favours that Allah has bestowed on you. He has provided you capacity to think and evaluate your reasoning. Observe everything around you, incuding the signs that lead you to reality. Distinguish the right from wrong! Seek His help and guidance, in patience. Recite His most beautiful names and Glorify Him. Recite often these verses from Holy Quran - 2:255, 2:285 and 286, 59:22–24. These verses abundantly increase your faith and patience.

He guides us to face the struggle:

"O you who believe! Seek help in patience and As-Salat (the prayer). Truly! Allah is with the patient ones." (2:153). Further He asserts, "Certainly I will test you with something of fear, hunger, loss of wealth, lives and fruits, but give glad tidings to the patient ones." (2:155). When afflicted with calamity, He requires us, to say: [إِنَّا لِلَّهِ وَإِنَّا إِلَيْهِ رَاجِعُونَ] "Truly! To Allah we belong and truly, to Him we shall return." (2:156). They are those on whom are the Salawat (i.e. blessings, etc.) (i.e. who are blessed and will be forgiven) from their Lord, and (they are those who) receive His Mercy, and it is they who are the guided-ones." (2:157).

Submit yourself to Allah, in entirety. Do not be in doubt about His Mercy. Allah claims, "And among mankind is he who worships Allah as it were, upon the very edge (i.e. in doubt); if good befalls him, he is content therewith; but if a trial befalls him, he turns back on his face (i.e. reverts back to disbelief after embracing Islam). He loses both this world and the Hereafter. That is the evident loss." (22:11).

Allah further exclaims, "Or think you that you will enter Paradise without such (trials) as came to those who passed away before you? They were afflicted with severe poverty and ailments and were so shaken that even the Messenger and those who believed along with him said, "When (will come) the Help of Allah?" Yes! Certainly, the Help of Allah is near!" (2:214)

"When harm touches man, he calls to Us (for help), then when We have (rescued him from that harm and) changed it into a favour from Us, he says: "Only because of knowledge (that I possess) I obtained it." Nay, it is only a trial, but most of them know not!" (39:49). Be grateful to the favours provided by His Mercy on you, as nothing is achieved based on your effort.

"Say (strongly): "Nothing shall ever happen to us except what Allah has ordained for us. He is our Maula (Lord, Helper and Protector)." And in Allah let the believers put their trust." (9:51).

Narrated Abu Sa'id Al-Khudri (RA) and Abu Huraira (RA): The Prophet said, "No fatigue, nor disease, nor sorrow, nor sadness, nor hurt, nor distress befalls a Muslim, even if it were the prick he receives from a thorn, but that Allah expiates some of his sins for that." [Sahih Bukhari, Vol. 7, Book 70, Number 545]

He assures in sura Al Balad, by guiding us to become the dwellers of Paradise: "And shown him the two ways (good and evil)? But he has made no effort to pass on the path that is steep. And what will make you know the path that is steep? (It is) freeing a slave or giving food in a day of hunger, to an orphan, near of kin or to a poor afflicted with misery. Then he became one of those who believed, and recommended one another to perseverance and patience, and (also) recommended one another to pity and compassion. They are those on the Right Hand (the dwellers of Paradise)" (Al Balad, 90:10 to 18).

Allah guides while you are in trouble to offer Sadaqa to orphans, poor and needy. Never lose your faith and hope on Allah. Do not allow the Shaitan to influence you. Help those in the trouble, by approaching them with pity and compassion. This approach will lead you to Paradise. Being His promise, Allah will always keep it up!

Our evil deeds and sins, attract trouble. Turn to Allah! Repent and seek His forgiveness. By undergoing struggles, our sins may be forgiven by Allah. Through one's good deeds, erase the bad deeds. "Whoever hopes for the Meeting with Allah, then [let them do good deeds]." (29:5)

Abu Hurayrah (RA) reported that the Prophet ﷺ said: "A strong believer is better and more beloved to Allah than a weak believer, although both are good. Strive to do that which will benefit you and seek the help of Allah and do not feel helpless. If anything befalls you, do not say 'If only I had done (such and such), the such and such would have happened', rather say: 'Allah has decreed and what He wills He does, for 'if only' opens the door to the work of the shaitan." (Sahih Muslim, 2664).

Remember the words of the Messenger ﷺ: "How wonderful is the affair of the believer, for his affairs are all good, and this applies to no one but the believer. If something good happens to him, he is thankful for it and that is good for him. If something bad happens to him, he bears it with patience and that is good for him." (Sahih Muslim, 2999).

Allah promises the Paradise:

Allah tests His slaves, He loves those who are patient, forgives their sins and gives them the glad tidings of Paradise. Therefore, one can face struggle patiently, awaiting the reward of Paradise.

O Those you who believe [يَا أَيُّهَا الَّذِينَ آمَنُو] pray whole heartedly, during Salath:

"Guide us to the Straight Way. The Way of those on whom You have bestowed Your Grace, not (the way) of those who earned Your Anger, nor of those who went astray." (Al-Fatiha, 1: 6 and 7). Surely you will be the one amongst those who dwell, forever in Jannah. Aameen!

الحمدلله

2. Do you know the good deeds which may weigh heavily in the balance, on the Day of Resurrection?

For Muslims (those who submit to Allah) it is made obligatory in believing Wahid (One) Allah; observing Salath; fasting during Ramazan; offering Zakath and Sadaqa, along with the performance of Hajj; Allahuthala thereby makes their balance heavy. Becoming the victims of the whispers of Shaitan, we become weak in faith and indulge in forbidden (evil) acts and thereby our balance becomes light. Thus, Allah commands us to believe and indulge in righteous acts, to change the weight of the balance in our favour.

The other good deeds weighing in our favour, are:

- **Constantly repeating (Dhikr) Tahleel - (لا إله إلا الله)**

One's dhikr will weigh most heavily in the balance. It was narrated by Abdullah bin Amr bin Al-Aas: that the Messenger of Allah ﷺ said: "Indeed Allah will distinguish a man from my Ummah before all of creation on the Day of Judgement. Ninety-nine scrolls will be laid out for him, each scroll is as far as the eye can see, then He will say: 'Do you deny any of this? Have those who recorded this wronged you?' He will say: 'No, O Lord!' He will enquire: 'Do you have an excuse?' He will say: 'No, O Lord!' So He will say: 'Rather you have a good deed with us, so you shall not be wronged today'. Then He will bring out a card (Bitaqah); on it will be: '[أشهد أن لا إله إلا الله وحده لا شريك له وأن محمداً عبده ورسوله] "I testify to La Ilaha Illallah, and I testify that Muhammad is His servant and Messenger." He will say: 'Bring your scales.' He will say: 'O Lord! What good is this card next to these scrolls?' He will say: 'You shall not be wronged.' He said: 'The scrolls will be put on a pan (of the scale), and the card on (the other) pan: the scrolls will be light, and the card will be heavy, nothing is heavier than the Name of Allah.'" At-Tirmidhi (2639).

- **Remembrance of Allah:**

Allah will be exalted by the reciting of Takbeer, Tahleel, Tahmeed and Tasbeeh. Takbeer is proclaiming 'Allahu Akbar' (Allah is Great!). Tahleel is stating 'La ilaaha illallaah' (There is none worthy of worship, except Allah). Tahmeed is pronouncing 'Alhamdulillah' (All Praise belongs to Allah). Tasbeeh is to glorify Allah by repeating 'Subhanallah' (Glory be to Allah).

It was narrated from Abu Hurayrah (RA) that the Prophet ﷺ declared: "Two words which are light on the tongue but will weigh heavily in the Balance and are beloved to the Most Merciful:" They are: "Glory be to Allah the Almighty, Glory and praise be to Allah." [سُبْحَانَ اللهِ وَبِحَمْدِهِ، سُبْحَانَ اللهِ الْعَظِيمِ] Al-Bukhaari (6406) and Muslim (2694).

It was narrated from Juwayriyyah (RA), the wife of the Prophet ﷺ that the he left her house one morning after he prayed Fajr, while she was praying. When he returned during forenoon she was still sitting at the same place. He exclaimed: "Are you still as you were when I left you?" She replied: 'Yes'. The Prophet ﷺ said: "After I left you I said these four words three times, which if they were weighed against what you have said today, they would outweigh it: "Glory and praise be to Allah, as much as the number of His creations, as much as pleases Him, as much as the weight of His Throne and as much as the ink of His words." [Sahih Muslim, 2726].
[سبحان الله وبحمده عدد خلقه، ورضا نفسه، وزنة عرشه، ومداد كلماته]

- **Regularly reciting adhkaar after the obligatory prayers:**

It was narrated from Abdullah ibn Amr that the Prophet ﷺ said: "There are two deeds that a Muslim does not do regularly but he will enter Paradise. They are easy but those who do them are few; saying (سبحان الله) Subhaanallah 10 times after every prayer, and saying (الحمد لله) Alhamdulillaah 10 times, and saying Allahu akbar (الله أكبر) ten times. That makes (5x30=) 150 on the tongue and 1500 on the Balance. Repeating Allahuakbar 34 times while going to bed during night, along with Alhamdulillah 33 times, and also Subhaanallah 33 times. That is 100 on the tongue and 1000 in the Balance."

- **Patience and seeking reward with Allah upon the loss of a righteous child**

It was narrated from Zayd, from Abu Salaam, from the freed slave of the Messenger of Allah ﷺ, the Prophet ﷺ declared: "Excellent, excellent, for there are five things, how heavy they are in the balance: Laa ilaaha illallah, Allahu akbar, Subhaanallah, Alhamdulillah, and the death of a righteous child whose parents seek reward (for their loss, with Allah).

- **Good attitude**

Abu Darda (RA) reported: The Prophet ﷺ said, "Nothing is heavier upon the scale of the believer on the Day of Resurrection than his good character. Verily, Allah hates the vulgar, obscene person." (Sunan al-Tirmidhi, 2002).

It was narrated from Abu-Darda that the Prophet ﷺ said: "There is nothing that weighs more heavily in the Balance than a good attitude (with people)." So also narrated by Abu Dawood (4799); which is categorized as saheeh, by Shaykh al-Albaani in 'Saheeh Abi Dawood'.

It has been narrated by Umm ad-Darda, who quotes Abud-Darda that 'I heard the Prophet ﷺ stating, "There is nothing that is placed in the balance that will weigh more heavily than a good attitude (with people); the one who has a good attitude will attain thereby the status of one who fasts and prays." Which has been also recorded in at-Tirmidhi (2003); and asserted as saheeh by al-Albaani in 'Saheeh at-Tirmidhi'

- **Staying during the funeral till the burial is completed:**

It was narrated from Ubayy that the Prophet ﷺ declared: "Whoever attends a funeral until the prayer has been offered for the deceased and the (burial) is completed will have two qiraats (of reward), and whoever attends until the prayer has been offered will have one qiraat. By the One in Whose hand is the soul of Muhammad ﷺ, it will weigh more heavily in his balance than Uhud." (Imam Ahmad 20256); classed as saheeh by Shaykh al-Albaani in Saheeh al-Jaamias-Sagheer. [الله اعلم !]

- **The dhikr upon entering the market places:**

Abu Huraira (RA) reported: The Messenger of Allah ﷺ, declared, "The most beloved of places to Allah are the mosques, and the most hated of places to Allah are the markets." [Sahih Muslim 671] Allah hates market places because Shaithan dominate there with lies, greed, exploitation and deceptions. While going there pray specially.

It was narrated by Umar (RA) said, the Messenger of Allah ﷺ assured: "There is no god but Allah alone who has no partner, to whom belongs the dominion, to whom praise is due, who gives life and causes death while He is living and does not die, in whose hand is good, and who is omnipotent," God will record for him a million good deeds, obliterate from him a million evil deeds, raise him a million degrees, and build him a house in paradise." [Mishkat al-Masabih 2431, also in Sunan ibn Majah 2235, and at-Tirmidhi 3428]

- **Quran recitation:**

Narrated Muhammad bin Ka'b Al-Qurazi: "I heard 'Abdullah bin Mas'ud saying: 'The Messenger of Allah ﷺ asserted: "[Whoever recites a letter] from Allah's Book, then he receives the reward from it, and the reward of ten the like of it. I do not say that Alif Lam Mim is a letter, but Alif is a letter, Lam is a letter and Mim is a letter." [Jami` at-Tirmidhi 2910].

Ayesha (RA) reported: The Messenger of Allah ﷺ assured, "The one who is proficient in the recitation of the Qur'an will be with the honourable and obedient scribes (angels) and he who recites the Qur'an and finds it difficult to recite, doing his best to recite it in the best way possible, will have two rewards." (Riyad as-Salihin 994 and also in Al-Bukhari and Muslim0.

الحمدلله

3. Do you know "the verse of sword" in Quran?

Answer: "[فَاقْتُلُوا الْمُشْرِكِينَ حَيْثُ وَجَدْتُمُوهُمْ]". The meaning of a portion of the fifth ayath, of surah At-Tauba is: "Kill the Mushrikun wherever you find them", is known as the "Verse of Sword" or "Sword verse." 'Mushrikun' refers to idolaters, polytheist, disbelievers, pagan Arabs etc.

The full ayath conveys that: "When the Sacred Months (the 7th, 11th,12th and Ist months; in their order) have passed, then kill the disbelievers wherever you find them and capture them and besiege them and prepare for them each and every ambush.

But if they repent and perform As-Salat and give Zakat, then leave their way free. Verily, Allah is Oft-Forgiving, Most Merciful." (Taubah, 9:5).

This Quranic verse has been treated for the first time, as a declaration by Usama bin Laden. Such a usage, is a latter invention, which is criticised as promoting violence against idolaters. The word "sword' is not at all mentioned, in the ayath referred. It is a wrong interpretation of that verse. Islamic extremists to justify their terrorism, joined hands with a few perpetuaters of violence, popularised this verse.

Opponents of Islam, claimed that: "the real Islam is violent, as it promotes repressive faith." On a proper analysis of the verse, it is crystal clear that Islam on the contrary, is tolerant and peaceful.

The preceeding verse, commands the Muslims to honor any peace treaty, entered with the disbelievers: "Except those of the Mushrikun with whom you have a treaty, and who have not subsequently failed you in aught, nor have supported any one against you. So fulfill their treaty to them to the end of their term. Surely Allah loves the pious." (9:4)

Then the next verse asserts that a peaceful disbeliever should not be considered as an enemy and Allah commands us to provide protection to him. "And if anyone of the Mushrikun seeks your protection then grant him protection, so that he may hear the Word of Allah, and then escort him to where he can be secure, that is because they are men who know not." (9:6).

Muslims should honor their treaty as long as the polytheists adhere to it. "How can there be a covenant with Allah and the Prophet ﷺ for the Mushrikun except those with whom you made a covenant near Al-Masjid- al-Haram? So long, as they are true to you, stand you true to them. Verily, Allah loves the pious" (9:7).

"They have purchased with the ayath of Allah a little gain, and they hindered men from His Way; evil indeed is that which they used to do."(9:9).

"With regard to a believer, they respect not the ties, either of kinship or of covenant! It is they who are the transgressors" (9: 10).

From the above ayaath, it is clear that they have been revealed as a defensive response against oppression. Verse 9:5 is meant for self-defense and does not authorize one, to kill all non-believers.

These verses are related to a historical event which took place, while the Prophet ﷺ was at Madhina. In A.H.9, Abu Bakr (RA) went to perform Hajj, leading a group of pilgrims. After his departure from Madhina, the ayaath 1-37 of Surah Thouba were revealed. Thereupon, the companions requested the Prophet ﷺ, to convey it to Abu Bakr (RA), requiring him to proclaim it on the occasion of Hajj. The Prophet ﷺ replied, "The importance and nature of the declaration demands that this should be proclaimed on my behalf by someone from my own family."

Thereupon, Ali (RA) was instructed to proclaim it openly before the pilgrims; to enable them to become aware of the new policy towards the mushrikun. Further he was instructed to declare that: (1) No one who rejects Islam, shall enter Paradise. (2) No mushrik should perform Hajj thereafter. (3) One is forbidden to perform thawaf; naked. (4) All the terms of the treaties enforced, will have to be faithfully observed till the expiry of their term.

This declaration of the observation of the treaties with the mushriks was made in accordance with the law enjoined in Surah Al-Anfaal: 55 to 62. The mushriks were always hatching plots against Islam, by violating the treaties and turning hostile and by grabing the first opportunity to commit treachery. Thereupon, Allah used harsh words to describe their deeds and the consequences arising therefrom. Allah is All Knower, Al-Ghafoor and Ar-Rahaman.

الحمدلله

4. Do you know the forewarning in the Quran and hadhees, to the Children of Adam?

1. To be beware of Shaitan and not to worship him: "Did I not enjoin on you, O, you Children of Adam, that ye should not worship Shaitan; for that he was to you an enemy avowed it?" [36:60].

"O, you Children of Adam! Let not Shaitan seduce you, in the same manner as He got your parents out of the Garden, stripping them of their raiment, to expose their shame: for he and his tribe watch you from a position where ye cannot see them: We made the evil ones' friends (only) to those without faith. (Al-Araf, 7:27)

2. To cover oneself, with the clothing of righteousness:

"O, you Children of Adam! We have bestowed garment upon you to cover your shame, as well as to be an adornment to you. But the garment of righteousness, - that is the best. Such are among the Signs of Allah, that they may receive admonition!"(Al-Araf, 7:26)

3. Avoid wastage:

"O Children of Adam! Wear your beautiful apparel at every time and place of prayer: eat and drink: But waste not by excess, for Allah love not the wasters. (Al-Araf, 7:31)

4. Follow the Messengers, who are sent to avoid fear and grief:

"O, you Children of Adam! Whenever there come to you messengers from amongst you, rehearsing My signs unto you, - those who are righteous and mend (their lives), - on them shall be no fear nor shall they grieve." (Al-Araf, 7:35)

5. Allah has honoured the Children of Adam:

"And indeed We have honoured the Children of Adam, and We have carried them on land and sea, and have provided them with At-Taiyibat (lawful good things), and have preferred them above many of those whom We have created with a marked preference." (Al-Isra, 17:70).

6. Allah's covenant with the Children of Adam:

"And (remember) when your Lord brought forth from the Children of Adam, from their loins, their seed (or from Adam's loin his offspring) and made them testify as to themselves (saying): "Am I not your Lord?" They said: "Yes! We testify," lest you should say on the Day of Resurrection: "Verily, we have been unaware of this." Or lest you should say: "It was only our fathers aforetime who took others as partners in worship along with Allah." (Al-Araf, 7:172)

7. Allah created them based on such a Fitrah:

"So set you (O Muhammad ﷺ!) your face truly towards the religion, Hanifan. Allah's Fitrah with which He has created mankind. No change let there be in Khalq-illah." (Ar Rum, 30:30)

'Muslim' records that Iyad bin Himar narrated that the Messenger of Allah ﷺ delared: "Allah said `I created My servants Hunafa' (monotheists), but the devils came to them and deviated them from their religion, prohibiting what I allowed"

Call of Tawheed, continues to urge within oneself to believe in the Oneness of Allah, as a natural inclination (fitrah).

Therefore, O Children of Adam! Do not forget the covenant, promised to Allah. You share with all, including your family members.

الحمدلله

5. Why most Prophets are shepherds?

The climate and rainfall of middle east was such that it contained vast grazing land with minimum rainfall, with no cultivation possible. The major occupation there was rearing of sheep, cattle and camels. Most of the Prophets, having born in the middle east, carried on the occupation as shepherds, herding their own sheep or that of the others.

The importance of sheep:

- Sheep are weaker than other domestic animals.
- Unlike camels and cattle, the sheep spread out more easily.
- They are usually not tied.
- They always obey the orders of their masters.
- Formerly, every commoner used to own sheep.
- The livelihood of most, was based on rearing sheep.
- Many of the family members involved themselves in grazing sheep.

Shepherds, while herding sheep, developed certain qualities:

- Developed patience, caring, tolerance and responsibility.
- Emotions like lenience and compassion increased.
- Spending most of their time in loneliness were separated from the society were attracted towards spirituality.
- Shifting the sheep to the grazing land; regrouping them was indeed a laborious job. Protecting them from wild animals and thieves, especially during grazing was a streneous job. Thus they became accustomed to hard work.
- They became merciful towards the weak.
- They gained knowledge to treat the injured sheep.

🐑 They became aware of the different categories of sheep; their nature and to deal with them accordingly.

With the rearing sheep, the Prophets:

- developed the nature of caring, being responsible, lenient and compassionate,
- maintained patience, whenever the people due to their weaknesses, disagreed with one another,
- maintained tolerance during oppression,
- they were always merciful towards their followers,
- consoled their followers, when they were found to be depressed,
- gained experience by understanding the changes in nature and differences arising in the minds of human beings.
- They adhered to a simple and humble life in the society and therefore, they became dearer to Allah.

Abu Hurairah (RA) narrates: "the Messenger of Allah ﷺ said, "Allah did not send any prophet that did not herd sheep." "Did you herd sheep too, O Messenger of Allah ﷺ?" they asked, He said, "Yes, I also looked after sheep for the people of Mecca in return for some qirat (amount or name of a place)" [Bukhari, Ijara 2; Muwatta, 18 (2, 971); Ibn Majah, Tijarah 5, (2149).]

Jabir (RA) narrated that: "I remember collecting the fruit of arak tree called kabas in Marruz-Zahran with the Messenger of Allah ﷺ. The Messenger of Allah ﷺ told us, "Collect the black ones; they are better!" Therfore, I enquired "Have you also herded sheep?" I further enquired. "Do you know any prophet who did not herd sheep?" was his answer to me." [Bukhari, Atima 50, Anbiya 29, Muslim, Ashriba 163, (2050).]

The following is recorded in Nasai: "Sheep owners and camel owners boasted about it. The Messenger of Allah ﷺ said, 'Moses (AS) became a prophet while he was a shepherd. Dawood (AS) became a prophet while he was a shepherd. I also became a prophet while I was herding my people's sheep in Jiyad."

الحمدلله

6. Why Razi-Allahu anhum (رضي الله عنهم) (RA), is added as a suffix to the names of the companions of the Prophet ﷺ [Sahabas]?

Razi-Allahu anhu (in short as RA), is an Arabic phrase used to revere the companions. It means "May Allah be pleased with him." For females, it is used as Razi-Allahu anha (رضي الله عنها) and in plural is Razi-Allahu anhum. (رضي الله عنهم)

Allah سبحانه و تعالى directed the believers to refer this suffix, whenever the names of the companions are mentioned.

Allah سبحانه و تعالى was well pleased with:

◆ Muhajirun (those who migrated from Makkah to Al-Madhina); and

◆ the Ansar (the citizens of Al-Madhina who helped and provided aid to the Muhajirun)

◆ and also to those who followed them exactly (in Faith).

Because:

- They were the forerunners in their belief and righteous deeds.
- Their physical, financial and religious sacrifices were in abundance.
- They obeyed Allah and His messenger ﷺ, by following their dictates about the change in the Qibla and jihadh.
- They proved to be the best Ummath, in their worship.
- They were prepared to sacrifice their lives and wealth, for the sake of Allah.
- They were the ones who pledged (baithul rhidhwan), under the tree to sacrifice their lives, for the sake of Islam.

Abdullah (RA) and Ayesha رضي الله عنها in their narrations observed that the Prophet ﷺ stated that: "The best people are those of my generation, and then those who will come after them (the next generation), and then those who will come after them (i.e. the next generation), and then after them, there will come people whose witness will precede their oaths, and whose oaths will precede their witness." Sahih Al Bukhari Vol. 5:3, Vol 8: 437 and Sahih Muslim 6159 [4].

Allah سبحانه و تعالى has strongly acknowledged the gratitude of the Sahabas in two places of the Glorious Quran. The suffix razi-Allahu anhu is derived from the following two verses:

"And the first forerunners [in the faith] among the Muhajireen and the Ansar and those who followed them with good conduct - Allah is well-pleased with them as they are well-pleased with Him. He has prepared for them Jannah under which rivers flow, to dwell there-in forever. That is the supreme success." (At-Taubah, 9:100)

"Indeed, Allah was pleased with the believers when they gave their Baia (pledge) to you (O Muhammad ﷺ) under the tree, He knew what was in their hearts, and He sent down As-Sakinah (calmness and tranquility) upon them, and He rewarded them with a near victory". (Al-Fath, 48:18).

الحمدلله

7. "And with Him are the keys of the ghaib (all that is hidden), none knows them but He" (6:59). What are the keys of the ghaib?

Allah continues this ayath with: "And He knows whatever there is in (or on) the earth and in the sea; not a leaf falls, but he knows it. There is not a grain in the darkness of the earth nor anything fresh or dry, but is written in a Clear Record." Allah further says, "(He Alone) the All-Knower of the ghaib (unseen), and He reveals to none His ghaib (unseen)." (Al-Jinn, 72:26)

Once, Warith ibn Amr, a Bedouin, came to the Prophet ﷺ and raised the following questions, seeking replies about the Last Hour and its timing. Then he wished to know, "Our lands are dry, so when will it rain? I left my wife while she was pregnant, so what will she give birth to? I know what I earned today, so what will I earn tomorrow? I know in what land I was born, so in what land will I die?"

Allah Subhanahuthala revealed in response to this quiary, as recorded in the surah Luqman, verse 34. "Verily, Allah! With Him (Alone) is the knowledge of the Hour, He sends down the rain, and knows that which is in the wombs. No person knows what he will earn tomorrow, and no person knows in which land he will die. Verily, Allah is All- Knower, All-Aware (of things)."

Allah has countless and limitless ghaibs for his creations, which He alone knows. He further ordains, "Allah was not going to leave the believers in the state you are in until He distinguishes the evil from the good. Allah would not let you know the unseen (ghaib), but He chooses whom He wills of His messengers. So believe in Allah and His messengers. If you believe and be pious then you will have a great reward." (3:179)

Even Prophet Muhammad ﷺ was instructed to convey to the people that he has no knowledge of the unseen: "Say [O Muhammad ﷺ!]: I do not say to you that I have the treasures of Allah nor that I know the unseen (ghaib). And I do not say to you that I am an angel. I only follow what is revealed to me." Say [O Muhammad ﷺ!]: Are the blind and the seeing equal? Do you not think?" (6:50)

The disbelievers always required to know, "When will the Hour come?" For which the response from the Almighty was; "The disbeleivers say, 'The Hour will not come to us.' Say [O Muhammad ﷺ!]: 'Yes, by my Lord, it shall come to you. He is the One who knows the unseen. Not the weight of an atom in the heavens or in the earth shall escape from him, nor smaller or bigger than that but is in a manifest book." (34:3). Say: "None in the heavens and the earth knows the Ghaib (Unseen) except Allah, nor can they perceive when they shall be resurrected." (27:65)

The knowledge of 'when the Hour will occur' is not known to any Prophet or any angel who is closer to Allah. Allah holds that: "None can reveal its time but He" (7:187). Even the angel awaiting to blow the trumpet for the Day of Resurrection, is holding his trumpet in his lips awaiting Allah's command.

Allah Subhanahuthala enquires: "O man, you do not have the knowledge even about those things with which you were most closely and intimately concerned in life. How then can it be possible for you to know as to when will the whole world come to an end?"

Similarly, no one but Allah knows when rain is expected. Its entire regulation is as per the desire of Allah. The angels who are entrusted with the task of bringing rain, obey Allah's command. He pours down the rain in correct measure, at a particular place and at a particular time. He is well aware of the fact as to which land can remain without it and which will be adversely affected.

None, except Allah knows what is in the womb of the mother. Applying modern technology, we may identify the sex of the fetus, whether fully formed or defective but we are unaware as to whether it is to be blessed or doomed, black or white or it will survive its full term or there will be a miscarriage. The angels are entrusted with the knowledge of it, which fact is also made known to a few selected amongst His creations.

Urwah is said to have narrated that Az-Zuhri conveyed the fact that Abu Bakr (RA), on his death bed while referring to his "will" informed Ayesha (RA): "You have two brothers and two sisters." Whereas she responded: "I know about my two brothers, and one sister but who is the other one?" The reply was: "What is in the womb of the daughter of Khaarijah; I think it is a girl, so take good care of her." And that girl was Umm Kulthoom.

None knows as to what he will earn tomorrow, while in this world with regard to the rizk, wealth, health, deeds, worship etc or in the Hereafter.

None knows as to the place of his death. None is aware as to how and when he will die? Those selected by Him, alone will be aware of those facts. The Prophet ﷺ informed his daughter Fatimah (RA), while he was ill that he would die due to that affliction.

The Prophet ﷺ conveyed that: "The area between my grave and my minbar is one of the gardens of Paradise." He declared: "No Prophet is buried in the place where he dies." This indicates that he was aware of the place of his death and burial. He also assured to his daughter Fathima (RA) that among their relatives, she will be the first one to meet him in Paradise.

Being ignorant of the unknown, we should not question Allah like the people of Jahaliya (ignorance). We have no option but to depend only on Allah's Decree. Allah ﷻ declares; "And to Allah belongs the Ghaib (unseen) of the heavens and the earth, and to Him return all affairs (for decision). So worship Him (O Muhammad ﷺ) and put your trust in Him. And your Lord is not unaware of what you (people) do." [Hud, 123].

الحمدلله

8. Islam does not persuade polygamy but permits it, on certain conditions. It requires marriage with only one woman. Why?

Polygamy is, 'one person having more than one spouse.' Polygyny: 'applies to a man having multiple wives'.

A common attack against Islam is that it permits polygamy. Polygamy existed in the early days of human history. Islam did not initiate or propagate it. Arabs of the Jahiliyah (ignorance) period married as many women as they wished; and later subjected them to injustice and oppression.

Polygamy is allowed in Islam only as an exception but not as a rule. Islam approves polygamy, under exceptional and unavoidable circumstances. After wars fought for the sake of Islam, the propotion of widows and orphans increased. Men were affected due to work related accidents, resulting in death. Boy babies being comparatively weak in resistant power, they die early affecting the male-female ratio. At present, all the countries are alarmed due to the variation in male-female ratio. In future, the condition may be still worse.

Under these circumstances, polygamy is preferred. Anticipating this, Allah had permitted a man to marry four women, at a time. Some men desired to marry orphan girls considering their wealth or beauty, thereby avoid providing maher as there will be none to claim on their behalf. After marriage few men treat the orphans unjustly. If they fear they will cause injustice to the orphan girls, the Muslims are directed to marry other girls, whom they desire.

Allah has revealed the following ayath, after the battle of Uhad: "And if you fear that you shall not be able to deal justly with the orphan-girls, then marry (other) women of your choice, two or three, or four but if you fear that you shall not be able to deal justly (with them), then only one or (the captives and the slaves) that your right hands possess. That is nearer to prevent you from doing injustice." [An-Nisa, 4:3].

Islam fixes a limit to the numbers of wives that a person can have at one time — maximum of four wives. Marrying more wives than one is permitted with the condition that he treats them equitably.

This is to avoid:

- committing injustice,
- financial hardship,
- poverty,
- having too many children,
- treating all wives unequally with injustice.

Few human beings retain such qualities of justice and fairness. The Quran itself, in the same Chapter 4, verse 129, declares: "And you do not have the ability to do justice between the wives, even though you may wish (to do so) ..." (4:129).

So the Divine command upholds that: "then marry only one."

Polygamy is intended to avoid:

- ◆ Extra-marital affairs

◆ Prostitution

◆ Rape

◆ Higher divorce rates

◆ Abandaning of families

الحمدلله

9. Allah will enquire: "What number of years did you stay on earth?" (23:112). Do you know what will be your answer?

Answer: "They will say: 'We stayed a day or part of a day: but ask those who keep account.' Allah will assert: 'You stayed not but a little, - if you had only known!'" (Al Muminun, 23:113 and 114).

Allah states in the other parts of Holy Quran as:

★ "And on the Day when He shall gather them together, as if they had not tarried (on earth) longer than an hour of a day: they will recognize each other" (Yunus,10:45).

★ "On the Day when He will call you, and you will answer (His Call) with (words of) His Praise and Obedience, and you will think that you have stayed (in this world) but a little while!" [17:52]."

★ "On the Day when they will see that (torment) with which they are promised as if they had not stayed more than an hour in a single day" (Al-Ahqaf, 46:35)

★ "We know very well what they will say, when the best among them in knowledge and wisdom will say: "You stayed no longer than a day!" (Taha, 20:104)"

★ "And on the Day that the Hour will be established, the Mujrimun will swear that they stayed not but an hour, thus were they ever deluded [away from the truth]." (Ar-Room, 30:55)"

★ "The day these people see it; they will feel as though they had stayed (in the world or in the state of death) only for the afternoon of a day or its forenoon. (An Naziath, 79:46)"

The Prophet ﷺ, too, stated, "The life of this world compared to the Hereafter is as if one of you were to put his finger in the ocean and take it out again then compare the water that remains on his finger to the water that remains in the ocean" [Sahih Muslim (2858), Grade: Sahih].

Ibn Umar (RA) quoted that: The Messenger of Allah ﷺ, took me by the shoulder and told me that: "Be in this world as though you were a stranger or a traveler/wayfarer." [Sahih Muslim (6053)]. All our Messengers have warned that the life in this world is transitory and for one's tests and trials. If the believers had been patient; worshipping Allah, performing righteous good deeds and forbidding evils during their short stay in this world; they will attain supreme success like many of His pious servants.

Otherwise they will lament on the Resurrection day, as Allah asserts in His Holy Quran:

- "Oh, I wish I had not associated with my Lord anyone." (18:42)
- "Oh, 'We' wish we had obeyed Allah and obeyed the Messenger." (33:66)
- "Oh, we wish that we could be returned [to life on earth] and not deny the signs of our Lord and be among the believers." (6:27)
- "Oh, I wish I had not been given my record" (69:25)
- "O woe to me, I wish I had sent good ahead for my life."(89:24)
- "Oh, I wish that I were dust!" (78:40)
- "Oh! I wish I had been with the believers; then I would have achieved a great success." (4:73)
- "O my Lord! send me back (to life), -"In order that I may work righteousness in the things I neglected." (23:99 and 100)

These are the impossible aspirations that cannot be fulfilled, after death.

We should not prefer extremes of this worldly life, abandoning everything. Let not be our preparations for the Hereafter, by neglecting our duties to our families in this world. With out delay prepare and endeavor for the present life, as well as for the Hereafter!

Prayer:

Say: "O my Lord! grant Thou forgiveness and mercy for Thou art the Best of those who show mercy!" (23: 118)

الحمدلله

10. Allah Exalted has mentioned four books of records, in Quran. Do you know what are they?

Answer: Al-Lauh Al-Mahfuz, Book of deeds, Illiyyun, Sijjin

1. Al-Lauh Al-Mahfuz:

Al-Lawh al-Mahfuz means "The Preserved Tablet." [Al-Burooj 85:22]. It is a divine record containing the whole program of the universe. Allah Subhanahuthala created 'Qalam' (the pen) first and commanded it to write and it did so. The past, present and future till the Last day, is recorded. Hence it is also referred as 'Kitabul-Qadar.' It is a book, beyond human imagination. None can touch or see, except the purified angels. None can change its content except Allah, the Almighty. Its width is equivalent to covering a distance of a hundred year walk.

Scholars of Tafseer, as well as others had mentioned some reported citations on the authority of Ibn Abbas (RA): "It is of red rubies, with its upper end tied to the Throne (of Allah) and its lower end on the lap of an angel. Its script is light, and its pen is light. Allah, The Almighty glances at it three-hundred and thirty-six times every day. With each glance, He does what He Wills; He exalts a humble person, humiliates an honored one, enriches a poor person, impoverishes a rich person, gives life to someone, causes death to another and does whatever else He Wills. There is nothing worthy of worship except Him."

Its words and letters are so well protected that the meaning of its content, can not be twisted. It is a clearly recorded book. Shayathaeen, have no power to reach it. Subhanallah! Like Zaboor, Taurath and Injeel, none can delete or add or change the verses of Quran, since it is preserved in Al-Lawh al-Mahfuz.

Al-Lawh al-Mahfuz is referred in the Holy Quran, as follows:

- "And with Him are the keys of the Ghaib (all that is hidden), none knows them but He. And He knows whatever there is in (or on) the earth and in the sea; not a leaf falls, but he knows it. There is not a grain in the darkness of the earth nor anything fresh or dry, but is written in a Clear Record. (Al-Anaam, 6:59)
- "And there is nothing hidden in the heaven and the earth, but is in a Clear Book" (i.e. Al-Lauh Al-Mahfuz). {An-Naml, 27: 75}

- "Verily, 'We' give life to the dead, and 'We' record that which they send before (them), and their traces, and all things 'We' have recorded with numbers (as a record) in a Clear Book." (Ya Seen, 36:12)
- "No calamity befalls on the earth or in yourselves but is inscribed in the Book of Decrees (Al-Lauh Al-Mahfuz), before We bring it into existence. Verily, that is easy for Allah." (Al-Hadid, 57:22)
- "We know that which the earth takes of them (their dead bodies), and with Us is a Book preserved (the Book of Decrees). (Qaf, 50:4)
- "And Verily, it (this Quran) is in the Mother of the Book (i.e. Al-Lauh Al-Mahfuz), before Us, indeed Exalted, full of Wisdom." (Az-Zukhruf, 43:4)
- "That (this Quran) is indeed an honourable recital. In a Book well-guarded (with Allah in the heaven i.e. Al-Lauh Al-Mahfuz). Which (that Book with Allah) none can touch but the purified (i.e. the angels)." Al-Waqia, (56: 77 to 79).

Al-Husayn bin al-Fadl was questioned as to whether: "Has Allahuthala not pre-destined the decrees of everything before He created the heavens and earth?" The reply was, "Yes." So it was said, "Then what is the meaning of Laylat-ul-qadr?" He replied, "Bringing the decrees of everything to their appointed times and executing the decrees of the pre-destined."

Ibn Kathir explains in his tafseer:

"On that night every matter of wisdom is ordained." [Al-Dukhan 44:4] "It means that on laylatul-qadr, the decrees are transferred from al-Lawh al-Mahfuz to the (angelic) scribes, who write down the decrees of the coming year including life span, health and sickness, provision, poverty and wealth, or any other calamities, good yields and drought, wars, earthquakes, rain and everything that will happen until the end of the year. Allahuthala says "Therein descend the angels and the Ruh [Jibreel {AS}] by Allah's Permission with all Decrees" [Al-Qadr, 97:4]

The Prophet ﷺ urged us to worship in a manner which will tend to increase a person's lifespan; uphold the ties of kinship and he also declared that such a worship can change the divine decree. It was narrated from Thawban that the Messenger of Allah (ﷺ) said: "Nothing increases one's life span except righteousness and nothing repels the Divine decree except supplication, and a man may be deprived of provision by a sin that he commits." [Sunan Ibn Majah 4022].

Ibn Abbas narrated: "I was behind the Prophet ﷺ one day when he said: 'O boy! I will teach you a statement: Be mindful of Allah and He will protect you. Be mindful of Allah and you will find Him before you. When you ask, ask Allah, and when you seek aid, seek Allah's aid. Know that if the entire creation were to gather together to do something to benefit you- you would never get any benefit except that Allah had written for you. And if they were to gather to do something to harm you- you would never be harmed except that Allah had written for you. The pens are lifted and the pages are dried." Al-Tirmidhi (2516).

Al-Tabaraani narrated with his isnaad from Abu Uthmaan al-Nahdi, Umar bin al-Khattab (RA) while circumambulating the Kabah was weeping and seeking this dua: "O Allah, if You have decreed that I should be doomed or commit sin then erase it, for You erase whatever You will and You confirm (whatever You will) and with You is the Mother of the Book, so make my life filled with happiness and forgiveness."

Al-Tabarani The Tabi`i Abu Wa'il Shaqiq bin Salamah, often used to supplicate with these words: "O Allah, if You have decreed that we be doomed, then erase it and decree that we be blessed. If You have decreed that we be blessed, then confirm it for us, for You erase whatever You will and You confirm (whatever You will), and with You is the Mother of the Book."

"Praised be unto He Who decreed the destined measures (muqadir) of all things in Mighty, Preserved Tablets" (AQA 4:317-320).

2. Book of deeds:

The honorable writers (angels called Raqib and Atid) record our deeds, both which are evil or good. "And each and everything they have done is noted in (their) Records (of deeds)." (54:52). And it will be fastened on our neck on the Day of Resurrection. People destined to go to Paradise receive the record with their right hand and the sinners will receive the book with their left hand.

The following verses of Al-Quran confirm it:

[82: 10 and 11] "But verily, over you (are appointed angels in charge of mankind) to watch you, Kiraman (honourable) Katibin (scribes) writing down (your deeds)"

[45:29] "This Our Record speaks about you with truth. Verily, 'We' were recording what you used to do."

[18:49] "And the Book (one's Record) will be placed (in the right hand for a believer in the Oneness of Allah, and in the left hand for a disbeliever in the Oneness of Allah), and you will see the Mujrimun (criminals, polytheists, sinners, etc.), fearful of that which is (recorded) therein. They will say: "Woe to us! What sort of Book is this that leaves neither a small thing nor a big thing, but has recorded it with numbers!" And they will find all that they did, placed before them, and your Lord treats no one with injustice."

[17:13 and 14] "And We have fastened every man's deeds to his neck, and on the Day of Resurrection, 'We' shall bring out for him a book which he will find wide open. (It will be said to him): "Read your book. You yourself are sufficient as a reckoner against you this Day."

[84:7 - 12] "Then, as for him who will be given his Record in his right hand, He surely will receive an easy reckoning, and will return to his family in joy! But whosoever is given his Record behind his back, He will invoke (his) destruction, and shall enter a blazing Fire, and made to taste its burning."

3. Illiyyun:

"Nay! Verily, the Record (writing of the deeds) of Al-Abrar (the pious who fear Allah and avoid evil), is (preserved) in Illiyyun. And what will make you know what Illiyyun is? A Register inscribed. " (Al- Mutaffifin, 83:18 to 20)

4. Sijjin:

"Nay! Truly, the Record (writing of the deeds) of the Fujjar (disbelievers, sinners, evil-doers and wicked) is (preserved) in Sijjin. And what will make you know what Sijjin is? A Register inscribed." (Al- Mutaffifin, 83:7 to 9).

الحمدلله

www.ingramcontent.com/pod-product-compliance
Lightning Source LLC
LaVergne TN
LVHW070521070526
838199LV00072B/6671